THE HORSE IN IRELAND

IN MEMORY OF MY BROTHER JOHN AND MY FATHER
WHO GAVE ME EVERY ENCOURAGEMENT

BRIAN SMITH

THE HORSE IN IRELAND

WOLFHOUND PRESS

First published 1991 by
WOLFHOUND PRESS
68 Mountjoy Square, Dublin 1

© Brian Smith 1991
Illustrations © as credited

British Library Cataloguing in Publication data :
Smith, Brian
    The horse in Ireland.
    1. Ireland. Livestock : Horses. Breeding, history
    I. Title
    636.1'082'09415

ISBN 0-86327-153-7 hardcover
ISBN 0-86327-311-4 limited presentation edition

FRONT COVER
Laytown Races (*Inpho*) with (left) Paul Darragh (*Horseman Photography*);
top right: Connemara pony (*Liam Blake*);
and below: *Dawn Run* and *Desert Orchid*, 1984 (*Gerry Cranham*).

BACK COVER
Supreme Edge, Reserve Champion Stallion for the Croker Cup at the RDS, 1991.
Owners Nigel and Charlotte Moore, Crumlin, Co. Antrim (*photo: Nigel Moore*).
Author photo: Pat Cowman

Design by Jan de Fouw
Typesetting by Type Bureau Ltd. Make-up by Redsetter Ltd.
Colour separations by Graphic Reproductions Ltd.
Printed in the Republic of Ireland by Colour Books Ltd.

A WOLFHOUND PRESS PUBLICATION

Contents

Foreword

While preparing this book I received assistance and encouragement from many people including family and friends. Here I would like to thank them.

William Micklem, Maeve McDonald, Patrick Connolly, Seamus Ó Síocháin and Michael Keogh read parts of the typescript. All their suggestions and corrections were greatly appreciated.

For help in typing the manuscript I am grateful to Helena Hever, Vivienne Floyd and Deirdre Simpson.

I am grateful also to Tim McCarthy and the staff of the IHR section of the Department of Agriculture for their help with photographic material. Special thanks are due also to Louise Garland and Captain Tommy Ryan for their advice and help in this and other respects.

I would also like to thank Maymes Ansell, Catherine Benson, Ned Campion (SJAI), Colonel Ned Campion, Margaret Coffey, Francis Connors, Grace and Michael Duncan, Dermot Forde, Joan Forde, Sean Gaffney, Richard Gerrard, Jessica Harrington, John Hassett, Maura Hussey (Bord Bainne), Ralph Keady (Bord Failte), Larry Kearns, Iris Kellett, Martin Leahy, Tom McCormack, Teresa Morley, Colm Mullen, Nicholas O'Hare, John O'Keefe, Tony Parkes, Charles Powell, Brian Reed (RDS), Colonel Billy Ringrose, Ruth Rogers, Maxi Scully, Gordon Standing (*Irish Times*), Doreen Swinburn, Fiona Smith, John Wright, the staff and residents of Cara Cheshire Home and the staffs of Cavan County Library, the Dublin County and City Libraries, the National Library of Ireland and the Library of Trinity College Dublin.

I am grateful to Seamus Cashman, Siobhan Campbell, the staff of Wolfhound Press and the editor Jeanne Marie Finlay for their patience and encouragement.

In particular I would like to thank Eugene Callan for his work in word-processing part of the manuscript and his constant advice and help, Nollaig Ó Muraíle for the numerous valuable suggestions and references and for reading the typescript and Raymond McGovern who nursed the project from its inception and was always generous with practical guidance and encouragement.

July 1991   Brian Smith

1

Horse Worship in the Earliest Times

THE HORSE AND THE OTHERWORLD

THE CELTS—and these included the Irish—believed in life after death. But the Otherworld to which their dead go is not the gloomy place inhabited by the pale shades of the classical tradition. Rather it is a place where full-blooded people live in happiness. In this vision death is seen not as a termination but as a continuation of this life, if at a more exalted level. Even the principal diversion of heroic life, warfare, frequently disturbs the peace. This Otherworld is a place of plenty and the warriors fight among themselves for the prize portion at the Otherworld feast. Over this feast the God of the Otherworld presides. One such god is Manannán mac Lir, literally Manannán Son of the Sea. Manannán's transport by land and by sea is provided by horses.[1] His residence in the Otherworld lies under the sea and in a twelfth-century Irish text called *Acallam na Senórach* or *The Colloquy of the Old Men* we read how his magnificent horse is used to transport one of the mythical band of warriors, the Fianna, and two other men to this place. The three men, the story goes, are in a boat at sea when a storm rises. They fear for their lives. Suddenly they see a warrior on a dark grey horse reined with a bridle of gold moving on the waves. For the space of nine waves he was submerged but he would rise on the crest of the tenth, managing all the time to keep his body dry. He will rescue them, he promises, if they will serve him. This they gladly agree to do. So he takes them out of the currach and on to the horse and they accompany him safely to the Otherworld.

Other tales in Irish tradition similarly describe how a marvellous horse carried people by sea to the Otherworld. In the story of the Death of Fergus, Esirt takes the poet Aed to his own Otherworld country. They reach the sea and a wonderful, coloured horse comes galloping over the waves and takes them on its back over the ocean to the Otherworld. As the story about Manannán mac Lir illustrates, there is sometimes an element of compulsion in the offer of transport to the Otherworld. Elsewhere in Irish tradition we learn that anyone touching one of these magical water horses sticks to it and the animal immediately plunges into the water with the victim firmly attached.[2] So deeply rooted in Irish tradition is the association of the horse with the sea and the Otherworld that current Irish language usage sometimes translates 'waves' as *Groigh mhic Lir*, literally the horses of (Manannán) mac Lir. An echo of this ancient tradition is also contained in West of Ireland

Top : Chariot warrior. Celtic coin which could well be an illustration from an early Irish epic. The naked and long-haired warrior hurls a spear while in retreat from the enemy. In his left hand is a shield. His charioteer, crouching well forward on the pole, urges the paired horses on.

Bottom : Horse and female rider. Gold coin used by Celtic tribes living in an area extending from Bohemia to the Lower Danube. The female rider may be Epona.

folklore. A poor man's equine stock, we learn, is miraculously upgraded when a marvellous stallion emerges out of the sea and covers his mare. In the famous ancient Irish story about the Cattle Raid of Cooley, *Táin Bó Cuailnge*, the storyteller likens the hero Cú Chulainn's horse to those Otherworldly giants, the Fomorians, who were reputed to have invaded Ireland. The Fomorians were sea-farers who in later Irish tradition came to be regarded as centaurs, that is half-horse and half-man. Their king was Eochaid Echcend, literally Eochaid Horsehead, whose name, as we shall see later, helps to throw light on the horse's eminent position in Ireland. Somewhat nostalgically, the storyteller in *Táin Bó Cuailnge* reflects that Cú's horses were the last of the Fomorians.[3]

The Otherworld is not exclusively located in water. It may be under ground, it may be a house or palace which appears or disappears with equal suddenness, it may be a hill or it may be reached through a cave. In most cases there is a fundamental link between these versions of the Otherworld and horses. In a tale about the destruction of Dá Derga's hostel, which is in reality an Otherworldly dwelling, the hero Conaire is lured to his doom there by three men riding horses which cannot be overtaken. The three horsemen, the Trí Deirg, have red hair, red accoutrements and are mounted on red steeds—red is the colour usually associated with death in the Celtic world. "We ride," says one of the horsemen, "the steeds of Donn Detscorach, though we are alive we are dead." In Irish mythology Donn was ruler over the dead. In another tale we learn how an Otherworld ruler, Giolla Deacair, carries off some of the Fianna to his dwelling. He releases a scraggy ugly grey horse among the horses of the Fianna and it proceeds to fight and maim them with ferocity (the Otherworldly significance of horse battles we will see later). It requires fourteen men to mount it before it can be moved. Once mounted, these men find that they cannot dismount, and they are carried off to the Otherworld.[4]

Two Irish legends of the twelfth century and a legend recorded in the eighteenth century make it clear that the horse in Irish tradition is not limited to providing transport to the Otherworld. The horse himself begins to embody the Otherworld. In these stories the hero is warned before he returns from the Otherworld that if he dismounts from the horse he will die or suffer extreme old age. In other words, while he is mounted on the horse he enjoys an Otherworldly existence even in this life. Once dismounted, he ceases to have this privilege. In one of the stories, the hero Oisín's girth snaps when he comes to the land of the living and he falls from the horse and immediately suffers the ravages of extreme old age. In another of the stories the warning is heeded and the hero remains on the horse's back. Safely mounted there, he is, in essence, in the Otherworld, despite his terrestrial surroundings, and may return at will to his Otherworld dwelling, provided he does not dissociate himself from the Otherworld by dismounting.

Such a key role in relation to the Otherworld could only be given to the horse in Irish literature and folklore which spanned a thousand years if the horse enjoyed

ABOVE:
Reverse of a first century BC silver coin of the Boii, found near Bratislava, Czechoslovakia.

Reverse of a denaruis of L. Cosconius, dated early second century BC. A Gaulish warrior standing in his chariot hurls a spear while the horses are at full gallop. Normally however, as in the Irish literary tradition, the warrior would have been accompanied by his charioteer.

OPPOSITE:
Reverse of a first century BC silver coin, possibly of the Taurisci, from Trifail, Steiermark, Austria.

Reverse of a third century BC coin, possibly from Northern Romania.

A bronze horse mask found in the excavations of the great tribal capital of the Brigantes at Stanwick, Yorkshire. it may have formed an element in a chariot decoration. (*British Museum*).

inordinate public esteem in real life. Because of the horse, the people believed, the impossible became possible. The chariot to which the horse was harnessed also reflects the prestige associated with the horse.

THE CHARIOT

In the earliest Irish tales horses are not ridden but are harnessed in pairs to chariots. In the popular imagination, as represented in these ancient tales, chariots drawn by horses had sacred properties. It could be argued that there was more than one reason for this. For example, chariots made use of the wheel which, since its invention in Mesopotamia some four thousand years before the Irish legends were written down, had made great advances in travel and working methods possible. The Celts as a result came to regard the wheel as sacred. The most outstanding Irish goddess, Medb, had as her messenger Mac Roth, literally Son of the Wheel. He is a supernatural figure who travels in a horse-drawn chariot made of white and lustrous gems. To those who travel in this chariot the night is as bright as the day. In it Mac Roth flies through the air and completes his journey around Ireland within a day.[5] St Aed mac Bricc goes one better than these pagan aeronauts and flies through the air in a one-wheeled chariot. The chariot, in this way, is seen to have supernatural connotations in Irish tradition. But the main reason why the chariot acquired sacred properties in the popular imagination was not the extraordinary powers of the wheel but the association of the chariot with the horse that drew it.

The characters in the ancient Irish tales did not think in terms of mounting on the horse's back in order to benefit from its power and prestige. True, the horse could be used to convey them from place to place in a manner which was faster and much more convenient than travel on foot. But this was achieved by attaching the horse to a vehicle which would intervene between the passengers and the animal. Harnessing a horse to a chariot did not encroach on religious susceptibilities to the same extent as riding him would initially have done. The ancient Irish, figuratively, took off their shoes before daring to approach the sanctuary of the horse.

The sense of wonder produced by a vehicle which made extraordinary feats of speed possible and enabled its driver to level or override natural obstacles in his path found expression in a passage in *Táin Bó Cuailnge*, the flagship of early Irish prose literature. The passage deals with the use of the chariot in the highest pursuit open to a young man in a heroic age, warfare. This chariot which belongs to Cú Chulainn is not an ordinary vehicle. Its axle is made of silver. The chariot pole when broken is replaced with a branch cut from a sacred tree.[6] A Rolls-Royce among chariots, powered by horses, emerges from the description:

Every inch of the chariot bristled. Every angle and corner, front and rear, was a tearing place . . . [It] bristled with points of iron and narrow blades, with hooks and hard prongs and heroic frontal spikes, with ripping instruments and tearing nails on its shafts and straps and loops and cords . . . He [Cú Chulainn] had the chariot driven so heavily that its iron wheels sank into the earth. So deeply the chariot wheels sank into the earth that clods and boulders were torn up, with rocks and flagstones and the gravel of the ground, in a dyke as high as the iron wheels, enough for a fortress wall.[7]

The tale of *Táin Bó Cuailnge* is built around the common pursuit of the aristocratic ruling caste in the first few centuries of the Christian era—cattle raids. Warfare, consisting in large part of cattle raids, was the preserve of this elite, raising its participants almost to the level of gods. Young men wishing to become warriors had, therefore, to pass stiff tests to prove their fitness for the new level of existence. Appropriately, the horse-drawn chariot symbolises this state and plays a part in the initiation ceremonies. As we shall see later when we come to consider the inauguration ceremonies relating to kingship, such ritual tests frequently took the form of mounting the chariot. Cú Chulainn during his initiation as a warrior in *Táin Bó Cuailnge* is required to do this. But he goes further. He makes use of the vehicles supplied to him, to serve notice that he is not going to be an ordinary warrior. The way he does this is by breaking seventeen of the chariots as unworthy of a warrior of his potential. Only when he receives the most prestigious chariot, that of the king Conchobor, does he desist from his destructive orgy. Later, he makes use of the chariot, again that of the king, to indicate that even his king will not constrain him. He drives out in the chariot and symbolically takes possession of the king's domain by encircling it three times.[8]

Gold coin of the Redones, from France.

Detail, from the sixth century BC, of punch-decorated sheet bronze from a couch-back, showing horse-drawn wheeled vehicles, from Eberdingen-Hochdorf, Kr. Ludwigsburg, Germany.

Entering the chariot has the same purpose for Cú Chulainn as mounting the horse had for the characters in the tales mentioned earlier. By virtue of it he can enter the Otherworld. His chariot-driver is none other than Manannán mac Lir, the God of the Otherworld who, as we have seen, provides transport with horses over the sea. When cast in the role of charioteer, Manannán is known as Laeg mac Riangabra, literally Laeg son of Sea Horse. As well as travelling to the Otherworld in a chariot Cú Chulainn also returns in one. The chariot is vitally important to him. It symbolises the fact that he has been to the Otherworld and that he is armed with its life and power. It is his most important weapon. Towards the end of *Táin Bó Cuailnge*, rising from his sick bed he finds himself without any of his accustomed weapons. He raises his chariot on to his back and kills three men with it. With the chariot, the wounded warrior, despite his debility, had the Otherworld in his hands.[9]

THE HORSE AS MYTHICAL ANCESTOR

In attempting to understand the belief in the otherworldly character of horse and chariot which *Táin Bó Cuailnge* and other tales convey, we have to broaden our search beyond Ireland and her literature and traditions. In doing so we cannot expect much assistance from sciences such as archaeology for, as we go further back in time, the evidence becomes more scanty and less specific and it lacks the back-up of literary sources. We move into the world of the nomad where a life of bare subsistence and continuous movement from place to place ensures that no artefacts are produced and no traces of the type of life being led are left behind for the archaeologist to study. To gain an insight into the existence of prehistoric nomads and hence to learn how an animal like the horse could occupy a key position in their world we must turn to research done on primitive nomadic societies in the modern world.

The work of the eminent sociologist Émile Durkheim is of particular interest to us. Durkheim's concern was to discover the origins of man's religious impulse and his research, based on anthropologists' field studies, led him to highlight the efforts made by man to order and explain his universe. Durkheim found that, among the primitive peoples whose habits he studied, animals played a key role in these efforts and in the growth of religious sentiment.

People in the clans which make up the primitive tribes studied by Durkheim do not think of themselves as individuals with an identity distinct from the clan. Without the clan the individual is nothing. It is the clan that gives him his identity and strength, it makes him what he is, he depends completely on it for his existence. In the clan man first comes face to face with a power greater than his own, a power which, according to Durkheim, inspires in primitive man his first religious sentiments.[10]

The clans in some of these primitive tribes identify themselves with a plant or animal called a totem with which, as a group, they feel a deep sense of kinship.

Cross of the Scriptures, Clonmacnoise, showing war chariots and horses at its base. (*Commissioners of Public Works, Ireland*)

Epona relief from Beihingen, Württemberg. Above, the seated goddess is flanked by triads of horses and a pig is sacrificed.

Reconstruction of an old Irish chariot.
(After Liam de Paor)

The survival of the totem is vital for the clan. One rite, for example, practised among some Australian tribes, is geared to ensuring that the kangaroo species will reproduce itself and survive as the rainy season approaches. The animal's dung is burned and, as the fire grows, sparks, considered to be the germs of life of the totem, spread and fertilise the earth ensuring growth and prosperity in all things. In other rites, the elders of the clans imitate the kangaroo with a view to achieving the same result.[12]

The benefit of the revival of the totem has to be shared among the clan members. After an initial period of abstaining from eating the animal's flesh, a hunt takes place and the animal is killed. This is done when the animal is at the height of its powers and the first fruits of the harvest are being collected. The people of the clan assemble and ritually eat its flesh.

In the clan mythology it is claimed that the clan ancestor is responsible for the birth of new members. It is believed that he was originally an animal, hence the clan's involvement with an animal as a totem. The ancestor's spirit entered the earth on death, in a place which subsequently became sacred to the clan, and from that place enters the body of a woman causing human generation.[13]

They share its name and, they believe, its nature. Their fate is linked to it. The power which the clan represents becomes associated in the popular mind with the totem. This is brought home to the members of the clan very forcibly when the clan which is normally scattered because of economic pursuits holds an assembly in one location. The rallying point for these gatherings is the totem of the clan whose image is everywhere placed on view. On such occasions the members of the clan are released from the constraints and dullness of everyday existence. Joy and sorrow take on exaggerated forms and are expressed in dancing and loud voice. The clan, numerically no different, is transformed.[11]

This totemistic framework within which Durkheim places the relationship between clan and animal enables us to see Irish practices and beliefs in relation to the horse in a clearer light. Parallels can be drawn between the Irish beliefs and those studied by Durkheim. Placename lore in Ireland, for instance, preserves the names of Horse Gods and Goddesses who entered their otherworldly abode at certain locations.[14] In addition lore preserved in a 10th-century Irish document reflects the belief that an animal was once the ancestor of a people. The document refers to one of the most famous of the Irish gods as Eochaid Ollathair—Eochaid Great Father. The god's animal origins are conveyed in the name Eochaid which is derived from the ancient Irish name for horse, *ech*, and his role as an ancestor in his epithet Ollathair, Great Father.[15]

Some early population groups in Ireland, to judge from their names, thought of themselves as descendants of the horse. It was said that Corc mac Luigthig, for instance, ancestor of the powerful Eoganacht dynasty in Munster, was called Mac Láire, Son of the Mare, after his foster-mother, An Láir Dhearg, the Red Mare. Another of the Láir Dhearg's alleged foster-sons, Niall of the Nine Hostages, was also the ancestor of a powerful dynasty, the Uí Néill. All but two of the kings who were designated Kings of Ireland from the second quarter of the fifth century to the Battle of Clontarf in the middle of the eleventh were from this dynasty. Niall's intimate connection with horses is further confirmed by his father's name and that of his alleged slayer. Both were called Eochu. There is also direct evidence that population groups claimed descent from Eochu or Eochaid, who as we have seen, came to be regarded as a great ancestor. The Uí Echach, who occupied an area of Ulster now covered by the diocese of Dromore, was one such group. Its name, which has Iveagh as its equivalent today, means literally the descendant of Eochaid or Eochu. Other names which preserve an echo of a similar claim were the Uí Echach Muaidhe in East Tirawley, the Uí Echach of Sliabh Breg and the Tuath Echach from Armagh. Even today names such as Keogh (Mac Eochadha), literally the son of Eochaid, and Haughey (Ó hEochaidh), the grandson of Eochaid, are still common in Ireland.[16]

One of the oldest and most enduring tribes known to us in the historical period was the Dál Riata. They were sufficiently powerful in the sixth century to establish from their base in Ulster a colony in Scotland. Their ancestor was also called Eochaid, in this case, Eochaid Riata, literally chariot or horse-riding Eochaid. Eochaid, whom Irish tradition regards as an ancestral god and who was, it would appear, a horse in the earliest formulation of the myths surrounding him, entered the earth on his death, as we shall see, through a lake which later bore his name, Loch nEchach (Lough Neagh). There are numerous Irish legends in similar vein telling how magical horses disappear into waters which they subsequently haunt. The waters provide an entrance to the otherworld, which the horse ancestor inhabits as a god.

The clan's mythical ancestor or totem can assume the proportions of a god in certain circumstances. As the members of the clan look outside the narrow confines of their own world and see the other clans of the tribe with similar religious beliefs and rites, the idea of the tribe's unity of origin grows, and with it belief in an ancestor who is of a higher order to that of the clan.[17]

The step from the idea of totem and mythical ancestor of the clan to that of the tribal god is a logical one, but that step is made possible by social and economic changes of very great importance. These changes in certain societies see the emergence of the Earth-Mother goddess. Central to these changes is the ownership and exploitation of land.

THE HORSE AND THE EARTH-MOTHER GODDESS

Peoples who recall how their great ancestors mark the end of their terrestrial lives by entering the earth and haunting it know what it is to own land. Sacred beings can be confined to the earth and localised only by people who possess the earth. In this, as in most other things, religion must follow social and economic developments, although the popular imagination would sometimes reverse this process. In Ireland possession of the land and the release which it must have brought to a nomadic people from the bondage of whimsical forces was so deeply linked in the popular mind with horses that horses were seen as the necessary cause of this possession. Later we will see that the link between horses and possession of land may be based in the historical experience of the Indo-European group of people as they spread out from their homeland to conquer new lands. The horse was essential for their success and, in their rituals, the Indo-Europeans preserved an echo of their dependence on the horse with respect to land. The Irish, who belonged to the Indo-European group of people, have a reflection of this in their legends and law. The early Irish law tracts indicate that horses used to be released on to land in order to test it to see if it had recovered after being grazed by another animal or to see if it met the full legal standard. If the grass did not stick to the horse's teeth or if briars, thorns and burdocks didn't adhere to his mane or tail then the land was considered to have passed the test.[18] We have already suggested that compatibility with the horse and chariot could be a test for warrior status or kingship and later we will

First century BC coin of the Curiosolites, from North Western France.

OPPOSITE:
Denarius of L. Hostilius Saserna, circa 48 BC. This might well be an illustration from one of the early Irish epics. The naked and long haired warrior hurls a spear while in retreat. In his left hand is a shield. His charioteer, crouching well forward on the pole, urges the paired horses on.

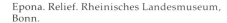

Epona. Relief. Rheinisches Landesmuseum, Bonn.

EARTH MOTHER OR FERTILITY GODDESS
This possession of land upgraded the status of woman. For nomadic people constantly on the move, children and the women who bore them could appear a liability. Women, with the children and uninitiated, were numbered among the members of the clan who could not attend the totemistic rites on certain occasions. This now changes with the possession of land. When the nomads settle down on the land women acquire a new prestige. The future of the clan is seen to depend on their fertility. The clan will cease to exist if it has no sons to inherit its land and work it. Without young members it has no future; others will take over its land. The procreation of children becomes an essential function in the life of the tribe but it is a function that is only imperfectly understood. For instance, the role of the father in procreation might not be fully appreciated. In some totemistic societies, as we have seen, conception is thought to take place when a woman goes to the clan's sacred place and comes under the influence of the soul of the clan's ancestor or its totem. What was appreciated was that the focus for the mysterious fertility forces at work was female. The woman was invested with the power and functions of the totem and in the process took on something of the stature of a goddess.

return to the subject. Here we are concerned with the possession and use of land, a subject which would have been of central concern to kings and warriors.

The law tracts stipulated that a person wishing to take possession of ground would first drive his horses on to it. A ninth-century poem in the *Calendar of Oengus* tells us that three Irish Saints—never ones to miss a pagan trick, particularly with horses—unyoked their horses on heaven. Later we will see how in an eighth-century legend concerning the kingship of Cashel an aspirant to the kingship unyokes his horses on the current king's land.[19] If, as we are arguing, the horse was one of the more important totems in the belief system to which Ireland was heir, then the changeover from a mainly nomadic life at some time in the past to a mainly settled agricultural existence would have been marked by a shift in the way society looked on the horse. In these new circumstances the spiritual principle in the clan becomes associated with the critical new element in the changeover from a mainly nomadic existence—the land. It is not so much that the totem slips out of view in communal life as that there is now a new figure in focus—the Earth-Mother goddess.

In Ireland the belief in the Goddess of Fertility is deeply embedded in the horse culture and finds expression in traditions which are related to kingship. Ownership of land has been important in Ireland since time immemorial. The preoccupation with land has continued to be so great that Irish poets and storytellers up to the present day frequently represent the land of Ireland as a woman. Sometimes they depict her as a beautiful girl, sometimes as an old hag mourning the loss of her spouse. Whatever her outward demeanour, her nobility is never in doubt. She is the companion of kings. In order to exercise sovereignty and rule the land a king must possess her. Towards the end of Yeats' play *Cathleen Ni Houlihan*, Peter Gillane asks his son whether he saw the mysterious old woman—"I did not," he replied, "but I saw a young girl and she had the walk of a queen". Clearly, in the boy's vision the land of Ireland was a worthy object of a king's attentions.

How is this marriage of king and goddess effected? In the main, it would appear, in symbolic terms. When Conn the grandfather of Cormac mac Airt is being inaugurated into the kingship, he is brought by a horseman to the Otherworld where the Goddess serves him ale from a golden goblet. But the sexual element is always, at least implicitly, present. Of Cormac Mac Airt it is said 'Nó cor faí Medb lasin mac, nibá rí Érenn Cormac'—'Until Medb had slept with the lad, Cormac was not king of Ireland'. Medb was the principal Irish goddess and the rites symbolising her marriage to the kings, the *Banais Rígi*, were carried out at Tara in Co. Meath. Her sexual prowess is legendary and it is one of the contributing factors to her prominent place among her sister goddesses. In her their function is most clearly delineated. They exist in mythology in order to ensure the fruits of the land and fertility in all things and this invariably means sexual congress and procreation, an area in which Medb has no equals.[20]

Medb's running is also of equine proportions for she can outpace the swiftest

On the list of Medb's sexual conquests, a list which, we are told, included the names of nine kings of Ireland, is the name of Fergus mac Roich, Fergus Son of Great Horse, King of the Ulaid, a man whose endowments do not belie his name. It takes seven women to satisfy him sexually. Medb, however, finds him lacking. Their encounters serve to draw attention, however, to another aspect of the goddess' nature which bears directly on the subject we are considering—how society ensured in a ritual fashion that its kings benefited from the sacred power of the horse. In highlighting the emergence of the Earth-Mother goddess to the forefront of societies which were changing from a nomadic existence to one of settled agriculture we observed that this need not necessarily mean the eclipse of the totem in clan consciousness. This is exemplified in the various stories about Medb where she is depicted as having distinct links with horses, links which Fergus strikingly confirms. As he reflects bitterly on his disappointed hopes and on his many failures with Medb, martial as well as marital, he chooses to represent her as a mare leading her herd astray: 'We followed the rump of a misguided woman. It is the usual thing for a herd led by a mare to be strayed and destroyed.' Whatever about the equity of blaming the failures of the Connacht men on Medb, the appropriateness of Fergus' designation of her could not be questioned.

Top : Fragment of lintel from Nages (Gard) in France, decorated by two severed heads and two galloping horses. Severed heads were venerated by the Celts. (*Musée Archéologique de Nîmes, France*)

Left : Wooden trackway, dated 148 BC, uncovered in a bog at Corlea, Co. Longford. The road was almost five eighths of a mile in length. With the growth, in early times, of bog throughout the country, this type of road would have been important to enable carts to provide transport. (*Barry Rafferty*)

Right : Decoration on a bronze snaffle horse-bit dating from the first century AD and found at Attymon, Co. Galway. (*Bord Failte*)

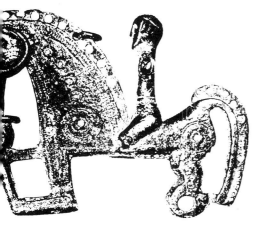

Fourth century BC bronze brooch from Iberia shows rider carrying a severed head (under the horse's muzzle).

horse, but the mode of transport which she normally employs is the horse-drawn chariot. In addition, her father, Eochaid Feidlech, like one of her suitors and her husband (Fergus Mac Roich), bears a name derived from the Old Irish word for horse, *Ech*.

The Indian epic the *Mahabharata* provides indirect evidence of Medb's close association with horses and her indispensability for kings. There we find that her father's counterpart is the great king Yayati and that Medb has many striking resemblances to Yayati's daughter Madhavi. In the epic, Madhavi is described as 'the door to the horses'. The reason for this is that she is sent by her father to sleep with kings in each corner of the world. Without her, they could not be kings for she alone can give them sons. They, in return for her services must each give back two hundred unique horses to the king. These horses had originally been dispersed throughout the world and it is clear that the possession of them by the kings in each part of the world was related to their acquisition of kingship.[21]

But Medb is not the only Irish goddess, and, like her, many of the others are never far removed from horses. Brigid, for instance, whose cult survived into the Christian era can, like Medb, claim horse-related ancestry. Her father's name is Eochaid Ollathair, the Horse-God extraordinary. The Caillech Bérri, the Hag of Berre, at the height of her powers, was the wife of the model of kingship, the God Lug. Now bereft of her beauty and youth she retains the memory of her days of glory, days which were filled with splendour and the excitement of horse racing:

> Swift chariots and horses that carried off the prize,
> once I had plenty of them;
> a blessing on the King who granted them.

One Irish Mother Goddess, Macha, actually races against the King of Ulster's horses when she is pregnant. The goddess Étaín is known as Echraide, Horseriding. Horses are drowned for her by a king and she is wooed by a succession of gods all of whom have definite equine links in Irish tradition. One of these, the magnificent horseman Eochaid Airem, a god associated with Westmeath and Longford, was, it was claimed, once King of Tara. His position at Tara, the story goes, could not be ratified until he had slept with Étaín.

The marriage of the would-be king to the Goddess is an Otherworldly affair and the stories which describe it confirm what we have already seen in the case of the goddesses themselves—horses are much in evidence. At Tara, traditionally the location where Kings of Ireland were inaugurated, a mist, we are told in the tale *Baile in Scáil*, envelopes Conn. A horseman comes riding towards him and takes him to his house which is, of course, the Otherworld. His grandson Cormac mac Airt has a similar adventure on his inauguration day. When he reaches the Otherworld the God who presides over the great feast is none other than the Horse God, Manannán mac Lir.

HORSE AND CHARIOT BURIALS

The Indo-European dispersal, believed to have taken place from an area of southern Russia to the north of the Black Sea, some time before the end of the third millennium BC, may have been responsible for the spread of totemistic practices and beliefs relating to the horse. The cultural similarities which existed between Ireland and India add weight to this suggestion. The people who issued forth from their homeland in southern Russia bequeathed vigorous religious beliefs to areas such as Ireland and India where their influence was felt. These areas would preserve in their language and ritual a memory of a past which may have been totemistic. To get a picture of the Indo-European attitude to the horse which was probably gaining influence in Ireland by at least 500 BC, we must turn to developments on the continent of Europe. Against the continental background, beliefs and practices in Ireland involving the horse form a more coherent pattern.

About the beginning of the first millennium BC an aggressive people mounted on horses was making inroads into Europe from the East. This was Homer's mare-milkers, the Scythians, who had made of the horse, when allied to the bow, an effective engine of war. A respect for ancient practice, attributable perhaps to the nomadic character of their existence, was a feature of their ways. It found dramatic expression in the sacrifice of the horse. The Scythians sacrificed horses and, in the manner of their Indo-European predecessors in southern Russia about 3000 BC, buried them in their graves with all their harness.[22]

Decorated bronze three-link bridle bit, now in the National Museum, Dublin.

The Celts who emerged in central Europe in the eighth century, like the Scythians, spoke an Indo-European language and belonged to the mainstream of the Indo-European horse tradition. But they introduced variations to that tradition, one of which relates to the practice of burying horse chariots in graves with human remains. As in Ireland, such chariots were seen to share in the sacred character of the horse but what was distinctive about the Celtic chariot graves was the status of their occupants. They were not ordinary people. They were chieftains and leaders who, in a stratified society, carried the fortunes of their tribes beyond the grave.

The Celts were to have a major effect on developments in Ireland some centuries before the Christian era. They play a leading role in the unfolding of the story of the horse as a quasi-religious force in society. The custom of vehicle burial may have never reached Ireland—Yorkshire in the second century BC provides us with the nearest recorded instance of it—but the belief in the otherworldly character of horse and chariot underlying it gained, as we have suggested, a firm foothold.[23]

A frieze of horse heads on the lintel of a portico of the Celto-Ligurian sanctuary of Roquepertuse (Bouches-du-Rhône).

2

The Horse in Irish Celtic Society

CELTIC HORSE GODDESS

As WELL AS finding a place in the burial practices of the continental Celts, the horse also figured prominently in their artistic work. Given the totemistic framework we have been suggesting, the representation of horses may have been intended to promote the common good. This would appear to explain the presence of the image of the horse on the helmets of Celtic warriors.[1] In the Roman armies Celtic auxiliaries also carried on their banners the representation of the goddess, Epona, who was closely associated with the horse. Like the name of the God Eochaid, that of Epona is derived from the Indo-European word for horse, *ekuos*. Epona was the homesick soldier's pin-up girl extraordinary. She represented the good life at home.

Epona's name or image is recorded on over one hundred and twenty monuments on the continent. In many of these representations her protective role is emphasized. She is the mother goddess responsible for the life of the foals placed in her charge. In her, fertility finds an outlet. In one representation of her—a bas relief from the Côte d'Or—Epona is not shown in human form with the foals. Rather, she is a mare suckling them. Clearly the sculptor saw no reason to depict the Goddess separate from the mare. It is a confusion that has its parallels in Irish tradition and may have been inspired by a belief in a mystical link between horse and people, a belief that preceded the emergence of the goddess.[2]

An association between Epona and a population group is suggested by the ancient name of the people of Kintyre in Argyll (Scotland), the Epidii, a name derived from the same root as Epona. The presence at Uffington in Berkshire in England of a large white horse, carved in the chalk scarp near a pre-existing Iron Age hill fort, suggests that the people of that region also identified with the animal. This white horse, thought to be the work of the mainly Celtic settlers known as the Belgae in the first century BC, may be a representation of Epona. One Scottish family unrelated to Epona, the McLeods, was considered at some stage in the past to be descended from the horse. 'Síol a' Chapaill' was the name by which this family was known.[3] The British evidence for such beliefs is, however, scanty and we must return to Ireland which because of its location has frequently preserved traditions lost elsewhere.

Before investigating further the various traditions and beliefs which have grown

Bronze statuette of a horse, found at
Châlons-sur-Marne, France, Gallo-Roman
period.

Below : Tara, Co Meath, the most famous
hill-fort in Ireland, built around an ancient
burial cairn, was the seat of the Ui Neill kings.
At Tara, according to mythology, rites
symbolising the marriage of the Goddess
Medb to the king were carried out. Here also,
we are told, the God Lug performed feats of
horsemanship to establish his claims to
kingship. *(Commissioners of Public Works,
Ireland)*

up around the horse in Ireland and which offer parallels with traditions and beliefs outside Ireland we must look at the type of society illustrated by the earliest records in Ireland. For the organisation of such a society and its degree of sophistication determine attitudes to religious forces like the horse; changes in that organisation, as we have noted, give rise to new ways of looking at the horse.

EARLY IRISH SOCIETY

The Irish world of the first centuries of the Christian era, which the largely fictional events of *Táin Bó Cuailnge* are thought to reflect is markedly aristocratic. It is peopled by kings and queens, warriors and beautiful women, all conscious of their rights and possessions. It is a Celtic world, quick-tempered and self-indulgent. In it the common people have no place. In the description of battles in the ancient tales they feature only as chariot fodder—the story teller, with unconscious irony, numbering them on occasions with the slaughtered horses.[4]

The *tuath*, meaning tribe or people, was the smallest and basic unit of this society, and each *tuath* had its king. The internal government of the *tuath* was in the hands of the king aided by an ancient system of detailed laws. The laws had been handed down from generation to generation and interpreted, developed and jealously guarded by a professional class of jurists which had its parallels throughout the Indo-European world. The great respect which the laws and jurists commanded within the *tuath* was a major factor in the observance of the laws. The king had little power to enforce judgement and was mainly concerned with matters external to the *tuath*. His main governmental duties were as war leader and to preside over the *aonach* of the *tuath*, or assembly.

Gold coin of the Bituriges Cubi, from Berry, France.

Detail from a fourth century BC frieze on bronze situla, from Slovenia, Yugoslavia.

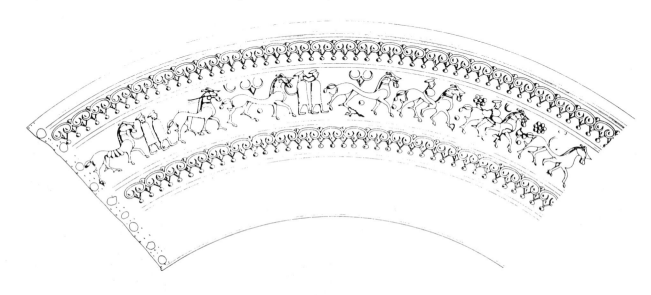

Source: Liam Blake.

Images of the horse. *Sources*: LEFT and BELOW DoA; RIGHT Bill Doyle; BOTTOM Turlough Smith.

The Gundestrup Cauldron found in a peat bog in Denmark dates from the
first century B.C. The scene on the inside right features the God
Cernunnos as Lord of the Animals, a scene which has a parallel on the
North Cross at Ahenny Co. Tipperary. On the left, horsemen pass by a
scene of ritual sacrifice.
Source: Danish National Museum.

Bronze pony-cap from Kircudbrightshire. Found deposited in a lake, probably as a votive offering. Style of ornament typical of the early Celtic. (*National Museum of Antiquities, Edinburgh*).

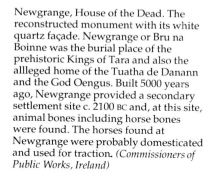

Newgrange, House of the Dead. The reconstructed monument with its white quartz façade. Newgrange or Bru na Boinne was the burial place of the prehistoric Kings of Tara and also the allleged home of the Tuatha de Danann and the God Oengus. Built 5000 years ago, Newgrange provided a secondary settlement site c. 2100 BC and, at this site, animal bones including horse bones were found. The horses found at Newgrange were probably domesticated and used for traction. (*Commissioners of Public Works, Ireland*)

BOND WITH HORSES

In the centuries before kingship became the focus of its welfare, the *tuath* was, in all probability, held together as a social unit by a mystical bond the nature of which must now be a matter of speculation only. Some of the names of population groups in the period before the seventh century do give an indication of the type of bond this may have been. Some are called after colours, some after the occupation of the members of the group, but those which are of interest here are those which received their names from animals, people like the *Artraide*, 'Bear People', *Osraige*, 'Deer People' and, more especially the *Grecraige*, 'Horse People'. Their names do constitute some evidence for the identification of groups of people with animals and in particular with the horse and, as we have seen, this identification is one of the characteristics of a totemistic society.[5]

Bearing in mind that names in ancient times attempted to capture the essence of that which they signified, we must consider whether there is any evidence from other sources which would suggest that an identification with horses is part of the Irish inheritance. Folklore, for its part, has put forward the belief that the horse's body had a human rib and that the horse could converse in human speech.[6] Ancient Irish literature also provides many instances of the belief that its depicted characters are linked very closely to their horses. The kinship which Cú Chulainn enjoyed with his horses is at times beautifully evoked. His chariot horses are called *Liath Macha* and *Dubh Sainglenn* and in a passage from the eighth-century tale *Aided Con cCulainn*, his relationship with them is almost taken for granted. The children of

Cailitin have searched the entire province of Ulster for Cú Chulainn. They come eventually to the Valley of the Deaf where

> They saw the *Dubh Sainglenn* and the *Liath Macha* at ease at the bottom of the valley and Laegh Son of Riangabhra (the charioteer) in charge of them beside; and they understood that Cú Chulainn was in the valley.

Cú Chulainn's link with the horses commences at his birth which coincided with a mare giving birth to two foals. The foals are presented to him and from that moment his fate is linked to theirs.[7] In addition, we are told that his human father was Sualtaim mac Roích, Sualtaim Son of Great Horse. His divine father was the god Lug who also had many equine associations as we shall see.

At times the story-teller of *Táin Bó Cuailnge* lyrically suggests the relationship between man and horse, the behaviour of the animals evoking, as in this passage from the *Táin Bó Cuailnge,* the powerful feelings of their owners. Cú Chulainn is alone with his father, Sualtaim. "Their horses grazed the pillar stone at Ard Cuillen, Sualtaim's steeds cropped the grass down to the soil north of the pillar stone. Cú Chulainn's steeds cropped the grass down to the soil bedrock south of the pillar stone."

The equilibrium is shattered for Cú Chulainn when he goes to fight his boyhood friend Fer Diad. Here again the behaviour of the horse suggests the mood. After the first day's battle Cú Chulainn and Fer Diad are still friends: "Their horses were grazing in the same paddock on that night," but by the end of the third day tempers had frayed and a barrier had arisen between the friends: "Their parting [from battle] was that of two sad dispirited ones. Their horses were not in the same paddock that night."[8]

This identification of horse and hero is not confined to Cú Chulainn in the *Táin Bó Cuailnge* but is universal in Irish literature. We are told that during his life Cú Chulainn killed many mythological figures bearing the name Eochaid or Eochu. So firm is the link between one of these, the splendid mythical horseman Eochu Rond and his horse that Cú Chulainn has merely to kill the horse in order to dispose of its owner. The tradition of a close relationship between man and horse is so secure that it survives into relatively modern times. Later we shall see that seventeenth-century folklore portrays the Earl of Desmond as a horse. Even a Christian saint, Colmcille, shares in the tradition and would seem to enjoy a similar relationship with his monastery's cart horse as Cú Chulainn's lover Emer had with the horse Liath Macha. When Cú Chulainn died his horse went to bid farewell to Emer, laying its head in her lap.[9] Saint Colmcille, the story goes, was resting after visiting his fellow monks shortly before his death in 597 when the white cart horse approached him. We are told that: "It pressed its muzzle into his bosom, whinnying plaintively and shedding tears, its mouth foaming."[10]

In the absence of strong centralised government and in conditions of pastoral

Coin of the Osismii of Armorica (Gaul).

The obverse side features an abstract representation of the human head.

The reverse side (page 27) shows a horse with human head and an acrobatic rider galloping over a prostrate human figure.

nomadism a common identification with an animal such as the horse could, at some time in the past, have constituted a bond which would link people together in a community, giving rise to the instances in myth and story we have been discussing. But settled life, as well as pastoral nomadism, influenced the popular lore concerning horses. The *Dindsenchas*, a compilation of traditional lore about famous places, both on land and on water, contains legends dealing with the origins of these places and their names. Horses figure prominently in these legends and are the basis of some of the placenames.

UNDERWATER HORSE GODS

As we have seen in the early part of this chapter, water was regarded in Irish tradition as one of the gateways to the Otherworld and horses often provided transport across the waters for mythical figures making the passage. Stories in the *Dindsenchas* elaborate on this theme. Sometimes, as in the case of Loch Gabhar (Lagore), they record how horses are drowned in lakes. These lakes are then the otherworldly dwelling places of the horses which are depicted in the popular imagination as the ghosts haunting the waters. Loch Gabhar, literally the lake of the steeds, on which the well-known crannog of Lagore was located, got its name when two mares, called *Grian* and *Gaoth*, belonging to Eochaid Cenn Maircc, literally Eochaid Horsehead, a king of the Corce Loígde in West Cork, were chased by a stallion and drowned in the lake.[11] In the popular mind such steeds however did not cease to exist. On the contrary, as we shall see later, there were great popular expectations of their return. Irish folklore contains many stories about water horses and their otherworldly properties.

In these tales we are not very far removed from the monster that rules the waters of Loch Ness in Scotland. At a point in the North-East of Ireland not very far from Scotland lies the country's largest lake, Lough Neagh, which the traditions tell us was once possessed by a horse. In the twelfth century, a Welsh visitor whom we shall meet again, Gerald de Barry, otherwise known as Giraldus Cambrensis, recorded claims by local fishermen that on a clear day buildings, presumably the Otherworld dwellings of a god, could be seen beneath the waters. These claims found their way into one of Tom Moore's popular melodies, 'Let Erin Remember the days of Old':

> On Lough Neagh's Bank, as the fisherman strays,
> When the clear cold eve's declining,
> He sees the round towers of other days,
> In the wave beneath him shining.

The stories about the origin of Lough Neagh, one of which is quoted below, provide a basis for these claims. Reading between the lines in these stories, it is clear that it was once believed that a horse was drowned in this lake and that this horse was or became a God. The stories differ,[12] but they all have this in common: they are peopled by gods with very definite equine associations, gods who jealously guard their domains, be they land or water. As we might expect, these gods are depicted leading a horse, an indication that they possess the land on which they are located. But it indicates more, as we have seen. There is a confusion between horse and god. The horse is a god.

The background to the Lough Neagh story is that the race of Gods, Tuatha Dé Danann, were banished to the Otherworld, namely the mounds and lakes of Ireland. In the following version of the story the god in question is Oengus, Mac Ind Óc, the son of one of the Tuatha Dé Danann, Eochaid Ollathair, the Horse God par excellence. Oengus is patrolling his Otherworld territory, the burial mound of Brug na Bóinne or Brug meic ind Óic, at Newgrange in Co. Meath with his great horse when he meets two brothers. As the story indicates, he gives his horse to one of them and from this gesture comes the origin and possession of Lough Neagh:

> Echu and his brother Ribh went westward . . . and set up on the plain of Mac Ind Óc. He [the Mac Ind Óc] went to them in the shape of a land holder, with his horse, and told them that they should not bide on the plain. They said to him that they had no way to carry their load of goods without pack horses. 'Put' says he 'the fill of the plain wherein you stand into bundles with their straps upon the horse and he will carry them with you to the place where he will lie down thereunder'. So they went thence till they reached Liathmuine. There the horse lies down beside them and there he stales and made of his urine a well which came over them. So that is Loch Echach, that is Echu, the king, and his horse's water, which there spread out.[13]

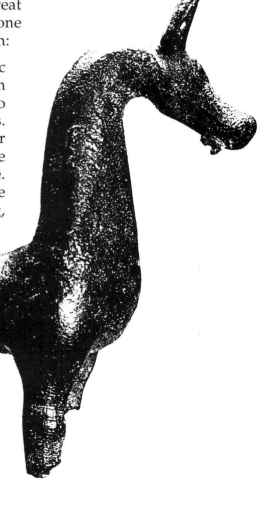

Fifth or fourth century BC bronze horse fugurine from Freisen, Kr. St Wendal, Germany.

In any society the changeover from a nomadic and totemistic existence to one of settled agriculture involves not only social but religious changes. The totem fades into the background but it does not die. It still haunts sacred places and continues to look after the welfare of society albeit in a new guise. In Ireland, as we have remarked, a drowned horse was believed to have been deified and to be living an Otherworld existence under certain Irish lakes. As one of the gods banished to the Otherworld, it was expected to return to intervene in man's affairs from time to time. Its return to land was anticipated with that mixture of longing and fear reserved for the gods.[14]

Water horses were able to upgrade a man's equine stock, likewise they could also take his children away from him. In the main, however, belief in the entry of the Horse God into the Otherworld gave reassurance to people. But the harnessing of the power of the horse on a day-to-day basis posed a problem which the Irish religious imagination had to tackle. True, the drowning of the horse constituted a rite which, having taken place in the past, was believed to have significance for all time in the future. The benefits of that once-off rite, namely the ownership and fruits of the land, would continue to be available, but this alone would not be sufficient. The benefits would have to be seen to be made available. Religious imagination demanded, so to speak, sacraments, regular re-enactments of Otherworldly drama.

HORSE SACRIFICE AND THE KING

Horse sacrifice was the means whereby the power of the horse would be harnessed. In ancient Rome the horse most pleasing to Mars, the God of War and father of Romulus the progenitor of the Roman people, was sacrificed. Society, if it had a

Panel from the first century BC Gundestrup Cauldron, found in a peat bog in Denmark. The scene shows a victim being ceremoniously sacrificed by being drowned in a vessel of liquid as horsemen pass by. The God to whom the sacrifice was offered may have been Teutates.

totem, could offer no more valuable victim to the gods than its totem. Horses were offered to the Germanic equivalent of Mars and, in Gaul, the rites involving his equivalent there, Rudiobus, also centred on the horse. In the second century AD the people of Cassiciate, literally the land of the mare or of horses, on ceremonial occasions offered a bronze horse to Rudiobus.[15] In the limestone rock of the portico of the Celto-Ligurian shrine of Roquepertuse (Bouches du Rhône) in France, which is believed to be dedicated to the Celtic God of War, the heads of horses have been carved. Not only have the horses been sacrificed, the sculpture tells us, but their heads have been preserved as a continual source of life for the god.

But settled life required not only gods but kings or leaders who would protect the land possessed and, in Ireland, ritual frequently involved the king who provided the focus for communal attempts to achieve prosperity. Kingship, it would appear, was the medium through which the horse remained an active force in Irish society—the separation of religion and politics being an invention of the modern world—and custom would find various ways of harnessing that force. As we might expect from our preceding discussion the most outstanding of these ways was horse sacrifice followed by the eating of the horse's flesh.

The king's sacrificial communion with the horse takes place at his inauguration. Inauguration rituals are concerned with validating the king as ruler over land and subject peoples. The Indian kingship ritual, the Asvamedha, makes the connection clear between horse sacrifice and conquest. For a year before it is sacrificed a prize stallion is allowed to wander over whatever lands it wishes. When it is killed the king's rule over these lands is confirmed. In Ireland the land is synonymous with the Earth-Mother Goddess. The king had to be assimilated to her and this is achieved by the killing of the horse. The fortunes and fertility of the land are thus linked to that of the king and welfare assured.

The evidence for horse sacrifice in Ireland is speculative but worth recounting since it is based on practices which probably had their origins in the Indo-European past. On the death of a Scythian king, according to Herodotus, a period of mourning began which culminated in the sacrifice of the king's horses. The method of staking the horses after they have been killed has a parallel in Irish legend. Herodotus' account is as follows:

> Fifty of the best of the late King's attendants are taken and are strangled, along with fifty of the most beautiful women . . . Then strong stakes are run lengthways through the bodies of the horses from tail to neck . . . Each horse is given a bit and bridle, which is later stretched out in front of the horse and fastened with a peg.

Later we read how the attendants who have been killed are placed on the horses' backs and, supported by stakes, riders and horses are ranged around the king's tomb.

Irish legend similarly describes a horse which has been staked, this time by the pole of the chariot to which it is harnessed. In the legend we are told how Cú Chulainn, hearing a terrifying cry at night, rushes from his bed outside and is confronted by a fantastic scene. A chariot, to which a single red horse is harnessed, having one leg only, and having the chariot-pole passing through its body and held in place by a peg in the middle of its forehead, carries a red woman, wearing a long red cloak (red being the colour usually associated with the Otherworld). When Cú Chulainn tries to find out from the woman who she is, everything disappears.[16]

There is some evidence that the ritual killing of a horse may have been followed by the consumption of its flesh. Archaeological evidence from settlement and other sites throws some light on the practice of eating horses. The presence of animal bones which have been broken, presumably to extract the marrow, is accepted by archaeologists as evidence that the animals in question were being eaten. As we might expect, the bulk of the bones found at habitation sites in all periods belonged to cattle. Only on one rath site, Boho, in Co. Fermanagh, does the amount of cattle bones fall below 70 per cent of the total. By way of contrast, the figure for horse-bones varies between a half and three and a half per cent of the total generally (where the percentage goes as high as nine per cent as at Garranes Ring Fort, the sample is very small).[17] At Cahercommaun Stone Fort in Co. Cork, dated AD 600–800, the contrast between horse and cattle bones was particularly strong. Cattle bones found there amounted to ninety-seven per cent whereas horse-bones only came to half a per cent of the total. Clearly horses did not rival cattle as a source of food. We are struck, nevertheless, by the frequency with which horse-bones, albeit in small numbers, occur at the habitations. In some of the sites, particularly from post-Christian times, the horses found may have been used for traction or riding and not necessarily as food. But the presence of broken horse-bones at the Beaker settlement at Newgrange dated about 2000 BC and at levels in Ballinderry crannogs with dates extending from early Christian times to about AD 1100 suggests the continuity of the practice of eating horseflesh from pre- to post-Christian times.[18] Excavations in tenth-century Dublin have also uncovered horse bones, probably indicating that some horseflesh was eaten, although this may reflect Scandinavian and not necessarily Irish taste.

In an 11th-century description by Gerald de Barry of the inauguration rite of a king in the north-western part of the country, the eating of horseflesh is dealt with in detail. In this account Gerald describes how a mare is killed, her flesh eaten and the king mated with her in her capacity as Earth-Mother Goddess. It is an account which has some parallels elsewhere in the Indo-European world but only in Ireland and India is the sexual element explicitly present. Despite the fact that in the Indian ritual, Asvamedha, it is the queen, and not the king as in Ireland, who is the focus for the sacred marriage there is little doubt that both cases have a common basis in a ritual mating of king and equine goddess.[19]

We see therefore that the power of the horse could be occasionally harnessed in a public manner by having potential kings joined in a symbolic union with a Mare Goddess, a ritual that culminated in the sacrificial eating of the animal's flesh. We are told nothing in this account about the mare except that she was white, a colour associated with one of the horses in the Roman races on the Campus of Mars. An indication that she may have taken part in a race and emerged triumphant is contained in a Fenian tale which features Fionn mac Cumhaill, a mythological figure who came to be seen as a leader of a band of soldiers. In the tale Fionn and his warriors have been horseracing and a present of the winning steed is made to him. Later the horse is killed and offered to him to eat by an old hag from the Otherworld. Such old hags or *caillechs* were disguised versions of the Goddess whom the king must espouse by accepting what food or drink she offers. In the case of Fionn the offering from the goddess is the flesh of the winning horse.[21]

Traditionally, it would appear, in the Irish popular imagination, horseracing and the destruction of the animal were not necessarily incompatible. People believed that the Otherworld, to which the slain horse would go, was very close to the forum in this life where he could be seen to best advantage—the racecourse.

The Irish practice which Gerald described in the passage given below had a certain shock value in the twelfth century. He wrote in the knowledge that extravagant examples of Irish behaviour would be politically useful to his Norman masters and that they would reward him for his services. However, despite the bias against the Irish which is evident in his writings, his account of the inauguration rite has an authentic ring to it. As he describes how the king, in an orgy of possession, is united with the Mare Goddess, very little of the detail is omitted:

A NEW AND OUTLANDISH WAY OF CONFERRING DOMINION AND KINGSHIP

There is in the northern and farther part of Ulster, namely in Kenelcunnil (Tyrconnell) a certain people which is accustomed to consecrate its king with a rite altogether outlandish and abominable. When the whole people of that land has been gathered together in one place, a white mare is brought forward in to the middle of the assembly. He who is to be inaugurated, not as a chief but as a beast, not as a king but as an outlaw, embraces the animal before all, professing himself to be a beast also. The mare is then killed immediately, cut up in pieces, and boiled in water. A bath is prepared for the man afterwards in the same water. He sits in the bath surrounded by all his people, and all, he and they, eat of the meat of the mare which is brought to them. He quaffs and drinks of the broth in which he is bathed, not in any cup, or using his hand but just dipping his mouth into it round about him. When this unrighteous rite has been carried out his kingship and dominion has been conferred.[20]

A fight between horses urged on by men at the side, on a memorial stone dated about AD 500 from Häggeby, Sweden. (*National Historical Museum, Stockholm*).

THE IMPORTANCE OF HORSERACING

As evidence of this link between horseracing and the Otherworld, the communal assemblies which featured a great deal of horseracing were often sited on ancient burial grounds, traditionally the entrance to the Otherworld, and included games which were funerary in origin among their programmes.[22] Nor was this phenomenon confined to Ireland. In the *Iliad* of Homer the funeral games after the death of Patrokles included a chariot race and among the Scythians, funeral games were characterised by horseracing.[23] To understand the relevance of horseracing to early Irish kings, we rely in part, as we did in relation to horse sacrifice, on the wider Indo-European background.

In ancient Rome, an Indo-European centre, the sacrifice of a horse, the October Equus, was linked to racing. Horseracing which took place on the Campus of Mars in March, at the beginning of the season of warfare, was considered to be vital for Rome's welfare. The horses in the race symbolised the different skills which society needed and competition between these horses was essential. The winning horse in the race was sacrificed to Mars, the God of War, in October, when the warfare season had been concluded. The horse's body, representing society's essential skills or the spoils of war, was presented to the king. 'The mystical benefits of competition' to quote the scholar Dumézil, were made available to him. When the fighting was over he was seen to be in charge.[24]

The forum in which racing took place in Ireland was the *aonach*, or communal assembly. A great variety of business was transacted during these gatherings reflecting the interests, both cultural and commercial, of the *tuath*, but they were held primarily because it was believed that tribal welfare would be mysteriously put at risk if the *tuath* did not come together in this way. These gatherings which took place at key points in the agricultural calendar resembled in many ways the totemistic clan assemblies considered at the beginning of this chapter, in that they afforded the *tuath* an opportunity to renew and assert itself and gave an animal,[25] the horse, a key role in the process. Part and parcel of this renewal process was the element of competition which pervaded the *aonach* and which, as we have seen, made horseracing in ancient Rome of prime importance to its king and people.

Of all events at the *aonach* the most important was horseracing. One of the most famous of the great *aonaig* was that at Carman which was held by the King of Leinster like many of the *aonaig* in August, a month whose Irish name, Lugnasad, still reminds us of the god Lug to whom the first day of the month was sacred.

Lug's feast was originally a harvest festival which celebrated his victory over the Fomorians, from whom he captured agricultural skills.[26] It was thus an appropriate festival for horseracing. We are told by an eleventh-century poet that seven of the eight days on which the *aonach* was held featured racing:

On the Kalends of August free from reproach, they would go thither every third year; they would hold seven races for a glorious object; seven days in a week.[27]

Ample testimony to the importance of horseracing is provided by the preparations which were made in advance of it. Some indication of the size of these preparations is conveyed by the poet's description of Carman. The *aonach* there was held only every third year, the other two being spent in preparation for it. In the Irish law tracts we read that the roads were specially cleaned before horseracing time. There are also other indications of the importance of racing. For instance, it continued at many sites long after the other activities of the *aonach* had ceased to occur there. An undoubted factor in the prominent place which horseracing held in the life of the *tuath* was the fact that it offered a forum for competition. The small independent *tuaths* into which Ireland was fragmented (up to 150 it is believed) were engaged almost until the eclipse of the Gaelic order in the seventeenth century in a continuous round of petty warfare. There was a strong element of ritual in this warfare, its object being, as a recent commentator has put it 'to sting and stun but not to kill'. Instead of destroying, it upheld the social order, enabled status to be asserted, righted wrongs, real or perceived, and bonded the *tuath* together. At the *aonach* such competitiveness could be channelled into games and horseracing in relatively peaceful fashion. At the fair of Carman, for instance, 'Suing, harsh levying of debts, satirising, quarrelling, misconduct are not dared during races'.[28] Organisers of hurling or football matches throughout the country today no doubt expect a similar restraint among spectators and hope that violence will be channelled into the cut and thrust of the game.

Because of the otherworldly location of the racecourse and the intense efforts which competition elicited from those racing there, the horses were seen to cross over the threshold to the Otherworld. Fertility was the result. The ancient fairs of Tara, Carman and Emhain Macha were held to promote fertility, and it is clear that for this reason, the kings were obliged to hold them frequently.[29] Of Aonach Carman it was said:

For holding it the Leinstermen [were promised] corn and milk and freedom from control of any [other] province in Ireland; that they should have men, royal heroes, tender women, good cheer in every several house; every fruit like a show and nets full [of fish] from waters.[30]

As we might expect, the king was closely involved with the *aonach* or *feis* in ancient Ireland. It was at such a gathering that he was inaugurated and it was he who presided over subsequent gatherings. Apart from this general involvement, he had a particular interest in the programme item which we have been discussing, horseracing. Some of the background to this had already been sketched in. The *feis*

Racing at Cheltenham (*Gerry Cranham*)

or the *aonach* has close parallels with totemistic clan assemblies. Both give rise to intense feelings and assertions of communal identity and are held in the belief that their proceedings are bound up, in some mysterious way, with the welfare of the group and both accord a central position to an animal in those proceedings. It remains for us to examine more closely the king's involvement in racing in the light of what we have seen of its purpose in the Indo-European world. As we noted with regard to the Roman races, the 'mystical benefits of competition' on the racecourse had to be seen to be appropriated by society, in the person of its king, at the end of the warrior season. In Ireland the king was the leader of the *tuath* and the symbol of its strength in war and, therefore, might be expected to be involved with horseracing in much the same way as his Roman counterpart. Reading between the lines of the story about Macha, the Irish Goddess who races against the king's horses when she is pregnant, we begin to get an insight into that involvement.

There are many indications in the story that the underlying impulse is to assimilate, as in the Roman and Asvamedha rituals which we have been considering, a king to a winning horse which embodies all-embracing powers. The calamity that overtakes the Ulstermen when their king is thwarted at the racecourse is an indirect testimony to this. Moreover, it is possible to see in the racecourse struggle a struggle between skills, as symbolised by horses, similar to that which has been noted in the Roman race of the 14th March, which had as its logical conclusion the conferring of the winning horse on the king in October.

In the story of Macha the warrior function and skills are pitted against those of breeders and cultivators among whom Macha, married to a rich farmer and pregnant with divine equine twins to whom she gives birth as she passes the winning post, is clearly numbered.[33] Macha wins and her success means that the Ulstermen are temporarily deprived of their warrior powers. Instead of conquering and possessing they are conquered and possessed by the woman—through her sickness. The equine goddess opposes the king and deprives him of his association with the winning horse. Her actions run directly counter to those of the Irish king in the inauguration ritual we have discussed. In this ritual he mates with the equine goddess in the time-honoured Indo-European manner and, by so doing, maintains the social order. Macha, the equine goddess, on the other hand, in our story places the social order at risk; Ulster is left undefended.

There is one saving grace, however. The birth of divine equine twins provides the sequel, it would seem, to the sacred marriage of an equine goddess and king in Indo-European mythology and would seem to be responsible for restoring order to the chaotic condition in which Ulster finds itself. The value of the twins to the province is indicated by the reference to them in the name of the site for the assembly of the Ulstermen, Emhain Macha, the Twins of Macha, known today as Navan Fort in Co. Armagh. The birth of the two foals is made to coincide in another tale, as we have seen, with the birth of Cú Chulainn, son of the god Lug, who emerges as the

MACHA, THE IRISH GODDESS, RACES THE KING'S HORSES

The occasion is, according to the legend, a fair in Ulster, on a plain known subsequent to the events as Emhain Macha, the Twins of Macha. During the day horseracing has been taking place and among those competing have been horses belonging to the King of Ulster. As the proceedings draw to a close, the king's horses have emerged as winners:
"Never before have two such horses been seen at the festival as the two horses of the king; in all Ireland there is not a swifter pair", the people cried.[31]
But a man called Crunniuc comes to the racecourse and disdainfully asserts that Macha, his wife, would be faster than the king's horses. This is a rash claim and one that earns him a spell in prison. Very great pressure is brought to bear on Macha to race. She is told that her husband will die unless she agrees to race and can substantiate his claims. On the other hand, not only is she pregnant but, if she does as she is requested and beats the King's horses, she will have undermined the King's stature. A cloud of disaster will hang over the Ulstermen once the symbol of their fortunes has been thus eclipsed. She has been placed in an impossible position. Reluctantly she races and, as she passes the winning post in the pangs of labour, she pronounces the wrath of the gods:
"As she gave birth she screamed out that all who heard that scream would suffer from the same pangs for five days and four nights in their times of greatest difficulty. This affliction, ever afterwards, seized all the men of Ulster who were there that day."[32]
Clearly, the accepted order had been violated by Crunniuc's claim, later substantiated by his wife, that the king's horses were not invincible. The result was that at the time of greatest need the warriors of Ulster are struck with pregnancy sickness as Macha had been and are thus ineffective.

saving hero, is mated with the Earth-Mother goddess, in the manner of kings, for a year, replaces the disabled king Conchobar and revives the fortunes of the province.[34] Cú Chulainn is unaffected by the debility which afflicts the Ulstermen and protects them from their foes, hence the events of *Táin Bó Cuailnge*.

The similarities which exist between the story of Macha's race and that of the Roman circus suggest that, in the Irish context, the king also had to be associated with the winning horse if he was to maintain his kingship and the social order. As with so much else relating to Irish tales, details of the religious and ritual background, in this case those relating to sacrifice and ritual union, are obscure if not missing, and have to be recovered by reference to the wider Indo-European mythology. There are indications that people in Ireland considered it essential for the social order that the king attend the races. He was, for instance, required to go there once a week—every Friday—if we are to credit the artificial list of his activities presented to us in the early Irish law tracts.[35] But there was more to it than that. The people of the *tuath* believed that their king was supreme in all things, and on the racecourse where the horse symbolised all-embracing powers this supremacy was critical. The king's business was principally war against the *tuath*'s enemies and he had to marshal his resources for this on the racecourse by possessing the winning horse. Perhaps his subjects saw in the victory of a champion—like the crowds that gather at Cheltenham racecourse to cheer on an *Arkle* against a *Mill House*—their own triumph.[36]

3

Christianity and Horse Ritual

W E HAVE CONSIDERED the ritual killing of the horse and its assimilation to the king in some detail because the people of the *tuath* considered it to be of great importance to the *tuath* and because many of the attitudes to the horse over the centuries can be traced back to this. Frequently the continuity in these attitudes is not obvious. The horse was seen to be closely linked to society from the earliest times but over the centuries society underwent fundamental change. It was, therefore, almost inevitable that the perception of the horse's role in Irish society would also change to meet the new circumstances. This change however, as we explore it, will be seen to be superficial. For there were conservative forces within the country which were determined to limit any change, particularly one being imposed from outside.

It may well be asked why the horse should attract attention from people abroad seeking to gain a foothold in this country. An answer to this lies in the material we have been considering. Any attempt to gain control over the hearts and minds of the Irish people had to take into account the place which the horse occupied in their ideology, a place which is closely linked to that occupied by kingship. When the Irish, in their mythology, depicted the king going to the Otherworld on a horse, or in their inauguration rituals had him ceremonially mated with a mare which he later ate, they were saying something very important about their identity and the horse's prominent place in it. Kingship and inauguration rituals celebrate and validate a way of life, as anyone who observes, even in a passing way, the importance attached to the royal family in Britain will confirm.[1] In Ireland, we suggested, totemism provided one possible explanation for the people's identification with horses and the place which horses had in their way of life but, whatever the origins, there can be little doubt about the position which horses occupied in the image which the Irish had of themselves. Anyone attacking and attempting to dislodge the horse from this position ran the risk not only of failure, but also of further consolidating the horse as a symbol of the 'good life' or Otherworld to which the Irish aspired. For an oppressed people the status of such otherworldly symbols cannot be overestimated.

In considering how different facets of the horse tradition came to the fore in ritual and lore as society adapted to changed and frequently adverse circumstances, we will be concerned in particular to learn what impulse lay at the basis of horse sacrifice, providing a continuity in Irish thinking about horses over the centuries and a perspective on attitudes to the horse in modern Ireland. One of the most far-reaching influences ever to be brought to bear on the country, and one which would affect the horse tradition, was that of Christianity. It therefore provides us with a logical starting point.

SAINT PATRICK

The relationship between Christianity and the old pagan ways in Ireland was characterised by compromise as a modus vivendi between the two was evolved. Saint Patrick, the person popularly associated with the introduction of Christianity to Ireland, would seem however to have been ill-fitted to accept even the most innocuous of the pagan traditions. A citizen of Roman Britain, he wanted the Irish not only to be Christian but Roman as well. The world of Roman civilisation which he admired was very different to that of Ireland which was a stranger still to the written word and firmly attached to its oral traditions. In one of the most important of the tales which would have circulated in oral form before being consigned to

Base of the Cross of the Scripture, Clonmacnoise, showing war chariots and horses.

writing, *Táin Bó Cuailnge*, we have already seen indications of a people's sense of kinship with the horse. In some of the lore concerning Saint Patrick the mood is altogether different. In the legend dealing with the origin of the placename Brí Graige, it would appear that the saint's disposition inspired fright rather than confidence in the native equines:

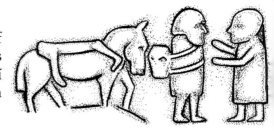

Panel from cross at Dromiskin, Co. Louth.

> When Loegaire mac Néill, King of Ireland, went to Ferta Fer Fecce to meet Patrick, when he came to plant the faith in Ireland there came, through the miraculous power of Patrick, great thunderings and lightnings so that all the studs of Erin were thrown into a panic. And thus they were found there by the mountains. So hence it is called Brí Graige, that is, the Hill or Height of the Horses. [2]

The horses' alarm at the saint's firepower was not, it would appear, without justification, for when he was at Ferta Fer Fecce he had clearly targeted them. "Some put their trust in chariots and some in horses but we will remember the name of the Lord our God," he is reported to have said.[3] This approach was unlikely to be helpful to the Christian mission to Ireland. Better to hijack the complex of beliefs surrounding the horse in Ireland and thereby to nudge the public imagination, in which they were firmly embedded, into Christian paths than to attempt to destroy those beliefs outright. The Christian scribes who wrote down the accounts of the exploits of the other saints seem to have realised this and tried to gear their writings to their audience. They were at pains to reconcile much of the old pagan past with the new religion, and eagerly seized upon pagan symbols which, they felt, they could christianise. One of these was the horse-drawn chariot.

In the legend-encrusted lives of the saints the chariot is the usual means of transport. The saints, like the warriors and kings of pagan times, were seen to share in the supernatural properties of the vehicle. St Fechín of Fore, we are told, not only used the chariot as his daily means of transport but when one of his horses died he replaced him, not with an ordinary horse but with a water horse which originated in a local riverpool. The horse, the story goes, eventually returned to the pool, but not before Fechín had incurred the wrath of the local king who clearly felt that such animals should be the playthings of kings only and not of saints.[4] The old pagan beliefs about horses and chariots, in common with many other facets of the pre-christian traditions, accommodated themselves to the Christian ways and survived in Ireland. These beliefs were able to strike responsive chords in the Christian as well as in the pagan era because their kernel was of vital interest to society. It concerned the process whereby men transcended the limitations of ordinary life and the key symbolic role that the horse and chariot had in that process. A Christian purpose could be served by the horse, the churchmen would appear to have believed, if it was handled in the correct way.

The Horse Museum at the Irish National Stud. Included in this view is the skeleton of *Arkle* and the old weighing-in chair from the Curragh Racecourse. *Source*: Bord Fáilte.

TOP LEFT: Horse dealer. *Source*: Inpho. TOP RIGHT: Connemara Pony Show. *Source*: G. A. Duncan. BELOW: Connemara Pony Show. *Source*: G. A. Duncan.

RIGHT: *Source*: Liam Blake. Ponies at Killarney.
BELOW: Goffs Sales in Kill, Co. Kildare. In 1975 Goffs, whose first sales took place in 1887, moved its activities from Ballsbridge, where the RDS has its headquarters, to Kill. *Source*: Inpho.

Source: Inpho.

HIGH CROSSES

To explore further the relationship of the Churchmen to the horse tradition, we turn from the literary sources to figure carvings on some of the high crosses and pillars to be found near monasteries in Ireland from the eighth century onwards. The scenes on these, many of them biblical in inspiration, were taken, it would seem, from an arsenal of material generally available in the Christian world outside Ireland. They were didactic in purpose, sermons in stone, one might say.[5] As such

Panel from the High Cross at Moone, showing the Flight into Egypt. *(Commissioners of Public Works, Ireland)*

they had to combine the best elements of the crafts of storytelling and modern advertising—suggesting, rather than telling, by drawing on the previous experiences of the audience—so that the impact of the message would be immediate and lasting. Not surprisingly the Irish Christian apologists recognised the potential of the horse, with its record as an enduring symbol, for such purposes. The resultant carvings are, to modern eyes, sometimes enigmatic but, when taken in conjunction with their pagan background, a picture begins to form which is consistent with our story.

The image of Jesus riding on horseback into Jerusalem on the Arboe Cross in Co. Tyrone sets the standard. The horse clearly is not taboo as a means of transport in Christian representations. A panel at the base of the eighth-century cross at Moone in Co. Kildare underscores this and goes much further. It shows the Flight into Egypt with the Blessed Virgin Mary riding in a manner which bears a striking resemblance to carvings of Epona, the Horse Goddess, whose cult, as we have seen, forms an integral part of the Celtic horse tradition. In linking Epona to an episode which was central to the Christian story, the sculptor was, it would appear, implicitly declaring the horse tradition, in all its pagan manifestations, fit for Christian development. For Epona is a goddess in which that tradition finds its richest expression.

The high crosses portray the Christian mission as a battle in which the saints were warriors fighting against the forces of evil. Scenes on the cross at Kilrea, a cross which also features an image of Epona, and on the cross at Killamery, show men mounted on horses or in chariots ready, it would appear, for war. Additional panels which are on these crosses identify the enemy of the men on horseback. In these panels a stag is being hunted by horsemen. The fact that the stag is indeed the object of the churchmen's attention is confirmed for us by the cross at Banagher in Co. Offaly, which features a stag caught in a trap and nearby a man mounted on horseback with a crozier in his hand. Linguistic usage gives credibility to the image of the churchman as a rider of horses. 'Marcach' is the word in Irish for rider but at an early stage it acquired the connotation of messenger. A poem in the twelfth-century Book of Leinster refers to 'marcachaib canoni', 'knights of canon law' or probably more accurately 'those bearing the message of the canonical scriptures'. In similar vein an eleventh-century bishop is called in one document 'marcach soiscéla' or 'messenger of the gospels'.[6]

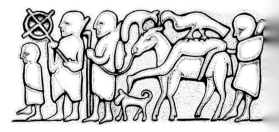

A funeral scene from a carving on the North Cross at Ahenny, Co. Tipperary.

Crosses other than those at Kilrea and Killamery also feature horsemen in pursuit of a stag. There are scenes on the crosses at Tuam, Monasterboice, Kells and Kilkieran of horsemen and chariots, and of a horseman hunting a stag at Dromiskin and Bealin. The precise significance of the stag is probably open to debate but the scenes which we find at Clonmacnoise suggest the explanation which seems best to accord with the consistent picture which we have of him as the enemy of Christianity.[7]

Hunting scene from the cross at Dromiskin, Co. Louth.

Near the monastery of Clonmacnoise there are several crosses with representations of horsemen and chariots. We look in vain for the stag until we come to a pillar nearby. Here we do not find the hunted animal familiar from other crosses but rather the sinister and threatening figure of Cernunnos, the Stag God. He is a much different figure from the figure of the fleeing stag shown on other crosses. But the difference is only one of emphasis. Probably the churchmen felt that if they were going to show the stag as an enemy of Christianity they had better, in at least one of his representations, establish the formidable character of the opposition which he provided. Even the Horse God needed his foil.

There is plenty of evidence for Cernunnos in early Irish sculpture but to get confirmation that his juxtaposition at Clonmacnoise to the horses and their riders is not haphazard we have to travel outside the country. His representation has been found in various Celtic contexts abroad, including one in a chariot grave as a decoration for horse trappings or a chariot, but the most significant from our point of view is that of the Gundestrup Cauldron from Denmark. Not only does one of the scenes on this cauldron, which feature Cernunnos, bear a close resemblance to one of the panels at the base of the North Cross of Ahenny in Co. Tipperary, a cross which, as we shall have occasion to note later, is particularly rich in horse symbolism, but it also shows him in close proximity to images of sea horses, a winged horse and horsemen passing by the scene of a sacrifice. Since these images strongly suggest the Horse God this juxtaposition was probably the inspiration for the Christian work on the High Crosses we have noted. The Christian sculptors could effectively show their Irish audience the struggle between light and darkness, good and evil, Christianity and Paganism in terms of the conflict between horse and stag.

Cernunnos was a worthy adversary for a God with the stature in the Celtic world of the Horse God. He was identified with Dis Pater, the God from whom, according to Caesar, all Gauls traced their ancestry and, like the Horse God, he had also strong fertility associations. His deep-rooted and widespread cult in the Celtic world must have made him a prime target of the Christian Church which saw him as the symbol of the anti-Christ and of the pagan forces which it wished to eradicate.[8]

In brief, therefore, the Church harnessed the symbolic power of the horse in depicting its mission to Ireland which it saw as the bringing of the faith and the battle against the forces of evil. It must have been reasonably successful in imprinting its message on the Christian imagination for that message surfaces, in the same form as on the Irish crosses, in a land where Irish monks ministered. On some of the Pictish tombstones in Scotland there are examples of mounted figures with some of them in pursuit of the stag.[9]

The presence of such scenes on tombstones is completely consistent with what we might expect of a Christian version of the horse tradition, involving as it does the Otherworld. The early Christians unlike their pagan contemporaries linked the Otherworld exclusively with death. Since Christian saints in Ireland wished to be associated in their mission with an otherworldly animal, the horse, and since that mission was seen on the crosses as a battle, it was logical that the horse should be seen to be associated with them in death. Success for the Christian missionary involved martyrdom sometimes—returning from the battle dead—and this is what seems to be the theme on one of the panels of the cross at Dromiskin in Co. Louth. The panel in question which can be seen as a sequel to the fight against evil depicted in the stag hunting scene also on this cross, features a horse bearing a headless corpse and a figure handing over the severed head to another. A similar panel on the cross at Ahenny confirms that the figure accompanying the corpse is Christian. He carries a crozier. The scene at Dromiskin, therefore, represents a christian being taken on horseback to the Otherworld, as in the pagan 'Ride of the Dead'.

We have tried to find out how the horse tradition would evolve in the face of Christianity which was potentially, at least, a threat to it. We have suggested that Christianity did not attack directly that part of the tradition which saw the horse providing transport to the Otherworld. Christianity could be seen to absorb the symbolic power of the horse as a means of transport. But there were other related elements in the horse tradition which discovered that Christianity did not provide such a hospitable environment. We are particularly interested in these since they revolve around horse sacrifice and since, according as they were exposed to increasing attacks, they would become more entrenched as symbols of resistance. Our concern is to isolate the form in which they do this.

HORSEMEAT

It is a small step from the idea of the 'Ride of the Dead' to that of horse sacrifice, whereby the horse is killed so that it might be available for the journey to the Otherworld. People outside Ireland in fact sometimes took that step and interred horses with their dead masters. But the fact that Christianity could comfortably absorb the 'Ride of the Dead' into its sculpture did not imply that the sacrifice of the horse could ever become an acceptable part of Christian ritual. Christianity might continue to allow the horse to be seen as a means of transport to the Otherworld without taking the further step of seeing the horse as the embodiment of that world.

There were of course, from an early date, compelling reasons other than the religious for not killing the horse. We need hardly stress that its role in agriculture, transport and warfare placed a great premium on it in many parts of the world. Because of this, horse sacrifice sometimes took on a symbolic character which left open the possibility of ritual benefits but avoided the loss of the animal. Hence the

Shaft of a cross at Clonmacnoise depicting a hunting scene with horseman and three lions.

In parts of Ireland it is still recalled that the death of a man was the signal for the selling of his horse. The basis for this custom is suggested by an entry in the *Annals of the Four Masters* in the year 1156 which tells us that 'Toirdhealbhach Ua Conchobhair, King of Connaught . . . and of all Ireland . . . died . . . after having made his will, and distributed gold and silver, cows and horses among the clergy and churches of Ireland in general'. Seventh-century regulations regarding burial fees stipulated that the standard gift to the Church was a garment, a horse and a cow, but that, in the case of the death of someone of the highest rank, two horses, a chariot, the dead man's bed trappings and drinking vessels were required.[11] Adequate provision for the 'Ride of the Dead' it would seem! Practices outside Ireland show a similar sanitising process at work. Among gypsies it was customary for the sacrifice of the horse to be part of the burial rites after a death but this apparently could be commuted into a less destructive form. At the funeral in the 1360s of the French gypsy Philipe de Rouvre the dead man's horses were brought up to the altar and in the nineteenth century the custom was noted among a primitive gypsy tribe in the Caucasus of having a dead man's servant for several days saddle his horse before dinner. In Britain, throughout the middle ages and even into the Reformation period, a man of means donated his best horse in his will to the Church. When he died, the horse followed his funeral to the grave, a custom which we have seen re-enacted on such notable occasions as the deaths of Winston Churchill and John F. Kennedy when a riderless horse, complete with saddle and stirrups, followed the gun carriage bearing the coffin. The horse donated to the Church by a rich man was not dispatched to the Otherworld immediately, as would have happened in more ancient times. It was sold and the proceeds were given to the Church.[12]

presence of representations of the horse where we might have expected to find its bones. In parts of Britain, for example, clay images of the horse were burnt as a substitute for sacrifice. In a Hindu ceremony figurines were used instead of horse victims, and, in France, the temple of Roquepertuse has a portico decorated, as we have seen, with horses' heads carved in stone.[10] But practical necessity alone cannot explain the tendency to avoid, where substitution was possible, the ritual killing of the horse. In Ireland there is a relic of a custom, also found in Britain and elsewhere, indicating that Christianity was at pains to outlaw the pagan practice of killing the horse.

In the ritual context, therefore, in which it had a key place at one time, we find horse sacrifice reduced to an innocuous relic—the selling of the horse to raise funds for the Church's benefit. In Ireland the early Church was quite explicit in condemning any practice which was related to horse sacrifice. In the tenth-century legend of Saint Brendan's Voyage we learn that Saint Ita counsels Brendan that his adventure would only succeed if he built a wooden ship and did not use, as in his first attempt, one in whose construction blood had been spilled. The saint's remarks on this occasion were probably directed against the use of horse hides which were frequently used, even into modern times, in the manufacture of boats.[13] The practice, however, which bore the closest relationship to horse sacrifice, and more than any other would appear to equate the horse with the Otherworld, was that of eating the flesh of the animal.

The eating of horseflesh has always been taboo in the Judaeo-Christian tradition. The Mosaic Law prohibited the eating of the flesh of any of the animals of the horse family. In that law the reason given was that their flesh was unclean because their hooves were not cloven and they were not ruminants.[14] Canon Law followed the Mosaic prescription and recommended excommunication for the breaking of the taboo. All the evidence points to the effectiveness of the law. Horseflesh may have been eaten ritually in central and southern areas of England in the eighth century but down to the present day the practice has never become established. An attempt made there during the last war to popularise horseflesh as a food failed completely. In Iceland the practice managed to survive along with other pagan remnants into the eleventh century. By that time it had come under Christian pressure and could only take place in secret. In Ireland also the practice of eating horseflesh was strongly opposed. We learn in the sagas that when a person ate horseflesh ritual uncleanliness ensued, a condition which prevented him driving a chariot for weeks. Disobedience in relation to the rule against the practice merited severe penance according to an early Christian penitential. "Anyone who eats the flesh of a horse," it stipulated, "does penance for three years." But if the Church attacked the practice strongly and directly it could also employ the subtle influence of the parable with a more conciliatory approach in view. The writer of the *Life of Saint Moling* tells us, for example, that the saint changed horsemeat into mutton when he was a guest at a meal where the unacceptable fare was provided.[15]

Horse-related beliefs and practices were, as we have seen, of central concern to society, a concern which may have had its basis in totemism. When christianity wished to strike roots in Irish society it had to be seen either to appropriate the symbolic power of the horse in a manner which the High Crosses indicate or to negate the force of some of the beliefs in the horse's role in society. Horse sacrifice and communion with the animal had played a central role in kingship rituals and provided a clear target for the attacks of the Churchmen. However if, as we suggest, rituals and beliefs which were central to kingship also occupied a central place in people's view of themselves and their society, we might expect that elements in that society would fight back. Our concern, as we note the efforts of society to defend what it considered important in the horse tradition, will be with the underlying meaning for the Irish of sacrificial communion with the animal. In order to do this we first have to note who, in Irish society, was seen to spearhead its defence.

Stag hunter and war horse from Pictish tombstone. (*Daphne Machin Goodall*).

HORSE AND HAG

The goddess to whom kings had to be married has continued to exist in popular thinking up until the present day despite the attacks which Christianity made upon what she represented. In a Fenian tale we observed that she took on the form of an old hag urging Fionn mac Cumhaill to eat horseflesh. In thus urging the leader of the Fianna to adopt the ancient practice, the old hag was attempting to turn back the clock and recover a glorious epoch when she, like her equivalent in the ninth-century poem 'Caillech Bérri', shared the company of kings who needed her. The ancient kingship ritual had however been disrupted by attacks such as that of Christianity and instead of the image of a fertile goddess enjoying the embrace of her suitor, we have, in the Fenian tale, an old hag spurned and defiant.

Folklore has retained the image of the old hag or *caillech* as defender and representative of a belief system which held out the hope of control over the apparently meaningless pattern of life's good and ill fortune.[16] Inevitably the Church had to come to grips with her for the Church too had its belief system and its priests.

The focus of the conflict between priest and *caillech* was control of the horse. In Ireland, for reasons which we shall see later, there was a particular consciousness of the otherworldly forces influencing the horse. Both priest and *caillech* tried to gain control of these forces. Many stories in the folklore record concern a horse stopping inexplicably on the road and refusing to move. In the following story the horse in question is the priest's horse and the priest is on a sick call:

> One night the late Father Maher, curate of Killimor, was going on a sick call. The Priest was coming on a sidecar and had his servant boy with him. As they were going along a black dog came before the horse on the road, and the horse

Mounted warrior in armour. Period of the battle of Dysert O'Dea, 1318. (*Journal of Galway Archaeological and Historical Society, xvi, 84*)

stopped and wouldn't move, no matter how much they beat or coaxed him. The boy was too much afraid to get down off the car, so the priest got down and put on his stole. The dog was still standing on the middle of the road. The priest began to read, and in a few minutes the dog slinked away. The belief was that it was the devil that stopped the priest on the road.

Here, clearly, the priest was able to gain control of whatever otherworldly forces were at work. Christian efforts in this regard could resemble superstition very closely at times, and it would seem that, as with so much of pagan tradition, a deliberate effort was made to christianise practices relating to horses. We learn, for instance, that in Kerry it was the custom to place blessed palm in the horse's collar as a protection, a practice which was very close to superstitions which involved decorating the animal's harness. It was generally believed that protection for the horse would be achieved by making the sign of the cross on the horse and an account from Kerry tells us that a christian prayer, 'Bail ó Dhia air', would prevent the overlook.

This overlap of superstition and christian belief was very common in Ireland. Even the wise old woman, Biddy Early, instructs the priest, in one story, to recite the words, "In the name of the Father, and of the Son and of the Holy Ghost," when attempting to get the horse to move. When malevolent forces struck, however, there was sometimes little that anyone could do, and a priest's horse was clearly not guaranteed immunity from such forces. About the year 1737 a fine horse belonging to a Co. Limerick priest, Father Nicholas O'Donnell, died and, according to traditional manuscripts, his death was due to the overlook. The event was of such significance that it occasioned a great deal of poetic activity at the time, as we shall see.[17]

Most of these incidents reflect the vulnerability of the horse and priests' or people's attempts to resist the malevolent forces attempting to gain control over the animal. But christian assistance to horses wasn't apparently geared solely to the prevention of death. The horse could also be helped to achieve great feats of prowess which were of such importance to the community, feats such as that performed by the *Paidrín Mare* in 1760 in beating *Black and All Black*. The *Paidrín Mare*'s real name was *Irish Lass* but she reputedly got her name from an incident during the race when a rosary beads (paidrín) was placed around her neck. The race achieved epic proportions in the public imagination and was seen as a struggle by *Irish Lass* against the Devil. Her rider and owner who figures in the following account of the race was known as Biorán:

When Biorán was riding into the field he heard the other horse saying to his rider 'Bear me up the hill, spare me down the hill, and whip me on the level.' Biorán went immediately to the priest and told him what he had heard. He told him to make a necklace of 'Apple Praties'. When the necklace was brought to him he blessed it and put it on the horse's neck. Then he told the jockey if he did not get the start on the other horse he was to retire, if he did he would hold it all the time and win in the end. The two horses lined up, and the jockey managed to get the start on the other horse and maintained it all the way. When the other horse was beaten he fell dead on the course. Ever after Biorán's horse was called the 'Paidrín Mare'.

Despite successes such as this, the priest is consistently shown in the folklore record coming off second best when he is pitted against the *caillech* in relation to control of the horse. Máire Caitlín Conway was a wise old woman living in Inbhear Mór in Co. Wicklow. The priest's horse had collapsed in her locale and nobody, including the priest, was able to get it to rise. The wise woman, noticing what had happened, only had to shake her apron and the horse got up off the ground.[18] Many such stories were collected in this century reflecting the endurance of the theme of the old woman's ascendancy over the horse in different historical circumstances.

Another influential group in early Ireland who, like the *caillechs*, exercised control over the horse and had an important role in conferring sovereignty was the poets.

The Tote Cheltenham Gold Cup 1986 winner, *Dawn Run* ridden by Jonjo O'Neill. *Source*: Gerry Cranham.

HORSE AND POET

The poets' involvement with kingship probably had its roots in a period when the king had all the functions of priest, leader in war, judge and lawgiver. Indo-European ritual would seem to reflect this, for, as we noted, it required that the king appropriate these various functions through the medium of the horse. By the time of the earliest written records in Ireland the priestly function had evolved to the point were it was represented by a figure separate from the king, the druid. This figure was concerned with the interpretation and application of the law. Further evolution occurred with the poets or *filidh* inheriting the functions and, in particular, the enduring and very close link with kingship which the druid once had. Without the *file* a man could not be king. The reason for this lay in the predominantly sacral character of kingship. In the main, the king was not an executive. Rather he embodied for his people the otherworldly powers controlling the fortunes of society. Access to these higher powers was given at the inauguration rite to the king by the poet who was seen as an intermediary between this life and the otherworld.[19] The gift of kingship from the poet was a spiritual matter and was conveyed through symbols. As we might expect from the Indo-European background to Irish kingship, one of the most important of these symbols was the horse. In the sacrifice of the October Equus which, as we have seen, consolidated the ancient Roman kings in their kingship, the horse was killed by the *flamen* or priest. Its body was then brought to the king's house. In a thirteenth-century inauguration ritual in Ireland we also find a horse being given as a gift to the chieftain or king, McMahon of Oriel, for the ceremony. Here, as it happens, it is not the poet who makes the gift but a subchief. But the corresponding gift from the poet also involved a horse.[20] The difference was that he made that gift in a manner particularly suited to his craft.

One of the factors behind the belief in the supernatural powers of the poet was his reputation for great learning, which commanded enormous respect in Ireland. So great was the power of his words that, in certain circumstances, they were as effective as weapons. The poet Conor Teigue Mac Rory from Clare, for instance, was credited with knocking a crow out of a tree with his verse. We have already seen something of the power of the word in our consideration of horse names in Ireland. The personal names Eochaid or Eochu embodied ancient traditions of ancestral links with the horse and people felt that these names renewed such links for them. Eochaid and Eochu were the second most popular names in early Irish society and were much in vogue with kings, particularly those from Ulster.[21] A king's legal entitlement to rule, however, was, in the main, dependent on the traditional lore and genealogical material which surrounded his ancestors and on his own personal fitness for kingship, and it was in these matters that the power of the learned men or poets was most in evidence. We have already noted some of these ancestors and their involvement with horses. In the ninth-century tale *Baile in Scáil*, for example, Conn of the Hundred Battles goes on horseback to the Otherworld where he is inaugurated and where the God Lug foretells to him the names of his descendants who will rule Ireland. His descendants were the members of the powerful Uí Néill dynasty who were very active in having their learned men develop their claims to political power in tales and genealogies.[22] Without a body of learned material, such as is found in *Baile in Scáil*, establishing their relationship to the original king who rode to the Otherworld to wed the goddess of sovereignty, the ambitions of the Uí Néill would have come to naught.

The symbolic gift by the poet of the horse to the king was made particularly in his poetry. The belief underlying the praise which a poet bestowed in his poetry on the king was that the king was married to his territory or stronghold. The praise of kings, which was essential to their power, could take the form, therefore, of praise of these places. A poet conferring an association with horses on a territory was giving praise indeed to its king. For example these are the terms in which the passing of Emhain Macha, the seat of the Ulster kings, is described in the thirteenth century:

> In bright Emhain of the fresh grass . . .
> many the vehement rider of a dun steed . . .
> Evil for us that the Dubh Sainglenn *[Cú Chulainn's horse]*
> Is no more in the brilliant stud of Fingal.[23]

The context for associating the king's territory or stronghold with horses was frequently the inauguration itself where his marriage to the kingdom was symbolically carried out. The inauguration ode which the poet composed was a critical element in the inauguration ceremony itself. It praised the king and everything associated with him, not in a factual way, but in terms of the ideal qualities of a ruler. It was a gift from the poet to the king signifying that the otherworldly powers had accepted him as king.[24] In this the poet's words were taken as gospel. They achieved what they described.

Even more widespread in poetry is the direct association of the king with horses. We read of Corc mac Ughaine na n-Each, of an eleventh-century king of Connacht called Tadhg an Eich Ghil who was given a gift of a white horse, of 'Ailill, son of Russ of the Raths, the fosterling of Connacht, of the curly maned steeds', of 'Eochu whose steeds are noble' and of 'Niall's scion of the horses'.[26] The terms in which praise was expressed could, however, be swiftly turned to a curse as in the *Testament of Cathaír Már*, a document in verse in which a prehistoric king is seen to wrathfully thwart the ambitions of his son Eochu Timmínne, ancestor of the Uí Buidhe of Leighlin in Carlow:

> No one of his children equal in rank
> will be a king rich in herds at the horse festivals.[27]

In the poem written for the inauguration of Aedh O'Connor, King of Connacht in 1224, O'Connor's fitness to rule is associated not only with his descent from former kings but also with the quality of his dwelling place Cruachain, capital of the kings of Connacht. It is described as 'horse rich Cruachain'. Elsewhere we read of 'Lofty Cruachain of the horses', and in a poem by Giolla Brighde Albanach the Connacht territories are described as 'extensive flowering plains in which are many horses'.[25]

The Kilkenny team winners of the Pony Club Games, RDS Horse Show 1980. (*Horseman Photography*)

Effectively, Cathaír was placing Eochu's descendants beyond the pale.

In the public mind the line between possessing horses and horsemanship skills was a fine one. Frequently the poets ascribe these skills to kings and potential kings. In this they took their lead from the exemplary king, the God Lug who invented horsemanship and brought it to Ireland. When he went to Tara to establish his claim to kingship, the training of horses was one of the feats which he offered to perform. One of the great kings whom Lug names as his successor at Tara was Niall of the Nine Hostages, son of Eochu Mugmedon. In a twelfth-century poem written for one of the O'Connor kings we are told that 'Niall's horseracing was fair'. The thirteenth-century King of Connacht, Cathal Crobhderg O'Connor, we are told in a praise poem, was 'good on horseback, excellent on foot'. A ninth-century genealogical tract *De Shíl Chonaire Móir* depicts with more generous detail a great king, Conaire, establishing control over horses. Like Lug, Conaire, who was reputed to be ancestor of many Munster tribes, had to go to Tara to establish his claim to kingship. The ability to control the horses which the poet ascribes to Conaire here was critical for this and would have had favourable implications for his descendants who, no doubt, saw to it that the poet formulated his account:[28]

There was a king's chariot at Tara. To the chariot were yoked two steeds of the same colour which had never before been harnessed. It would tilt up before any man who was not destined to receive the kingship of Tara, so that he could not control it, and the horses would spring at him. And there was a king's mantle in the chariot; whoso might not receive Tara's sovereignty the mantle was ever too big for him. And there were two flag-stones in Tara; 'Blocc' and 'Bluigne'; when they accepted a man, they would open before him until the chariot went through, and Fál was there, the 'stone penis' at the head of the chariot course; when a man should have the kingship of Tara, it screeched against his chariot axle, so that all might hear.

Conaire, we are told, mounts the chariot safely and dons the coat which fits him. He drives the chariot towards the stones. They open for him and the Lia Fáil cries out.[29]

By ascribing in this fashion control over horses to kings and ancestors the poet was making a very significant statement regarding their worthiness and that of their descendants for kingship. But his gift to them was not altruistic. He expected a return, and this also involved the horse.

The standard form of gift from king to poet was the horse. At his inauguration, power was mediated through the horse and the king, in turn, had to reciprocate during the ceremony by giving a horse to the poet. If he failed to be generous in this way the functions appropriate to kingship were forcibly taken away from him. The symbolism of the horse in this respect is finely caught in a fifteenth-century poem which compares Maguire Lord of Fermanagh with Mac Dermott of Moylurg. Maguire has been less than generous to the poet and is therefore seen by the poet in an unfavourable light. He is not in the poet's eyes without a horse but, what amounts to the same thing, his horse does not measure up to the usual royal standards:

> A lame big bellied hack carries Maguire when he goes out,
> he puts his rotten pillion on its skinny hump . . .
> Maguire without vigour or brilliance on the stinking yellow hack.

Mac Dermott, by way of contrast, has been 'open-handed to poets':

> A lovely-eyed spirited colt carries Mac Dermot when he goes out;
> the hero's slender horse as it flies makes a break for the clean wind.[31]

The main obligation which a king had to fulfil was that of generosity. Without generosity he could not be king. The reason for the vacancy in the kingship of the Tuatha Dé Danann which led to the accession of Lug, for instance, was that the previous incumbent Eochaid Bres failed to be generous in return for the dues which his people had given him. The contract between king and people essential to society and kingship was broken. Eochaid lost power in relation to all three functions—priesthood, warfare, and agriculture—which as we have seen found symbolic expression in the horse. His poet Cairpre mac Edaine, who should have been in receipt of a gift of a horse from him, expresses the displeasure of the Otherworldly powers by satirising him.[30] Symbolically the king is deprived of his horse.

Because poets were indispensable to kings for reasons which we have discussed they could rigorously apply the rules of generosity, so favourable to themselves. Assisting them in this was their privileged custodianship of a great body of laws which commanded great respect in early Irish society. These specified that a poet was entitled to a horse as a fee for his poetry.[32] The poets never forgot this. *The Annals of the Four Masters* in 1338 has an obituary for Rory an Einigh, Lord of Fermanagh, "who had bestowed much silver apparel, steeds and cattle on the learned men and chief professors of Ireland". In fourteenth-century Ireland the learned men referred to would have been the poets themselves and the obituary

Shergar's **first foal.**
(*Horseman Photography*).

which they penned for a chief would be a charter for his descendants to rule. According to the sixteenth-century English commentator Thomas Smyth even the retinue of the poet got horses from the patron:

> Now comes the rhymer . . . with the Rakry . . . Also he hath his barde . . . who also must have a horse given him; the harper must have a new safern [saffron coloured] shurte, and a mantell, and a hacknaye; . . . and the rhymer himself a horse and harness with a nag to ride on.

We find, therefore, poets over the centuries using the horse as their usual means of transport. Praise was lavished by the poets on their patron and his territory in return for his generosity with horses. In a lament attributed to Gormflaith, the wife of several kings, there is praise for the territory of Cashel "in which horses used to be bestowed". One of Gormflaith's husbands, Niall Glundubh, is lamented as

> A man who would give steeds for a poem—God reward him for it!
> —If I should speak well of Niall, the poets would speak far better.[33]

Giolla Brighde Albanach in the poem referred to praises O'Connor for giving him 'blue steeds'. But such praise could turn to burning satire if a poet's hopes were disappointed:

> I have heard that he does not give
> horses for songs of praise
> He gives what is natural to him—a cow,

an unknown ninth-century poet wrote of a boorish patron.[34] In subsequent centuries the position of the poets became less secure and their disappointments more frequent. In the *Magauran Duanaire*, or family poem book containing verse dating from the fourteenth century, there are lines written by a poet to his patron Brian Mag Shamhradháin in which he bemoans having to go about on foot and begs him for a horse. His predicament finds an echo in that of a seventeenth-century poet Diarmait Mac Carthy from Blarney in Co. Cork. His old horse had died ignominiously, causing the poet great grief. He links his own plight after the horse's death to that of the country with the Gaelic social order which supported him crumbling. A country, he claims, in which no chieftain can be found to make a gift of a horse to replace the one that has died, has reached a low ebb. Far across the sea are the leaders who would have rewarded him for his verse with a horse.[35] Later we shall look more closely at the hope which the poet entertained of recovering a golden age with the return to Ireland of the banished heroes and at the horse's role as a symbol in their dream.

In the early mediaeval period, however, the poet still retained the function of priest of the inauguration rite and of kingmaker. Even in the fifteenth century we find the king of Connacht being inaugurated by a poet, Ó Maol Chonaire. In the late fifteenth- or early sixteenth-century tract on the Uí Fiachrach, or O'Dowda's territory of Tireragh, we read that O'Dowda's horse is given to the poet Mac Firbhisigh "the day Mac Firbhisigh shall give the name of Lord to Ó Dubhda". The well-known *History of Ireland* by Geoffrey Keating which was completed around 1634 also recounts how the Irish chieftain Mac Murrough was inaugurated, the ceremony culminating in the gift of his horse to his poet.[37]

The living link between poet and king which the gift of the horse expressed constituted a threat and a barrier to those wishing to achieve their own form of control over the country and the Gaelic order. The antipathy of the English to the Irish inauguration rite was illustrated in graphic form when after O'Neill's defeat at Kinsale in 1601 the English commander Mountjoy destroyed the throne of stone slabs at Tullaghogue near Dungannon in Co. Tyrone where the O'Neills from the eleventh century on had been inaugurated. Churchmen, as we have noted, tended to be more circumspect. From the thirteenth century on they were active in intruding themselves into the ceremony of inauguration with all its pagan paraphernalia, thus appropriating the function of the poets. St Maedóc, for instance, was patron of Ua Ruairc of Breifne and his coarbs acted as the officiating priests at his inauguration, receiving in return the chief's 'horse and robes'.[38] Churchmen, like their pagan equivalents, would appear to have been prepared to see the inauguration as a symbolic marriage in which gifts were exchanged.

The link in the poet's mind between the availability of a horse to ride on and the old Gaelic order with its generous royal patrons was not fortuitous. It was a living link which the poets on occasion saw as a marriage between themselves and the representative of that order, the king, a marriage which was solemnised at the inauguration rite. It was this ceremony which gave the exchange of gifts and specifically the gift of the horse, between poet and king, meaning. That meaning could become obscure as over the centuries the custom of giving a horse to the poet was torn away from its ritual context and the gift was increasingly seen as payment for a poem. This shows up in a pointed fashion in the accusation made against Gofraidh Ó Dálaigh by a fellow poet, that he had written a quatrain in praise of the Earl of Thomond "not because of love but for a horse".[36]

HORSE GIFTS AND OVERLORDSHIP

To this point our concern in discussing the horse's symbolic function in the Gaelic order has been with the mystical and sacral nature of kingship. We have observed how the priestly function, through the person of the poet, was essential to the reign of a king. When the king measured up to the criteria set by the poet, the poet gave him his sanction, symbolised by the horse, and a prosperous reign resulted. Failure to meet these criteria spelled the end of a king's reign. A whole body of traditional material including genealogy, lore and laws, hallowed by respect for immemorial custom, helped to maintain this system of government. When the native political structures, however, proved vulnerable from the ninth century on to the invasions of the Scandinavians who had little respect for the customary law which governed these structures, the nature of kingship changed. Naked power rather than customary right came increasingly to the fore in determining who would be king. The fact was that behind the institution of gift-giving which was central to the relationship

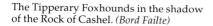

The Tipperary Foxhounds in the shadow of the Rock of Cashel. *(Bord Failte)*

between poet and king lay the reality, at times only thinly disguised, of power. The poet's gift of kingship through the medium of the horse was not so much an invitation as a demand to the king to provide him in turn with a horse. If the king refused he lost all. Viewed from the point of view that he was master of the sacred, the poet was superior to the king, and could make such demands. The king, for his part, increasingly was prepared to exercise force in order to gain the submission of other kings and thus acquire power outside the immediate area of his own tuath where he exercised his kingship as of right.[39]

The change was reflected in the inauguration rituals, particularly in the 14th and 15th centuries when, instead of the poet, the principal subchief of the king performed the ceremony. What this indicated was a change from the original perception of the inauguration rite as a marriage between king or chief and the *tuath* to the less mystical view of it as the proclamation of a dynastic leader by his most powerful subchief or vassals and their acceptance of his right to collect rents and other dues. We can see in practice, in the account of O'Dowda's inauguration, the transition from poet to subchief as minister of the ceremony. Ó Caomháin, whose line had once held the chieftainship, performs the key elements of the ritual and is the first to receive the apparel and steed of O'Dowda the new chief. These are later passed to the poet who is clearly being pushed to one side. The necessity to appease a potentially powerful political rival, in this case Ó Caomháin, and gain his acceptance and loyalty took precedence over the claims of the poet and what he represented. In some later tracts there is no reference to the poet as celebrant at all. The subchiefs alone command the right to inaugurate and receive the chief's gifts. In the case of the Mac Mahon subchiefs these gifts were rider's suits—an amalgam of the horse and apparel normally given.[40]

The usual context for gift giving, as in the *Book of Rights*, was the *aonach* where the community feeling was reinforced by the extravagant exchange of gifts and the mutual obligations which it implied. "There they would discuss with strife of speech the dues and tributes of the province . . . every legal enactment . . . was settled." For peoples normally scattered geographically such opportunities for coming together for ceremonial sharing involved a great outpouring of emotion as noted at totemistic assemblies. The resulting social cohesion benefited the king.[44]

Gift giving was an appropriate activity for a king. "Honour him like a god with gifts" was the conventional wisdom in Homeric Greece. The gift of horses in Ireland was particularly appropriate. The Indo-European background to this has already been sketched in—the dispersal of horses throughout the world by a great king who divides the world among subkings.[45] In the *Timna Cathaír Mair* or *Testament of Cathaír Már* the prehistoric King of Leinster, Cathaír Már, makes bequests in the manner of Jacob to his sons. As we have seen, the son whom he curses, Eochu Timmínne, will not have horses to pass on to his descendants. To Bressal Enechglass, ancestor of the Uí Enechglass who settled near Arklow, he grants, on the other

Pat Taaffe and his daughter Elaine with *Captain Christy*. (Gerry Cranham)

Outside the context of the inaugurations, gifts were made by kings or chiefs to subordinates who accepted them as an indication that they recognise the king as their overking. In the *Book of Rights*, dating approximately from the twelfth century, we get an idealised picture of the gifts and counter gifts made by kings. In most cases the gift to a subordinate consists of horses, in contrast to the tributes from the subordinate which are mainly in cattle. In Xenophon's *Anabasis* there are descriptions of similar gifts being given in Persia. Cyrus bestows gifts on the King of Tarsus when he reduces him to submission. These include a horse with a golden bridle, a golden chain, armlets, a golden dagger and a Persian costume. By accepting the gifts the king had, in effect, publicly acknowledged Cyrus to be King of Persia.[41]

Gifts such as these, in the manner of gifts in less developed societies the world over, established the superiority of the donor, but they also brought benefits to the receiver. In the first place, they were of value in themselves.[42] In addition, they were gifts fit for a king and this had its importance. The *Book of Rights* tells of gifts of "seven gilt chariots which he [the King of Laigin] brings with him to a banquet," of "fifty horses properly harnessed," and of "bridles with splendid ornaments of precious stones".[43] It was believed in early societies that gifts carried the personality and prestige of those who gave them—in some instances being even accredited with genealogies. Later we will see the precautions which a purchaser of a horse had to take in order to prevent it returning to its original owner of whom it was still believed to be a part. In similar vein, those who received a horse as a gift, acquired a part of its owner and this, in the case of a king's *tuarastal* or stipend, would mean a share in his sovereignty. The greater the king's authority, i.e. the greater the number of subkings attached to him, the greater the prestige of those who by virtue of their submission to him shared in his sovereignty.

hand, his own six horses:

> Many hounds and horses
> are thine and well-watered land
> beauty upon the women of thy race.

A king's attempt to disperse his horses could sometimes fail to produce the expected results. Coirpre Luachra, son of the King of Munster, Corc Mac Luigthig, we are told, arrived with thirty horsemen at Cashel and unyoked them on Corc's land with the intention of taking possession of it. But when he slew one of Corc's officers he was banished. The disappointment of another of Corc's descendants, Feidlimid, is captured in the following lines she is said to have uttered:

> Anyone would be greatly surprised
> that my two horses were barred from Cashel
> they would be astonished to learn
> of the shutting of Cashel against my horses.[46]

There was a coercive side to the symbolic unyoking of horses as we have seen. Prior to the Asvamedha ritual the Indian king's wandering horse had to be given free

Mare and foal. (*Horseman Photography*).

access by local rulers to the lands it wished to enter. By this means the king was seen to acquire lordship over them. It is perhaps no coincidence that the word used in old Irish in relation to a king's act of ruling has as its primary meaning 'stretches' or 'extends' and that this word in the early law tracts forms the basis of a term for a trespassing horse.[47] When a king sent a gift of horses to a subchief it could be refused because of what it implied. In the fourteenth-century text *Caithréim Thoird-healbhaigh* we are given a description of such gifts being refused because neither of the leaders involved, O'Neill and O'Brien, wished to recognise the superiority of the other. O'Brien had sent a stipend of 100 horses to O'Neill. O'Neill proudly countered with 200 horses "with their gold adorned white edged bridles" only to have them sent back by O'Brien with a company of armed men to enforce acceptance of the gift. Where a subchief did not grant submission to a king, the king would generally go on a cattle raid in his territory. This did not mean all-out war, rather it was a ritual test of the king's valour and ability to obtain submission by force where gifts had clearly failed. Without such a test a subchief had no guarantee that the superior would be able to protect him from others.[48]

Under the civilised veneer of gift giving which we considered earlier, therefore, lay the threat of warfare to achieve submission. The close relation between gifts and war is placed in sharp relief in a homeric context when the heroes, Diomedes and Glaucus, cease from battle and exchange armour. Frequently the booty taken by Irish chiefs in their raids included horses. An elegy for Mathgamhain, brother of Brian Bóroimhe, found in the twelfth-century compilation *Cogadh Gaedhel re Gallaibh* refers to the significance of this kind of booty:

> When he carried off a black steed of a stud
> Which belonged to Tadhg, son of Maelcellaigh,
> We thought that he would not have left his body,
> Until he had become sole king of Éirinn.[49]

Clearly the horse's past was to be of significance to its captor's future. Whereas cattle taken on such occasions would generally be valued in bulk, an individual steed, particularly if it was the steed of a noble with all the prestige that that implied, could be the excuse for a raid. In 1495 Con, son of Hugh Roe O'Donnell, accompanied by a small force, probably no more than two hundred including battleaxe men and some thirty horsemen, marched to the residence of McJohn of the Glynnes in Co. Antrim. McJohn had the finest steed, wife and hound in the neighbourhood and when Con demanded them, understandably McJohn refused. Con then proceeded to take them by force. The booty here was not retained by Con. He had, it would appear, promised the steed to one of his people. Wealth was of little use once basic needs had been satisfied except to achieve power over people, through redistributing it as gifts. Thus the circular flow of wealth considered essential to heroic society would be maintained and the power and prestige of the donor increased.[50]

HORSEMEN AND THE RETENTION OF LAND

There was a practical side to the chiefs' need to disperse horses. Their herds of horses, many of which were acquired as booty, were frequently very large. When the celebrated chieftain Grace O'Malley was captured in 1586 the herds of cattle and horses which were confiscated from her numbered 1000. When her son Owen was captured on his island by the English, "4000 cows, 500 stud mares" formed the booty. On one occasion about this time O'Ruairc of Breifne went on a raid in Tireragh and captured 3000 cows and 1000 mares. Such enormous herds required land on which they could graze. Theoretically a lord could not directly utilise the land of his subchiefs as this land was held corporately by the clans. But there were practical difficulties in the path of subchiefs trying to protect their lands against the depredations of a strong lord. He generally demanded as part of the contract between lord and subchief, to which we have alluded, enormous tributes from his subchiefs' lands. The difficulty with these crippling impositions was compounded by the necessity for a subchief to have herds and tenants to maximise the use of the land. Herds and tenants were his capital. From Norman times into the sixteenth century population levels were, however, low and tenants were difficult to acquire and retain. Time and time again we see Irish chiefs brought to their knees "for the sake of the cattle and the people" who were his most valuable assets. Without them he was completely at the mercy of an acquisitive overlord. Failure to pay the exactions which lords demanded meant that frequently the lords got compensation through gaining possession of the lands which defaulting subchiefs were forced to cede to them or through gaining the use of lands lying waste and underutilised for the reasons mentioned.

Such lands were invaluable to lords who possessed a large herd of horses. One such lord was the Earl of Thomond who demanded large exactions from the McBrien sept which had more than 4700 statute acres of land in Thomond but was eventually forced to cede it to the earl in the second half of the 16th century. "The land lay waste without tenants," we are told, "and was grazed by the Earles studd." There was always the prospect that lands ceded in this way, on a temporary basis, might in time become part of the lord's inheritance and be passed on to his descendants. In any case, the lord needed to have such lands at his disposal in order to ensure that his followers did not desert him.

There were good economic reasons for a lord attempting to retain vassals of some standing and resources who could guarantee a supply of tenants and full utilisation of the land. It is perhaps in this light that we should read Turlough Luineach O'Neill's complaint in 1567 that two 'horsemen', Patrick O Donnill and Patrick McAgirr, both of good surnames in Tyrone, were 'unjustly detained' from him by his cousin Conn Buidhe.[51] But there were reasons other than the purely economic for Irish chiefs valuing their horsemen.

Such noble vassals would have shared a common background with the lord and it was natural that he should surround himself with them. In the earliest times in Ireland, as reflected in the law tracts, the *rí tuaithe* or petty king entered into a contractual relationship with free clients by giving them a fief of cattle. They, in turn, paid him onerous rents and personal service by attending him as part of his retinue. In parts of Ireland, especially Gaelic Ulster, which had never known English rule in the middle ages, this system would seem to have survived.[52] The clients, who became known as the lord's *Lucht Tighe* (Household Troops) because of their personal service to him, lived on 'mensal lands' which consisted of a special tract of land providing the food for the chief's household. From among the *Lucht Tighe* the chief made appointments to positions within his household.

From the point of view of the *Lucht Tighe*, the conditions of the contract which they had with the chief were onerous in that the food rents which they paid were high. But their participation in the contract was free. As horsemen they had the privilege of turning down the gift of the king's horses. In the *Cogadh Gaedhel re Gallaibh* we see how independent in this respect horsemen could be. It depicts Brian Bóroimhe's great rival for the kingship, Maelsechlainn, accompanied by twelve score horsemen going to submit to Brian. The submission takes the form with which we are familiar. Brian gives him twelve score steeds which would, in the normal course, be passed on to his horsemen followers but

(Ruth Rogers)

there was not one of the twelve score men who accompanied Maelsechlainn who would deign to carry a lead horse with him.

A visitor to Muff Fair, near Kingscourt in Co. Cavan, 13 August 1990 (*Irish Times: Frank Miller*)

When they gave their service to a chief or king horsemen, however, as relatively free agents, would appear to have given it wholeheartedly. The picture that emerges from Sir Toby Caulfield's account in the early 17th century of O'Neill's *Lucht Tighe* is of horsemen who served their master with enthusiasm:

> For the butter and other victualling provisions they were only paid by such as they termed horsemen, called the Quyness, Haugans, Conelands, and Devlins, which were rather at the discretion of the giver, who strove who should give the most to gain Tyrone's favour, than for any due claim he had to demand the same.[53]

The *Lucht Tighe* were very privileged in comparison with other clients of a lord in that the mensal lands were not subject to the periodic subdivision among the chief's kinsmen which was the fate of the ruling sept's lands. They had a certain security of tenure, a security which was emphasised by the location of their lands. In the 16th century when the words *Lucht Tighe* had become a placename, we find it on maps in its anglicised form, Loughty, Loughtee or Lotie, in proximity to the lord's stronghold—in the case of O'Neill, between the inauguration site at Tullaghogue and his castle at Dungannon and, in the case of O'Reilly, the Barony of Loughtee contained his chief residence near Cavan Town.

The closeness between *Lucht Tighe* and lord found expression on the battlefield. From the twelfth to the fifteenth century the annals depict the *Lucht Tighe* as the chief's most faithful followers, playing a prominent part in his battles as they fought alongside him. The most dangerous location in which warriors could be during a cattle raid was at the rear of the cattle. Many of the kings died there. It was a privilege to fight at the rear and it is there that the horsemen were generally found.[54]

The horsemen were the elite of the king's forces. Much less numerous than his footsoldiers or 'kernes', they were recruited in the main from the native nobility. "The O'Neales are all horsemen," an account of Ulster in 1586 reported. Also in Ulster, O'Reilly's retinue of horsemen consisted only of O'Reillys. When Toirdhealbhach O'Reilly challenged the ruling O'Reilly, Maelmordha, at his inauguration, his cavalry of 21 horsemen included seven of his own kin. Even in such small numbers these horsemen made formidable opposition. Land hunger was often the motivating force behind such attempted interference with the succession of a particular member of a clan to the chieftainship. In the barony of Clanmahon, on the principle that the winner and his descendants take all, one of Maelmordha's sons, Philip the Prior, was attempting to establish himself as a landowner despite competition from the sons of previous rulers. One of his strategies to achieve this was the familiar one of giving gifts of horses.[55]

4

Irish Horsemen and their Mounts
from Norman times to the Williamite Wars

THE NORMANS

THE INDICATIONS ARE that the Church felt it necessary, in order to gain a foothold in Ireland, to come to grips with customs involving the control and gift of horses. These customs had political and, as we have seen, military significance. Men who had horses, it would appear, could control the land. We might expect therefore that the Normans, and later the English, would show a similar sensitivity to these customs in their efforts to gain control of the country. If we are correct in suggesting that the gift and control of horses had critical and long-standing significance for the institutions which bound society together, then attempts to overthrow such institutions would inevitably involve those aspects of the horse tradition.

from *Giraldus Cambrensis.*

Indeed one of the starting points for both the Church and the Normans in Ireland was approximately the same. King Henry II was described in the Bull *Laudabiliter* as "bringing the truth of the Christian faith to a rude and unlettered people". This Bull provided the legal basis for Henry's interference in Ireland in 1169 and was issued to him by Pope Adrian IV, the only Englishmen ever to sit on the papal throne. Giraldus Cambrensis, who travelled to Ireland with Henry and who supplied details of the inauguration rite which lies at the heart of our story, claimed that the Irish were "so barbarous that they cannot be said to have any culture". He goes on in like vein claiming that they are "a most filthy people, utterly enveloped in vices, most untutored of all peoples in the rudiments of faith . . . practising always treachery beyond all other races: they keep their plighted faith to no man". Such comments of course had their propagandist side: they justified conquest. But they were also the words of someone who had difficulty understanding and knew that there would be difficulty in conquering. The Norman world, which was feudal, was highly organised. The King gave his tenants-in-chief land and protection, in return for which they owed him in the main military service. The tenants-in-chief in turn had their tenants and the relationship was duplicated. This pyramid structure within society had a certain order in it. Control was possible. The Gaelic Irish world offered no such apparent order.[1] Hence Giraldus' and other commentators' strident utterances.

On the face of it, Norman claims to superiority were reflected on the battlefield. Compared to them the Irish were amateurs. The Normans, to quote the words of

From *Giraldus Cambrensis.*

the historian Curtis, saw war as "a business proposition and their enterprise a joint-stock company out of which profits were expected". In Ireland war brought an immediate return. They had learned their great skills of horsemanship in the plains of France, plains which were ideally suited to the cavalry charge which was being perfected in the 11th century. Ireland was not so well suited to it for it consisted of many forests, mountains and bogs in which the Irish could take refuge. But the Normans who came to Ireland had been schooled in an environment which closely approximated to that in Ireland. They had triumphed in the difficult Welsh terrain. They managed to combine with the fighting power of their knights the effective skills of archers, mounted and unmounted. Highly mobile and able to attack their opponents from a distance with their longbows, the archers were invaluable in Ireland. When they were placed among the knights, the archers were able to counteract the lightning attacks of the Irish, by alternately rushing forward and retreating sufficiently quickly to avoid casualties. All of this was to pay dividends early in the Norman story in Ireland. At Dublin in 1170 the Norman archers shot gaps in the solid phalanx of axemen drawn up to defend the city, before the horsemen moved in and overran them. When confronted with the might of the Normans, the initial response of the Irish was fear. At Wexford the inhabitants moved out of the town to attack the forces of Robert FitzStephen, recently arrived from Wales, but they quickly retreated back to the town, burning the suburbs. The unfamiliar sight of the serried ranks of knights and archers with horsemen on each wing "resplendent with breastplates, swords and helmets all gleaming" had quickly convinced them that defence was their best policy. Eight years later when the Norman leader de Courcy led a force of 22 knights and 300 other soldiers to conquer east Ulster he achieved rapid success against the much greater numbers of the Ulstermen who, according to one set of annals, "retreated without a blow when they saw the Englishmen with their horses in full battledress". Even a hundred years later, according to the Irish annals, charging knights in open country could still terrify the Irish into flight without ever a blow being struck.[2]

The Norman knights had enormous power as shock troops. They wore byrnies or hauberks of mail—long skirted coats of iron rings or of quilted fabric or leather reinforced with metal studs. They had heads or coifs of mail over which they wore conical iron helmets, and some wore leggings or chausses of mail. Their shields were kite-shaped giving them complete cover on the left hand side as they rode. They carried a lance, a long straight-bladed sword, and sometimes a club or mace. Mounted on their destriers or heavy horses which they rode skilfully into battle they dominated their opponents in the field. Against this superb fighting machine the Irish, as always disunited, were practically helpless. We have already noted the limited character of Irish warfare. A king saw warfare as an opportunity to impress his subjects and his enemies—not to destroy them.[3] They were of little use to him dead. When he had achieved the immediate object of battle he retired. During certain times of the year he did not fight at all as his levies had to tend to their crops. On the battlefield the most striking limitation on the Irish related to their equipment. By way of contrast with the heavily armed Norman knights, the tanks of mediaeval warfare, the Irish, in the words of Giraldus Cambrensis, were naked as they rode into battle:

> They use woollen trousers that are at the same time stockings, and these are mostly dyed. When they are riding they do not use saddles or leggings or boots. They drive on, and guide their horses by means of a stick with a crook at its upper end, which they hold in hand. They use reins to serve the purpose of a bridle and a bit. It does not prevent (as it usually does) the horses from feeding on the grass. Moreover they go naked and unarmed into battle.

Where the Normans had mail the Irish wore a linen tunic. They carried a short sword, a battle-axe they had borrowed from the Norsemen—their only concession to modernity—spear, javelin and slingstones. They were no match for the far-flying arrows of the Welsh followed by a charge of knights and the methodical operations of disciplined foot-soldiers.[4]

Such weapons as the Irish had were suited to close hand-to-hand combat and not to cavalry operations. Irish battles such as that at Clontarf in 1014 had been largely foot battles and we have few references to the part played by horsemen in them. Irish leaders, however, rode on horseback and may have even worn armour. Diarmaid Mac Murchada, the Irish leader responsible for inviting over the Normans, had horsemen in his retinue and we read of the Normans capturing horses and occasionally armour from the Irish. *The Book of Rights*, probably written in the twelfth century, has many references to cavalry. But the earliest evidence which we have of horses being ridden in Ireland occurs in the Irish law tract *Críth Gablach* which was probably written in the eighth century. It is clear from this and other law tracts that it was the prerogative of the noble grades to ride horses, and this may have been narrowly interpreted until Norman times.[5]

The high degree of professionalism which the Norman knights exhibited on the battlefield did not have a political counterpart. When compared with the conquest of England which was 'systematic, ruthless and complete', that of Ireland was almost casual. King Henry was willing to give Diarmaid Mac Murchada help for his struggles in Ireland provided that it did not cost him anything. Henry's interest was not focused on Ireland but he realised that Diarmaid might be useful to him in ridding him, at least temporarily, of powerful barons who had little scope for their ambitions in his domains. The Norman knights who came to Ireland, for their part, were footloose adventurers who had no particular national allegiance. They were not chivalric figures but professionals whose service was given as a commodity by lesser lords to the king and other lords in return for land. They fitted easily into the Irish polity where shifting alliances were the order of the day. Their initial success was astounding. By the year 1250 three quarters of the country had been overrun by them. But there was very little co-ordination of their activities. Not only was the king concerned with events elsewhere but he was suspicious and acted against such leaders as de Courcy who threatened to develop sufficient power and prestige in the country to make himself king of Ireland. Their progress in the absence of royal support was dependent on individual effort. The Normans outside Leinster were sparse on the ground and in order to survive or prosper had to form alliances with the native Irish.

But their approach to conquest, such as it was, was not purely military. After they had built fortresses designed to ensure that they held the land which they conquered they proceeded to utilise the land for agricultural purposes, and for the first time Ireland knew systematic agriculture and estate management. For the Normans conquest would be a failure if they did not succeed in exploiting the land and, for this, the co-operation of the Gaelic Irish was essential. The ordinary people would be required to remain on the land to herd the cattle and to till the soil. It was inevitable that the Normans would displace some of the Gaelic aristocracy from their lands but alliances, including considerable intermarriage, were also features of their interaction. The intermingling of the two races also resulted in the Normans adopting the lighter Irish horse which suited warfare in the Irish terrain.[6]

Norman knights from the Bayeux Tapestry, late 11th century.

THE HOBELAR

It is against this background that we have to consider the development in Ireland of the hobelar, a fighter who was to make a considerable contribution to the advance of medieval warfare. Countries like Ireland and Wales had highlighted the limitations of the mounted knight. He was immensely powerful as part of shock troops but against an enemy which would not stand and fight he was at a great disadvantage. This is borne out by the Norman experience in Ireland where their settlements were generally limited to lowland areas. Above 600 feet and in the more inaccessible parts of the country, in particular the woodland and bog, where the nimble Irish could find refuge from the charging knights, there is little evidence of their occupation. The disadvantages of the heavily clad knight were brought home to the Norman king Edward in his Scottish wars when he was opposed by Robert Bruce, King of Scotland. The latter used guerrilla tactics against him. He had his soldiers mounted on ponies and he used these ponies to avoid battle. While the English starved he retaliated in lightning quick raids. When the English king realised that he needed troops which could catch the Scots and bring them to battle he sent for the hobelar to Ireland.

The hobelar is of interest generally, for one particular reason. He played an important part in the evolution of the most effective fighting man of the middle ages—the mounted archer. He represented a half-way house between the out-moded knight and the mounted archer. He was a light cavalry man who could mount and dismount at ease and scout if necessary, and the first references which we have to him indicate that he originated in Ireland. The key to his ability was the light horse or pony which he rode—the hobby.[7] Descriptions of it abound over the centuries and are in the main full of praise. One of the earliest references is that of an Italian visitor Raphael Maffeus Volaternus in the sixteenth century:

> Ireland possesses nothing worthy of mention but corn and excellent horses which the inhabitants call Ubinos.

The first reference to hobelars occurs in 1296 when 260 of them were among a contingent of Irish troops led by John de Wogan, the Justiciar, who was determined to make Ireland a source of aid for the king's wars in Scotland and France. They seemed to have made a good impression on the king for, even though the rest of Irish force went home, the hobelars remained. A small number were used regularly in the Scottish wars subsequently for such duties as scouting and patrolling. In 1300 King Edward had requested 300 hobelars from Ireland for muster at Carlyle, but by 1302 his expectations had greatly increased and he wanted a force of 1000. During the period 1300 to 1304, however, the number serving in Scotland never exceeded 503, but the value placed on them was great since they were much better suited to skirmishing and pursuit than the more heavily armed cavalry. The fear

The Irish for their part did not value their own horses as highly as did others. In the Irish law tracts we read that it was a British horse which was valued as a gift, and there is considerable evidence of horse imports into Ireland for breeding purposes. The Normans brought their own horses to Ireland despite the fact that this required elaborate preparations of the ships transporting them. To take the destrier or heavy Norman horse which carried the knight, special stalls had to be fitted, bridges built to take them on board and the ship had to be reinforced against the animal. It is clear, however, that from an early stage the Normans prized the smaller and faster Irish horse. After his expedition to Ireland in 1171 Henry II took some such horses back with him to England. Edward I got six 'hobbies' for his own use and there is evidence that from these early beginnings a steady export of horses to England and the continent built up. Over the centuries Irish horses were in use in the king's service and frequently laws had to be enacted to prevent their export and use for other purposes. The difficulties of transporting Irish horses abroad for the king's service were also very great and frequently the ships available in Ireland were found to be inadequate. When preparations were being made for the dispatch of Irish troops for Edward's Scottish wars in 1303 many of those that were available were too small or needed repair. The work of fitting out and reinforcing a boat which was capable of carrying at a maximum thirty horses could take several weeks. Hurdles made of pliable wood woven together had to be provided for stalls or to protect the sides of the frail boats and the work, although inexpensive, was very time consuming. Despite the difficulties, however, hobbies and hobelars were regularly withdrawn from Ireland during the 13th and 14th centuries to aid the English king and it is to that period that the decline of the Anglo-Norman colony, suffering greatly from its lack of defence, can be dated.[8]

was that the Irish hobelars would return to Ireland leaving the English king in difficulties. In July 1299 Robert de Clifford sent an urgent request that wages be paid immediately to Robert le Brut, "an Irish hobelar, retained to spy the passes and haunts of the enemy by night and day and who has been on duty six weeks and three days, lest he take himself off for want of sustenance." Unpaid wages, in the case of a hobelar 1s 6d per day, were a feature of such campaigns. Irish hobelars were still being sought by the king even when he had developed his own English hobelars. On the eve of the Bruce invasion of Ireland in 1315 we find small troops of Irish hobelars in the king's service in Scotland when clearly the Norman lords in Ireland would have needed them for defence purposes. As late as 1347, fifty of them fought in the king's service under the Earl of Kildare at the siege of Calais. By that time, however, the need for hobelars outside Ireland was passing. They had been superseded by the mounted archer as the most effective fighting man of his age, for he combined in one fighting unit the hobelar's great mobility with the firepower of the longbow. In Ireland, however, where the winds of change did not blow strongly, the hobelar was to endure for many centuries.[9]

GAELIC IRISH WARFARE AND HORSEMANSHIP

The success of the Irish hobby and hobelar and the fascination which they exercised for the leaders of the Norman central government in England facilitated the process whereby the Irish horse and rider became the focus of English frustration in trying to gain control of Ireland.

The horse myth grew, and in the process many of the factors in Irish life which the English found incomprehensible and uncontrollable became absorbed in it. Admiration for the horse and horseman in Ireland became imbued with an instinctive fear of what they represented. Not for the Irish, for example, the chivalrous ideal of the Norman knights of standing the charge on the battlefield. To the English the Irish proclivity to take to the bogs, mountains and woods when the going got rough was akin to the 'treachery' described by Giraldus. From the Irish point of view, given the type of terrain in Ireland and the equipment which the Irish fighting men used, it made perfectly good sense to rely on such escapist tactics. The Normans had, after their great successes on the battlefield in Ireland, built castles and towns but the Irish had no such centres of defence or points from which attacks could be launched. Only when Irish chiefs had acquired gallowglasses or heavily armed footsoldiers in the second half of the 13th century were they able, in some way, to make up the deficit. Because of their heavy armour the gallowglasses could provide an attacking party with a moving line of defence from which the horsemen could emerge to make their sharp charges and behind which they could retreat when pursued.[10]

The characteristic feature of Gaelic Irish warfare in the middle ages was the plunder or defence of the moving *creaght* or cattle herd. Raids on herds of cattle depended for their success on surprise. If warning was given then the cattle and the people could be moved to safe ground and the attack would be unsuccessful. Having horses which were light and fast, ridden by horsemen who could mount and dismount with ease and who could exercise efficient control over their horses, was a necessity. One has only to note the conditions in the average Wild West film to appreciate the essential characteristic of partnership between horse and man in conditions where cattle driving is involved. Sir Henry Christede, who gave an account of King Richard's campaign in Ireland in 1399, provides an indication of how the Irish used their knowledge of the terrain and of horsemanship to foil their enemies :

> It happens quite often, however, that from their minute knowledge of the country they find a favourable opportunity for attacking their enemies: they are very alert on such occasions and no man at arms, however well mounted, can overtake them so light are they on their feet: they can even leap up onto a horse, drag the rider to the ground, or else pin his arms behind him so that he cannot escape for their own arms are immensely strong, and when they have the worse of any skirmish, they scatter and hide in hedges or bushes, or underground, and seem to disappear without trace.

To this picture of the 'wild' Irishman Christede then adds an account of his own experience of Irish horsemanship in which the Irish ability to take control of the animal is vividly illustrated. On an occasion when he is accompanying the Earl of Ormonde on horseback on campaign his horse takes fright and gallops into the midst of the Irish enemy:

> and in passing though the Irish one of them by a great feat of agility, leaped on the back of my horse and held me tight with both his arms, but did me no harm with lance or knife. Turning my horse he rode with me for more than two hours till we reached a large bush in a very retired spot, where he found his companions, who had retreated thither from the English.

He subsequently spent seven years among the Irish, married the daughter of the local chief and adopted the Irish language and customs, illustrating in many respects how the English government's fears about its subjects succumbing to what it saw as the Irish contagion were justified.[11]

Leaping on the back of a moving horse was a much prized skill among the Irish. In an amended form, it was an important part of the games which featured at the fairs and assemblies in early Ireland where competitors vied with each other in leaping over a horse's back. Indications in the Irish law tracts suggest that this game may have originally been played by warriors. A German account of the Williamite commander Marshal Schomberg's campaign which commenced in August 1689 draws attention to the control which the Irish who practised leaping on to their horses had over them:

> The Irish here train their beasts to complete obedience; they jump on them in full armour, being swift and agile.

In Norman times the Irish did not use a saddle. Certainly the high Norman saddle would have been out of the question for even the most agile Irishman attempting to mount a moving horse. Both mounting and dismounting were made very cumbersome for the Normans because of it. On the other hand a saddle with stirrups was essential equipment for a horseman if he was to stay the charge of mounted knights or in turn make such a charge on his enemy.[12]

The Irish reluctance to have equipment distancing the horse from its rider is evident in relation not only to saddles but also to other pieces of equipment. The earliest Irish horsebits were snaffles which would have interfered very little with the horse. Indeed Giraldus had been so struck by the contrast between what he saw in Ireland in this respect and the curb then in use in France and Britain, with its long

Winter racing scene (Inpho)

cheek pieces, that he was prompted to suggest, as we have seen, that the Irish did not use bits at all. The development of the snaffles in Ireland does show a tendency to increasing severity over the centuries but, at the time Giraldus was writing in the twelfth century, nothing as severe as the curb with its strong lever action was employed. As Giraldus's comments also show, neither was the spur in use. The earliest reference to a spur in Ireland comes at the beginning of the 14th century and, in a contemporary picture of Art McMurrough, the Irish chieftain, leading his men from the woods to attack the Earl of Gloucester's forces in 1399, we see what is probably a rowel spur attached to Art's bare foot. Although by the sixteenth century the spur was being worn by the Irish over their boots it is clear that its use was still regarded as a mark of anglicisation and therefore suspect.[13]

Control of the horse has been traditionally seen, the folklore record in Ireland makes clear, as exercised by virtue of an empathy between man and animal. A man riding the horse bareback will be conscious of his closeness to the animal. Lacking spurs and the other tools of coercion, he will be inclined to foster a relationship with the animal which produces co-operation rather than demand submission by exerting force. It was his closeness to the animal and his skill which, we can surmise, enabled Christede's captor to take control of his horse.

THE STATUTE OF KILKENNY, 1366

We may well ask whether the sequence of events in the story of Christede's adventure—his exposure to Irish horsemanship leading to his absorption into the network of Irish life and customs—had a general application to the English experience in Ireland. A body of legislation, the Statute of Kilkenny, enacted in 1366, would seem to indicate that it had. Before turning to this it is necessary to recall the general context in which this legislation was seen to be necessary. Irish warfare had a ritual character designed to elicit submission. The legal theory in Norman England by which war was waged only on the king's behalf and land was given by the king in return for feudal service had little application in Gaelic Ireland. There the basic unit of kingship had once been the local and highly autonomous *rí tuaithe*. Over the centuries such kings or chiefs strove, through alliances and through the submission of rivals, to add to their power and prestige. Into this world of shifting alliances the Norman knights who came to Ireland fitted easily for they gave allegiance freely to no one, least of all to a king who tried to curb them. Absorption into the Gaelic Irish world offered them the possibility of increasing their power. Not surprisingly English kings and their representatives in Ireland felt it necessary to control the relations between the Gaelic Irish and the Anglo-Normans in Ireland who were in danger of succumbing to Irish influence. The way in which they attempted to do this was to defend the frontier which separated the Anglo-Norman colony where the king's writ ran from Gaelic Ireland where "the wild Irish our enemies" lived.

This frontier was, in the 14th century, continuously being pushed back as the

Anglo-Norman settlers were being swamped culturally and their identity threatened. Eventually the colony or Pale would consist only of a narrow strip of country centred around Dublin. The Statute of Kilkenny was an attempt to halt this process of infiltration of the Pale and some of its enactments centred on the horse.

(*See marginal note page 74.*)

There were, of course, military reasons for the Anglo-Normans retaining their horses. They would be available for the king's service and could be used in defending his subjects if necessary. But it is doubtful if the Gaelic Irish would be greatly hampered by the Anglo-Norman refusal to deal in horses with them. The heavy Norman horse, the destrier, had little function in the Irish terrain and the Normans themselves had adopted the Irish hobby of about 12 to 14 hands for the purpose of warfare. More important than the specifically military side to the supplying of horses was the fact that, as we have seen, it created bonds between people, bonds which, in the government's view could become military alliances.

There can be no doubt about the seriousness with which the government viewed the sale or gift of horses to the Irish. One of the duties of the Keepers of the Peace in each region was to ensure that such occurrences did not take place. In 1468 the Earl of Desmond was executed for breaking the Statute of Kilkenny, one of the charges laid against him being that he had supplied the Irish with "horses and harness and men". The Earls of Kildare who were intent on increasing their personal power in much the same fashion also bestowed horses lavishly. Both Desmond and

A *cavalry* skirmish (English on left; Irish on right) Woodcut probably by John Derrick 1581.

Kildare were descendants of the original Norman settlers but what saved Kildare was that he was sufficiently powerful not to have the full rigours of the law used against him. English sensitivity on the subject, however, did not abate with time. As late as 1584 a passage in a *Treatise on Ireland* recommended that "no horse be sold by any subject to the Irish without lycence of the governor". The exchange of horses among the Irish themselves was also a source of concern to the government. In 1549 Conn Bacach O'Neill gave eight horses together with some armour to Maguire in order to attach him to his service, and some fifty years later we find a spy reporting to the government about horses being exchanged between the Irish rebels as "a bond of devotion".[15]

If the exchange of horses conjured up for the English images, however ill-defined, of the pernicious and forbidding world of ancient Irish kingship and alliances, so also, we might expect, would the horsemanship and manner of controlling the horse which the Irish exercised. In Irish tradition, as we have seen, horse gifts and horsemanship were linked and seen as belonging as of right to kingship. The preamble to the Statute of Kilkenny highlights the Irish manner of riding as one of the factors leading to the 'degeneracy' of the English in Ireland:

> whereas at the conquest of the land of Ireland and for a long time after, the English of the said land used the English language, mode of riding and apparel, and were governed and ruled . . . by the English law . . . Now many English of the said land, forsaking the English language, fashion, mode of riding, laws and usages, live and govern themselves according to the manner, fashion and language of the Irish enemies and also have made diverse marriages and alliances between themselves and the Irish enemies aforesaid: whereby the said land and the liege people thereof, the English language, the allegiance due to our lord King, and the English laws there, are put in subjection and decayed.[16]

Some of the thinking which lay behind the English concern with Irish horsemanship may be gleaned by reference to the other facets of Irish life which are also highlighted in this preamble. An English treatise remarks with regard to the Irish language: "This vulgar Irish tongue induceth the habit, the habit induceth the conditions and inordinate laws, and so tongue, habit, law and conditions maketh mere Irish."

For an Anglo-Irish chronicler writing in 1399 images of a strange language, local kingship and a 'wild people' riding practically naked in an inhospitable environment were all part of one composite nightmare.

> a wild people who speak a strange language, and dwell always in the woods and on mountains of the country and have many chiefs among themselves, of which the most powerful go barefoot and without breeches, and ride horses without saddles.[17]

The horse might seem an appropriate focus for legislation designed to protect frontiers. Traditionally in Ireland it was used to invade another man's land. What threatened the Pale, however, was rather the gradual encroachment of a network of Irish customs which eroded the basis of governmental control. To the English these customs had all the characteristics of disease—they were both contagious and destructive. Fosterage, for example, was seen as being particularly dangerous since it established close bonds between people. Bonds were also established by the exchange of horses in Gaelic Ireland, and one of the enactments at Kilkenny was aimed at this. This enactment forbade the English in Ireland to sell or give horses to the Irish in time of peace or of war.[14]

The linking of horseriding and apparel here and in the preamble to the statute is hardly fortuitous. A consistent feature of indentures between the English government and Irish chiefs in later centuries was to be stipulations about the Irish chiefs wearing English clothes. In 1573 the 14th Earl of Desmond symbolically cast off his English apparel as he returned from enforced exile in London to his castle at Lough Gur and put on the dress of an Irish chieftain. His action was a signal to the English queen that he was no longer her humble servant. In Ireland, in mediaeval times and before, kings at their inaugurations gave gifts of horses and clothes to their subordinates in order to ensure submission. Horses and clothes, for the Irish, had very great symbolic significance. They represented a way of life which would not be surrendered easily. Sir Henry Christede who, as we noted, lived among the Irish for several years, gives an account of his efforts to instruct four Irish chiefs who had submitted to the king—O'Neill, McMurrough, O'Brien and O'Connor—in the customs of England. He was put in a house with them and remarks:

> They had another habit, which I know was common in their country, of not wearing breeches, so I had some made for them and for their people, to which they soon grew accustomed. At first I had difficulty in persuading them to wear clothes of silk trimmed with fur, for till then they considered a rough Irish cloak sufficient. They always rode without saddles or stirrups, and I had great trouble in getting them to use them.[18]

While the government was conscious of the risks to Anglo-Irish identity inherent in exposure to the network of customs symbolised by horses and clothes, the Gaelic Irish, through their poets, had little hesitation in asserting and celebrating their own identity by means of the same symbols. There is no doubt in the mind of the 16th-century poet Laoiseach Mac an Bhaird, in his description of two sons of an Irish chief, about the significance of horses and clothes. One of the chief's sons has adopted English ways but the other, Eoghan Bán, has remained Gaelic, earning the praise of the poet:

> Little he cares for gold-embroidered clothes
> or for a high well-furnished ruff,
> A troop of horse at the mouth of a pass
> A wild fight, a ding dong fray of footsoldiers,
> These are some of the delights of Donnchadh's son,
> And seeking contests with the foreigners.

English horsemanship is repugnant to Eoghan:

> He would hate to have at his ankle
> a jewelled spur on a boot, or stocking
> in the English manner

Eoghan Bán's brother, on the other hand, is a figure of fun:

> men laugh at you as you put your foot on the mounting block,
> It is a pity that you yourself don't see your errors,
> O man who follows English ways.[19]

The thirteenth-century King of Connacht, Cathal Crobhderg O'Connor, also strongly asserted the preference for vaulting on to the horse's back and dispensing with equipment which interfered with the Irish manner of controlling the animal. He did this in the presence of King John who had come over to Ireland in 1210. John was proceeding in a triumphal march along the east coast when he was joined by Cathal who accepted a richly caparisoned steed from him. This was an act of submission on the Irish king's part but it was one which he was quick to qualify. He did not mount the steed until he had first removed the heavy Norman saddle from it.[20] It was almost as if O'Connor was giving King John a coded message indicating the extent of his submission. He would accept the steed from him and recognise him as his overlord but there were aspects of Irish life which were considered to be sacrosanct and which would remain impenetrable to the English. Even today, techniques of horsemanship and modes of dress on horseback which have their provenance abroad arouse feelings of antagonism in Ireland, particularly, as is often the case, when they are advocated by English personnel. Carelessness and bravado with regard to horses acquire overtones of nationalism. When the government in 1366 acted sternly against the English in Ireland adopting Irish horsemanship techniques it was, no doubt, helping to mould Gaelic Irish attitudes of defiance. It was also reacting to a threat which it greatly feared:

> No Englishman who has the value of one hundred shillings of land or of tenements by the year shall ride otherwise than on a saddle in the English fashion: and he that shall do to the contrary and be therefore attaint his horse shall be forfeited and his body shall be committed to prison until he make fine.[21]

Over the centuries the Irish clung firmly to their custom of not using a saddle. On a visit to Niall Óg O'Neill's camp in 1397 the Spaniard Count John de Perilhos noted: "He has indeed forty horsemen, riding without saddle on a cushion and each wear a slashed cloak, moreover they are armed with coats of mail, and wear them girded, and they have throat pieces of mail and round helmets of iron."

The contemporary picture which we have of Art McMurrough leading his men from the woods to attack the Earl of Gloucester's forces in 1399 is the earliest representation of the Irish wearing mail. The contrast with the English forces in it is, however, very pronounced—the Irish on their ponies, with no saddle or stirrups, bearing aloft their javelins and throwing themselves at the massed ranks of Gloucester's forces with their larger horses and their mail protection from head to toe. Twenty years later, Irish horsemen under Thomas Butler, the Prior of Kilmainham,

English fears that the Irish style of horsemanship would, if unchecked, continue to gain ground within the Pale proved to have not been without foundation. As one commentator has observed, the Irish horseman of the sixteenth century presents a remarkable illustration of how an inefficient or obsolete practice can not only survive but actually extend itself at the expense of a more efficient one. In the Pale, horsemen were more heavily armed than elsewhere in Ireland and were equipped with a saddle and stirrups, and against them, in open fighting, Irish horsemen continued to fare badly. The Gaelic Irish, on the other hand, frequently succeeded by wearing down their opponents rather than by risking all on a charge and subsequent cavalry mêlée. Despite the weakness of the Irish manner of riding it continued to gain ground within the Pale, a fact which was given tacit recognition in 1495 when all the stipulations of the 1366 Statute of Kilkenny were renewed with the exception of two—those relating to Irish horsemanship and language. The government must have considered that there was little point in attempting to control these any further.[23]

were taking part in the French campaign of Henry V and laying siege to Rouen. A French chronicler tells us that they "had no saddles, but rode excellently well on small mountain horses."

By 1600, according to the English writer Dymmock, the position had not changed very much. In noting that Irish horsemen "ride upon paddles, or pillowes, without stirrups and in this they differ from ours," he pointed out the disadvantage of not having stirrups. The Irish horseman bore his stave 'above arme' and not 'under arme and so put it to the reste'. In making a charge, forces like McMurrough's would have lacked the necessary weight to make an impact on an enemy drawn up in formation.[22]

(See marginal note page 76.)

The prestige of Irish horsemanship is reflected in the praise which it attracted from commentators. De Perilhos noted in 1397 of O'Neill's cavalry: "For a long time they have been fighting with the English and the king of England cannot get the better of them." Most of the praise, however, comes from English sources. One hundred and fifty years after De Perilhos' visit the Lord Deputy in Ireland wrote to King Henry: "I thinke that for ther feate of warre, which is for light scoorers [skirmishers] there are no properer horsemen in Christian grounde, nor more hardie nor yet that can better indure hardenesse."

Durlas Eile, ridden by Major Eddie Boylan, at the Sheepwash and Rails during the Three-Day Event European Championships at Punchestown in 1967. This combination took the individual title during the championships. (*Horseman Photography*).

Accordingly to Fenton, the English commander writing in 1585, the Irish "do greatly overtop us, as well in numbers as in goodness of horses". By the time that Fenton was writing the English had paid the ultimate compliment to the Irish horsemen. They had employed them in their armies in Ireland.[24]

FEAR OF IRISH HORSEMEN AND ENVIRONMENT

But beneath the admiration which the commentators expressed lurked the feeling that the horsemen were strange and incomprehensible. The Irish people in general adhered to beliefs and customs which to English eyes frequently had an air of primitive savagery. One such custom was the eating of horseflesh which was taboo in England since early times and which attracted the ire of the English writer Fynes Moryson. He was writing in the early years of the seventeenth century when prolonged periods of war had resulted in great scarcity of food. The Irish, he claimed, "were ready to tear out one another's throat for a share" of a horse.

Much the same conditions of scarcity existed in 1397 when De Perilhos noted that the people ate "oxen and cows and good horses". The crack fighting unit among the Irish, the Gallowglasses, we are told, were forced to eat horses because "other vittels were scant" as they struggled in the service of the doomed Earl of Desmond in 1583. Incidents took place about the same time, in the very difficult circumstances in which Munster found itself, which show the Irish as eager to acquire the horse for food. Beggars in Waterford slew dispatch riders from Youghal and ate their horses. The horse of an English official named Fenton was burned when his stable in Dublin caught fire and "before it was half roasted" the horse was pulled from the flames in front of his eyes by the people and eaten. The horse of Vice-Treasurer Wallop which had died of sickness "was devoured, entrails and all, without any preparation". Conditions became so severe that horsemeat became a common staple and horse numbers for cavalry purposes were correspondingly reduced. English troops sold their mounts to butchers who, in turn, supplied the tables of officers who little realised that they were depleting their own cavalry when they sat down to dinner.[25]

Moryson, however, maintained that it was not only necessity but choice which encouraged the Irish to eat horseflesh. "Yea (which is more contrary to nature) they will feed," he claimed, "on horses dying of themselves, not only for upon small a want of flesh, but even for pleasure." In a subsequent passage he shows his hand. In speaking of the custom of the Irish of drinking the blood of their cattle in times of hunger he draws a comparison: "A man would think these men to be Scythians, who let their horses' blood under the ears, and for nourishment drink their blood".[26]

Writers might well imagine that the horsemen among the Irish had more in common with distant and possibly primitive people than with their contemporaries in Western Europe. De Perilhos described "their manner of warring" as "like that of the Saracens" and in a letter to Lord Burleigh in 1579 Sir William Drury wrote of the impression made on him by O'Reilly's horsemen:

> How strange the view of these savage personages, most of them . . . armed in mail, with pesantoes and skulls and riding upon pillions, seemed to us strangers.

The fear of the unknown played a considerable part in the instinctive reaction of the English to Irish horsemen. Militarily these horsemen were centuries behind their time and should have posed little threat. But the myth of the Irish horse and horseman was compounded in the English mind by another factor and this was the terrain in Ireland.[27]

In the sixteenth century bogs were said to cover one quarter of the area of the country. Woods covered one eighth. To judge from English accounts, moreover, the country outside the Pale consisted only of bogs and woods. Such terrain was a metaphor for Gaelic Irish society, exposing the inadequacies of English methods of control and used by the Irish to their own advantage. Sir Henry Christede had commented in 1399:

> Ireland is one of the worst and most unfavourable countries in which to carry on warfare: it abounds in deep forests and in lakes and bogs, and most of it is uninhabitable. It is often impossible to come to grips with the people, for they are quite ready to desert their towns and take refuge in the woods, and live in huts made of branches, or even among the bushes and hedges, like wild beasts.

Most of the country was impenetrable, at first to the heavily armed Norman and later to the English, except through the passes which they were able to open up. The Irish, for their part, from Norman times could impede the progress of troops by plashing the passes, i.e. obstructing them with felled trees and thus throwing troops into confusion and leaving them open to ambush. In difficult country Irish horsemen could manoeuvre easily on their light horses and carry out lightning strikes on the enemy if they dared to try to penetrate their fastnesses:

> Wherefore it is not to be wondered at
> If the brave knights
> dreaded those people
> who were swift as the wind.

To the image of the Irishmen, at home on horseback and able to make a co-operative partner of the horse, was added the image of woods, bogs and mountains which were likewise the home of the Irish and which, by turns, the Irish could use as part of their defensive style of warfare.[28]

Between the twelfth and sixteenth centuries the Irish terrain had not changed substantially but continued to provide a haven from which horsemen could make lightning attacks mounted on their nimble horses. The unchanging character of their environment was a factor in the conservatism of the Irish horsemen. They had little reason for altering their equipment and methods. The absence of a saddle, for instance, was a positive advantage in terrain where mounting and dismounting the horse was, of necessity, swift and frequent. Small wonder that at least one aspect of the terrain, the woods, assumed large proportions in both English and Irish eyes.

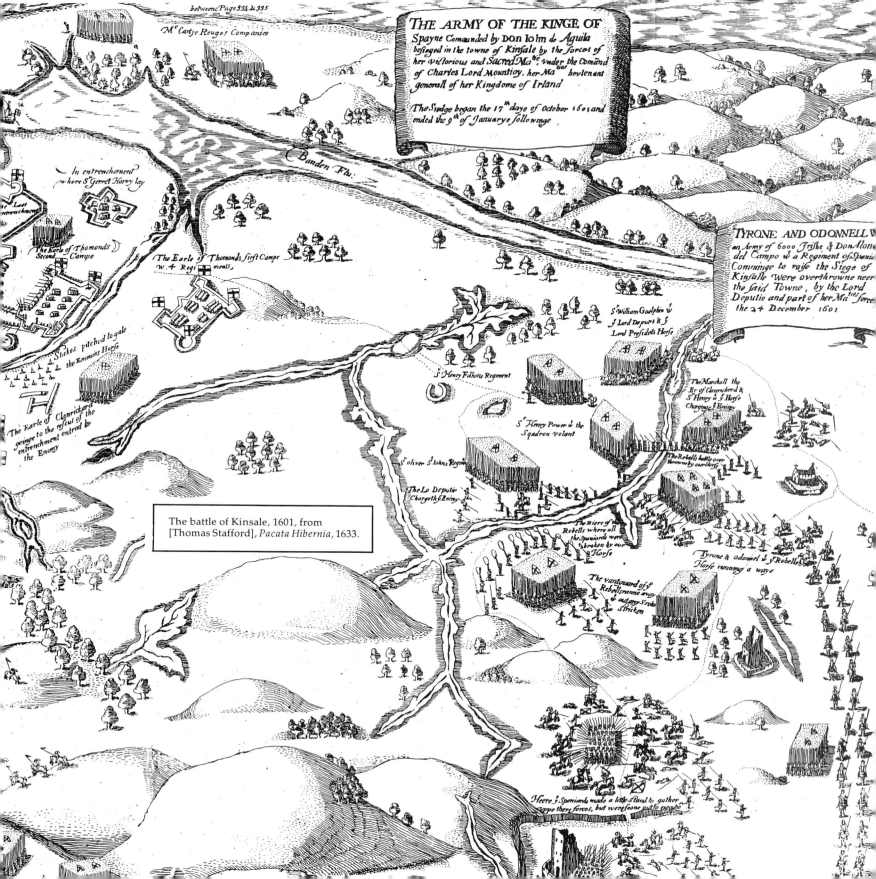

between Page 334 & 335

Mr Cartye Reuges Companies

THE ARMY OF THE KINGE OF Spayne Comanded by Don Iohn de Aguila besieged in the towne of Kinsale by the forces of her victorious and Sacred Maᵗⁱᵉˢ vnder the Comand of Charles Lord Mountioy, her Maᵗⁱᵉˢ heutenant generall of her Kingdome of Irland

The Siedge began the 17ᵗʰ daye of October 1601 and ended the 9ᵗʰ of Ianuarye followinge

In entrenchment where Sʳ Gerret Harry lay

Banden Flu:

Last entrenchment

The Earle of Thomonds Second Campe

The Earle of Thomonds first Campe wᵗʰ 4 Regiments

Stakes pitched to gale the Enimies Horse

The Earle of Clanrickard goinge to the rescui of the entrenchment entred by the Enimy

TYRONE AND ODONNELL Wᵗʰ an Army of 6000 Irishe & Don Alonso del Campo wᵗʰ a Regiment of Spanie Comminge to raise the Siege of Kinsalle Were overthrowne neer the said Towne, by the Lord Deputie and part of her Maᵗⁱᵉˢ force the 24 December 1601

Sʳ William Godlphin wᵗʰ ȳ Lord Depurs & ȳ Lord Presidets Horse

Sʳ Henry Folhotts Regiment

The Marshall the Eᵉ of Clanrickerd & Sʳ Henry wᵗʰ ȳ Horse Charginge ȳ Eniny

Sʳ Henry Power wᵗʰ the Sqadron Volant

The Rebells battle over throwne by our Horse

Sʳ oliver Sᵗ Iohns Regimᵗ

The Lo Depute Chargeth ȳ Eniny

The battle of Kinsale, 1601, from [Thomas Stafford], *Pacata Hibernia*, 1633.

The Riere of ȳ Rebells where all the Spaniards were broken by our Horse

Tyrone & odonnel wᵗʰ ȳ Rebells Horse ronning a waye

The vantgouard of ȳ Rebells ranne away ad any Sᵗ rube ȳ Stricken

Heere ȳ Spaniards made a little Staard to gather ȳ pe there forces, but were soone put to ȳ exᵉᵗᵒ

Over the centuries much English effort went into removing the woodland cover enjoyed by the Irish, whilst in Irish poetry the passing of the woods is seen as a calamitous event.[29]

In Ulster the alliance between horseman and terrain was particularly forbidding for the English and their influence least effective. Any army entering Ulster had to travel through passes surrounded by mountains and bogs which provided effective cover for ambushes and for continuous harassment by the enemy. Woods such as that of Glenconkeyne in Co. Tyrone, approximately 200 square miles in area, provided invaluable shelter for native armies and the flocks which sustained them while those armies slowly exhausted the advancing enemy by successively carrying out fleeting attacks and retreating. In this difficult environment in the sixteenth century Shane O'Neill, and later Hugh O'Neill, perfected defensive tactics firmly based on the nature of the terrain and wore out the English armies trying to take issue with them. Only when Hugh deviated from such tactics did his struggle come to an end.

NINE YEARS WAR

Hugh had devoted much effort to improving his army, using English trained men and English captains to help him. This work was mainly directed towards the infantry. Horsemen generally comprised only one half or one quarter of the total manpower of Irish armies and this, allied to the primitive character of their weaponry and equipment, greatly reduced their impact on the battlefield. However, during the Nine Years War which ended in the Treaty of Mellifont in 1603 the potential of O'Neill's horsemen as a backup to the infantry was fully exploited. The opening blows of this war were struck at the siege of Enniskillen, not however by O'Neill but by two other Ulster lords, O'Donnell and Maguire, who would later be prominent as the leader of the Irish cavalry. Enniskillen was one of a number of castles which had been garrisoned by the English in Ulster in an effort to facilitate conquest of the province but which, by virtue of Ulster's isolation and terrain, was liable to be cut off from supplies by the Irish chiefs. At Enniskillen in 1594 the Irish developed the tactics of ambush on a relieving force which would be frequently used during the war. Near the ford over the river Farney, later to be called the Ford of the Biscuits because of the supplies which the English had to abandon there, the relieving army was continually harassed by Maguire's troops, pouring musket fire on it under cloak of darkness. As the English army approached the ford its cavalry was rendered useless by the nature of the terrain and had to dismount. The horses sank in the marshy ground and the army crossing the ford in confusion was at the mercy of the Irish troops. Horses, arms and baggage were abandoned to the Irish as the army fled in terror, leaving Enniskillen to surrender to O'Donnell.[30]

The following year O'Neill entered the war. The effective use which he made of his cavalry in harassing the enemy in a series of running engagements can be seen before the battle at Clontibret in 1595. Bagenal, the English commander, was anxious to relieve the English garrison at Monaghan and his troops set out on their journey from Dundalk with a convoy of supplies. Several times O'Neill emerged on horseback with his troops, attacked and disappeared again before Bagenal could retaliate in a decisive fashion. During the battle itself modern and orthodox tactics were employed by the Irish with the horse and foot drawn up in formation and complementing each other. O'Neill had trained his troops in the use of muskets and pike in place of the old-fashioned bow and halberd, and when Bagenal sent out his cavalry they were confronted by musketmen and calivermen protecting O'Neill's horse. Victory for the Irish was followed by the surrender of the castle at Monaghan.

Another garrison in danger was that at Armagh and it was here, against Sir John Norris who was attempting to open up a channel for supplies in September 1595, that O'Neill's tactics were seen to best advantage. Norris had come to Ireland in May of that year and had made the mistake of thinking that the Irish horsemen were good only "to catch cows". Near Newry he was exposed to their adroitness. Time and time again he charged with his own horse when his rearguard came under attack to find that O'Neill's force of horsemen had wheeled and avoided him, taking up another position in formation.

The castle of Portmore which was situated near Armagh had been captured by O'Neill in 1595 but had fallen back into English hands and was again under threat from the Irish in 1598. The English commander Bagenal's march to relieve it again afforded an opportunity for the use of the classic Irish tactics. His cavalry, his guns with the trains of oxen and horses, his pack horses carrying supplies for the fort at Portmore and probably materials for making causeways through the bogs, were sitting targets for O'Neill's harassment. While he marched O'Neill attacked from behind the shrubbery and trees along the way. Because of the nature of the terrain, Bagenal's cavalry was totally impotent and, like the foot, was easily picked off.

When the English reached the open plain their cavalry charged only to find that O'Neill had dug pits and trenches as traps for them, disguising them with brambles and hay. As Bagenal's army tried to recover, the light-armed Irish horse, which in different circumstances would have been little match for the English cavalry, charged, "wheeling their horses again and again returned to the fight inflicted many wounds but giving ground, however, all the time". The battle proper took place at the Yellow Ford in terrain which particularly suited O'Neill. On both sides were marshes, and between these O'Neill had prepared the ground. Here during the battle, when the English wings caved in under the combined action of O'Neill's horse and foot, the Irish leader saw his opportunity to charge with his horsemen. Bagenal himself was killed, a third of the English army was destroyed and the rest driven back to Armagh.[31]

Until now O'Neill had been fighting on his own terms. Ulster enjoyed good natural defences, woods, mountains and lakes, as we noted, and behind these barriers he could carry on a war of attrition without ever having to expose himself to battle in terrain which did not suit. As we have pointed out, the strength of Irish armies lay in defence. Even at the Yellow Ford the battle was principally won against an army on the move and with its divisions strung out. O'Neill's troops were good guerrilla fighters. Despite their leader's efforts, however, they still suffered from a lack of experienced officers, and the troops themselves had no experience of pitched encounters where they would need considerable organisation and discipline in order to press home a charge and not to panic. The cavalry, although successful in the particular circumstances of the Yellow Ford, was still weak when judged against the standards of contemporary armies. The Spanish commander at Kinsale in 1601, Don Juan del Aquila, was very critical of his Irish allies, remarking on their small horses ridden by men with no stirrups using only 'half pikes'. Within the context of Ulster such forces were, as O'Neill had proved, more than adequate. The context however had changed. He had allied himself to O'Donnell and other Ulster chieftains and his success at the Yellow Ford had put the Queen on notice that she was no longer dealing with a recalcitrant subject. It was a national rebellion and was likely to become part of an international conflict. It had to be crushed, at whatever cost, and O'Neill would have to emerge out of Ulster if he was to meet the challenge a determined queen would pose to him.[32]

When Spanish assistance did come it was late and ineffective. Four thousand landed at Kinsale in September 1601 and were quickly besieged by Mountjoy, placing O'Neill in the difficult position of having to march the length of the country in order to come to their assistance. Estimates of the Irish force differ widely, but by Irish standards it was a big army. O'Neill himself was accompanied by about 3000 foot and 400 horse. Tactics, however, not force of numbers were to play the main part in the outcome of the struggle. The horses of the English commander Mountjoy's besieging army were lacking in forage and both men and horses were dying. Such horses as remained were exhausted and the cavalry, the mainstay of Mountjoy's troops, would soon have been forced to go to Cork for supplies. All circumstances encouraged O'Neill to wait and not allow himself be forced into battle. The Spanish, however, were insistent. They had come without any horses and this was their greatest deficiency in trying to counter the besieging English who daily rode up to the walls of Kinsale under the Spanish gaze and took cattle and corn and destroyed the mills. The Spanish had however brought saddles and bridles with them from Spain and after the debacle at Kinsale it was claimed against del Aquila that he could have mounted two hundred men by purchasing horses locally for between 50 and 60 *reals* and thus have prevented the English from replenishing their stocks. The Spanish opinion of the Irish horses we have already noted, but the battle indicated that the Irish horses alone were not necessarily the problem.

When Mountjoy showed that he was going to attack them outside Kinsale the Irish tried to draw themselves up in the massive formations which had proved so

Top : Eddie Macken on *Carroll's Royal Lion. (Horseman Photography)*.

Bottom : Paul Darragh and *Carroll's Heather Honey. (Horseman Photography)*

Top: *Garraí Eoin* and Capt. Ned Campion.
(*Ruth Rogers*).

Bottom: *Bellevue* ridden by
Col. Raimondo d'Inzeo.
(*Ruth Rogers*).

successful to the Spanish allies on the continent. The cavalry had even been supplied with trumpets and the infantry with drums. However, the horsemen had never fought in the accepted manner of the time. They had remained light horsemen, able to manoeuvre to perfection, and were unable to bear the shock of a charge or, except in very favourable circumstances, charge to effect. By way of contrast, Mountjoy's best troops in such an open field were his horsemen. The Irish cavalry was no match for them and fled the battle. The desertion of the cavalry was critical to the final result of the battle for it not only demoralised the infantry but, as it left the battlefield, it also fell in on the infantry and disorganised its ranks. One after another of the unwieldy infantry units fell as Mountjoy swept forward.[33]

There was more to the behaviour of the horsemen on this occasion than their apparent fright when confronted by the English horse. There were tensions within the Irish forces which had their basis in much earlier times. These tensions meant that the normal format for an army at the time of going into battle, i.e. the horse leading the foot, was not observed, and the forces were not in order during the attack. In fact, the indications are that the cavalry was at the rear and played very little part in the battle.

ELITE HORSEMEN

Some of these tensions which surfaced at many Irish battles were based on class distinction. As we have pointed out, from the earliest times in Ireland horseriding was the prerogative of the noble classes and, in the mediaeval period, only the more prosperous elements of the landowning classes could afford to be horsemen and to form part of the elite horse element in a lord's 'rising out'. The poorer elements made up his kerne or footsoldiers. Although the horsemen did not have the elaborate equipment of their English counterparts they were still expensive to provide for. They had, for example, at least two horses, often three, each with a groom or horseboy who often took part in battles with his master. The difference between the value placed on them and on the kerne is seen in the divergence between fines imposed in the late 16th century for defaulting on the obligation to join in the lord's 'rising out'. For horsemen it amounted to three cows or 15s in lieu, whereas for the kerne it was one cow or 5s. Along with their membership, as part of a lord's forces, of a small well-to-do elite went great prestige, remarked upon by the Anglo-Irish writer Stanyhurst in the sixteenth century: "To be a horseman . . . is the chieftest next the lord and capteine". As a rule they came from the ruling class in society.[34]

Inevitably, such men exercised a leadership role in the army. In a fictional account of the invasion by the Norman leader, de Courcy, of Ulster in the 12th century we are told that during a battle with him, the Irish chief O'Donnell was driven beyond a narrow pass with his horsemen and separated from the footmen who always looked for the king and the aid of their horsemen, amongst whom were all the gentlemen, in whom the footmen had all their trust.

Without the horse to back them up the footsoldiers were defenceless. Up to the end of the seventeenth century the horsemen were the natural leaders of the Irish armies. As such, they could play a decisive part even in battles which were predominantly foot. Their influence was in the main psychological and operated on their colleagues in the infantry and on the enemy. Their leadership role in mediaeval warfare had found expression, as we have seen, in the privileged position which they occupied at the side of the king in the most dangerous location at the rear of the war party. There was, however, a divisive side to this. Their separation from the foot expressed a divergence of interests and came to be institutionalised. Irish horsemen fought separately from the foot and usually against other horsemen only. In the class-conscious Gaelic world this was not a matter of tactics only. On the approach to Kinsale, for instance, the horsemen were, it would appear, all gathered together even though they belonged to different leaders among the Irish, and were separate from the foot.[35]

The battle of Benburb in 1646, however, continued the tradition of battle evident at the end of the 16th century, when horsemen, cleverly deployed in terrain which was strange to the English, played an inspiring role in victory. The Irish horsemen's equipment had not changed much since the 16th century although they probably now carried their staves couched and not overarm as formerly. During the battle at Benburb, nonetheless, the horsemen of the skilful Irish general Owen Roe O'Neill performed effectively in driving back the cavalry of the English leader Munroe. In his report of the battle Munroe complained bitterly of Myles the Slasher O'Reilly and the "Lisnagarvie Irish horse . . . cutting a swathe through the ranks". Later, with six horsemen, Myles died valiantly attempting to cut off Munroe's retreat. Meanwhile, Irish horsemen who had been sent to Dungannon had returned victoriously to Benburb "in great haste in a gallop, all in a sweat both horses and men" to assist the Gaelic Irish to a great victory. This time it was the English cavalry which rode off leaving the rest of their army to be cut to pieces.[36]

The victory did not, however, provide the pattern for the second half of the seventeenth century. Events occurred which tended to exacerbate the divergence of interests separating the horse from the more lowly infantry in Irish armies. From 1641 the Anglo-Irish who had been traditionally loyal to the English crown, found that their Catholic religion placed them under increasing suspicion from the king and the parliament. With the deterioration in their constitutional and social position they found themselves driven into making common cause with their co-religionists, the Old Irish. Towards the end of the seventeenth century, therefore, we find that many of the officers in the Jacobite army belonged to the Anglo-Irish landed aristocracy. Sarsfield, for instance, had inherited the family estates of Lucan. Such men were at home in the saddle with a tradition of cross-country riding and hunting behind them. They were men of substance who were conscious of being part of a tradition which was composed of both Irish and English elements. Between them and the Old Irish there were considerable divisions. The Old Irish sought not only a return to religious freedom but the restoration of confiscated lands to the Irish. What the Anglo-Irish wanted was moderate terms with the king and a restored kingdom under him ruled by themselves as a landed aristocracy controlling the Irish parliament.

The question of land was crucial. In 1641 Catholics had owned about three-fifths of the land of the country. By 1688 that proportion had been reduced to one-fifth and worse was to come. For the Old Irish ownership of land was, in the main, only an ancestral memory. They would have to get rid of the English in order to recover their estates. The Anglo-Irish for most of the second half of the seventeenth century still retained the hope of holding on to their estates under the English king. Despite the body blows which the English delivered to their loyalty they still considered an accommodation with the government possible. Their attitudes were a crucial factor in the behaviour of the cavalry. Only three years after O'Neill's great victory at Benburb much of the Irish cavalry deserted the infantry at the battle of Dungan's Hill.[37]

WILLIAMITE WARS

Irish defeats were not however always marked by the failure of the cavalry. Its performance in the service of King James at the battle of the Boyne in 1690 made it feared and respected by the Williamite generals for the rest of the war. As the forces under King William crossed the river Boyne at Oldbridge, King James' infantry came under intense pressure. The Irish horsemen successfully came to its assistance, charging several times, no longer mounted on the small native horses but on chargers of some substance. Until the end of the battle the cavalry stood by the infantry and, particularly at Plattin Hill, fought with a recklessness which earned it the praise of both its enemies and allies. Even the wounded remained in the ranks. King James, despite the defeat suffered, paid tribute to his horsemen:

> . . . though they did not break the enemy's foot, it was more by reason of the ground not being favourable than for want of vigour, for after they had been repulsed by the foot they rallied again, and charged the enemy's horse and beat them every charge.

Although the Irish were defeated and James left for France, the cavalry action on this occasion prolonged the war for eighteen months.

In what remained of the Williamite war after the battle of the Boyne, the figure of the Irish cavalry officer Patrick Sarsfield stands out. A member of a prominent Anglo-Irish family on his father's side, and a grandson, through his mother, of Rory

The Battle of the Boyne. Painting by Jan Wyck. (*Courtesy: National Gallery of Ireland*).

O'Moore, a prominent Gaelic Irish rebel leader, he had received his military education on the battlefields of France. He thus combined in his background most of the conflicts of interest in the Irish camp as it moved back to the line of the Shannon after the defeat at the Boyne. His reputation and that of his horsemen were such that the Williamite general, Douglas, marched away from Athlone on news of his approach. Sarsfield was to prove Douglas' fears justified. At Limerick, where the main Irish army had taken its stand, its leader Tyrconnell and the French General Lauzun argued for making terms with the Williamites. Sarsfield was, however, defiant and urged that the city should hold out. The Williamites were, however, bringing a huge siege train from Cashel and were confident that the walls could not hold out for long against their firepower when it was brought up. The destruction of the siege train was of the utmost importance. Such an enterprise required, however, a great deal of knowledge of local terrain. The siege train was approaching via Ballyneety in east Limerick. At this point it would be temporarily vulnerable. The direct route to Ballyneety was some fifteen miles but a troop approaching that way would be subject to immediate attack from the Williamites. To negotiate the alternative but difficult route of about ninety miles across the mountains, north, east and south, Sarsfield enlisted the help of 'Galloping' Hogan, so called because of the fine large mare which he rode.

It was a significant alliance and one which was to point the way, as we shall see, to the future. In the short term, the daring ride across the mountains was a complete success, its heroic character heightened by the ever-present possibility of Williamite detection.[38] The siege train was blown up, the Williamite cavalry disabled and Limerick temporarily saved.

It was an incident, however, which stood out alone as an example of the full utilisation of the potential of the Irish cavalry. The tragedy was that between the battle of the Boyne and that of Aughrim in 1691 the cavalry had been allowed to remain inactive due to disagreements among the Irish high command. As we have noted, however, the reputation of the cavalry was so great that its presence alone was enough to tie down the Williamites to a great extent. Ginkel's main preoccupation at Athlone was to guard against the possibility of cavalry raids to his rear. Lanière's attempt on Lanesborough failed through fear of an attack by Sarsfield from the rear. Ballymore had been fortified because of the fear of an Irish attack from Lanesborough. Athlone itself had been attacked against every rule of war from the Connacht side because of the Williamite fear of an attack from the Irish horse. In view of the reputation of the cavalry it was logical, as Sarsfield suggested, to use it in Leinster after the fall of Athlone to cut Ginkel's communication lines with Dublin. But the view of the French general St Ruth prevailed and all was staked on a pitched battle at Aughrim in East Co. Galway. The ground was favourable for the classic Irish tactics. Openings had even been cut in the field boundaries, and, as the Irish lured the English forward, deliberately retreating and using these boundaries as field works behind which they could fire on their opponents, the cavalry could emerge and attack through the openings and again retire behind the infantry and hedges. The success of the cavalry, however, was later thrown away when St Ruth who was leading it was killed and his horsemen thought only of saving themselves. But the Irish collapse on this occasion could not be ascribed solely to the death of the general. There was a large number of the cavalry who felt that they had more to gain from bargaining than from further resistance. They had estates which still might be saved. This expressed itself on the field of battle in their desertion of the poorer classes in the infantry.

The main body of the cavalry was now in Clare. Morale was low and some of the men were beginning to desert. To the besieged in Limerick the line of communication which they had with the cavalry was, however, still very important. Psychologically it was their umbilical cord. Ginkel knew from deserters that he had to cut that line if he was to take the city. This he did. The negotiations for surrender began and culminated in the Treaty of Limerick. Sarsfield, the leader of the Irish cavalry, went abroad.[39]

Cudama at Naas in 1980. *(Tony Parkes)*

5

Violent and Heroic Horsemen

T HE POET Dáibhí Ó Bruadair wrote of his contemporary, Patrick Sarsfield, as "the warrior bold who protects his spouse". We have noted two of the ways in which the Irish cavalry leader discharged his responsibility in this respect. He allied himself with a band of Rapparees or outlaws living in the mountains and woods and led by the horseman 'Galloping' Hogan, and he went abroad. In this chapter we will be concerned to show how Irish horsemen tended to conform to such a pattern as Sarsfield followed and, in the process, became for an impoverished people heroic figures representing an otherworld beyond the boundaries of society.

One of the factors which led Irish leaders in the seventeenth century either to take to the hills where the King's writ did not run or to go abroad was the break-up of Gaelic Irish institutions. This forced many of the leaders into the position of being outlaws, *personae non gratae* within the ambit of the English administration.[1] These leaders were violent men. Gaelic society, as we have hinted, had been run largely on the basis of violence. Gaelic institutions were capable not only of absorbing violence but of turning it to good account. Society profited from the wild energy of its warriors, energy which frequently ran to excess. In the absence of institutions such as tribal kingship this violence would get out of control and propel the warriors beyond the limits of society.

Our argument will be that the horse is a factor in the violence of the horseman, whether one considers him in the context of warfare in early or mediaeval Ireland or whether one moves to a later period and considers outlaws, steeplechase riders or huntsmen. A man in a horse-drawn chariot or mounted on a horse's back is likely to be more violent than his counterpart who does not have a horse at his disposal. The greater the power the greater the violence which is possible and, indeed, encouraged.

THE HORSE AND THE ELEMENTS

To date, as we examined the folklore and mythology surrounding the horse, we have referred to the power of the horse mainly in a communal context. The horse, for instance, was killed so that, through its king, society might benefit. But there is another complementary side to this and this relates to violent horsemen who appear not as part of a homogeneous crowd but as highly individualistic figures frequently standing apart from the community. Folklore, mythology and psychoanalytical experience cast some light on the motivation of such figures. The content of dreams, for instance, has frequently revealed how the horse was associated with sex and with elements such as thunder, lightning and the wind. In Lusitania it was believed that mares were fertilised by the wind and a German legend depicts the wind as a lustful huntsman in pursuit of a maiden.[2] Like all instinctive animals lacking higher consciousness, the horse is subject to panic and as a result comes to represent animal impulses in man which bear him away with great force. In Ireland this untamed energy has been traditionally associated with stormy weather. The tradition, which was strong in German and Norse areas, of a wild hunt led by the God of the Dead, Odin, riding his eight-legged horse, Sleipnir, has its parallel in Ireland. The Irish counterpart of Odin was Donn Fírinne who is depicted as a horseman riding at a gallop through the sky followed by his troop. Bad weather was said to be due to his raging rides among the clouds. An Irish poem of the eighteenth century states, in describing disturbed skies, that "Donn Fírinne of the Otherworld hills is mad with fury. Gearóid Iarla with his followers travels in angry clouds." The legends concerning Donn Fírinne became attached to Gearóid Iarla, the Third Earl of Desmond, and through him to the whole Desmond dynasty. In Irish folklore, Gearóid is shown leading a band of ghostly horsemen through the countryside. For reasons which will be our main concern in this chapter, wild horsemen raging through the countryside in a destructive orgy became associated in the popular mind with the good life or Otherworld and became part of the myth of the Desmond Geraldines. For a long period after the murder in 1583 of the last true earl, a man who frequently rode to hounds—even when consigned to gaol—Munster people would ask travellers, when the west wind blew, to listen to the sound of the 'Desmond howl'.[3]

my Stack. *(Gerry Cranham)*

THE SINGLE-COMBAT WARRIOR'S FRENZY

Early horsemen in different parts of the world frequently created the impression that they were monsters or centaurs—wind gods who were half men and half horse—before whom everything crumbled. In the *Táin Bó Cuailnge*, a tale which provides a 'window' on early Irish warrior society, the hero Cú Chulainn is transfigured as he prepares to mount his chariot to go into battle. This is due to the frenzy which took possession of him on such occasions. A similar transformation occurs when he encounters his friend Fer Diad in single combat, the storyteller even comparing him to one of the Fomorians, a mythical band of invaders who threatened Ireland and who, as we have noted, were sometimes seen in Irish tradition as centaurs.[4]

Such was the intensity of Cú Chulainn's battle ardour that it could pose a threat not only to his enemies but to the society to which he belonged. We have already seen how, in the course of his initiation, he shattered seventeen chariots given to him. Initiation into the warrior life involved a young man going to the frontiers of the tribe's land in his chariot and defending them. While there, Cú Chulainn's violence finds an outlet, but a danger also arises. At the frontiers he is close to the Otherworld and, by virtue of his superhuman violence, he is in danger of slipping out of control and out of society. In this respect Cú Chulainn in his chariot is akin to test pilots who "ride the rockets" to the outside of the earth's atmosphere. A peril of their job was that they would push their craft too far and go out of control. It was believed that at fifty miles altitude the boundary between the earth's atmosphere and space was located. Test pilots had to know where the "outside of the envelope" of air was but the challenge was "the part where you reached the outside and stretched her a little" without breaking through. Such men had to be violent to themselves, their vehicle and their environment for they travelled in uncharted territory.[5]

Cú Chulainn is typical of the single-combat warrior common across the whole Indo-European world. When such warriors were gripped by frenzy in battle their features became distorted and they were able to do impossible things. In one of the Indo-European centres, Rome, the single-combat warrior, however, became an anachronism and gave way to the disciplined operations of the massed Roman legions when the city became a great power. Among the Germans and Celts, also Indo-European peoples, single combat nonetheless managed to retain its importance.[6]

(Horseman Photography)

RECKLESS HORSEMEN

The Irish horsemen who fought against the Normans and later against the English soldiers had shown scant regard for the conventions of warfare as understood by their opponents. With some notable exceptions, the Irish in their armies were prepared to rely almost exclusively on individual valour and on the lightning attack and retreat instead of on a tightly-knit fighting force in which the individual's identity was submerged and which stood its ground or advanced in accordance with its leader's intentions. Irish horsemen were prepared recklessly to gamble away their lives in violent and frenzied attacks for the sake of honour, and their day-to-day lives reflected their behaviour on the battlefield. They were larger than life.

Horsemen in Ireland, particularly if they had few material resources, felt the need, according to the Anglo-Irish writer, Stanyhurst, to engage in extravagant flourishes: "These horsemen, when they have no staie of their own, gad and range from house to house like errant knights of the Round Table and they never dismount until they ride into the hall, as far as the table".[7]

In the mid nineteenth century, the Knight of Glin, known as 'Cracked Jack', whose ancestors had been faithful followers of the Earls of Desmond and who had acquired a great reputation as a horseman, used to ride into drawing rooms when visiting friends and even tried riding up stairs on occasions.[8] As we shall see, he

Countryman and Wolfgang Mengers competing at the Punchestown Three-Day Event in 1990. *(Inpho)*

was not the only eccentric horseman to come from this family whose lands were situated along the banks of the Shannon in Limerick.

We may well ask why horsemen engaged in reckless behaviour of this kind and to what purpose. In order to get an answer we turn to another activity, gambling, which has also characterised the history of the Glins and which was, according to Stanyhurst, much favoured by horsemen: "There is among them a brotherhood of carrows (gamblers) that prefer to plaie at cards all the year long and make it their onelie occupation." Gambling by carrows was frequently criticised by English commentators as a concomitant and cause of lawlessness. When gambling was taking place the normal rules of behaviour were put in abeyance. Gambling involved honour and status for it was part of the network of customs and practices which had as their basis competitive gift giving. The size of a man's wager was his estimate of himself and the one who was prepared to risk the most, to ride, as in the case of test fighter pilots, "on the outside of the envelope", was the one who emerged triumphant. Gambling, therefore, was a peaceful form of warfare in which violent instincts were engaged. Even today at Cheltenham racing festival, where the Irish congregate to challenge once again the English, it is not unheard of, off course, for possession of a dwelling house to hang on a hand of cards.[9] It is perhaps no coincidence that Irish jockeys at Cheltenham are frequently fined by the English turf authorities for excessive use of the whip.

Extravagant gift giving frequently takes place in an atmosphere of heightened excitement and conviviality. Drink often flows freely. Communal life involves honour, it is believed, and honour is being asserted. But the underlying seriousness of gambling and risking all is not in doubt. It is akin to the fighter pilot's desire to "dice with death". So strong is the urge to rise above the rest of mankind that people of a competitive disposition will do anything to satisfy it, even to the point of risking death.[10]

Irish horsemen had a similar leadership role, copperfastened over a period of a thousand years, to uphold. In addition, the horseman, united with the animal bearing him along, felt, for reasons which we have discussed, that the energy placed at his disposal by the horse was his energy. It had to find an outlet.[11]

Tom Woulfe in his book on test fighter pilots and astronauts quotes an American commander's glowing description of his men and the risks they took over Korea: "Like olden knights the F-86 pilots ride up over north Korea to the Yalu River, the sun glinting off silver aircraft, contrails streaming behind, as they challenge the numerically superior enemy to come on up and fight!"

MAURICE FITZGERALD

The close connection between the horse and lawlessness is seen in the activities of Maurice Fitzgerald, the First Earl of Desmond. As we consider him and other Anglo-Norman nobles in Ireland we will note how, from an English perspective, they drifted away from the centre of government and became increasingly lawless and uncontrollable. A key factor in drawing them towards an Otherworld of lawlessness was their alliance with 'wild' Irish horsemen. Maurice Fitzgerald who became Earl of Desmond in 1329, according to complaints made against him, attracted 'wrongdoers' to his banner with the prospect of plunder from many parts

Pony stallion at the Connemara
Pony Show at Clifden Co.
Galway. *Source*: Tony Parkes.

LEFT: *Source* Inpho
BELOW: Sally Harrison and
weanlings at the Irish National
Stud. *Source*: DoA.

Con Power in trouble at the Puissance
Wall with *Young Diamond. (Inpho)*

of Ireland. These men equipped themselves with horses after joining Maurice's 'rout' and, armed with letters patent from the Earl, proceeded to engage in 'highway robbery'. Desmond always remained within the ambit of English authority—one of his last acts before he died in January 1356 was to send horses and other gifts to the king in England—but through his activities he was frequently close to stepping over the borderline and becoming the king's enemy. His descendant, the seventh earl, as we have seen, took that further step and suffered death in 1468 because of his involvement with Irish 'rebels'. Maurice went a considerable distance along the same road. His arrest, for instance, in 1333 was due to his involvement with the Irish chieftain O'Brien, and with other 'rebels' but his violence was not geared to making himself an enemy of the king. Like the violence of Gaelic Irish chieftains, it was intended to impress both friend and foe with fear and respect.

The symbolic character of the violence was seen when Maurice and his followers attacked Limerick and were refused entrance. Like a young man being initiated and having to prove his prowess in his first struggle, Desmond forced his way with his men into the suburbs where they set fire to the gates, pulled out the "hooks, crooks, twists and locks" from the gates and rode off with them. His tactics on other occasions were those of the rural terrorist, killing, robbing and trampling the wheat and oats of his enemies under the horses' hooves. His violence could be of a particularly brutal kind. It was said that he had the Constable of Bunratty Castle seized and mutilated for leaving his charge. He put his own kinsman in prison and left him to starve to death there.[12]

In a violent society where fortunes shifted as a matter of course lords and chieftains needed to align themselves with violent men. Such men would become available to a leader's enemies if he did not allow them attach themselves to his retinue and avail of whatever spoils could be obtained. There were always such violent men available, men who perhaps had lost out in a succession struggle for the chieftainship and saw their prestige and possessions, and those of their descendants, slipping through their fingers.[13]

IDLE HORSEMEN

Encouraging such men in mounting their horses and joining the retinue of a war lord was the belief that the life of battle was more in keeping with their noble birth than that of tilling the soil which was suited to "mere churls and labouring men, (not) one of whom knows his grandfather", as Conall Mageoghegan commented scornfully in 1627. Crops were very vulnerable in times of strife so that men of war had another incentive to live a pastoral existence, following herds of cattle which provided a war band with a mobile canteen. Industry, for the Normans, meant cultivation of the soil and the cattle-rearing Irish are constantly described in English documents as 'idle'. It was a word that within a warrior aristocracy had honourable connotations. "To be idle" Herodotus remarked in relation to the Thracians, "is

An Irish lord prepares to go on a cattle raid, c. 1575. His horseboy is on the right. Woodcut probably by John Derricke, 1581. *(Derricke's Image of Ireland)*

accounted the most honourable thing, and to be a tiller of the ground the most dishonourable. To live by war and plunder is of all things the most glorious." In a society where honour was the highest value, the life of warfare, considered as if it was a birthright, would not easily give way to something more menial. According to Sir Edward Phyton in 1587, poor people were in dire conditions because of shortage of food "but yet so idle as they will not worke because they are descended eyther of kerne, horsemen or gallowglasses, all three the very subvertion of this lande". Included among those categorised as 'idle' men were those who engaged in gambling and who encouraged 'idleness' among others. Clearly the fear was that a proliferation of 'idlemen' would overrun the land.[14]

Even among the Anglo Irish the problem of the well-born 'idleman' or *occiosus* with few resources to support him existed. Such men were a source both of energy and of disruption in a feudal society and were much feared by the government. They either attached themselves to the retinue of a lord in the hope of spoil or became a burden on their own kin and its subordinates. In the latter case they could become the pretext for onerous impositions and taxes such as those which the Gaelic Irish, according to ancient custom, applied to their subordinates.

We have already seen the English fear of Gaelic customs, some related to the horse, spreading in the English colony in Ireland. A similar fear was aroused by 'idle' men and their horses being loosed to wreak havoc on English subjects in Ireland. Two years after the Statute of Kilkenny had been enacted we find a parliament summoned as a result of complaints that:

> The Irish and other our enemies rode in hostile array through every part of the said land, committing homicides, robberies and arsons, pillaging, spoiling . . . so that the land was at point to be lost, if remedy and help were not immediately supplied.

An order made in November 1234 that "bands of malfactors who rode through Ireland to perpetrate fire, robberies and other injuries" be arrested reflects a similar sense of all-pervading danger from horsemen.[15] Horses in Ireland, as far as the English were concerned, unless they were firmly controlled, brought violence in their wake in a manner which we will see later.

COYNE AND LIVERY

One of the main focuses for English governmental attacks from the fourteenth century on was the system whereby man and horse in a chief's or lord's retinue were supported by the inhabitants of the chief's territories. This system of support came to be known by the English as 'coyne and livery' referring respectively to food for man and horse. According to Sir John Davies, Maurice Fitzgerald was the first "English lord that imposed coigny and livery upon the King's subjects". It was alleged that he used it to support the men in his 'rout' as they ravaged the southern counties in the 1320s.[16] As we discuss this system and the related abuses which horses, horsemen and their attendants perpetrated on both English and Irish people in Ireland we will be concerned to a large extent with two dynasties, that of Desmond and that of Kildare, for on them we will see the effect which lawlessness had in gradually placing them 'beyond the Pale' of English control. Working in tandem with these abuses we will see that the earls' alliance with native Irish horsemen fighting in the main in the mountains and woods would help to confer on them and their violence a heroic and otherworldly character.

The custom of coyne and livery had its origin in Irish exactions which lay at the basis of the Irish system of authority. Under these, a lord was entitled to free entertainment from his clients for himself and his retinue at a certain period of the year. Like all occasions when gifts were exchanged, this was a festive period, the client providing a feast for his lord in return for the protection which he enjoyed from him. The survival into mediaeval times of the custom of free entertainment should not surprise us. The tenth century glossarist, Cormac, marks its importance by claiming that at the time of such entertainment the roads were cleaned so that chariots en route to it would not be soiled. The other two occasions on which,

Commandant Con Power on *Rockbarton* and James Kernan on *Condy* hold aloft the Aga Khan Cup after the Irish team won it outright, RDS Horse Show 1979. *(Ruth Rogers)*

according to him, this work was done was 'time of horseracing' and 'time of war'.

There was a military side to this custom of free entertainment particularly from the Viking period on. The lord's soldiers were frequently billeted on the country-side. The First Earl of Desmond even went a step further and gave letters patent to his men to levy not only food and drink but their wages "as well within his lordship as outside it", with consequences which we have seen.[17]

Horses had also to be catered for when the lord's retinue was being billeted. "Summer oats" were exacted yearly to feed the lord's chief horses i.e. war-horses. This could be a considerable burden as a chief horse consumed, according to one source, a bushel of oats every four days. An indication of what this might entail in

the case of the most powerful lords is given by the requirement that the Earl of Kildare, when he was Lord Justice about the middle of the fourteenth century, "should find twentie great horses to serve in the field". An indenture in 1524 between Garret Óg, son of the Great Earl of Kildare, and the English King specified that the amount which he could exact from the king's subjects in the Pale for 'every chief horse' was '12 sheeves for a nyght and a daye.' Another account tells us that 24 sheaves were taken. But more than the lord's chief horses came into the reckoning. Complaints made in 1606 by freeholders against their lord O'Dunne of Iregan in Co. Laois listed among his extortions:

> Item 16 horseshoes unto O'Dunne yearly and 8 horseshoes to each of his horsemen of every smith dwelling upon the freeholder's lands. Item, that O'Doyne every year laid upon every freeholder all his horses twice a year at which time they were to give every chief horse 24 sheeves of oats and to every hackney 16 sheeves.

At one time knights had not only to maintain war horses but also lighter saddle horses as well as draught and pack horses. The Irish in mediaeval times had no knights but an account in 1480 would seem to suggest that their horsemen were also well supplied with horses. "Every horseman hath two horses sume three", we are told and all these had to be supported. In the second half of the sixteenth century one peck of oats costing 7d was allowed each horseman in the English army in Ireland 'for his chief horse and for his hackney'. Unlike the Gaelic Irish horseman, he bore this cost out of his pay of 9d per day.[18]

The onus of supporting all of Kildare's horses which totalled at least 200 fell on "the contrey". There were specified provisions which he was entitled to claim for his hackneys or trotting horses and when he was in the Pale, we are told, he could take for each 'bereing horse . . . eight sheeves'. It was customary also in some lordships to make provisions for the lord's wife's horses. (*See marginal note.*)

Horse stealing in Ireland was very common and both the Gaelic Irish and the government took action against it. The damage to those who lost their horses could be very grievous. The value placed on a plough horse in the sixteenth century varied considerably. The loss to the Earl of Ormond's estates in Leinster during his quarrel with the Earl of Desmond was, according to a document dating from 1567, two thousand eight hundred and twenty seven "plough garranes" valued at £3,769 6s 8d. It seems that those engaged in horse stealing were frequently either the servants or kinsmen of the great lords. Such men would, as we have seen, have something to prove, for they were in a position to have ambitions greater than their means.[20]

At times of feasting the numbers of Kildare's horses which the country had to support would increase to 500. He would use the occasion to entertain 'strangers' —no doubt those whom he wished to convert into allies—and their horses would, in addition to his own, be supported by his tenants. The violent character of these impositions involving horses is indicated by the fact that even if these 'guests' did not come to share in the lord's merrymaking "some send their horses. Also his servants' plowe horses must be cessed under colour of his owne to make up a number". Complaints were also made against Kildare that if his servants did not manage to get coyne and livery they would steal 'garrons' or plough horses from farmers leaving them in difficulties regarding their work in cultivation. One way or the other, it would appear, the people would have to pay for the lawlessness of their lord and his servants.[19]

Joe Griffin leading in his *Early Mist*, ridden by Bryan Marshall, after winning the Aintree Grand National in 1953. Vincent O'Brien (with binoculars) is on the right. *(Hulton-Deutsch Collection)*

HORSEBOYS

To judge from both English and Irish accounts, the most violent figure in the retinue of the lord was the horseboy. "They are the very skumme, and outcaste of the countreye, and not lesse servicable in the campe for meeting and dressinge of horses, then hurtful to the enemy with their dartes", Dymmock noted in 1599. The bishop of Rosse wrote of them during the Desmond rebellion in the second half of the sixteenth century that "amongst the heathen there is no more wicked soldiers". According to Edmund Spenser writing at the end of the century the basis of the problem was the sense of noble ancestry which the man who had fallen on hard times entertained. "If he can derive himself from the head of a sept", he would not "work or use any handy labour . . . but thenceforth either become a horseboy or stocagh to some kerne, enuring himself to his weapon, and to his gentlemanly trade of stealing (as they count it)." The young Hugh O'Neill found himself working as a horseboy before becoming a chieftain and the leader of the great Ulster army. Even today in Ireland looking after horses is considered a step above other manual work and may, in circumstances where it is linked to riding, carry social prestige. In Fenian literature it is clear that a horse groom was of low social status but such an attitude did not prove very resilient.

Undoubtedly a factor in this was the opportunity for battle which work as a horseboy provided. His skills with horses made him particularly suited to the type of warfare which was the norm in Ireland, something which even the English appreciated and used. They employed Irish horseboys to assist their cavalry troopers by foraging for them, tending to their horses and carrying their arms. The value of Irish servants, particularly those employed in England to look after horses, was much stressed by sixteenth-century English writers whom we might otherwise expect to be hostile. But there was another factor which made English captains eager to recruit horseboys in Ireland. They were cheap. They could be employed at a rate lower than the normal and the captains could keep the difference. This, however, meant that the horseboys plundered from the people.[21]

Spenser was prepared to admit that because of the lack of inns in the country where horses could be looked after, horseboys were a necessity but he, in common with other English commentators, viewed them with suspicion. They typified the danger to which the English interest in Ireland was exposed. For instance, a writer in the State Papers in 1515 commented on the change in the retinue of the Earl of Kildare, who was then the King's deputy in Ireland, in terms which make it clear that employing large numbers of horseboys who demanded coyne and livery represented a drift away from English to Irish control. Kildare, he claimed, used to bring with him wherever he rode

a strong garde on horseback of sperys and bowes, well garnysheid, after the Englishe maner, that payde trewly for ther meate and drynke, wherever they

A moment of informality at the Connemara Pony Show on 24 August 1989. (*Irish Times: Joe Shaughnessy*)

dyd ryde; Nowe garde of Kynges deputie is none other but a multytude of Iryshe galloglaheis, and a multytude of Iryshe kernes and speres, with infynyt nombre of horseladdes . . . and with extortion of coyne and lyverye consumeth and devoureth all the substance of the poore folke, and of the comen people all the kinges subjettes.

The emphasis here on the great number of horseboys is significant. In the first place the damage done to those on whom horseboys were billeted was a function of their numbers. Part of the complaints against O'Dunne by his freeholders was that they had to supply "meat and drink for twenty-four horseboys in summer, and so also in winter". The more powerful lords could assign, with apparent impunity, as many boys as they wished to each of the horses, which the country had to support. "If there be four or five boys to a horse, and sometimes ther be, the tenant myst be contented therwith, and yet beside reward the boys with money," one observer noted in 1603. The bishop of Ossory claimed that in Kildare there were three boys per horse, while another account claimed that with regard to Kildare's 200 horses there were two boys assigned to each. All agreed that the number was excessive and in his Breviate of Ireland, written during King Henry VIII's reign, Baron Finglas specified that there should be only one boy per horse. In an indenture with the king which he signed in 1524 on becoming Deputy, Kildare agreed to limit the number of his boys to this.[22] Allied to the impoverishment brought by their great numbers there was a second and related reason for concern over the numbers of horseboys and this was that they constituted the enemy within.

Many of the horseboys had been brought in to the Pale as youths and grew up there "among Englishmen and soldiers, of whom learning to shoot in a piece, and being made acquainted with all the trades of the English, they are afterwards when they become kerne, made more fit to cut their throats." It was Spenser's belief that they promoted subversion. "Out of the fry of these rakelly horseboys", he wrote, "are their (Gaelic Irish) continually supplied and maintained." Two hundred of them were in the employ of Kildare to look after his horses and, by virtue of his privileged position as Lord Deputy, enjoyed immunity from retribution by the people on whom they preyed. In addition, such men could easily slip into and out of the Pale and, by supplying their countrymen with information, leave the Pale very vulnerable to the Gaelic Irish.

HUNTING

One of the occasions when Kildare would send "his horses and idle boys into the contrey" would be when he went hunting. According to the custom of Gillycon (Giolla Con i.e. keeper of the dogs) and Gillycree (Keeper of the horses), earls like Kildare could quarter their huntsmen on the people and have their hounds and horses provided for. The hounds, it was even said, got "bread and butter like a man". Complaints were made about the severity of this imposition. It was claimed that "his houndes and huntesmen must have meate as often as he dothe appoynt, to the number of 40 or 3 score". This was, we are told, "more prerogative than any Christian prince claymethe".[23]

The demand that the country support the hunt of its lord fitted into the general pattern of coyne and livery which had its roots in the Gaelic system of authority. For instance a subchief like O'Sullivan, the most important vassal of McCarthy of Clancare, was expected, in return for protection and a key role in his overlord's appointment and inauguration, to provide in Bantry among other things food for his horses throughout the year. Where subchiefs did not have the resources to utilise their lands fully and provide such services, the stud keepers, it would appear, in Munster at least, were entitled to come with their horses "and pasture and graze upon the said wast land and to take meate and drinck of the next inhabitants for themselves, and to be in number so many as please the lord to appoint".[24]

Complaints against the lords' hunting exactions were, it would appear, confined mainly to Leinster and Munster. In counties Kilkenny and Tipperary Piers Butler, Earl of Ossory, engaged in deer hunting, with "the king's subjettes" bearing the cost of supporting the hunt, "the hole charges whereof surmounteth two thousand markes by yere". Hares and martens were also hunted there. In Waterford, Lady Eleanor Butler who had married into the Power family there aroused the ire of the 'commoners' because her hounds and stud keepers were cessed on the country and "the said stood pastureth over every grounde paying nothing therefor". These complaints were not directed at hunting as such but at the burden which it placed on the people. Indeed it was even claimed that hunting was necessary in order to get rid of wild animals such as wolves and deer "that do injury". The claim hardly carried much weight with the people who were burdened with the exactions. While hunting the deer was undertaken by the lords, the less profitable animals such as wolves and foxes were left to the inhabitants themselves to hunt.

CURBING EXCESSES

In considering coyne and livery and in particular the custom of cessing horses, horseboys and the lord's hunt on people, we have stressed the violence being done to the people who had to bear the exactions. Much of the complaints against them came from within the Pale and found an answer in attempts by the government to control them. The horse was at the centre of a network of demands with Gaelic roots and these demands were increasing rather than being brought under control. Instead of acting in the government's and its subjects' interests, magnates like Kildare and Desmond were using coyne and livery to increase their own power base. What made the exactions reprehensible to the government and people in the Pale were the abuses which were a feature of them. The size of the demands was based not so much on hereditary right or laws setting forth the entitlements of lords

A famous period print of an Irish hunting scene in 1850.

vis-à-vis their tenants but on the lords' power. They took from their tenants what they wished or what they could take. Tenants frequently felt, as we have seen in the case of billeting of horseboys, that if an onerous exaction was imposed by a powerful lord there was little they could do about it. Lords coming for a night's entertainment often stayed for several nights and invited their friends along. These additional guests increased the number of horses which had to be supported, as we have seen. The English reacted strongly to this apparent lack of control over the exactions and the abuses which were a feature of them. Some of their proposed solutions were therefore sweeping. "They should be cut off", Spenser wrote in relation to the horseboys. A life of cultivating the soil, it would appear, could be expected to provide a channel for violent energies and bring order to the ranks of the 'idle' horseboys engaged in warfare. "Into the plough, therefore, are all those kerne, stocaghs, and horseboys to be driven". It would appear, however, from an edict which the English commander Perrot issued in the late sixteenth century, that the ranks of these engaged in cultivation had to be protected from disaffection: "If the son of a husbandman will become a kerne, gallowglass or horseboy or will take any other idle trade he shall be imprisoned for a twelve month and fined." Baron Finglas suggested a regulation forbidding lords of the Pale from keeping Irish horseboys, with a fine of £10 for those breaking it.[25]

It was mainly the powerful Anglo-Irish lords like Desmond and Kildare who were excessive in their demands on their tenants. An estimate made on the basis of a survey in the late sixteenth century indicates that Desmond's irregular exactions amounted to ten times as much as the regular rents in money and cattle which he received from his freeholders. Since the execution of the seventh earl in 1468, subsequent earls had drifted further and further away from loyalty to the Crown into alliances with the Gaelic Irish designed to increase Desmond power. In Finglas' words they were no better "than the wild Irish". A similar drift was evident in the case of the Earls of Kildare but where they were concerned there was a constraint. From 1478 to 1534 an Earl of Kildare was the King's Deputy in Ireland. It was a constraint which each earl turned to his own account, however. To increase his power, he needed to be able to acquire powerful allies and to increase the numbers of his followers. This necessitated, at a ceremonial level, bestowing gifts and, in a more humdrum way, leaving the way open for his allies or followers to acquire booty. His position as Deputy enabled him to do this with impunity. To add to the government's indignation, Kildare's allies were in the main Gaelic Irish.

Under the guise of defending the Pale, Kildare, we are told in 1534, sometimes invited his Irish allies to ride through it. These strangers with their "horsemen, horses and boyes" took not only coyne and livery, but, as we noted, considerable spoil as well as they passed through under the guidance of the horseboys.[26]

McMURROUGH KAVANAGHS

Principal among the Gaelic Irish who were allied to Kildare and who were noted for their depredations on the Pale were the McMurrough Kavanaghs. In the 1530s the towns in the south-east of the country were complaining about *'garrons'* or plough horses stolen by them, and in Ross we read that a hackney worth £4 was taken. There were, as we have seen, easier ways of acquiring horses and a magnate like Kildare was quite anxious to cement his alliances with powerful clans like the McMurrough Kavanaghs with gifts of horses. The advantage to Kildare of such gifts made to men from this clan was seen in the case of Cahir Mac Inycross to whom he presented a 'sorrel' in 1523. By attaching Cahir, who was probably illegitimate and a great grandson of the famous Art McMurrough, to him, Kildare gained influence in the succession to the McMurrough Kavanagh kingship. Against the claims of a rival he had Cahir installed as McMurrough in 1531.

The story of the McMurroughs, from Art in the fourteenth century to his name-sake in the nineteenth, is one of superb horsemen. They were also rebels, who Sir John Davies saw as living a life untouched by English law in Carlow. "They dwell by west of the law that dwell beyond the Barrow," he wrote, conscious no doubt of the significance of their geographical location and its possible repercussions. Kildare's alliance with them, for instance, led him also "beyond the Pale".[27]

Like most Irish rebels the McMurrough Kavanaghs' strength lay in their occupation of mountain and woodland areas. From their fastnesses in Carlow they were able, particularly in the fifteenth century, to apply great pressure on the administration by controlling communications between Dublin and the south-east of the country. Over the centuries the clan produced a number of remarkable figures. Donall Óg for instance who was King of Leinster in the early part of the fourteenth century had very great ambitions to increase his power, wishing "to flaunt his banner within two miles of Dublin and then traverse all Ireland". But the outstanding leader in the McMurrough Kavanagh story was Art who came to the kingship some time in 1370. During the first visit of King Richard to Ireland in 1394 he had learned a useful lesson. After being driven out of the woods he was forced into submission. When the king returned in 1399 Art was careful not to allow himself to be pinned down and placed in a similar position. According to a history of King Richard's reign, Art had a superb horse, *Tree Leaper* by name, which, if we translate the value ascribed to it, would be worth at least £8000 sterling today:

He had a horse without saddle or saddle-tree, which was fine and good, it had cost him, they said, four hundred cows. In coming down it galloped so hard that I never saw in all my life hare, deer, sheep or any such animal run with such speed as it did. In his hand he bore a great long dart, which he cast with much skill.

In the second half of the sixteenth century the ruthless Tudor onslaught had taken its toll in Ireland. The Earls of Kildare were destroyed and it would appear that the Kavanaghs too had taken a beating. "There is none of them able to make (up) eight horsemen of his own byinge; and everyone of them enemy unto the other; but they have theeves on foot to steal from the Queen's trewe subjects," a report in 1572 noted. Yet, to the English historian Camden writing about the same time, the danger from the Kavanagh horsemen was ever present: "The land is full of Kavanaghs, good soldiers, famous horsemen, still breathing the spirit of their ancient nobility in their abject poverty." Although that spirit was no longer directed against the might of the English, it would appear to have been sufficiently resilient to have survived, for it emerged two and a half centuries later, this time from an unlikely quarter.

Meeting between Art Mc Murrough and the Earl of Gloucester, June 1399. *(Royal Irish Academy)*

Art McMurrough, the nineteenth-century Kavanagh heir, needed all the courage and energy of his ancestors for he had been born without arms or legs. On horseback he defied all the limitations his condition imposed on him. Since the age of two he had been fascinated by horses and, with the aid of a specially-designed saddle, he became an excellent rider, developing a reputation as one of the best horsemen in Leinster and a fearless rider to hounds. During the 1848 rebellion he consistently outwitted the rebel horsemen—the Kavanaghs were now in the position of being on the side of the law—as he rode around on horseback. In the political sphere he also defied the conventions and became an MP. But perhaps his greatest triumph over his limitations was his extensive travel abroad—as far afield as Russia and even India, where he hunted lions. The secret of his ability to transcend difficulties, which were formidable even for the strong-limbed, seems to have been his closeness to horses, evident in Kurdestan when he slept under his horse during a snowstorm, and his remarkable power over them. The Indian servants whom he employed during his sojourn in that country were willing to do anything for him. They considered him a worker of miracles.[28]

The English had reason to fear the alliances which Kildare, before his downfall in the first half of the sixteenth century, made with horsemen of a similar spirit to Art. A report in 1537 claimed that the three hundred horsemen which Maurice 'the woodkerne' Kavanagh, in conjunction with his kinsmen O'Byrne and O'Toole, could muster were unsurpassed in Ireland "for hardiness". These, allied with six or seven hundred kerne also available to him, made up a force which exceeded what the king's five shires of Leinster could draw up.

We have seen earlier how Sir Henry Christede in the late fourteenth century made efforts to tame Irish chieftains including McMurrough Kavanagh. Their horsemanship was one aspect of their lifestyle which he tried to change. Indentures made by the government with the Irish reflect a related concern with horses and horsemen. The government fear was, it would appear, of horsemen riding around at will within the Pale under no ones control, free to steal from the people. This fear was the basis of the objections to the abuses surrounding coyne and livery. Such Irish 'extortions' left the Pale like a wasteland. In order to protect it, men of substance were expected to maintain horsemen and legislation was enacted stipulating this. In 1297, for instance, all men with land worth £20 per annum had to have an armoured war-horse and suitable weapons. Those less wealthy were expected to have hobbies or other unarmoured mounts as their resources permitted. Keepers of the Peace were required to ensure that such legislation was enforced and to "assess and array all men . . . to horses and arms, hobelars and footmen, so that they be ready and prepared to set out in the king's service . . . to fight felons and rebels as well English as Irish, invading those parts."

Their powers enabled them to arrest 'idle' hobelars wandering through the country and damaging the king's subjects. The Statute of Kilkenny makes it clear that "kerns, hobelars or idlemen" could not be kept "in the land of peace" but only in the border areas of the Pale at their lord's own expense. In that way they might act in the defence of the Pale rather than undermining it. To the English government having horses available for service when required and, presumably out of the hands of 'idlemen', necessitated the provision of stables. The Lord Deputy, Bellingham, who was appointed in 1547, for instance "kept sundrie stables of horses: one at Leighlin, one at Lex, and some in one place and some in another, as he thought most need for service". In circumstances where the people of the Pale were generally too impoverished from the depredations of the magnates and of their Irish allies to be able to afford "armed" horses which could pursue felons escaping from the Pale with their booty, such preparations were necessary. Regulations required that the army hold a muster each month to check, among other things, that the numbers of horses were sufficient.[29]

Efforts to control the McMurrough Kavanaghs included provisions for regulating in a detailed way the deployment and use of their horses. Cahir Mac Airt and other Kavanagh leaders indicated in the early fifteen forties that they were prepared to accept, as a condition of an agreement with the government, the abolition of coyne and livery, "the cause of the number of Ydlemen, which fall to roberies and felonies . . . but to make his house after English sort, and have at least twenty horses in a stable, and every horseman to have but one horse and a nag . . . and he himself and his contree for one year forth to have English apparaill to their habilitie". The Kavanaghs agreed to cultivate their lands and banish "their idle men. And that no one of them for the future shall ride armed, save only a captain or officer of the Crown for the time being." Clearly the emphasis was on putting order, according to English lights, where there had been disorder, by insisting on "stables and a certain standing householde". In 1549 we learn that it was hoped that Cahir "have such a stable of horses as never was seyne in Ireland . . . he may well keepe four score chief horses in his stable, and four stables, to be divided in four severall quarts of the countre, and all the chief horses that shall be in that stable . . . then shall ye have no horsemen robbers (as they have been wonte to be)."

O'BYRNES

The web of alliances which drew Kildare towards the McMurrough clan and away from government control also included the O'Byrnes who as we have seen provided horsemen for McMurrough. The O'Byrne movements over the centuries are obscure as befitted a clan dwelling in the mountains of Wicklow and carrying out opportunist raids on the Pale. South County Dublin, which was the focal point for their attacks, lying under the shadow of the Dublin mountains, was an area where the sense of frontier in mediaeval times was very strong. Areas like Crumlin, Tallaght, Saggart and Dundrum were defended from the thirteenth to the fifteenth centuries as the last outposts against the encroachments of the mountain Irish and against the threat of an alien way of life on the Pale. The O'Byrnes, frequently aided by the O'Tooles and acting in support of McMurrough, represented such a threat and attracted many moves by the government against them. These Gaelic Irish had the great advantage that the large massif of mountains running from south Dublin into Wexford afforded them an impenetrable haven. By the early fifteenth century the O'Byrnes had become lords not only of the mountains but also of the coast from Bray to Arklow, stretching inland to Shillelagh.

The character of the O'Byrnes is captured in the figure of Fiach McHugh O'Byrne who led the Irish rebels in the midlands and Wicklow in defiance of the English government's plantation policies during the second half of the sixteenth century.

Winter in Wicklow. *Source*: Liam Blake.

Red rosette for a winner at the Connemara Pony Show in 1989.
Source: Louise Parkes.

A splendid horseman, he has come down in Irish tradition as a great folk hero:

> Feagh McHugh of the mountains
> Feagh McHugh of the glen
> Who has not heard of the Glenmalure chief
> and the fears of his hard-riding men?

Glenmalure, the wildest and most impenetrable defile in Wicklow, was the O'Byrne stronghold and from there he controlled the mountains. It had been the graveyard of many an English expedition in former times but despite this the Deputy in 1580

Children at Smithfield Horse Fair, Dublin, 3 January 1988. A growing phenomenon at this fair is the purchase of horses and ponies by children from urban areas. In many cases these children lack the skills and resources to care for the animals. *(Irish Times: Matt Kavanagh)*

moved into the mountains to attack Fiach and his allies. The battle was a classic case of the Irish totally familiar with the environment and able to use it to their advantage, routing an enemy hopelessly weighed down with pikes and body armour and strangers to that type of countryside and warfare. Nineteen years later history repeated itself when Fiach's son Phelim inflicted a defeat also on an English force at Glenmalure.[30]

If Glenmalure represented for the English in a particular way a treacherous Irish otherworld which engulfed them, for the Irish it provided a refuge. Fiach made the future O'Donnell, Red Hugh, welcome there on his escape from Dublin Castle in 1591 and provided him with the horse, "a white bobtayle", which enabled him to return to Ulster to be inaugurated. Hugh was later one of the leaders of the Ulster forces at Kinsale and became a figure of heroic proportions in Irish tradition. The image of the hero returning on horseback—in Hugh's case to his stronghold in Ulster—to claim his inheritance was a potent one to which the Irish clung avidly as a source of hope. It could, as we shall see shortly, even become the hallmark of the great Anglo-Irish dynasties with which the Gaelic Irish, particularly from the sixteenth century, had a common cause.

With Fiach McHugh O'Byrne some of the elements in that image were being put together. English sources show him stealing and bestowing horses and, in the process, acquiring a great reputation among the Irish. One of those to whom he gave a 'chief horse' was Hugh O'Ferrall who was, according to a spy in 1599, "with a great number of idle knaves riding up and down the county of Longford". In Irish tradition Fiach is shown always on horseback. In fact his dependence on the horse for his power was considered to be so great that in the legend of his death, a legend which has also become associated—subject to a slight variation—with his brother-in-law, the O'Toole chieftain, Phelim, his separation from his mount was seen as the occasion of his death. This legend bears a striking resemblance to that of Oisín, seen earlier, in which Oisín, who inhabits the Otherworld, is brought face to face with the ravages of mortality when he alights from his horse. In the case of Fiach we are told that it was his practice to use a girth of steel on his horse when he went riding. On the one occasion when he neglected to do this and his horse was wearing a leather one, a sword cut through it, thus unseating him, and he was killed.

THE EARLS OF KILDARE AS HEROIC HORSEMEN

In order to achieve heroic stature in Ireland warriors had to be seen to escape the grip of English authority. Fiach achieved this by being mounted on horseback in the mountains and woods. The house of Kildare, we have tried to show, achieved much the same position through alliances with such men as Fiach and through lawlessness frequently associated with horses. The process of distancing themselves from the English culminated for the Kildare Geraldines in 1534 when the Earl's son Thomas, known as Silken Thomas on account of the raiment of his horsemen, rode "accompanied with seven score horsemen . . . through the citie of Dublin" to the chamber of St Mary's Abbey where the King's Council was in session. This could have been a Gaelic chieftain making his presence felt and substituting, for a brief period, the boisterous activity of an Irish assembly for the formality of the council proceedings. "When the Lord Thomas was set in councell", Stanyhurst wrote, "his horsemen and servants rusht in to the councell chamber armed and weaponed, turning their secret conference to an open parlee". Even Thomas' poet was there with verses "in commendation" of his lord. The poet was ever in Ireland the spur for violent men.[31]

Stephen Craine and *Corwyn Bay*, trained by Tommy Stack, after their victory in the Cartier Million in 1988. *(Inpho)*

In their verses, as we have seen, poets praised the violent deeds of former kings and ancestors. Violence was made respectable by reference to the past and even tolerated by those who suffered from it. There would appear, for instance, to have been relatively little complaint from the Gaelic Irish against coyne and livery. This may reflect to some extent the lack of opportunity which they had to voice their grievances but it probably also indicates that a form of violence with its roots in a Gaelic past, which increasingly came to be seen as a golden age, had its rationale. A lord who had the power to take great booty or dues from his people would also be capable of defending them against the depredations of another lord. The abuse which people suffered at the lord's hands was their guarantee of security—hence the praise lavished on a lord, in the early fifteenth century *"ara chaithem agus ara chosnam"*, for his spending and defending. When the Earl of Kildare in the early sixteenth century proposed to the 'lords and gentry' of Kildare and Carlow that he be their 'defender and spender', he was in fact offering to be a king in the Gaelic manner.

Such violent men as Kildare and his horsemen commanded great prestige in Ireland by virtue of their lifestyles. At the battle of Knockdoe in 1504, for instance, the instructions of the Great Earl of Kildare to his captain in relation to the lowly footsoldiers offered to him in support of his horsemen was reportedly "Let them stand by and give us the gaze". The horsemen were the warriors who dashed in headlong, broke the rules, took the risks and rode, in the manner of Tom Woulfe's test pilots, on the "outside of the envelope". They were a source of inspiration to those who stood to one side and watched them as they risked their lives. The reaction to an astronaut "about to hang his hide out over the edge in a hurtling piece of machinery" according to Woulfe was palpable:

> It was a look of fraternal awe, of awe in the presence of other men at a base when a test pilot or combat pilot headed for the aircraft for a mission when the odds were known to be evil . . . It was the look that came over another man when one's righteous stuff triggered *his* adrenalin.

Like astronauts or test pilots, the horsemen were single-combat warriors who knew that they risked their lives on behalf of others—there was of course more to it than that—and that the fate of others depended on their violence.[32]

PROPHECIES

In times of popular disturbance or difficulties when people would feel helpless in the face of some calamity, the need for heroic figures increased. Such figures held out the hope of vicariously transcending the difficulties. To a lifeless and dispirited people they were capable of bringing life. Prophetic messages which predicted the emergence of such great figures and dynasties were a feature of Gaelic culture from the earliest times, and in times of threat people seized on these messages, many of

Right: Brian Dardis making a horseshoe, assisted by Declan Cronin. (*Horseman Photography*). Left: Photo *Ruth Rogers*.

Shoeing a horse is often seen in legend as part of a leader's preparation for battle. We may speculate about its precise meaning in the case of the belief about Hugh O'Neill. We have seen that driving a horse on to land was part of the procedure for taking possession of it in early Ireland. According to Jung, even the horse's hoof mark, in the folklore with which he was familiar, had a function in this respect also. It too established the right of possession and determined boundaries. The horse's shoe was equivalent to its hoof—hence its function in warding off ill-luck—and therefore could, as in the O'Neill story, be part of the ritual associated with the capture of Tara and consequently of the kingship of Ireland. But it is not to the O'Neill dynasty but to that of the Geraldines from which the Earls of Kildare and Desmond were sprung that we have again to turn in order to see the role of the horse in the expectations of the return of the lost leader.[33]

which had been attributed to saints in order to give them validity. Saint Patrick, for instance, was believed to have prophesied that no foreign race would rule Ireland forever. Prophecies in the 12th and 13th centuries dealt with a mysterious figure, Aodh Eangach, a royal deliverer who would win a great battle at Tara. When Conn of the Hundred Battles had ridden, as we noted, to the Otherworld to be inaugurated, the god Lug had foretold to him that Aodh would be one of those who would succeed him as King of Tara. So Aodh became the long-awaited one who would come to claim his rightful inheritance and inaugurate a golden age. In 1593 it was strongly believed that Red Hugh (i.e. Aodh) O'Donnell was Aodh Eangach. His fellow leader Hugh O'Neill was also the subject of this prophetic belief. A report in 1593 when O'Donnell and O'Neill were in rebellion indicates the sense of expectancy. The Irish, we are told, were converging on Tara, fully believing the old prophecy that if Hugh O'Neill should shoe his horse there he would be king of all Ireland.

Prophecies concerning a royal deliverer who would defeat the enemy and become king of Ireland were initially specific to a particular dynasty—in the case of Aodh Eangach, the O'Neill dynasty. As well as catering for the popular need for reassurance, the prophecies provided a morale boost for the particular dynasty concerned. But they inevitably were appropriated by other dynasties which also had claims to greatness. The Geraldines, in particular, were the focus of prophecies over the centuries, a process that dated as far back as Giraldus Cambrensis' history of the Norman conquest which first brought the Geraldines to Ireland. Giraldus had moulded his story of the conquest to accord with the prophecies of Merlin Silvester, thus hoping to give the Normans and, in particular, the Geraldines, a predetermined significance in Ireland's history. Giraldus claimed, for instance, that one of the Normans, John de Courcy, fulfilled Merlin's prophecy that "A white knight astride a horse, bearing a device of birds on his shield, will be the first to enter Ulaid, and overrun it with hostile intent".

Many of the legends which subsequently became attached to the Geraldines are told in relation to both Desmond and Kildare earls. However, it is the Desmond story which is most clearly defined. Part of the reason for this lies in the critical turn in the fortunes of the Desmond dynasty about the middle of the fifteenth century. Thomas the seventh earl represented the high point of Desmond power. It was claimed that he wished to assume the sovereignty of Ireland but, as we have seen, he was executed in 1468.

GEARÓID IARLA AS LOST LEADER AND GHOSTLY HORSEMAN

From 1468 on the Desmonds were disloyal to the king in England and the belief grew that an Earl of Desmond would conquer the English. Prophecies and legends supporting that belief were encouraged by the Geraldine earls themselves, for they got hope and status from popular credulity in this regard. In the middle of the sixteenth century, for instance, an English report stated that the people "would sooner a Geraldine come among them than God".

There was another factor behind the emergence of the Desmond Geraldines as the focus for legends of lost leaders. Their chief castle was at Lough Gur which was only twelve miles away from Knockfierna, where Donn Fírinne, the God of the Dead and mythical huntsman was said to live. As we have seen, the Desmonds attracted much of the lore attaching to Donn. Equally potent in helping to elevate the Desmonds to supernatural significance was their proximity at Lough Gur to Knockainy (The hill of Áine) which was reputedly the home of Áine, the earth goddess associated with the sovereignty of Munster. In poetry, Maurice, the First Earl of Desmond, was seen as the rightful spouse of Áine. Munster, or more generally Ireland, could therefore easily be seen as awaiting his return to claim his bride and release her from bondage. At times of great difficulty, for example at the siege of Limerick in 1691, people believed that the earls like the gods and goddesses

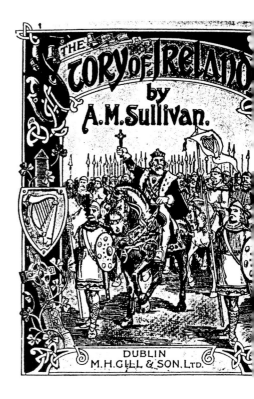

The late nineteenth-century Celtic revival saw publications such as this history book which featured a drawing of Brian Boru bearing the cross aloft and mounted on a noble horse. Many heroes in Irish history—Brian was the victor at Clontarf in 1014—were shown on horseback, frequently fighting a battle on behalf of Christianity.

of old were dwelling in the mountains and lakes of the countryside and would return on horseback to intervene in human affairs.[34]

These beliefs coalesced in particular around the figure of the Third Earl of Desmond, Gearóid Iarla, who because of his poetic ability was considered to have supernatural power. His death in 1398 is shrouded in mystery and provides the basis for many of the beliefs surrounding him. In popular tradition he was considered to have drowned like many of the other Desmonds. Fortifying this belief, perhaps, was the tradition that Donn, Gearóid's exemplar, had also drowned. One scholar has even suggested that Donn was identical with Eochaid Ollathair, the horse god. Earlier we saw that in Irish tradition the drowning of a horse was considered to have benefits for the community. It did not die but inhabited the waters as a horse god and protected the territory of the tribe. In this context we saw that horse and man were not seen as separate but as a unity. Gearóid after his disappearance in 1398 was also believed to have inhabited the Otherworld under a lake. Legends tell of him sinking to the bottom of Lough Gur with all his court and continuing there under a spell in anticipation of the time of his release from the enchantment. In the Otherworld he is seen accompanied by horses, or, according to one story, as a horse. His disappearance to the Otherworld was linked, by some of those living at the time of his death around Lough Gur, to his galloping horse:

> They saw his horse, which he used to ride furiously, gallop swiftly by them.
> But the Earl was not to be seen on its back, and has never been seen since.

Gearóid's perceived benevolence towards the people and intervention in their affairs took different forms. It was believed, for instance, that his stallion broke out of its Otherworldly stable in the lake and covered an ass. The resultant progeny was a mule considered very valuable by the community for its racing and work ability. Popular feeling was frequently engaged in resistance to high-handed landlords in the eighteenth and nineteenth centuries and stories about Gearóid reflect this preoccupation. A Kerry Chief, Donal O'Donoghue, entered into a wager with a boastful landlord who had three great hurlers among his tenants that he could find three better hurlers. At the time both gentry and common people took a great interest in hurling. O'Donoghue risked his estate on the bet, but on the day of the proposed hurling match he failed to produce the hurlers. Just as he was about to concede defeat three strange horsemen came on the scene and offered to play for him. He accepted and the three horsemen thrashed their opponents in the game. The horsemen, one of whom was Gearóid Iarla, later explained to O'Donoghue that they had done this for him because it was his custom to leave three tubs of oats beside the Lakes of Killarney for their horses each year. The legend of Gearóid and his horse had spread to these lakes where it was also believed that horsemen lay under a spell.[35]

Much of the conflict in Ireland from the fifteenth and sixteenth centuries on, when

the Desmond legend became the focus for popular credulity, was about land. A great sense of wrong grew up among the people as a result of the seventeenth-century confiscations. In 1641 fifty nine per cent of the land had been in Catholic hands but by 1703 that figure had been reduced to fourteen per cent. Through story and legend this wrong could be put right. The Irish were never keen to underplay the value of a good story. Old scores could be vicariously settled through the action in a story of the Earl of Desmond. In the nineteenth century, we are told, a man named FitzGerald—the Desmond family name—was walking near Lough Gur on lands which had once belonged to his ancestors when the agent of the landlord, Count de Salis, ordered him off. FitzGerald was very upset and turning towards the lake asked the enchanted earl, believed to be dwelling there, to remove the agent. When the agent, enraged at this, mounted his horse in order to call the police it shied and galloped under a tree dashing the agent against it, and killing him. Intervention by Desmond in the land question, however, the people expected, would be in an even more fundamental fashion than this legend implies. The unconscious wish of the people was that the furious horseman would return, for he accorded with their image of the righteous king, the figure who expressed their identity most fully and the spouse for whom Ireland was waiting so that he might make a decent woman of her. Messianic prophecies, therefore, grew up around him depicting him returning and, in a manner which was in line with the Irish tradition of the horse, taking possession of the land.

We have already seen how the image of Gearóid Iarla was influenced by that of Donn Fírinne, the wild huntsman. The messianic prophecies owe much also to the supposed Florentine origins of the Geraldines. The Florentine nobles in the thirteenth century were supporters of the Emperor Frederick II who, after his death in 1250, was popularly expected to return to fight a battle with an army which lay with him under a spell in Mount Etna. In order for such a spell to be broken the mounts of the soldiers, it would appear, had to be shod completely with silver. Tales concerning Gearóid depict him with his horses and horsemen waiting in his Otherworldly abode for the spell to be broken. But he does more than wait, according to tradition. Every seven years he rides around Lough Gur, as we have seen, on a horse partially shod with silver, as a huntsman with his followers. There are stories of him visiting a blacksmith anticipating the day when the spell will be broken. We learn that he has three shoes and that he is awaiting the fourth, his 'fourth green field' as it were. His recovery of the kingship of Ireland was seen, as we have noted in the case of Hugh O'Neill, to be bound up with the shoeing of his horse in preparation for a battle.[36]

THE FOURTEENTH EARL OF DESMOND

The strongest impetus to the messianic prophecies surrounding the Desmonds was given during the events of the life of the Fourteenth Earl. There was nothing heroic about him but events, coupled with the fact that he fitted the pattern of a violent huntsman prepared to risk all in one final great battle against the odds, conspired to thrust heroism upon him. The second half of the sixteenth century was a period of great resentment against Tudor encroachments, chiefly in matters of religion and land. In the hope of pacifying the Queen, Elizabeth, Gerald had ceded his huge estates to her in 1568, thinking that he would receive them back. Instead, the English adventurers moved in to take possession. In the parliament of 1569 coyne and livery in relation to "horsemen, footmen, galloglasses, kerne, hackbuttier, horses, horseboys, hunts, studkeepers, officers or adherents", the basis of Irish lords' authority, was abolished. It was a scheme in the grand manner in which the new landowners would compel the Irish, "even wildest and idlest" into "obedience and civility" or kill them.

Pressure on Gerald grew to join those offering resistance led by his cousin James FitzMaurice FitzGerald. Messianic hopes ran high for a saviour among the Geraldines. Gerald's future pattern of behaviour is finely caught in his actions in 1573 in Dublin where he had been imprisoned. On the pretext of going hunting he escaped the attentions of his gaoler and returned to Lough Gur donning the garments of an Irish chief. It was a journey beyond the Pale into the Irish Otherworld but it was six more years before the Earl unwillingly and in great pain from his wounds saw its logic through and openly rode to war. In October 1579 he was lifted on to his horse and embarked on a struggle which could only end in death. The violence was uncompromising. Desmond's harshness to others including his diminishing band of retainers was matched only by his cruelty to himself. Time spent in the saddle was extremely painful for him.

As the Earl took on the mantle of heroism he could almost be seen to reincarnate the spirit of Gearóid Iarla. Even his wife, Eleanor Butler, bore the same name as Gearóid's wife. An excellent horsewoman, she did not hesitate to brave the wrath of the English in a chase across country designed to lure them away from her husband's hideout. There were many escapes from the English forces. Gerald was almost captured on one occasion, we are told, when he and his eighty gallowglasses were surprised while preparing a horse for dinner. Gerald and his men had the advantage of excellent horses to ride but the end of a ritual struggle in which one man fought practically alone against impossible odds could only be temporarily delayed. What was important however was that the struggle took place and that the image of the returning huntsman be kept alive. When the end came it was not through capitulation but through betrayal by one of his followers. In a version of the Desmond legend attaching to Gerald collected in 1926 the earl on his horse throws a purse containing a thousand silver pieces, the price of his betrayal, to the man who asks to shoe his horse on the night of his return with his horsemen. Then the ghostly horseman disappears again.[37]

BALLDEARG O'DONNELL AS HORSEMAN-SAVIOUR

The idea of the lost leader returning on horseback to win the final great battle took on a variety of forms in accordance with historical circumstances. In the early seventeenth century with the cataclysmic event of the Flight of the Earls, Hugh O'Neill and Red Hugh O'Donnell, to Europe, the continent assumed the properties of the Otherworld in the popular mind. The heroes would return bringing salvation for the people. Given the mythology which surrounded Ireland's past and the pervasive influence of the learned classes in perpetuating it as the framework within which the Irish mind operated, it is easy to see how a vibrant hope of help from across the water could exist. Early Irish history was seen as a series of invasions which featured great battles. In one of these invasions the Tuatha Dé Danann, a race of gods who later inhabited the mountains and lakes of Ireland, conquered the Fir Bolg and then the Fomorians in two great battles, thus releasing Ireland from enslavement. A key figure in the second of these battles was the god Lug who went to Tara, offered to perform feats of horsemanship and of all the other skills, became an exemplary king and hero leading the Tuatha Dé Danann to victory. Christian respectability would necessitate that the Tuatha Dé Danann, pagan gods in the tales, be seen to be defeated but the old gods remained in the public imagination nonetheless, ready, it was hoped, to intervene in human affairs when the need arose.

The man who capitalised most spectacularly on this amalgam of mythology, fabrication and prophecy concerning a golden age about to be inaugurated by a returned leader was Balldearg O'Donnell who had gone to Spain and joined the army there. After the Battle of the Boyne he returned to Ireland, claiming that he was the messianic figure Aodh Eangach returned to free Ireland in accordance with the prophecy. Balldearg and his message struck chords in the unconscious of many of the Irish among whom the sense of "collective calamity and demand for collective deliverance" was strong. The poets composed verses proclaiming him in the traditional manner as the prophesied one who would save Ireland. Within a short period he had 10,000 followers.

A prophecy which played its part in Geraldine messianism stated that the final great battle against the forces of evil would be fought at the Hill of Singland near Limerick and Balldearg, true to his mission, went there at a time when the Irish were staging their last great stand in Limerick. The rest of Balldearg's story after the fall of Limerick makes inglorious reading. He deserted the Irish side and was granted the title Earl of Tyrconnell by the government before returning to the continent.

Our concern is not with Balldearg himself, who in any case did not prove a great messiah, but with his 'uncanny' appeal, with his charisma, or with the "subconscious communication between leader and led" which his story exemplified. That communication had little to do with the greatness or otherwise of the leader or hero. As we have seen in the case of the last 'true' Earl of Desmond, when it came to heroism, almost anyone would do. Rather, what lay at the basis of Balldearg's appeal was the people's need for heroes to compensate for the misery of their own existence. Our interest here is in the form which those heroes took in the popular mind and with the enduring character of that form. A radio interview in June 1984 with an elderly lady from Kinvara in Co Galway revealed how resilient the image of the horseman hero returning to bring salvation could be. At some time, she believed, a leader would emerge out of a fairy fort and lead his horsemen to take over the country.[38]

Into the nineteenth century many Irish revolutionary movements were permeated with millenarian fervour coupled with the belief in foreign invasion. Towards the end of the previous century Charles Walmesley ('Pastorini') published his commentary on the Book of Revelations claiming that with the Second Coming heretics would be punished. His work found a ready market in Ireland where the heretics were identified with Protestants and peasants were only too anxious to fight even to the death to bring in a new age. Early in 1822 in the Adare region in Co. Limerick the following prediction was noted:

The children of God are to be defeated with great loss in two first battles; before the third, on their march they are to meet with a white horse. They are then to come victorious and to chase the locusts to the north. A man with four thumbs is to hold the horses of four kings or four great generals at the battle, which is

The image of the returning heroes, embedded in the subconscious of those who responded to prophetic messages, invariably involves horses. In this respect Irish tradition has been copperfastened by the Apocalypse of John which greatly influenced the content of the continental prophecies to which we have referred. It was also very popular with early Irish churchmen among whom many Irish prophecies were reputed to have originated. In the vision of John, the Resurrection is seen to triumph over death and the Lamb of God emerges triumphant to inaugurate a golden age: "Then I saw the heaven opened and behold, a white horse! He who sat upon it is called Faithful and True".

Commandant Gerry Mullins and *Parkgate* clearing the Puissance wall at the RDS Horse Show. (*Inpho*)

Top: Connemara Pony competing at the RDS Horse Show. (*Ruth Rogers*)

Bottom Right: Bill Steinkraus and *Ksar d'Esprit* meeting the difficulties of the Puissance wall head on, RDS Horse Show 1962. (*G. A. Duncan*)

Bottom left: Irish draught stallion *Pride of Shaunlara* with Billy Cotter, left, and Dan Downey to whom he was sold as a three-old. (*Ruth Rogers*)

to be fought at Singland near Limerick. When all is over, the Spaniards are to settle a frame of government. Ireland was to be in after time in the possession of the Spaniards.

Given the biblical tradition among Protestants it is hardly surprising that a white horse would also be seen as heralding their liberation. King William, the victor at the Battle of the Boyne, is shown to this day on Orangemen's banners, mounted on a white horse.

By the Treaty of Limerick, King William offered to transport, at his own expense, the Irish army with its horses, to France. Those who remained behind had to surrender their horses. William was at war with France and it is a measure of his fear of Irish horsemen in their own terrain that he was prepared to present them to his enemy abroad. His action was counterproductive in another way also.

THE POETS AND THE HOPED-FOR RETURN OF THE HORSEMEN

The exile of the Irish troops or Wild Geese as they were known to the continent kept alive the hope of the return of the lost leader. Sarsfield was such a leader but two years after his departure he lay dead on a battlefield at Landen. Into the breach therefore came the Stuarts, the righteous kings, according to the poets, who would return to claim their spouse. Even in the nineteenth century, when Charles Stuart was dead and hopes of a restoration lay dead with him, the Munster poets were still referring to the proud young horseman who would bring back the golden age. One of those poets was Eoghan Rua Ó Súilleabháin, born about the middle of the eighteenth century at a time when Charles' cause had already collapsed at Culloden. In Eoghan's vision the arrival of Stuart would act as a catalyst for other horsemen:

> Should our Stuart come to us from beyond the sea
> With a fleet from Louis and from Spain
> In the sheer dint of joy I'd be mounted
> On a swift, stout, vigorous, nimble steed,
> Driving out the 'ospreys' at the sword's edge.

Another poet, Diarmaid Mac Carthaigh from Co Cork, saw the position in more local terms. His former patron, McCarthy, now the leader of the Irish Brigade in France, he expects soon to return and reinaugurate the golden age which was suspended with his departure across the seas. The poet had been deprived of his horse, the symbol of that age:

> Our mighty heroes swept from us beyond the sea
> It is that leaves the merry bards in straitened bonds,
> Else Ireland's nobles would not let me foot my road.
> An Oisín in the Fenian's wake, full pitiful.

The extent to which the horse is part of the image of the returning leader is conveyed in a folk epic, probably composed in the eighteenth century, about Balldearg. It describes how, imprisoned in Spain, he is given an opportunity to ride the king's stallion in a race. The horse wins against all odds and Balldearg gains a place in the king's household. The king makes use of Balldearg's proven skill with horses by sending him to Ireland to purchase horses. Balldearg sets his eye on a savage stallion in his mother's stable which no man had dared to take out and ride for seven years. He, however, is able to control the horse and when he goes out to its stable it gets down on its knees and allows him to mount. Having thus established his credentials, Balldearg returns to Spain where he rides the fierce stallion in a duel against a giant who threatens the country and kills him. The parallels between Balldearg in this account and Lug, the exemplary hero and king, who before he became king and won a great battle, performs feats of horsemanship at Tara, is clear. An additional element is also present in the story of Balldearg. He is cast in the mould of David who slays the giant Goliath and liberates Israel. Like the astronaut in the first manned orbital flight of the earth described by Woulfe, Balldearg was the "single combat warrior triumphant" who had risked his life and for whom, on his return the people would throng the streets, with "tears of joy and gratitude and awe". In the meantime, we are told, Balldearg waits in Spain with his army for such an opportunity when he can lead Ireland to freedom.[39]

Whereas poets such as Ó Súilleabháin and Mac Carthaigh looked to patrons across the water to provide access to the Otherworld and to supply them, in particular, with a horse, other people sought a refuge at home. Patrick Sarsfield, before he too went abroad, had pointed the way in this regard. He had taken his horsemen into the mountains and from there, in alliance with Galloping Hogan and his wild Rapparees, he scored a spectacular victory at Ballyneety against the English. The memory of his escapade on this occasion is still kept alive by many local traditions.[40]

TORIES, RAPPAREES AND OUTLAWS

Earlier we saw how in mediaeval Ireland figures like Kildare and Desmond were drawn away from the English sphere of influence into a life among the 'wild Irish' where they could be seen as folk heroes. Enabling them to make this transition into the Irish Otherworld were bands of Irish 'idlemen' under their chieftains, with whom the Anglo-Irish lords made alliances. These bands frequently lived in the mountains and woods, the least accessible parts of the country. With the flight of many of the Irish leaders to the continent in 1607 attempts made to transport some of their followers, who were the most spirited and reckless of the Irish and who now were leaderless, failed. The plantation policy pursued by the government during the course of the century provided a focus for the discontent of these lawless bands. From their wood and mountain fastnesses the Tories or 'hunted ones' as they came to be known descended on the plains to wreak revenge on the planters now in possession of their lands. To the English, such men as Redmond O'Hanlon in Armagh and the three Brennans in Kilkenny were daylight robbers who could be hunted with impunity. But as the Irish watched the violent and lawless men take to the mountains and woods, from which they frequently returned to rob and steal, they turned a blind eye to their excesses and failings, as they would do with Balldearg O'Donnell and as they had done with the Desmonds, and Robin Hood type legends developed. The turbulence of the seventeenth century had left the Irish hungry for heroes and there was much in the background and character of the Tories and later of the Rapparees to satisfy that need.

We have stressed the role of the Irish terrain as a part of the composite myth of the Irish horse. We have seen how the race of gods, the Tuatha Dé Danann, were believed to have been banished there and how legends of horse gods buried beneath lakes are common in Ireland. We pointed out that because of the immediacy of the Otherworld to the Irish people, even today, intervention by these gods in the affairs of men is not only expected but demanded. When Irish beliefs and way of life came under threat the mantle of the returning saviour fell on the Desmonds in the person of Gearóid Iarla who was believed to lie under enchantment with his horses and horsemen in Lough Gur. The Tories and Rapparees were seen in this tradition. They knew every inch of the landscape and could use it as a refuge when they were being pursued. The English from the time of their coming to Ireland were painfully aware of the cover which the terrain offered and frequently took the extreme measure of cutting down the woods to unearth their opponents. One Gaelic poet saw clearly the options which would face the Irish rebels when the woods had been removed. The good life could only be found abroad:

> Now the wood is being cut
> We will journey over the sea.

The English forces in the second half of the seventeenth century were not oblivious of the value of the terrain to the Irish. For instance, they hacked down Glen Woods in a bid to capture Redmond O'Hanlon, the most famous of the Tories, who used it as a retreat. The Rapparees who greatly assisted the Irish army in the late seventeenth century wars were known to the Williamites as 'bog-trotters' because of their ability in a part of the terrain which also posed problems for strangers. Indeed the initiation rites of the Rapparee leaders involved a test of a young man's ability to endure long periods of confinement in the inhospitable conditions of a bog hole. The Rapparees were capable, if necessary, of sinking entirely into a bog so that pursuers would be unaware of their existence. The wild terrain of Ireland was a part of the Rapparee, he faded imperceptibly into it when he wished and emerged swiftly out of it when about to make a raid.[41]

For such men as the Tories and Rapparees, horses were essential, but unlike the poets whom we have discussed they did not look to their leaders abroad to provide them. They stole them. Stealing horses, it would appear, was almost an initiation rite for members of a Tory or Rapparee band. Redmond O'Hanlon, for instance, was discovered trying to sell a stolen horse, to which he had attached a false tail, with the result that he had to go 'on the run' for the first time in his life. At the end of the seventeenth century Rapparees were a constant plague on the Williamite army which badly needed horses. At Ballyneety the Williamites lost 500 horses to the marauders who stampeded the animals towards Limerick serving the dual purpose of confusing the Williamites and supplying the Irish in Limerick with food and a means of carrying out construction work.[42]

The line of demarcation between outlaw and Rapparee was frequently nonexistent. The highwayman Charles O'Dempsey ended his days on the gallows in Maryborough in 1734 because of his fondness for horse-stealing. So closely identified was he with horses that he was known as Cathaoir na gCapall. One of his ploys when stealing horses was to switch the horse's shoes back to front to lay a false trail. In Irish tradition such a measure was standard procedure probably because there were occasions in Irish history when the English had tracked the Irish by their horsetracks. Sarsfield was reputed to have switched his horses' shoes, thus confusing the Williamites when he and his troops fell back on Limerick after the battle of Aughrim. When Cearbhall Ó Dálaigh, the fifteenth-century poet reputed to have composed the famous song "Eibhlín a Rúin" abducted one Eibhlín Kavanagh he

The Ward Union Hunt, St Stephen's Day Meet, Ashbourne. *Source*: Inpho.

Source: DoA.

also turned the shoes of his horse backwards.

Like O'Hanlon, O'Dempsey included in his repertoire of tricks methods of disguising the fact that he had stolen a particular horse. Substitution of horses, which is not unknown among horse dealers today, was even tried by him. The evidence in court against him on one occasion broke down when the 'horse' which the offended party swore to be his own property turned out to be a mare which O'Dempsey was able secretly to substitute for the stolen horse on account of the similarity between the markings on the two animals. Ability to use the horse with such facility in a life-and-death struggle demanded a great deal of self confidence with the animal and, of course, the ability to control it. O'Dempsey, it was said, could tame and master the wildest horses on account of a charm he was said to possess. One of the first Rapparees was reputed to have trained his own horse in such a way that he could mount it while it accelerated by catching hold of its mane and ear.[43]

The central place given to horses and horsemanship in the image of the hero is reflected in legends about many of the outlaws. To the folk mind, facility with horses made possible the return and, of course, the escape of its heroes, robbing the rich to give to the poor or striking a blow against the English soldiers. People trapped in poverty and oppression and unable to right the wrongs done to them developed stories of those who could exercise the required force. In the eighteenth and nineteenth centuries, production of romanticised versions of the lives of highwaymen like O'Hanlon and O'Dempsey was a growth industry. Redmond, for instance, was seen as being ubiquitous, mounted on his well-bred charger. This animal was so valuable to him and his trade that when, during the course of one robbery, he is deprived of it, he is made to look silly and ends up empty-handed.

Folklore had, of course, to admit that its heroes were vulnerable. The difficulties faced by people in their lives when confronted by oppressive authority were very great. The heroes, standing defiantly alone against authority, are inevitably overthrown in the end but, in a face-saving exercise, folklore shows the oppressive authority having to resort to foul means in order to achieve their defeat. The heroes, as we have seen in the case of the last 'true' Earl of Desmond, are betrayed frequently by those who are close to them. The horse in this context is cast in the role of protector.[44]

There are many instances, of course, of horses providing an escape for men in danger of capture and these do not necessarily involve well known heroes. At the end of the Cromwellian war, John O'Connor Kerry was on the run from his brother-in-law John FitzGerald and went to his sister, John's wife, Sarah. While he held Sarah's infant boy in his arms, he heard the child's nurse sing some lines from a song:

They soothe thee and smile,
But their hearts, full of guile,
Are plotting the while
How best to betray.
Leave the babe to its nurse.
Let the man to his horse,
And away! and away!

He took the advice, and jumping on his horse escaped to Ballylongford where he went to ground. In a story about Ned of the Hills, who as his name might suggest was a Rapparee, the horse is given a more central role. Ned, about whose life on the run a song, "Éamonn an Chnoic", has survived in Irish to this day, was, it was said, one of Galloping Hogan's band who helped Sarsfield at Ballyneety. He is recalled in tradition as one who helped the poor and outwitted the English. The threat of betrayal from among those who purported to be his friends was constant and we learn how he used always to leave his horse tied up outside any house in which he slept so that it might alert him to an attack. One night he was asleep in his cousin's house when the horse's neighing awoke him. He decided to ignore it even though the horse persisted. The warning from the horse proved to be justified however for, when the opportunity arose, Ned's cousin beheaded him.[45]

Going it alone: unlucky 13.
(*Horseman Photography*).

Nigel Moore of Crumlin, Co. Antrim, with *April Storm*, the National Irish Draught Broodmare Champion, 1990. Also champion in 1986 and 1988. (*Horseman Photography*).

Ruth McCullough with foal out of half-sister of *April Storm* (above) and sired by *Supreme Edge* (see back cover), the Reserve Champion for the Croker Cup at the RDS, 1991. Owners Nigel and Charlotte Moore, Crumlin Co. Antrim. (*Photo: Nigel Moore*).

"At the Start." The Conyngham Cup, Punchestown, 1872.
Riders from left to right: Mr Whyte riding *Bashful*,
Mr G. Moore riding *Curragh Ranger*, Mr Comerford
riding *Chisel*, Mr Exshaw, Capt. H. McCalmont
riding *Magenta*, Mr Oldham riding *Ireland Yet*,
Mr St. James riding *Lamp*, Mr Thomas riding *Star of the Sea*,
Capt. Smith (winner) riding *Heraut d'Armes*,
Mr T. Beasley riding *Hubert*, Mr Long,
Capt. Mac Farlane riding *Waterford*.

6

The Sporting Horse and Society in the Eighteenth and Nineteenth Centuries

THE VIOLENT HORSEMEN of the last chapter, we argued, were heroes. The Irish people moulded them in their own idealised self-image. They were skilled with horses and they used this skill to conquer their oppressors. But there was undoubtedly considerable divergence of outlook among the Irish. The horse, conceivably, could mean different things to different people depending on their economic circumstances and their background.

The poet Eoghan Rua Ó Súilleabháin, whom we have quoted, for instance, had little in common with the ordinary people. His thinking was aristocratic and his poetry that of the well-to-do who once patronised poets and aspired to a restoration of their estates. Such poets wrote of a return of the golden age when their patrons were powerful landlords. Tenants might not look forward to their return with such pleasure. The seventeenth-century wars and dispossessions in some instances left the ordinary people better off. Between the dispossessed aristocrats and the ordinary people there was however a sense of identity and racial consciousness stretching back to mediaeval times which the defeats at the hands of the English in that century only served to consolidate. An important factor in the common outlook of the poor and the dispossessed was respect for nobility of birth.

Even ordinary people cherished the belief that they were descended from royal ancestors and were outraged when they saw those of privileged position being undermined by those whom they considered their inferiors. Arthur Young writing in the last quarter of the 18th century refers to a landlord, Charles O'Conor of Clonalis House in Co. Roscommon, who was descended from the once powerful kings of Connacht but who had suffered in the 17th century: "The common people pay him the greatest respect, and send him presents of cattle etc. upon various occasions. They consider him as the prince of a people involved in one common ruin."

This was a mediaeval world and the presents given to O'Conor were the coyne and livery of earlier days when a lord got free entertainment at his tenants' expense. In this chapter we will consider how both landlord and tenant clung to many of the trappings of that world as a corrective to military impotence. Violence which could no longer be channelled into the building up of great lordships could find an outlet in the ritual struggles of the hunting field and in the entertainment which went with hunting. As in mediaeval times, the ordinary people were spectators who rejoiced at the sight of greatness on display.[1]

THE POETS' VIEW

Part of the service which the mediaeval lords obtained when they went hunting included, as we have seen, provisions for their horses and huntsmen and, in the poetry of the eighteenth and nineteenth centuries, we find echoes of this custom being celebrated. Even the possibility that, as in mediaeval times, such guests might prolong their stay, would not dampen the welcome which they received. In her elegy for her husband, Art Ó Laoghaire, Eibhlín Dhubh Ní Chonaill recalls how Art brought back his hunting companions and horses for lavish entertainment to his house:

> Where the tossing oats were which would make the steeds whinny,
> and the graceful long-maned horses with their grooms beside them
> —who would not be charged for the keep of their horses,
> though they stayed for a week.

Eibhlín Dhubh was a member of the proud O'Connell family from Derrynane in Co. Kerry which had managed to retain a mediaeval lifestyle among its tenants and which had, therefore, a vested interest in a retention of the past with its proud traditions of hunting and hospitality. The other aristocratic poets were also prime beneficiaries of that tradition. They depended on a patron's generous lifestyle and when the dispossession of those patrons became the reality they took refuge in a world marked by hunting and hospitality as a hedge against the ignominy of their position. They describe in loving detail the good company, the types of food, the drink, the music at festive gatherings in the great houses which made them honoured guests. Aogán Ó Rathaille, for instance, nostalgically recalled the house of O'Callaghan of Clonmeen in Co. Cork in these terms and then went on to describe the hunting:

> Often in that plain was heard the sound of war-bugles,
> The loud cry of the chase on the sides of the misty hills
> Foxes and red bucks were being wakened for them,
> Hares from the mead, water hens and thrushes.

Nor did he leave self-interest out of the picture :

> Steeds being bestowed on the ollamhs of Fodla, [the poets]
> Strong steeds in teams racing on the hillside.[2]

The poets knew, however, that for them the world had to change. As their patrons were dispossessed or went abroad the prospect of a free dinner went with them. If they were to survive they had to cater for popular taste and become more self-reliant. In their poetry they made frequent allusions to the plight that faced them. Given the horse's place in the symbolism of the old order which was swept away in the seventeenth century and its importance to the poets as a gift from their patrons, it is hardly surprising that it features in verses about the difficult transition which the poets had to make. The poetry in question, from which we have already quoted, revolves around the poet Diarmait Mac Carthaigh who has lost his horse. His loss is the subject of a Court of Poetry in Whitechurch Co. Cork, a kind of dressing-room post mortem held after the game has been lost to discuss tactics for the future. As the poets gather to ponder the death of the horse, *An Fhalartha Ghorm* (The Grey Ambler), they are ranged on two opposing sides. On one side there is Mac Carthaigh, vainly clinging to the old ways and supports, and, on the other, the younger breed of poets telling him to stand on his own two feet and clearly unperturbed by the fate of the old horse. For Mac Carthaigh the loss of his horse has been cataclysmic. He can't travel any more across the mountains or go to mass or to a funeral. The patrons who would have replaced "The Grey Ambler" are gone. His world has contracted. But there is a saving grace in the poetic wrangle. Through the verses written about it the old horse gets a new lease of life and achieves immortality among the people who would hear its story.[3]

When we move away from the aristocratic poets of Munster to poets who are closer to the ordinary people we are not conscious of any large shift in attitude to the horse or in what it represented. The thoughts of Peadar Ó Doirnín, a northern poet who lived in the first half of the eighteenth century, turn first to the loss of the right to hunt and fish when he considers the misfortune which befell the Irish on the English arrival. Likewise in his best-known love poem "Urchnoc Chéin Mhic Cáinte" one of the prizes which he offers his loved one if she will come away with him is "uaill na ngadhar", the sound of the hounds. Another poet with close sympathies with the ordinary people was Raftery, born in the last quarter of the eighteenth century. Like Eibhlín Ní Chonaill he too could rejoice in

> Fine racehorses, and steeds in stables
> Hunters there, tired out after being hunted;
> Smooth white oats in a fine wooden manger
> They have to get, though they should remain for a year.

In *The Midnight Court*, Brian Merriman perhaps expresses best what the sight and sound of the hunt meant to the ordinary people:

> This view would bring the heart to life—
> Be it worn with sickness, age, or strife—
> The sound of the horn and a glimpse of the hunt
> With the pack in chase and the fox in front.

Hunting in Ireland has its roots in pre-Norman times when men on foot followed

Left: *Arkle* in training with his regular work rider, Paddy Woods, at Greenogue, Co. Dublin, where Tom Dreaper had his stables. *(Bord Failte)*

Top right: The display of hounds and huntsmen has been a feature of the RDS Horse Show, as in this scene at the Double Bank in 1960. *(G. A. Duncan)*

Bottom right: Mrs J. Armstrong on *Slieve Bloom*, winner, and Mrs J. A. Wilson on *Mr X*, competing in the Kilkenny West Point-to-Point in 1949. *(G. A. Duncan)*

their hounds. Fenian poems describe the Fianna hunting on foot. Because of the wooded terrain in many parts of the country mounted hunts would have been difficult. As late as 1600 one-eighth of the country was covered by woods and the tradition of hunting on horseback instead of displacing hunting on foot was grafted on to it in many areas, and shared the affection which foot hunting enjoyed. This was true particularly of Clare, Merriman's birthplace. As early as the mid seventeenth century a pack of hounds which one writer described as the best in the world was found there and the love of hunting has survived to this day in the region. Around Ennis there is a high concentration of harrier packs most of which are followed on foot, and mounted hunting enjoys a similar popularity.

In the poetry of Raftery the impulse to glorify the hunting field was given free rein. There were good reasons why nostalgia should figure prominently in his poetry. He had been born in Killedan in Co. Mayo and was a frequent visitor to the house of the local landlord there, Frank Taaffe, but had been banished for drowning Taaffe's choice horse in a boghole. When Taaffe had sent him on an errand to fetch drink he had failed to take a turn in the road in time due to his blindness and horse and rider had landed in the bog. Killedan assumed in the poet's mind the aspect of an Otherworld and his verses about hunting have much the same character:

> Cellars without doors and drink for the world . . .
> The hind and her brood is there, the badger and the white deer,
> There they be, every day, and the hunt after them;
> Reynard is there, and the shouts and pursuit at his heels,
> And gentlemen out of every quarter observing the sport.

Raftery was not oblivious of the sectarian tensions of his age or of the gap that lay between rich and poor but in his vision these tensions are forgotten, rack rents are not spoken of, as the poet, whose father had been a cottier with less than one acre of land, describes the prowess of every landlord on the hunting field.[4]

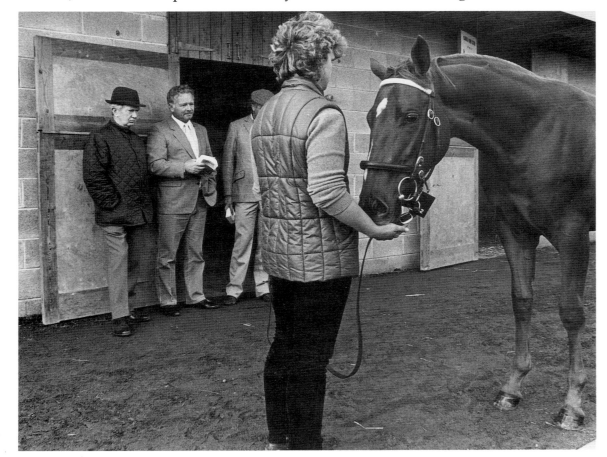

Vincent O'Brien and Robert Sangster with a prospective purchase at Goff's Bloodstock Sales. *(Inpho)*

Above: A ferry carrying men and a horse across the Foyle at Derry, as shown in an early seventeenth-century map of Derry.

Below: Turf sales in Dublin.

BUYE the dry Turf; buye Turf; buye the dry Turf—Here's the dry Bog-a-Wood.—Here's the Chips to light the Fire; Maids!

HORSE OWNERSHIP

There were good reasons why divisiveness should not enter into thinking about horses. The urge to own a horse, for instance, had never been the prerogative of the wealthy classes alone in Ireland. Writing in the second half of the seventeenth century Sir William Petty estimated that one third of Irish cabins possessed a small horse. The era of prosperity which commenced in the second half of the seventeenth century was probably responsible for the increasing incidence of horse-ownership. "The poorest now in Ireland," Petty noted, "ride on horseback, where heretofore the best ran on foot like animals." There is undoubtedly an element of exaggeration in this. Particularly during periods of famine and of war the horses of the poor were sold. Armies had great need of horses and there are frequent reports of their scarcity in the country and of the necessity to import them from England. However, it is clear from the comments of Arthur Young that even the people belonging to the poor cottier class who paid their rent in labour and often lived at a subsistence level, were very determined to keep horses. In Co. Westmeath he learned that "they are ill-clothed, and make a wretched appearance, what is worse, are more oppressed by many who make them pay too dear for keeping a cow, horse, etc." Young regarded the practice whereby the cottiers would pay for their cabin or horse with a certain number of work days as a great abuse and something which would not be tolerated in England. Further up the economic scale were the "common farmers" and in Courtown in Co. Wexford Young noted that "all keep cows and generally a horse, and pig or two."

The pattern of the poorer classes in Ireland keeping horses continued into the nineteenth century. The census of 1841, taken a few years before the Great Famine forced many of the poorest people to sell their horses, records that almost all 192,000 farms between 6 and 15 acres possessed a horse. Asses were however becoming very common on holdings of less than three acres and were being used for carrying goods. For heavier work, such as ploughing, horses (or oxen, as in the case of the English and Anglo-Irish farmers in Ireland) would be required and this was frequently done on a co-operative basis. The livestock census of 1849 revealed that there were about half a million horses in the country, a figure which towards the end of the century probably increased by about 20%. The submissions to the Commission appointed to enquire into the horse-breeding industry in 1896 confirmed that small farmers at that time were still deeply involved in horse ownership, one witness claiming that half the horses in the country were owned by farmers with less than 20 acres of land. These farmers, individually, would not own many horses, of course.[5]

Economically there were good reason for ordinary people to have a horse. In the seventeenth century the condition of many roads, particularly in the winter months, was appalling and some areas could only be reached by pack-horse. The growth in

trade in the eighteenth century led to an increase in road building activities and a great many small farmers, on a seasonal basis, were able to supplement their income from farming by carting goods locally. This, in turn, helped to expand the horse population and improve agriculture. The eighteenth-century poets who reflected the outlook of small farmers frequently expressed the belief that their lot could be improved through husbandry and depict the horse between the shafts of a plough:

> I'd be better off with a horse, a plough and harrow
> A ploughteam of horses ready and harnessed,

wrote Marcus O'Callanan. Even Ó Doirnín believed that with one or two horses, a cow, a goat or a sheep, his lot might be better than if he spent his time day-dreaming in a tavern. In this picture of level-headed husbandry, however, some of the thinking which we associate with the more aristocratic poets breaks through. A nostalgic memory of other pursuits for which in better times horses might be used asserts itself as we see in the poetry of Ó Maoil Chiaráin who is living in Co. Monaghan, away from his home:

> I do not see sheep grazing on the white plains or horses being trained as they pursue the dogs across the ditch.

It is clear that in Ireland the poor as well as the rich aspired to horse-ownership. Horses were an interest shared by both of these sections of society. Much the same could be said in relation to those in society who were separated by religion. The occasion of the composition of a series of poems written in the first half of the eighteenth century concerning the horse of Nicholas O'Donnell, a priest and poet, provides us with a more general illustration of the horse's capacity to draw people together. The horse *Preabaire* had died as a result of being overlooked by a spirit and, in order to comfort the priest over the loss, a group of poets, including the Protestant poet Micheál Coimín, gathered together in a tavern to compose poetry. Coimín added his sympathetic verses to those of the other poets and the effect of the whole offering is to make the priest forget his grief over his loss. The feeling of unanimity which the horse evoked was able to recreate the past in which the horse was alive.

The religious unity for which the horse was a focus on this occasion was a feature of most of the eighteenth century. As a rule Catholics and Protestants got on well together. The tensions of the nineteenth century however ensured that this would change. In what follows we shall be considering how the horse, as a focus for unity and cohesion within society, managed to override these divisions.[6]

Above : 'Taking the Bride Home' (1842)

Left : An Irish cart.

PENAL LAWS

Because of the religious character of the battles between the two kings William and James, the increasingly denominational character of bitterness and division between people in Ireland became apparent. Catholics and Protestants would try to deprive each other, given the opportunity, of their rights and property. An indication, in the midst of this polarisation, that the horse was becoming denominational came from a remark by King James in 1689 when he was presented with a horse of Irish breeding. James considered that the horse must have been a papist.

The subsequent conduct of the Williamite war reinforced the identification of horses with one or other of the two religions. Horses were one of the engines of war and during periods of war they were much sought after by the opposing Catholic and Protestant sides. In 1689 when the Catholic king's deputy, Tyrconnell, ordered that all serviceable horses be seized from the Protestants, the poet Dáibhí Ó Bruadair wrote a poem rejoicing at the humiliation inflicted on them. As the Williamite threat mounted in the country the action against Protestants became more extreme. Those in Dublin were ordered to hand over their horses and arms and so great were the abuses of the emergency powers which the Jacobites had taken in this respect that orders had to be issued forbidding the unauthorised commandeering of horses. The period of Catholic power was of brief duration and soon it was the Catholics and their horses which were under threat. The outstanding body of legislation geared to depriving the Irish Catholics of their rights was the so-called 'Penal Laws'. These were enacted soon after the Treaty of Limerick which brought an end to the Williamite war in Ireland. In every sphere of life, ownership of land or property, the professions, religion and the franchise, it was intended to deprive the Irish Catholic of his civil rights. The Protestant ascendancy was anxious not only to gain

(Ruth Rogers)

revenge for the difficulties which the Jacobites had caused them and to ensure that they might not recur but was also greedy to acquire and control Catholic wealth and power. Given the value placed by Irish people on having horses available to them, Protestants could deal a great blow to Catholic self-esteem by placing their horses under threat. Horses in Protestant hands could be seen as the symbol of victory and oppression. More than two centuries after the 'Penal Laws' were enacted the playwright Brendan Behan, who had been jailed in England for his republican activities, could refer to the ascendancy as "a Protestant on a horse" as if the two—Protestantism and ownership of a horse—were synonymous.

Among the 'Penal Laws' enacted was one which sought to achieve this. The act dating from 20 January 1695 stated that

> no person of the Popish religion shall be capable to have or keep in his possession any horse, gelding or mare which shall be of the value of five pounds or over; and if any Protestant shall make discerning on oath of such horse or horses to be in the possession of such Papists . . . to any two Justices of the Peace . . . any such Protestant paying or making tender of the sum of £5 5s. 0d. to the owner or possessor of such horse . . . for and after such payment or tender, the property of such horse or horses shall be deemed to be vested in the person making such discovery.

There were other provisions also enabling the civil officers to seize horses belonging to Catholics who would have to pay the expense of seizing and keeping them if and when they were returned. Any Catholic concealing a horse was liable to be imprisoned for three months and to pay a fine to the value of three times the horse's worth.

There were various incidences of the penal legislation being used or, almost as important, threatened against Catholic horse owners. At the racing which took place around the Commons of Armagh in 1731 the owners of good horses were warned that they would have to take £5 for their horses if offered it. What concerns us here is the manner in which the legislation was thwarted. In the first place it was, of course, only applicable to the small number of Catholics who could afford to keep a racing horse. A second factor limiting the impact of the legislation on Catholics was the weakness of the machinery for enforcing government legislation in the eighteenth century. There was no police force and the prisons were inadequate. The enforcement of the law in general depended on local conditions and we may deduce that the law concerning horses, in common with the rest of the penal code, was rarely applied universally. But perhaps the single greatest blow to the legislation on Catholics' horses was the co-operation which sometimes took place between Catholics and Protestants to defeat its objectives. In such instances the law achieved a unity where division was intended. On the whole it would appear country gentlemen wished to stay on good terms with their Catholic neighbours

Three generations of the Cash family at the East Galway Hunt. Left to right : Mrs Rose Lowe, Mrs Doreen Swinburn and her son Walter, the late Mr and Mrs Michael Cash (parents of Doreen, Myles and Patrick), Myles and Patrick Cash, Michael and Wally Swinburn. In front : Myles, Deirdre and Shane Cash. The Cash family today continues the horse-dealing tradition of Michael's brother Ned, who died in 1990. *(Ruth Rogers)*

and to maintain with them social and sporting relations, and they were prepared to involve themselves in stratagems to achieve these ends. A well-known story tells of one such effort to evade the law. A Catholic who owned one of the most famous racehorses in Ireland, reputed to be worth 200 guineas, was informed in advance that a Protestant was going to seize the horse and pay the statutory £5. On hearing of this the Catholic owner mounted his horse and took him to a Protestant friend who accepted the gift, "thus defeating the miscreant of this vile purpose". In what follows we will be arguing that equestrian sport and, in particular, racing continued to prove to be an Otherworld where divisions between Irish people were, however temporarily, suspended. [7]

POPULAR APPEAL OF RACING

During the eighteenth and nineteenth centuries ordinary people travelled in great numbers to fairs, patterns, races and other communal gatherings. In 1812 Edward Wakefield noted that "one third at least of the time of the labouring classes in Ireland is wasted in holydays, funerals, weddings, christenings, fairs, patterns, races, and other recreations". "If there be a market to attend," Nicholls, the Poor Law organiser and expert noted, "a fair or a funeral, a horse race or a wedding, all else is neglected and forgotten." A key characteristic of such festive gatherings was generally its contrast with everyday life. The normal rules of behaviour were abandoned as people gave themselves to revelry. For ordinary Irish people and particularly the cottier class life, in general, was difficult, affording little relief so that assemblies of different kinds had a great attraction. One night before the races in Kilkenny, for instance, a traveller in the first half of the 19th century noted that the main street of the city was crowded with "bagpipes snuffling, violins squealing, melancholy flutes blowing and ragged paddies dancing". For a short period such assemblies provided a refuge and an Otherworld.[8]

We may well ask why races should feature in this catalogue of attractions to which the ordinary people thronged. A good horse was the prerogative of a gentleman so that all others who were outside that category were necessarily excluded from active participation in racing. The character of some of those who, until recent times, owned racehorses provides us, however, with an indication of one feature of the racecourse which appealed to people. Earlier we discussed how for many Irish people resistance to the English offered the only possibility of sharing in the good life and how those who offered such resistance frequently acquired heroic stature. As attitudes among the racehorse-owning fraternity to the 'Penal Laws' would seem to indicate, the racecourse could also provide a forum for resistance to the English. Tom Ferguson, the breeder and owner of *Harkaway*, considered by many to be the greatest racehorse of the 1830s, provides us with a striking if unusual instance of this. Although popular with the nobility and gentry in the west of Ireland, Ferguson was no friend of the racing authorities in England whom he frequently tried to flout. His bitterest enemy was the self-styled dictator of the English turf, Lord George Bentinck, who wished to own *Harkaway*. Nothing, as we have implied, was more likely to anger an Irish person than efforts to deprive him of his horse. "Harkaway is my horse," Ferguson declared publicly, "to win money for me, and not for any damned fellow, either a lord by courtesy and a thief by the curse of God." Cheltenham, the scene of many an Irish battle against the ancient enemy, provided the scene for Ferguson's greatest victory over his arch-enemy. *Harkaway* defeated Bentinck's *Grey Nomus*, winner of the Two Thousand Guineas, St Leger, Ascot Gold Cup and other races. As he looked up at his enemy in the Jockey Club stand, Ferguson declared "That fellow with the buttons knows

Eventing at Watergrasshill, County Cork. *Source*: Louise Parkes.

TOP AND LEFT: *Source*: DoA. BELOW: Preparing for the start of the Meath Hunt at Dunsany Castle, Co. Meath. *Source*: Bord Fáilte.

Right : *Harkaway*

Below : *Red Rum* and Tommy Stack ready
to go at the start of the Aintree Grand
National, 2 April 1977.
(Ruth Rogers)

me now, and he won't like spancelling the kicking Irishman, I think."[9]

Another Irishman whom the English authorities had difficulties in spancelling was Boss Croker, the owner of *Orby* whose victory in the Epsom Derby in 1907 gave rise to such a wave of emotion among the Irish. It appeared to matter little that the horse had been bred in England, that its sire was English and that its dam had been bred in America. Rather what mattered with the Irish supporters was that, as he led the horse in at Epsom, Croker was striking a blow against the English establishment, some of whose members gazed disapprovingly down on him from their places in the Jockey Club stand. Even the usual privilege extended to owners of the winning horses on such occasions of meeting the king or queen was denied to him, creating a precedent which was not followed, in the case of another Irish 'rebel' later on in the century.

Croker's choice of the racecourse as the forum in which he could assert what can be seen as nationalist tendencies cannot be taken as an isolated instance. Political concerns and recreations in Ireland have always been closely related. At the *aonach* in early Ireland the overlap between the two found expression in racing activity which, as we have noted, had great significance for the king's reign as well as entertainment value. Such assemblies, we also observed, offered people an opportunity for asserting their identity and this in the changed historical circumstances of the eighteenth and nineteenth centuries helps to explain the nationalist colouring which activities at race meetings could acquire. The Fenians, for instance, used race meetings to conceal their activities in the second half of the nineteenth century, and the monster assemblies organised by the uncrowned king of Ireland, Daniel O'Connell, in the course of his efforts to repeal the Act of Union, have been compared by his biographer Seán Ó Faoláin to a race meeting.[11]

The atmosphere of licence which pervaded fairs and assemblies in Ireland over the centuries sometimes found expression in mistreatment of horses. The 'heroic horsemen' observed by Barrington, for instance, had, as we shall see later, little concern for the horses which bore the brunt of their gambols. Such abuse of horses could acquire for the Irish the added ingredient of defiance of English norms which rendered it not only acceptable but also an essential aspect of the festivities at assemblies. In England the outlook on animals differed significantly from that which was general in Ireland. An interest in scientific history had developed in the seventeenth and eighteenth centuries in England, encouraging an interpretation of man's position as lord of the animals which inclined people to take care of them rather than exploit them. Ireland, a country which was predominantly rural, did not experience a similar revolution in thought and feelings. To the Irish, horses were a means to an end which varied, as we have seen, from the ritual to the practical. Given their attitude of defiance, it is hardly surprising that with Croker and Ferguson the practical tended to overlap with the ritual. Of Croker, his trainer F. F. McCabe wrote:

The role of rebel fitted easily on Croker. Forced to emigrate at a very young age to America with the rest of his family because of the mid 19th-century famine, he had overcome the enormous disadvantages facing an emigrant at that time and succeeded, by fair means or foul, in becoming the boss of Tammany Hall, the organisation which controlled the Democratic Party in New York. Political activity offered the Irish the only channel in cities like New York and Boston to challenge the dominance of the WASP establishment, "where Cabots talk only to Lowells, and Lowells talk only to God". For this, it would appear, Croker was a natural, working successively as barman, blacksmith and professional pugilist in New York on his way up the Democratic Party ladder. When he moved to England in 1903 he once again confronted the establishment. He had brought his horses with him from America but the gates of Newmarket were closed to them. The racing authorities refused him permission to have them trained there. He transferred to Ireland but despite his great successes in racing he was never elected to membership of the Irish Turf Club.[10]

Mayobridge with Tony Mullins up. (*Horseman Photography*).

He wanted his horses always to win and wanted an explanation when they did not . . . And the hard fact that other people's horses were better on the day and at the weights was no explanation to him. His horses had won before and should always be capable of doing so.

Croker's attitude to his horses led to abuses of them and ultimately lost him races. After *Orby* had won the Epsom Derby, for instance, Croker instructed his trainer to prepare him for the St Leger although McCabe was very worried about one of the horse's legs. Despite the trainer's advice and protest Croker insisted on entering the horse for the race. *Orby* broke down and never ran again. Tom Ferguson similarly did not consider that he could afford the luxury of treating his horses well. He was not a rich man. His horses, he considered, had to earn their keep and he was not too scrupulous about the manner in which this was achieved. His treatment of his great horse *Harkaway* was far from sympathetic. On one occasion it pulled up lame at Liverpool having been run two days in succession. Because of Ferguson's frequent cheating in his efforts to make money, his horse was also often given greater weights in handicaps than would normally have been the case, placing a great strain on it.

If his activities placed Ferguson "beyond the Pale" as far as English officialdom was concerned, they did not interfere with his popularity in Ireland, particularly among the nobility and gentry west of the Shannon, many of whom were as hard on their horses as he was. Such gentlemen engaged heavily in steeplechasing and it is to that branch of the sport that we direct our attention as we try to unearth the complex of reasons for the appeal of the racecourse to the ordinary people in Ireland.[12]

STEEPLECHASING RITES

Again we see that English criticism provided the spice to whet the Irish appetite. Steeplechasing was a "bastard amusement" as opposed to the "legitimate sport" of racing on the flat. A late nineteenth-century work on the sport in England commented that "as the sport grew popular it grew inferior; it was indeed the refuge of all outcasts, human and equine, from the legitimate turf". There were other reasons, apart from the criticism levelled at it by the English, why steeplechasing in Ireland should provide a refuge for ordinary Irish people and, in our consideration in an earlier chapter of the importance of the inaccessible terrain in the country as an Otherworld, we have provided the background to this.

Woods and bogs had provided Irish horsemen for centuries with a safe haven from which they could mount attacks on the English. In a difficult environment they felt at home, whereas to their enemies that environment was lawless and forbidding, a 'no go' area. As English rule extended and became more thorough-going in the country, such inaccessible places acquired a quasi-sacred importance, they became the domain of marginal and legendary figures offering resistance. This tradition was a very strong one. We have argued that it traced its roots to mythology which viewed the terrain as the dwelling place of Gods who had been banished

French Tune ridden by T. Murphy, clearing the final flight to win the Mullacash Hurdle at Punchestown, 28 April 1971. (*Horseman Photography*).

from this life to the Otherworld. Steeplechasing, with its natural and difficult terrain over which horsemen galloped, was easily absorbed by this tradition. That terrain became sacred, and like the fairy forts where the gods were believed to dwell, it could not be interfered with. Henry Sargent, an expert on steeplechasing, writing about the nineteenth century remarked that the steeplechase courses "were laid out over a perfectly natural country; not a single sod or stone would be removed nor a fence trimmed, and there was no levelling of places, where the going was bad". Enclosed courses with made-up fences would eventually become a feature of steeplechasing as in England and men like Sargent would look back with nostalgia at the old courses and vent their spleen against course designers such as Thomas Waters for interfering with sacrosanct fences:

> When the old pillars of our sport died or ceased racing, orders went forth to Mr Waters for the pick and spade, the bill-hook and scalping shears to hack and to hew the natural fences, which were sacred from harm in the old men's days.[13]

In the early steeplechase races, the ride across country was a journey into the unknown. Such instructions as there were regarding the line of country to be

Monksfield with Dessie Hughes (left) and *Sea Pigeon* with Jonjo O'Neill, take the last flight in the 1979 Champion Hurdle at Cheltenham, which *Monksfield* won. (*Ruth Rogers*)

followed were of the vaguest kind. Like the horsemen and their test pilot equivalents whom we saw earlier, the steeplechase rider faced, in the main, uncharted territory in which the obstacles to be overcome could be very great and in which the unexpected frequently occurred. The contestants set out for some selected destination but on the journey out and back they were free to choose their own line of country and spectators, unhampered by vigilant officials, could interfere with the progress of a contestant in the interests of their favourite. John Dennis, known as "Black Jack", who was master of the Galway Blazers between 1840 and 1849, was on one occasion subjected to interference during a race. He was pelted with stones and when coming at the last fence—a wall five feet high—he found an ass and cart pulled across it. However, with a prodigious leap he flew the double obstacle. At a race in Kilkenny an open ditch, built up with dry gorse, was set alight and the competitors rode through the flames. Such obstacles and interference exposed the horse and rider to danger but this would appear to have heightened rather than diminished the attraction of the sport for the participants. Some of the dangers were self-imposed. To win a bet, "Black Jack" rode the steeplechase course at Rahasane, which included ten stone walls and 25 other fences, with neither saddle nor bridle, guiding his horse with a cabbage stalk. The absence of saddle and bridle and the primitive method of controlling the horse suggest not only confidence with horses and bravado but a return to the model of the horsemen who until the seventeenth century defied the English. Such heroic feats had an appreciative audience to encourage them. When Allen McDonough, one of the best known gentleman riders in the first half of the nineteenth century, had to ride in a steeplechase in Bandon, Co. Cork without "rudder or compass" due to his bridle snapping, his victory was greeted by the "waving of handkerchiefs from carriage windows and the cheers of everyone who saw him, including the backers of other horses".

The violence which elevated the riders took its toll on the horses. After a four mile steeplechase at Roscommon in 1846 "Black Jack's" horse was found to be stone blind. It was taken for granted that horses in steeplechases would fall at least once during the course of the race. *The Sporting Magazine* of April 1819 reported a steeplechase at Lismore which "was a complete tumble-down race. The winner got four falls; Dandy one; and Thrasher one—in all twelve falls, but nobody killed. Even betting at starting that there would be six falls". For the writer in this case Irish steeplechasing had its own particular character "for which the Paddies are particularly famous, and in which, unless the rider has pluck and his prad goodness, they cannot expect to get well home".[14]

We are suggesting that racing took place in an otherworldly environment in which, as in an earlier age, horsemen exposed themselves and their mounts to abuse. We have illustrated the pattern earlier in a different context, suggesting parallels with test pilots. The horsemen had a desperate need to transcend, to rise above their contemporaries and prove to themselves and others that they stood

Trials of strength between the gentry were frequent occurrences during the eighteenth and nineteenth centuries. Protagonists in many instances opted to settle their affairs with a duel where honour and prestige were involved. The struggle on the racecourse was sometimes carried over and became the pretext for a contest with pistols or swords. When *Black and All Black* was raced against the Earl of March's *Bajazet* for 10,000 guineas the impulse to cheat was too strong for the notorious earl. He instructed his jockey to wear a shotted belt which he could discard on the course, thus reducing his weight. After the match, Sir Ralph Gore, the owner of *Black and All Black*, challenged March to a duel. In this case the contest did not take place. The Earl lost his nerve and made a full apology to Gore.

apart from the general run of humanity. Violence was the means whereby they achieved this. They sought out a difficult environment where there would be obstacles which would pose great challenges to them, and they were prepared to do violence to themselves and to their means of transport in order to overcome the obstacles in their way. In steeplechasing there was the added factor of competition for the single-combat warriors who engaged in it. Steeplechasing originated in the 'pounding matches' of the seventeenth and eighteenth centuries when rivals used to jump their way across country until one or other had been 'pounded' to exhaustion. The ritual has been described as follows:

> On the appointed day, accompanied by their friends, their grooms and by half the countryside, they would ride to some very difficult piece of country, and then each in turn had the choice of a fence over which the other must follow or admit defeat. Large sums were often ventured on these ordeals, and in the effort to 'pound' an opponent the most dreadful obstacles were attempted.

The English made efforts to curb the 'pounding matches'. To them such contests reduced the participants to 'lawlessness'. There was also always the danger that in the heady atmosphere of the sporting field Catholic and Protestant might forget their divisions. An act was passed in 1739 prohibiting matches and making it illegal to run for any plate of less than £120 in value. Matches however continued to be held in spite of this.[15]

Violence and competition found outlets in other activities which were also related to the struggle on the steeplechase or 'pounding match' course. Matches often arose as a result of wagers made in the heat of a moment when "the merits of horses were being discussed, [and] some favourite owner of a great jumper would challenge a rival sportsman to the test". Gambling, as we have seen, was a highly competitive activity which had a long tradition in Ireland and which, in the eighteenth and nineteenth centuries, commanded a great appeal among gentry and peasantry alike. Violence also found an outlet in abductions. Among the upper classes those who engaged in steeplechasing were frequently from the hunting fraternity and it may be suspected that, among this fraternity, "a predatory hunt for the favours of a country girl" was often seen as an extension of the 'chase'. This is suggested by marriage customs—in existence well into the nineteenth century—which linked sexual conquest with horses and more specifically with a conquering huntsman. In common with peoples the world over, a bride was considered, in popular thinking, as the quarry and language usage reflects this. In Co. Donegal the word to describe a marriageable girl was 'insealga' which means literally 'fit to be hunted'. After a marriage ceremony, as the wedding party approached within a couple of miles of the bride or groom's home, the young men, mounted on horses, commenced racing, often heading at a gallop across country, clearing obstacles on the way. A bottle of whiskey was given to the man who reached the house first, and this was drunk on the spot. The empty bottle was then given to the bride who, in the manner of a ceremonial launching of a ship, had to break it against a stone. The number of splinters determined her fertility. In its original form, no doubt, the race itself was a struggle between prospective suitors, the prize being the bride. Abductions which were common among the upper classes and enjoyed considerable popular and upper-class support were, it would appear, the more violent counterpart of this. Such abductions were frequently carried out in the eighteenth and nineteenth centuries by force and on horseback with the chief protagonist being egged on by his followers. On such occasions, however, the proficiency of the abducted girl in horsemanship might be of assistance to her. A daughter of Thomas FitzGerald who became Knight of Glin in 1775 was abducted by one of the Brownes near Rathkeale in Co. Limerick. On his way to Rathkeale, Browne's saddle girth broke and while he was fixing it the girl jumped on the horse and returned to Glin. In respect of such activities the Glins were, however, in the main, more sinning than sinned against.[16]

Caroline Beasley, now training in England, with her horse *Eliogarty*, and Sheamie O'Callaghan from Newmarket-on-Fergus, Co. Clare. Caroline, with *Eliogarty*, was the first woman to ride a winner at the Cheltenham Festival. Her victory in the Foxhunter Chase there in 1983 was greeted by scenes of Irish jubilation reminiscent of that surrounding *Arkle*'s victories over *Mill House* nearly a decade earlier. *Eliogarty*, a very successful hunter chaser, was bred by Phil Sweeney from Thurles, Co. Tipperary, who also bred the 1983 Champion Hurdle winner, *Gaye Brief*, *Lucky Brief* and *Quare Times*. He was bought for Caroline, who had come over to Ireland from England, by trainer John Hassett from Quin, Co. Clare.
(Ruth Rogers)

The Glins provide us with a good illustration of a proud Irish family asserting itself and prosecuting its quarrels in the manner we have been suggesting. The family had its roots in the Geraldine past and could therefore lay claim to an honoured place among the gentry of the south-west even in the nineteenth century. A cousin of the Knight of Glin, for instance, took part in the first steeplechase in Co. Kerry which occurred in 1830. 'Cracked Jack' who became Knight in 1854 also took part in matches. He was an excellent horseman but a fall from a horse when he was young had left him eccentric. In this respect he was not alone among the gentry. A rival of the Knight was Colonel Henry Kitchener, father of the future field marshal, who reputedly insisted on one occasion when he was out hunting with his son that the young man remount his horse and continue hunting although he had just broken his arm in a fall. His harshness extended to his tenants and, as we shall see, this was guaranteed to bring out the pugilistic strain in the Knight. Many centuries after the Geraldines, the ancestors of the Glins, had established themselves in Ireland, other families arriving in the country from Britain had to face the same problems of adjusting to the inhospitable nature of the country's terrain, some of it inaccessible. Many of these families conformed to the way of life in the areas where they settled in order to survive. Some even tried to outdo their Irish counterparts in the extravagant lifestyle which they adopted, a lifestyle characterised by hunting and hospitality.

There was therefore a close link between the character of the landscape and the competitive nature of the sports in which the people engaged. The west of Ireland is a case in point. Of all parts of the country the west was the least accessible. Visitors who crossed the Shannon in the eighteenth century and ventured into parts of Connacht where there were few roads and many places difficult to reach had the sensation that they were entering another world where the nobility and gentry were a law unto themselves. But it was a world where Protestant and Catholic enjoyed good relations with each other. The difficulty of the terrain may have been influential in this respect. It prepared them, indeed whetted their appetite, for the 'rough country' of the steeplechase course where all obstacles could be overcome and divisions buried in a ritual show of violence. In any case it was from the gentry of this part of the country that the stimulus for 'pounding matches' and steeplechasing mainly came. It is necessary therefore to consider that gentry more closely in our attempt to arrive at an understanding of the people's liking for the racecourse.[17]

VIOLENCE AT THE RACECOURSE

One of the remarkable families in the west of Ireland was the Martins of Co. Galway. The family ruled an immense territory of more than half a million acres in the more inaccessible parts of western Connacht and Connemara. When Maria Edgeworth travelled to visit their castle at Ballinahinch in 1834 the horses of her carriage had to be unharnessed several times to drag them out of the bogs. The Martins were extremely combative. Having acquired their possessions by dispossessing the O'Flahertys, they become embroiled in a running feud with their old enemies and pitched battles were a frequent occurrence. Single-combat was a feature of some of these battles. Richard Martin, for instance, generally fought the O'Flaherty champion, Éamonn Láidir, with a sword while mounted on horseback like a mediaeval knight. His great grandson, Richard also, an excellent horseman, achieved fame through his duelling feats which merited him the nickname of 'Hairtrigger Dick'. His most famous duel was with another eccentric western nobleman, George Robert FitzGerald, a man who used to allow a bear to ride in his carriage with him and who hunted at night time, by the light of torches, in order to avoid the society of those whom he disliked.

What is significant from our point of view about the battles of the Martins and other families is the effect which they had on their tenants. These battles seem to have acted as a catalyst to violent impulses among them. Colonel Eyre, commander of the Galway Militia, wrote to Dublin Castle in 1747 that Robert Martin could bring to the town of Galway in twenty four hours "800 villains as desperate and as absolutely at his devotion as Cameron of Lochiel". Tenants, armed frequently with sticks, were mobilised into armies by the O'Flahertys and the Martins as well as other landed families such as the Frenches and the Taaffes in order to engage each other in battle. Wagers were sometimes placed on the outcome of these battles or faction fights at races and fairs in the eighteenth and nineteenth centuries.[18]

Such fights have to be seen as an expression of the excitement which characterised all assemblies in Ireland from the earliest times. Mr and Mrs Hall who visited Ireland in the 1840s saw faction fighting as "a necessary epilogue to a fair" and the diarist Amhlaoibh Ó Súilleabháin treated those fairs which did not feature fighting almost as curiosities. Violence therefore was seen as an inevitable consequence of people coming together for an assembly and when it did break out it followed a predetermined pattern:

> Oft have I seen two landlords at a fair,
> Where tenants with their sheep and cows repair
> A quarrel first betwixt themselves erect
> Then urge their clans to end their fierce debate.

This ritualised violence, although it could result in many injuries and deaths, did not attract the immediate censure of the authorities. Some of them seemed to have appreciated that it provided a useful outlet for feelings which, if not expressed through the rites of faction fighting at an assembly, might be directed against themselves. Local authorities, for instance, were suspected of conniving in the precipitation of the savage fighting at Balleagh Races in 1834. Races such as those at Mullingar in the mid 19th century were frequently the location for fights, for at them excitement and violence found a ready focus. Harry Sargent writing in 1894 noted the excitement which pervaded the steeplechasing course:

> Every fence and vantage point was thronged with frieze-coated farmers, their sons and labourers. Within a ten mile radius of the course not one of them could be found at home, except those too ill or too old. Wherever was fence more formidable than the other there would congregate the crowd in greatest numbers. Every man evinced the keenest interest in the sport, which was intensified when a neighbour's horse ran and if he won the excitement amounted to a frenzy.

What he does not mention here is the active part which, as we have noted, spectators sometimes took in ensuring that their favourite would win. This involvement of the spectators could frequently take violent forms. The correspondent of the *Sporting Magazine* reported in February 1833 from Nenagh for a mainly English readership:

> At these meetings the peasantry assemble in crowds, and generally have a favourite into whose cause they enter heart and mind. Riding a Steep-chase is on *your* side of the water considered to be a sufficiently dangerous thing per se; but here a man has to run the gauntlet at the risk of martyrdom—to put himself in the way of becoming a second St Stephen or, in plain language, being stoned to death. These self-elected and active partisans stick at nothing, and are no respecters of persons.

The partisanship and violence exhibited by Irish crowds at home could be transferred abroad, as observers at Cheltenham today may appreciate. In 1891, for example, *Come-away*, ridden and trained by Harry Beasley, beat *Cloister*, ridden by Captain Roddy Owen, in a controversial finish to the Grand National at Aintree. After the race Owen objected and the Irish crowd almost stormed the weigh room. Forty years previously *Mathew*, an Irish horse named after the Apostle of Temperance, Fr Mathew, had been the first Irish horse to win at Aintree and his success set off an orgy of celebration and drinking on both sides of the Irish sea and in the packets returning to Ireland. After the Widgers had won the Grand National at Aintree with their horse *Wild Man from Borneo* in 1895 they returned as heroes to Waterford where the whole community celebrated in style. Bands played, the ships in the harbour were bedecked with flags, bonfires blazed for days and whiskey flowed liberally.[19]

Because of the lack of control over steeplechasing in Ireland it was relatively easy for horses and their riders to be interfered with by members of the crowd. The crowds were not separated from the action on the field by stands and enclosures as in more recent times. Out in the country, far from the view of such stewards as there were, holes could be knocked in fences for the benefit of a favourite horse or one of the spectators on horseback could give it a lead over a fence. The *Sporting Magazine* correspondent mentions how a stranger taking part in a steeplechase in Limerick hit on a stratagem for turning the tables on the spectators who were ranged against him. At the start of the race he changed from his jockey's kit into an overcoat and hat. He then took the lead in the race calling on the spectators at each fence who were armed with stones to make way as the favourite was coming after him ahead of the rest of the field. Thinking that he supported the same cause as themselves the spectators allowed the stranger through unharmed and he won the race.

The leadership exercised by returning heroes has been the theme of a previous chapter and here we are suggesting that the gentry who went steeplechasing travelled to an Otherworld from where such a return could be possible. Clearly their character appealed to the ordinary people. Faction fighting provides us with a clue as to why this was so. Long after the gentry had withdrawn from the leadership of this fighting it continued at fairs and races. One example of it which was not gentry-led was the faction fighting which took place between the Caravats and the Shanavests in Munster in the early nineteenth century. What provoked this was the quarrel between two flamboyant characters, Hanley and Connors. The struggle between these two 'hard men' who, with their taste for violence, had much of the character of single-combat warriors, gripped the popular imagination and ensured that their followers would continue their battles and emulate their violence. The popular hero, it seems, was the one who not only used violence but also relished it.

Elizabeth Bowen, writing of her ancestor, Henry Cole Bowen, noted that despite his Cromwellian ancestry he enjoyed the affection of the people. She attributed this in part to Henry, who, as we shall see, was addicted to horses, "palpably having a good time". Robert, her grandfather, though in some ways dreaded, was popular also because he was a 'hard rider'. The affection in which the family was held among the tenants was seen when Elizabeth's father, Henry, got married. On his arrival with his bride at the gates of the family home in Co. Cork, Bowen Court, the tenants took the horses from the shafts of the carriage and drew it up the avenue. Bernard Fitzpatrick's picture of a typical warrior of mid 19th-century steeplechasing, Lord Clonmel, who served as Master of the Kildares in 1852 suggests much the same appeal as that exercised by the Bowens:

> Old habitués of Punchestown will remember Lord Clonmel as with long thong whip in hand, dressed in the scarlet uniform of the Kildare Hunt Club, and mounted on his favourite white horse, he cantered up and down the rails, cheerily rating the rustics with whom, as with those of his own rank, he was an especial favourite.

In a practical way many of the hard-riding gentry justified the affection in which their tenants held them. They not only 'spent' but 'defended'. One of those who, particularly in his youth, as we shall see, had been a 'hell raiser' on horseback was Lord Waterford. A writer, after his death in 1859, expressed regret that stories of "the mad exploits of his youth, when with other kindred spirits 'he heard the chimes of midnight', of his steeplechases and single combats . . ." had received more attention than the efforts which he made to relieve the distress of his tenants during the Famine years. One of the companions of his youth was an excellent horseman and a landlord also, George Henry Moore. He was notable among landlords for his kindness to the starving people of Co. Mayo during the great hunger. When his horse *Corunna* won the Chester Cup in 1847, for instance, his tenants and the poorest people living around Moore Hall received one thousand pounds from the ten thousand pounds prize. Moore used the balance of the money to ease his debts.

Likewise at Bowen Court there was a soup kitchen offering relief to the people in the neighbourhood. But perhaps the most significant example, from our point of view, of 'hard riding' gentry who defended their tenants was the Glins from Co. Limerick. During the famine of 1739-1740 the wife of the then Knight had even gone cattle-raiding in order to feed the starving people. John Fraunceis FitzGerald, Ridire na mBan, to whom we have referred, liked to socialise with his tenants and when famine struck in 1822 and again in the middle of the century he showed his concern in a practical way. A poorhouse was built in Glin and the Knight himself personally supervised the soup kitchens during the Great Famine. His son, 'Cracked Jack', as "good a man as any in Ireland to hounds" never forgot, despite his eccentricity, the tenants who in centuries past had been the followers of the Knights of Glin. He consistently acted in their defence against middlemen or landlords attempting to evict them.[20]

Death wagons in Co. Cork.

MEDIAEVAL EXCESSES OF HORSEMEN

With the Glin family the continuity with the mediaeval past was a fact of history. With other families such as those of planters like the Bowens this was not so, but the deference in which landlords were held and the reassurance which the ordinary people got from observing them rising to the challenge of the steeplechase or of the hunting field was mediaeval. Families like the Martins ruled their tenants absolutely but in a mediaeval world, as we have seen, tenants benefited from the protection which the landlord's power offered. Maria Edgeworth, who had an opportunity to observe the Martins and other Irish families at first hand, in her novel *Ormond* gives us a picture of the start of a hunt which graphically illustrates the relationship between the ordinary people and their leaders on horseback. As Cornelius O'Shane, known as King Corny, sets off to hunt he is followed on foot by an adoring mass of peasants and tenantry.

The connection between hunting and steeplechasing was intimate. Hunting, for instance, was frequently one of the entertainments which were available during the many week-long race meetings, as at Ballinasloe where foxes and hares were hunted each morning. It was the foxhunting fraternity, particularly in the west of Ireland, which nurtured the sport of steeplechasing. Challenges were often issued at hunt dinners "when the punch was smoking, spirits waxing high, and the merits of horses were being discussed". The first "regular steeplechase", held in Ireland in 1803, arose as a result of a conversation at such a dinner. We read that it was "a sweepstake with added money of a hogshead of claret, a pike of port and a quarter cask of rum". Particularly associated with an addiction to hunting was the practice of feasting and drinking. In keeping with many of his class in the 18th century, Colonel Cosby from Stradbally in Co. Laois who was descended from a Lincolnshire gentleman who fought in Ireland in the sixteenth century, would hunt "from morning to night" and "entertained lavishly". In October 1843, a steeplechase called, for reasons which will become clear, the New Melton Stakes, was run at the Marquis of Waterford's course at Curraghmore and the evening before it took place Waterford entertained 120 guests to dinner. Included among them were well known horsemen like the Third Earl of Clonmel, Valentine Maher, George Henry Moore and the First Marquis of Clanrickarde. Towards the end of the century the trainer Henry Linde and John Gubbins, the owner of the English Derby winners *Ardpatrick* and *Galteemore*, rode a private match over Henry Linde's schooling ground at Eyrefield Lodge on the Curragh for 100 guineas each, celebrating the stakes in whiskey and champagne.[21]

The close link between hunting and lavish hospitality recalls the mediaeval practice of coyne and livery by which lords availed themselves in a festive manner of free entertainment and hunting. We can speculate that lords in the eighteenth and nineteenth centuries harboured an unconscious desire to revert to the customs

Racing at Cheltenham, 1986. *(Gerry Cranham)*

of mediaeval times. Apocalyptic notions and ideas of a golden age returning were, as we have seen, certainly in the air and the commitment to drinking in hunting and racing circles would probably have fortified these. One balladeer who would have been heard at races and fairs promised in his song that he and his listeners would "daily drink beer" in 1825, the year after Pastorini's prophecies were expected to be fulfilled. About a century earlier people who attended the races around the Commons of Armagh, we are told, kept their spirits up "by consuming their liquour, the chief manufacture of the place". In Killarney also, it would appear, consumption of drink was high during the races there for when Lord Kenmare was forced to suppress them due to disorder among the peasants he had to compensate the local publicans for their loss of income. Similarly many contemporary poets, not content to look forward only to the drinking bouts which would be a feature of the reign of the Deliverer, spent their nights drinking his health and hoped that daylight might not come. A similar emotional investment in idleness and drinking was a feature of the hunting gentry. Barrington in his memoirs described how the hunting fraternity shut themselves up in a hunting lodge on St Stephen's Day with their hounds and fiddler for an orgy, lasting seven days, of drinking, feasting and cock fighting—a sport which was popular among the hunting gentry. He remarks how they closed the windows in order to shut out the light.

The reason for this uninterrupted match of what was called "hard going" was that the sporting gentlemen involved knew that the frost and snow might prevent "their usual occupation of the chace" and had made alternative arrangements. There was a certain logic to this. Given that hunting and its associated pleasures were seen as the Good Life, it was inevitable that they would dominate the lives of those involved. When not on the hunting field many of those who indulged in the sport would spend their time either recreating, somewhat in the manner of Barrington's friends, their hunting enjoyment or preparing, no doubt also over claret, for the next hunting adventure. Hunting became a way of life, akin as we have suggested, to warfare. It was totally absorbing and young men who wished to participate had to be initiated.[22] (*See marginal note.*)

One of the most remarkable of the group of Irishmen at Melton in the early part of the nineteenth century was the Marquis of Waterford who in his more mature years was not only to prove a careful and kindly landlord, as we have noted, but also one of the pillars of Irish racing, first as a rider and later as an owner and administrator. Dubbed the 'Wild Marquis' at Melton where he rode harder than most, he gave rise through his exploits to the phrase "painting the town red". On one occasion, he managed to get his horse to jump a five-barred gate in a Melton drawing room with "a blazing fire staring him in the face" for a bet of 100 guineas.

When he returned to Ireland he was determined to make Tipperary into the finest hunting country in the world, drawing on his Melton experience for the programme of covert-planting which he implemented. In 1841 he purchased a pack of hounds

Initiation gambols for young gentry entering 18th- or 19th-century society, where a premium was placed on combat skills, inevitably took a violent turn. Barrington tells how he and some of his fellow students from Trinity College Dublin were in the habit of driving about the city on dark nights in coaches, breaking windows of all the houses which they passed with coins flung from the speeding vehicles. He also tells us that he was initiated "into a number of accomplishments" appropriate to a "young sportsman". These included "riding, drinking, dancing, carousing, hunting, shooting, fishing, fighting, racing, cockfighting". In his novel *Charles O'Malley*, Lever wrote that a young man in the west of Ireland had to "ride boldly to hounds, to shoot, to swim the Shannon and to drive a four-in-hand". Some of the young nobility in the 19th century went even further than this, however, in order to cut their teeth. At Melton Mowbray, the fashionable centre of English hunting, we find young men making their mark who would later be prominent on both the hunting and racing fields in Ireland. The racing correspondent Charles Apperley, known as Nimrod, illustrates for us the character of the hunting field at Melton. Coming home from the hunt, the young bloods, he tells us, engaged in 'larking': "One of the party holds up his hat which is the signal for the start, and putting their horses' heads in the direction for Melton, away they go and stop at nothing till they get there."

Another of the intrepid Irish riders at Melton was George Henry Moore, a member of an independent Catholic family from Mayo whom we have already noted. His brother Augustus had met and defeated Lord Clanmorris in a celebrated 'pounding match' at Ballyglass but shortly afterwards, in the Grand National of 1845, he was killed in a fall from his horse. George who was one of the most successful steeplechase riders of his time was nearly killed also when riding one of Lord Waterford's horses at Cahir in 1843 but he survived, retiring from racing four years later to become MP for Co Mayo.[23]

and he kennelled them at Rockwell (now a well known school) which he leased as his hunting lodge. Something of his reckless youth remained with him on the hunting field. It was, for instance, a fall during a hunt which eventually led to his death. He hunted his pack at night as well as by day, and on one occasion, when his hounds killed a fox outside Thomastown Castle at night, the huntsman, Johnny Ryan, felt that he had been lucky to have only four falls.

Also at Melton about the same time as Waterford, was Valentine Maher, described by Nimrod as a "brilliant performer with hounds". He was even considered to be superior in this regard to either Waterford or Squire George Osbaldson who wrote that on many occasions "he and I have been the only two remaining with hounds at the end of a long day". The Mahers, an old Tipperary family, had a long association with hunting and racing. Valentine's cousin Matthew from Ballinkeele won the Aintree Grand National with *Frigate* in 1889 and, one year later, the Irish Derby with *Kentish Fire*.

A way of life into which young men were initiated and in which they might lose their lives could impose its own tyranny. Elizabeth Bowen's grandfather, Robert, was a great rider to hounds and all his friendships had their basis on the hunting

Commandant William Mullins jumping the last fence on *Charleville* at the 1956 Olympic Games in Stockholm. (*Associated Press*)

Difficulties at the Puissance Wall, RDS Horse Show, 1963. (*G. A. Duncan*)

field. Hunting activities proliferated around Bowen Court, the home of the Bowens, and two of his sons shared his passion for hunting with him. One of them was even killed by a horse. The eldest son, Henry, Elizabeth's father, however, stood apart from this group. Though forced to ride, he was, much to his father's annoyance, apathetic about horses. Once free from his father's authority, he never rode again. Aroon St Charles, the heroine of Molly Keane's novel *Good Behaviour*, is afflicted by a similar tyranny and it is through her sense of alienation from a community which saw hunting as a duty and fear of horses as a betrayal that we learn the extent to which the hunting field intruded on life.

The life of Aroon's father, an Anglo-Irish country gentleman, was dominated by horses. His son, whom he loved, was "admirable to him in the deepest sense. He rode beautifully, and with judgement and courage. He was all that Papa's friends most approved and all that Papa wished for in a son." Into her father's world, where "getting left behind in a hunt" was the equivalent of deprivation, Aroon does not fit easily. At the balls she notes the preoccupation of the men with hunting and their façade of courage:

> Never a heart-warming admission of cowardice, or hatred of a horse. No truth that could betray the myth. When I was twenty foxhunting was Wholly Holy and everybody was an apostle or a disciple. If you were a doubting disciple, so much the worse for you—keep quiet and show willing.[24]

Joe Widger.

For those within the hunting fraternity, the competitive forces to which we referred ensured that the preoccupation with hunting and hospitality would, of necessity, exclude nearly every other pursuit from life. Lord Buttevant from Co. Cork, according to George Edward Pakenham, drank enormous quantities of claret and "his abilities . . . reached little further than a pack of hounds, or horses, and such like . . ." Maria Edgeworth, describing the manners of the upper classes in Ireland in the 18th century, refers to the long tedious dinners, when everyone ate and drank to excess, and the conversation of the men dealt solely with horses and dogs. Edward Power, a magistrate in Co. Tipperary and known to the Tipperary bloods as "Beau Power", was described by his daughter, the Countess of Blessington, as very fond of "dogs, horses, wine and revelry, besides being very improvident and inattentive to all affairs of business".

The organisation of hunting in Ireland encouraged incessant entertainment. Until the development of subscription packs in the middle of the eighteenth century most packs which were followed on horseback were owned privately by wealthy individuals who invited their sporting acquaintances to hunt with them, dine and stay in their houses for as long as a week at a time. On hunting days little room was left for other pursuits. Arthur Weldon describes the regimen of hunting at Bishopscourt where the powerful Ponsonby family to which he was related by marriage had its seat and elaborate hunting establishment: "I went to bed last night at one of ye clock,

Humanity Dick Martin. *(RSPCA Library)*

was on horseback this morning at four, rid eight miles before daybreak, hunted a fox afterwards, came back afterwards here to dinner, and rid acoursing this afternoon till nightfall, and I thank God I cannot say I am much the worse for it."[25]

Of Humanity Dick Martin it was said that he could fight a duel before breakfast, ride all day to hounds over six-foot walls and entertain lavishly in the evening. In Co. Limerick the Glins were at the centre of a circle of hunting families who engaged in a wide range of social activities including balls, tennis and sailing parties. About the middle of the 18th century nearly all the gentry owned a pack of hounds. Indeed, we are told by the Reverend George Gubbins that his grandfather Joseph "kept three packs of hounds and no end of hunters". This meant that hunting was always available: "If the Buck Hounds did not take the field either the Fox Hounds or Harriers were ready at the call or taste of the hunters."

Stables built at Rallahine Castle, Co. Clare.

Within twenty miles of the Galtee Mountains in nearby Co. Tipperary there were 24 packs of buck hounds, "each pack being kept by the owner of a deerpark". Hunting parties were frequently very large, entailing large expenditure on entertainment. At Adare Manor the Countess of Dunraven wrote of her park being "overrun by the whole of the country of Limerick" in October 1826, and it was reported that seventeen brothers from the Massy family, famous for its foxhunting, used to appear together at meets of the Limerick Hounds.

The incessant hunting had an inevitable impact on families' fortunes. In Rathkeale lived Gerald Blennerhassett whose family was related by marriage several times to the Glin family. He himself was married into the Massy family and was the first Master of the Limerick Hounds. His hospitality, it was said, "knew no bounds" but his finances did not measure up to his lifestyle. His house had all the appearance of lack of care and resources. Provisions for the table were however the best:

> Chairs with broken legs, and rickety cabinets loaded with priceless china, never cared for, and never dusted . . . the best of everything that was going, a good bottle of claret after dinner, which we at once whipped off the table the moment the ladies disappeared and replaced by a bowl of steaming whiskey punch. The one thing always lacking was 'money', but that did not seem to affect life.

By the end of the 18th century the residence of the Eyres in Co. Galway, Eyrecourt, was showing signs of neglect. Lord Eyre, a descendant of a Cromwellian officer, though wealthy, lived, we are told, "according to the style of the country, with more hospitality than elegance." He spent most of his afternoons sipping claret.[26]

The unpaid bills are a recurring theme in Molly Keane's *Good Behaviour*. For the Glin family they even led to an Act of Parliament in 1801 to force the Knight to pay his debts. The lavish spending of the Bowens led to part of their estate being sold in 1788. Eventually court action was required to try and straighten out the financial mess. If the financial difficulties of families was a factor in the dilapidated condition of some of their houses it was not allowed to interfere with their stable building. Dineley's sketches around 1680 already indicate the upper class preference in this regard—the stables were more modern than the dwelling houses. Horse racing was coming to the fore and by the end of the century there were on the Curragh "several fine horses kept thereabouts for the race in stables built on purpose." A century later, when Henry Bowen was building his residence at Bowen Court he considered the stables so much an integral part of the house that he had cut stone saved for them. The proper housing of his children alone took precedence over that of his

Pat Hogan out with the Co. Limerick Foxhounds. *(Ruth Rogers)*

horses. Meanwhile at Eyrecourt, while the dwelling house was already falling into neglect, magnificent stables were built, at the very front of the residence. Few properties could aspire to the magnificence of the stables at Slane Castle which had been designed by Capability Brown in the Gothic style or the large stables at Curraghmore, the residence of the Marquis of Waterford, but most country houses in the 18th and 19th centuries had stable-blocks of some kind. It was not until the Land League troubles of the 1880s that the period of extravagant stable-building came to an end.

The concern to provide stabling on a grand scale suggests that landlords kept large numbers of horses. Since the mid 17th century horse breeding had been a focus for investment among the landed classes. Even King James had stud farms in Ireland. People like Colonel Daniel O'Brien from Co. Clare realised that with the popularity of racing, there were profits to be made from breeding. "I began to be the greatest breeder of horses in the king's dominions," he wrote, "for I keep about my house 16,000 acres for my mares, colts and deers". At about the same time Sir William Temple, a diplomat in King Charles' service, was trying to encourage the breeding of better horses in the country by having the king sponsor plates for racing in Ireland. Given the country's excellent soil, horses which were, he believed, a 'Drug' in Ireland could be improved 'to a commodity'. The 18th century saw a continuation of efforts to upgrade the quality of horses in the country with owners like Sir Edward O'Brien importing the best blood available. On his estate near Newmarket on Fergus in Co. Clare O'Brien had built a racetrack and, until his death in 1765, he maintained there a very large breeding and racing stud.[27]

In Young's view the Irish landlords' preference for "great numbers of horses and servants" was principally responsible for the great drain on their resources. Henry Cole Bowen, for instance, in the mid 18th century, insisted on having servants and horses in such numbers as he considered appropriate to his status. In his stables at Bowen Court there were sixteen horses and, despite worsening financial circumstances in the second half of the 19th century, the family managed to keep their stables full, catering for the continuous round of hunting and of carriage journeys to make social calls. Also in the second half of the 19th century, the Fifth Marquis of Waterford had thirteen hunters in his stables for himself in addition to those which he kept for his wife, twenty-one horses for his hunt servants, horses for the carriages and some young horses.

One of the most outstanding examples of the damage to a fortune due to an addiction to horses relates to the Second Marquis of Donegall who was born in 1769. His father, Arthur Chichester, an absentee, was the greatest landlord of his day in Ireland. He owned one quarter of a million acres of land, including that on which Belfast was built. Despite this his son was in continuous debt, much of it due to his gambling, racing and hunting interests. His debts to gamblers and horse dealers while his father was still alive amounted to £40,000. Brought up in England, his

Horses in the case of many of the landlords in Ireland did not augment resources, however, but proved a great drain on them. Families like the Glins may have bred horses but their main concern was not with business but with pleasure. The quantity of unproductive horses in the country particularly struck Arthur Young. "The number of horses may almost be esteemed a satire on common sense," he commented, expressing surprise that landlords, in a country like Ireland where it was possible to live well cheaply, were able to "spend their incomes" with such ease. Giles Eyre, the celebrated Master of the Galway Blazers from 1791 to 1829, immortalised by Lever in his novel *Charles O'Malley*, and a competitor in many pounding matches, afforded demonstration, if demonstration were needed, of how this could be achieved. His stables carried a complement of thirty or forty horses, and by the time of his death, he had nearly exhausted his large fortune and his estates were heavily encumbered.

Top : Huntsmen and hounds from the Ward Union, survey the Double Bank, RDS Horse Show, 1968. *(G. A. Duncan)*

Bottom left : The late Lord Daresbury out with the Limerick Hunt, of which he was Master. *(Ruth Rogers)*

Bottom right : The late Billy Filgate out with the Louth Hunt. *(Ruth Rogers)*

improvidence eventually forced him to flee from his creditors to Ireland in 1802 where he remained for the rest of his life. His spending on horses did not abate. In 1806 one of his creditors claimed that he kept a great number of "horses and carriages attended by a suitable retinue of servants". At his house at Ormeau in Belfast he had eight coach horses, two hacks and a hunter together with six coaches and carriages of various kinds and in various stages of repair. Also at Ormeau he had a 'race-course' built so that he could prepare his horses for the annual meeting at the Maze racecourse. The expenses of his establishment greatly outweighed his winnings however. In one year, for instance, the bill for forage from one provision merchant alone came to £1,600. Ormeau was not the only one of his houses with ample stables. At Fisherwick Lodge in Doagh he kennelled the hounds for the local hunt and kept a great number of horses.

His horses, hunting and entertaining proved a great drain on Donegall's resources, eventually forcing him to grant leases in perpetuity on his land—a measure of his desperation at a time of rising land values when landlords were generally careful to grant short leases. The short term gains to the Marquis, achieved at the price of future income, were sums equivalent to millions of pounds today. These Donegall proceeded to lavish on his hunting interests. Fisherwick Lodge was equipped with more expensive stabling and kennels and the supporters of the flourishing Doagh Hunt were entertained royally.

A feature of the Marquis' career and decline was his association with the O'Kelly family which had built its fortune on horses. In the 1720s Denis O'Kelly, a young illiterate who was skilled with horses, had gone to England from Ireland in the hope of making his career on the fringes of the sporting world. He was a resourceful gambler and adventurer and had soon secured enough finances, through a marriage to a leading brothel keeper, to purchase a remarkable horse called *Eclipse* which remained unbeaten from its first race, the Epsom Derby in 1769, until it was retired for an equally illustrious career at stud. The horse gave O'Kelly, known as 'Colonel' on account of his association with the Middlesex Militia, fame and fortune but it did not give him the status which he craved. He never realised his hope of being elected to the English Turf Club. His son Philip, however, became closely associated with the young Marquis while he was recklessly indulging his passion for racing in England. Philip seems to have regarded Donegall, who sent his mares to the O'Kelly stud, as fair game for his moneymaking adventures. He succeeded in persuading him to enter into unfavourable bonds for the purchase of horses. These bonds later provided O'Kelly's son, Dennis, with a pretext for seizing the contents of the Marquis' house in Belfast.[28]

STATUS SYMBOLS

Right : While stagecoaches connected Ireland's major cities by the end of the eighteenth century, methods of transport remained primitive, especially in remote western areas where roads were little more than dirt tracks.

Not all the landlords who, through horses, became associated with those beneath their rank were as ill-served as the luckless Donegall who, on his death, had squandered much of what his father had bequeathed to him. There were, however, many in Ireland who, like the emigrant O'Kelly, saw horses and horse-related activities as the means whereby they could aspire to the social standing of landlords. One index of status was the carriages which the gentry used for travel.

Travel on horseback had once been the only mode of conveyance in Ireland, a situation which was reflected in the toast 'Tottenham in his boots', commemorating

Colonel Tottenham who entered the Parliament building in Dublin for an important vote on one occasion in his riding boots straight from a 100-mile ride from New Ross. However, with the great improvement in roads, carriages were used extensively. One of the spurs to the road building activities of the 18th century which effected these improvements was the gentry's interest in travel for social purposes. Spas attracted many of them particularly when, as at Ballinspellin in Co. Kilkenny, the hunting was also good. Near Bowen Court was the Bath of Ireland, Mallow, famous for its spas and frequent race meetings during the summer months. Dublin was also a very important social centre in the 18th century. The very large and distinctive gentry which hunted together in Galway had their own drinking club in Dublin and during the social season transferred to that city. Barrington recounts how his father, a country gentleman, under pressure from his wife, a Galway lady,

Left : A Ringsend coach.

purchased a house in Merrion Square, "made up new wardrobes for the servants; got a fierce three-cocked hat for himself; and removed his establishment (the hounds excepted) to the metropolis of Ireland".

Before the advent of the Bianconi coaches in the early 19th century such travel was the prerogative of the wealthy, a factor which, no doubt, enhanced its popularity. Arthur Young estimated that it would require £500 a year to keep "a carriage, 4 horses, 3 men, 3 maids, a good table, a wife, 3 children and a nurse." Included in the expense of keeping a carriage was the tax which was levied on it. Towards the end of the century the exclusiveness of carriage ownership was revealed by the hearth money returns which indicated that out of 700,000 houses only about 3000 had a four-wheeled carriage. Only a few hundred households employed four or more manservants and had two or more carriages. The number of carriages was, however, on the increase. In the 1740s there were only four in the vicinity of Limerick city but thirty to forty years later according to Young the numbers were "183 four-wheeled carriages, 115 two-wheeled ditto".

Bianconi cars at Gorey, Co. Wexford.
(G. A. Duncan)

Left : The Bianconi routes, 1815-1877. The decade in which each of the routes was established is shown and the inset map indicates the position in 1877, when the 'bians' had become feeders to the railways. (*From* Bianconi, *Watson*)

Right : Hotel transport (Brake), Gap of Dunloe, Killarney, late 1940s. (*G. A. Duncan*)

Carriages were a status symbol and in the competition which took place between wealthy families no expense was spared in providing a long train, liveried servants and postillions. Mrs Martin, whose family divided its time between Dublin and Galway, always travelled to Dublin in style with a carriage of four and liveried outriders. In Dublin, according to Barrington, his "good and well-bred mother (for such she was) had her Galway pride revived and gratified; the green coach de ceremonie was regilt and regarnished, and four black horses, with two postillions and a sixteen-stone footman completed her equipage." The Cosby family, already mentioned, travelled in great style also. Colonel Cosby had the distinction, for instance, when he died in 1729, of having his hearse pulled by six horses. Some years later we learn that Lord Buttevant travelled from Dublin to his estate at Castle Lyons in Cork in a chaise and six with led horses alongside and three or four servants. In Dublin such vehicles would have probably been frequently seen on the North Circular Road, then one of the boundaries of the city and a fashionable promenade along which the carriages of the great used to travel. A short distance

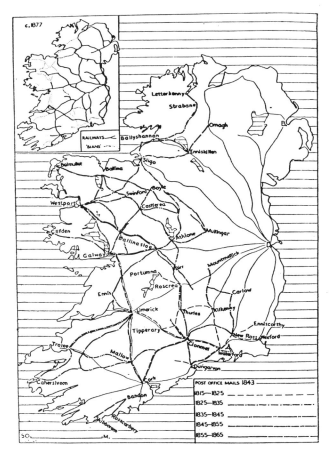

from the North Circular Road, just outside the city, lay the Phoenix Park. Here, according to William Makepeace Thackeray, a visitor in the middle of the 19th century, aspirants to the city's high society and its fashionable gathering places staked their claims. "If an Irish gentleman has a hundred a year to leave to his family," he commented, "they all become gentlemen, all keep a nag, ride to hounds and swagger about in the Phaynix."[29]

The rush to purchase carriages was not, it would appear, confined to the gentry. As towns like Belfast increased in wealth and population, merchants and shop-keepers grew in importance socially and insisted on the trappings which went along with their new-found status. One commentator complained of "rich upstarts" who "skipping from the counter to their carriage, run one down with force of wealth which sanctions ignorance and vulgarity, and now gives them a lead of fashion, who a few years since would have shrunk with awe from the notice of what is called good company." Hunting, as we might expect, also attracted new money. Success-ful business families sought out country houses in which to ape the manners of the landed classes and live extravagant lives, hunting and entertaining. Conditions in Cork in the 18th century encouraged the proliferation of such families. The growth of trade had been particularly pronounced there, with the port supplying provi-sions to every country in Europe. In the Cork area in 1834, Inglis found that "the disposition towards improvidence and display, amongst the upper and middle classes, [was] strongly manifest." The "passion for horses and hunting" was par-ticularly in evidence. "Everybody hunts who can possibly contrive to keep a horse, nor is the indulgence of the passion looked upon as at all inconsistent with business. This is very different from our English commercial habits."

The boost which hunting received from the wealthy in Cork in the 18th and 19th centuries is reflected in the number of mounted hunts which are found there today. A quarter of the total hunting packs which are followed on horseback in the country are in Cork. There were "country squires . . . distinguished by a taste for foxhunting" in other counties also, but it would appear that in Cork conditions were particularly suited to their emergence. In addition to the competition for status among the merchant classes in the city, there was competition also among the middlemen entrenched in the Cork hinterland.[30]

Connemara driving ponies. *(Ruth Rogers)*

Jaunting car, early 1900s. *(G. A. Duncan)*

Horse-drawn fire engine, early 1900s.
(G. A. Duncan)

Horse-drawn tram. *(G. A. Duncan)*

MIDDLEMEN

So far we have considered the popularity of horses and horse-related activities among tenants and landlords solely. We noted that horses provided common ground between both classes but did not relate this to an important factor in rural life in the 18th and 19th centuries—the middlemen to whom many landlords let their properties and who, in turn, relet them to tenants. Middlemen are of interest to us because, like the gentry, many of them were addicted to hunting. Although often despised, the middleman on horseback personified much of what attracted the ordinary people to the landed classes and played an important role in drawing the gentry and the poor together.

In the 18th century middlemen were of considerable use to landlords. Instead of letting their lands directly to small tenants, landlords had found it convenient to give leases to middlemen who were people of economic substance and who could, therefore, be relied upon to meet their obligations. The middlemen would then, in turn, sublet to smaller tenants. In less tangible ways also middlemen provided a service to landlords. Frequently they were closer to the ordinary people than the landlords were and therefore could fulfil a useful function for the gentry in the management of their estates. This can be seen particularly in the case of landlords who were descended from planters and who would therefore have difficulty in achieving acceptability among their tenants. Some of these landlords attempted to outdo the older families in hospitality and hunting with a view to gaining that acceptance. Their association with middlemen whose rakish lifestyle, as we saw earlier, would have struck responsive chords among the ordinary people, was also beneficial to them.

Part of the reason for the character of the middlemen's lifestyle was the competition which existed between them for status. They were originally members of the upper classes and they retained the ambition for a gentry-style life supported by the difference between the rents they paid and those they received. The competition became particularly intense towards the end of the 18th century and in the early 19th century when rents were no longer sufficient to fund their pretensions. A multiplicity of distinctions between the different grades of landholding people arose as a result of this competition and of the insecurity over land felt by them. According to Sir Jonah Barrington, gentlemen were divided into three grades, the lowest of which included 'half-mounted gentlemen' or middlemen who were "occasionally admitted into the society of gentlemen—particularly hunters—living at other times amongst each other, with an admixture of their own servants, with whom they were always on terms of intimacy."

Many of the Catholics who became middlemen in the south of Ireland were members of old Gaelic families which had been dispossessed but had retained enough capital to be able to secure leases and support an upper class style of living.

After 1800, tenants began to see many landlords as alien, and hunting came under attack.

"The State of Ireland: Stopping a Hunt".
(Illustrated London Evening News)

Families such as the O'Connells of Derrynane in south Kerry or the Mahonys of Dunloe still provided leadership for their tenants and still indulged in mediaeval hospitality. Inevitably, however, the indignity of the dispossessions left its mark and found expression in covert lawlessness. Members of such families were prominent in the organisation of the smuggling trade and frequently were involved in abductions. According to Sir Robert Southwell, an absentee landlord in the late 17th century, such families never turned "their minds to any industrious course, but expect to be regarded as unfortunate gentlemen, who yesterday lost an estate and were to be restored tomorrow."

The middlemen's activities brought them close to their tenants but it was with the gentry that they identified. According to Barrington the 'half-mounted gentlemen' armed with their whips kept the ordinary people in their places at the races: "Their business was to ride round the inside of the ground, which they generally did with becoming spirit, trampling down some, knocking down others, and slashing every body who encroached on the proper limits."

Undoubtedly Barrington was given to exaggeration but it is clear that in their day-to-day dealings with small tenants in the second half of the 18th century many of the middlemen were abusive. In the dairying areas of Cork and Kerry where archaic conditions favoured their proliferation they rented both land and cattle to dairymen in return for rents which were often paid in kind. In an era of rising prices this method of payment struck harshly against the dairymen whilst the middlemen prospered and developed a reputation for hard drinking, hunting and idle ways.[31]

A German visitor to the country in 1828, Prince Von Pückler-Muskau, confirms the quality of the horses ridden by the country squires on the hunting field: "They are unequalled at leaping, to which they are trained from their youth. They go to a wall with the most perfect composure, and mount it with their fore feet just like a dog. If there is a ditch on the other side they leap that also by giving themselves a fresh élan on top of the wall."

The prowess of the horses noted by the prince was very important to the riders, for the competition between them on the hunting field, although only implicit, was real. The day's hunting in which the prince participated was a very serious affair. He was on horseback by 6 a.m. and his companions, "six or seven sturdy squires" who "do not think much . . . had only dogs and horses in their heads." The competition during the hunt on this occasion was particularly intense. The size of the walls encountered astonished the visitor, but he noted that their formidable character "is not admitted as any pretext whatever for the riders to deviate from a straight line . . . Some gentlemen fell but were only laughed at; for a man who does not break his neck on the spot must look for no pity, but on the contrary ridicule." The hunt lasted until "the approach of twilight" at which time the participants prepared to transfer their competition indoors, where "a genuine sportsman's and bachelor's feast" was waiting. Here the drinking, which was a feature of many occasions in Ireland when men tested each other, "was on a vast and unlimited scale."[32]

Hunting and the combative activities with which it was associated became for many of the middlemen virtually full-time pursuits. Dressed in a beaver hat and

> Cutting a figure he never was used to
> In tan riding boots and thin polished spurs,

as Aodh Mac Cruitín described him, the middleman, whether on the hunting field or in the tavern, had to prove himself the equal of the best. Arthur Young saw him as belonging to the

> class of little country gentlemen; tenants who drink their claret by means of profit rents; jobbers in farms; bucks, your fellows with round hats, edged with gold, who hunt in the day, get drunk in the evening, and fight the next morning . . . these are the men among whom drinking, wrangling, quarrelling, fighting [and] ravishing are found as in their native soil.

The competition which lay at the root of the 'hard going' on the hunting field demanded that the middleman have at his disposal a good horse. Having a superior mount was a blow struck against the pretensions of a rival in a similar social position. In addition, it enabled its owner to negotiate obstacles on the hunting field a less wealthy or, perhaps, a less courageous rival might not attempt. "They generally had good clever horses, which could leap over anything", Barrington, who admitted to having a 'a bit of blood' in his own stables, noted about the 'half-mounted gentlemen', adding that their horses "had never felt the trimming scissors or curry comb". In Maria Edgeworth's novel, *Ormond*, White Connal, a penny-pinching grazier with no ability on horseback, spends a lot of money ensuring that he is "better mounted than any man at the fair."

Mary McGrath, granddaughter of the late Joe McGrath, drives the Lord Mayor of Dublin's coach, drawn by four Irish Draught Mares, down Grafton Street, Dublin. They are flanked by Charles Powell, left, former chairman of the Irish Driving Society and by Toddy White, groom to the McGraths. Each St Patrick's Day, the Lord Mayor is driven in this coach to the reviewing stand for the parade held in the city on that day.
Source: DoA.

ABOVE: Harness racing at the RDS Horse Show in 1983. *Source*: Bord Fáilte. RIGHT: Joe McGrath drives the landau carrying President Hillery at the RDS Horse Show in 1990. Part of the horse show ceremonial. *Source*: Bord Fáilte. BELOW: Old style transport at Ballinasloe Fair. *Source*: G. A. Duncan. OPPOSITE PAGE: Driving Competition at Birr Castle. *Source*: G. A. Duncan.

ABOVE: Concentration at the start, RDS Horse Show 1987. *Source*: Inpho.
RIGHT: Majella Doyle on *Molly Bawn*. *Source*: Tony Parkes.

ABOVE: David Broome and *Lannegan* on their way to winning the Kerrygold Welcome Stakes. *Source*: Horseman Photography.
RIGHT: The Aga Khan Cup, the trophy presented to the winning Nations' Cup team at the RDS Horse Show annually. The original trophy was presented to the RDS by the late Aga Khan in appreciation of the Irish tutors he had in his youth and of the enjoyment he had at the RDS Horse Show. *Source*: Inpho.

Thomas Fuchs (Switzerland) on *Tullis Lass*, bred in Ballinhassig, Co. Cork by J. K. Murphy. Born in 1970, she is by *Go Tobann*, the sire of *Pele* (Kerrygold). With Fuchs, she has been the top showjumping money winner in Switzerland on a number of occasions. In addition in 1981 she won the European leg of the World Cup in Berlin. In 1983 she was on the gold medal-winning Swiss team in the European Championships. *Source*: DoA.

Parade for the Grand Prix Competition at the RDS Horse Show. Among the Irish riders are Diana Conolly Carew and Col. Ned Campion (*Liathdruim*). In the sixties, when this photograph was taken, the double bank, single bank and stone walls were still a feature of the show. *Source*: G. A. Duncan.

Jaunting car.
Source: Liam Blake.

At the time that Young was writing the position of middlemen was changing in many places and their quarrels were acquiring a new urgency. Landlords were beginning to see that the middlemen and the boisterous lifestyle of lavish spending for which they stood were outmoded and could be dispensed with. They were no longer willing to grant them the long leases on which they had prospered in times of low prices. Middlemen had now to compete for leases with strong tenant farmers to whom landlords now preferred to let their lands directly.

The middleman's increasing insecurity over land tenure could open up old wounds and grievances which had their roots in the 17th-century plundering of Irish lands but the violence which resulted seldom flared into open rebellion. Disloyalty was an expensive business, a luxury which only those who had nothing to lose could afford. Such conflicts as arose had a ritual character and frequently assumed a religious colouring, as in the case of the Catholic Byrne family from Wicklow and Wexford and a Protestant leaseholder. As we shall see, the result of their struggle was single combat in the time-honoured way between the old and the new, the aggressor and defender, the noble and the upstart, and this took place within the narrow confines of the hunting field.

Intense family pride characterised the Byrnes. They saw themselves not so much as middlemen but as landlords in their own right. Myles Byrne who was involved in the rebellion of 1798 recalled in his memoirs how his father had often shown him "the lands that belonged to our ancestors now in the hands of the sanguinary followers of Cromwell." The decline in the fortunes of the Byrnes in Kilnahue was matched by the rise in those of the neighbouring Protestant Gowan family. To the Byrnes, Hubert Gowan was a parvenu. "He called his place Mount Nebo," Myles observed, "and planted his lands with trees of different kinds. He kept a pack of hounds and wished to be looked upon as a great sportsman; he felt much mortified when the neighbouring gentlemen refused to hunt with him." The confrontation between him and the O'Byrne patriarch, "puffed up with pride" and "dexterous in the use of arms" was inevitable and came when Gowan, during a hunt, invaded Garret Byrne's territory. Irish Catholic pride, as we have noted, was most vulnerable to Protestant attack, in the wake of the 'Penal Laws', in matters relating to horses. Myles Byrne recounts Gowan's transgression and subsequent humiliation at the hands of the old Byrne chief:

> He happened one day to be led by the chase some miles from his own place and fell in with Old Garrett Byrne of Ballymanus who, with his hounds, was in full chase. The latter enraged at being crossed in his sport by an 'upstart' as he called 'Hunter Gowan' gave him a horse whipping and told him never to presume to come in his way again.

We have already seen the horsewhip being used in circumstances which resemble those of the Gowan-Byrne confrontation. In full view of the crowd at Tralee races

Delivering milk to a creamery depot in the late 1940s. *(G. A. Duncan)*

Martin Leahy working at the anvil on a shoe for a Clydesdale. Martin, one of the leading farriers in Ireland, numbers among his clients the Irish National Stud and the Kildangan Stud. *(Peter Harvey)*

Horse ploughing competition. *(G. A. Duncan)*

Saving the hay, Summer 1964. *(G. A. Duncan)*

the Knight of Glin horsewhipped Colonel Henry Kitchener whom he regarded as an upstart and who had pricked the Knight's family pride by abusing tenants whose ancestors had been followers of the Knights. As a means of humiliating a rival, it would appear that there was no more effective weapon than the horsewhip. The threat of horsewhipping, for instance, was one of the factors which led Daniel O'Connell in 1815 to engage the Dublin councillor D'Esterre in a duel. But to a large extent the horsewhip was the badge of landlordism and was used arbitrarily against the ordinary people. It was not uncommon for cottiers, among the most vulnerable of the rural classes, to be struck out of the way with a whip by the landlord or landlord's agent as he travelled about. Wakefield recalled seeing a gentleman cut open a man's cheek with a whip at a racecourse in Co. Carlow. What surprised travellers in Ireland greatly was the submissive reaction of bystanders on such occasions compared to what would have happened in England if landlords or their servants had acted in such a high-handed fashion. The landlord and his whip, it would appear, were accepted as part of the status quo, and there were circumstances, as we have seen in the case of Lord Clonmel, when an imperious figure brought reassurance to ordinary people.

Given an opportunity, servants themselves would apply the whip. Thomas Cromwell travelling in the Kilkenny Coach in 1828 noted how the driver, overtaking three men on the road, applied the whip to their shoulders for the sole reason that they were within reach. Middlemen, as we have seen in Barrington's account, were even prepared to act as landlords' servants at races and whip the peasantry out of the way. With their "buck-skin breeches, and boots well greased, and . . . long thong whips heavily loaded with lead at the butt end', their identification with the landlord was complete.[33]

Typical of the middlemen of his time was Art O'Leary, hero of a well known Irish poem. His dairying activities in Co Cork brought him prosperity and his marriage into the O'Connell family from Derrynane provided him with the additional status such men craved. In his wife's poem for him we read the standard descriptions of the 'hard going' on the hunting field and of

> the fine-handed rider
> who used to tire out the hunt
> as they hunted from Greanach
> and the slim hounds gave up,

with the inevitable feasting to follow:

> Where knives were being sharpened,
> Pork laid out for carving,
> And countless ribs of mutton.

But, as have seen in the case of the Byrnes, the veneer could be quickly stripped from the conventional lifestyle of the middlemen, revealing a single-combat warrior willing to risk all in avenging the insults of the traditional oppressor.

The occasion when this dramatic change is precipitated in Art's life is when his horse wins a race at Macroom, defeating the horse of the Protestant Magistrate Abraham Morris. The 'Penal Laws' were still in force at the time, enabling the magistrate to seize the horse if he wished. Faced with such a threat Art has no option but to go 'on the run'. There is an inevitability about his death which follows. In taking to the hills with his horse, Art is in the tradition of the Rapparees and Tories fighting against insuperable odds. He becomes a hero and the poem his wife wrote, lamenting his passing, has survived in oral tradition to this day.

After going 'on the run', Art, instead of avoiding his enemies, sought them out as if he welcomed death. He taunted Morris and his soldiers by showing himself just out of reach of their guns until, on one occasion, he misjudges the distance and is shot dead. Death for such men represented a triumph, and for his wife, Eibhlín, there is still hope:

> Rise up again now, Art
> Leap up on your horse,
> Make straight for Macroom town,
> Then to Inchigeela-back,
> A bottle of wine in your fist . . .

Traditionally in Ireland the "Merry Wake" was an occasion for celebrating life. The dead person was not lost irretrievably in a world beyond the grave but was in an Otherworld which impinged a great deal on this life. In her poem, Eibhlín Ní Chonaill consoles herself with the thought that the spirit of the hunt would be in evidence as Art was laid to rest:

> That fierce troop of riders,
> Shaking their bridles,
> Would have been making a clatter
> As they came to your burial,
> White breasted Art.
> My love and my delight
> Kinsman of that wild troop of riders
> Who used to hunt in the glen.

Her horseman hero was not dead but was alive, offering hospitality and reassurance to all.[34]

Turnip, a celebrated gelding.

7

The Treatment of Horses
in Folklore and Practice

T O DATE we have been concerned with the question of the benefit which horses brought to Irish people. Our story, of course, will continue this theme as we enter the modern period. However we must also turn the question around—if only as a preliminary to observing how horses have been a force for good up to today—and consider how Irish people treated their horses over the centuries, how in general terms they approached the training of them and how they achieved the control over them which would ultimately redound to their benefit on the competition field.

CARELESSNESS AND BRAVADO

Violence, as we have seen, characterised Irish society over the centuries. From the earliest times the initiation rites of young men of noble blood about to enter society consisted of violent activities. It was to be expected that, in early Ireland, horses which were bound up with the activities of the elite in their pursuit of honour and glory would suffer some of the effects of their violence. In the story of *Táin Bó Cuailnge* which mirrors Irish life in the fourth century AD and in other tales Cú Chulainn is seen as a hard-driving chariot warrior. We read in the Irish law tracts which relate to a period many centuries after that of the *Táin Bó Cuailnge* that a boy was given a horse by his father when he was seven years old. Children of the nobility were placed in fosterage but this did not interfere with their equestrian education. The foster children were provided with horses. It would appear that horses could be abused at races, for the Laws specifically refer to this. It seems to have been accepted that in the struggle to win a race a horse could suffer and we are told that there was no fine imposed on such occasions. Likewise it was expected that horses in battle could be damaged or even killed and that horses pitted against each other in horse fights would injure each other. These were serious pursuits with a lot at stake and penalties were not levied.

This is not to argue that carte blanche was given to be cruel to horses. There was a penalty for overworking or even frightening horses. The Laws, which tended to delight in fastidious detail, even specified how to avoid tethering a horse improperly and a fine was imposed for failure in this respect. One of the great fears about horses in early Ireland was, for reasons which we have seen, that they would trespass, hence the concern about tethering them. At night-time horses, according to the Irish Law Tracts, had to be either tethered or in stables.[1]

Harness racing at Portmarnock. *(Ruth Rogers)*

From Norman times criticisms of Irish treatment of their horses were general. Giraldus Cambrensis, writing in the 12th century, claimed that the Irish provided no stalls for animals, although it is clear from the Laws that, in theory at least, this had not been the case. There are indications there that horses were sometimes driven into stables. A list of farm buildings in one of the law tracts, however, makes no reference to stables.

Another complaint of Giraldus, which was also echoed down the centuries by other commentators about horses, was that the Irish did not provide fodder for their animals. Horses were left out in the winter to fend for themselves, it was claimed by many observers, and this neglect was the main reason why the horses were often small. Undoubtedly these criticisms have some basis in fact but disregard for the animals may not have always lain behind the Irish behaviour in this regard. Economic necessity would have been one of the main reasons for keeping horses out in the open. Reports made in the late nineteenth century make it clear that small farmers with very little resources always tried to have horses in their possession, even though they could not afford to provide the stabling and forage required. In addition, in Ireland attitudes to horses differed from those in Britain. For the Irish, horses, until recent times, were of assistance in work as well as a source of income, whereas in Britain, for many, they were pets.[2]

Left : Floating a horse out behind a currach, in order to load him on a boat for Galway. Aran Islands 1954. *(G. A. Duncan)*

Right : The horse is lowered into the hold, having been hauled on to the boat from the water. *(G. A. Duncan)*

A factor, as we have seen, in the Irish adherence to their customs and practices in relation to horses, was the wish to act in defiance of the English. This was true, of course, of the Irish horse soldiers but it also applied where the ordinary Irish people were concerned. Defiance went hand in hand with violence in Ireland as the opium of the dispossessed. It gave ill-treatment of horses, where it existed, an added dimension. "The common Irish," Sir Jonah Barrington remarked at the end of the eighteenth century, "are the most heroic horsemen I ever saw—it was always one of their attributes." This comment was occasioned by his visit to Donnybrook Fair where those showing off their horses to potential buyers had to "leather their horses over . . . a large ditch with a drain, and a piece of a wall . . . and the tumbles which those venturous jockies constantly received, with the indifference wherewith they mounted and began again, were truly entertaining". Donnybrook Fair, in common with many other assemblies, attracted the criticism of both the Church and the English authorities, because of the general 'lawlessness' of the behaviour there. An atmosphere of licence pervaded such fairs and assemblies and, as Barrington observes, this sometimes found expression in mistreatment of horses: "Coming from fairs, I have often seen a couple or sometimes three fellows riding one bare-backed horse as hard as he could go, and safely—not one of them, if they were on their own legs could stand perpendicular half a minute".

From a more objective quarter—Barrington was not the most reliable of witnesses—we get confirmation of some of this picture. "Two beggars were seated on a horse," the German Prince Von Pückler-Muskau noted at Donnybrook Fair during the course of his visit to Ireland in the period 1828–1829, "they had no saddle, and a piece of twine served as reins".[3]

PLOUGHING BY THE TAIL

Comments from such travellers make it clear that Irish horse harness was still somewhat different from what was the norm on the continent and in England. Fourteen years after the Prince's visit his compatriot Kohl visited the Gap of Dunloe in Co. Kerry where horses are still offered to the visitor on his tour of the Lakes of Killarney and there he noted "an entire harness of plaited straw; and what is more remarkable is, that it was not a mere makeshift, or the whim of an individual, but the general custom throughout the whole west of Ireland". It is clear that the use of straw to make saddles, or 'soogauns', and of twigs twisted into ropes, known as 'gads', to provide halters was motivated not only by economic considerations but by a determination to resist conditions imposed by the English. The most notorious instance of Irish resistance in this respect was the practice of ploughing with the tail of the horse attached to the plough by 'gads' or straw ropes rather than with a yoke or collar on the horse. Most English commentators considered this practice cruel and proposals were made in the early seventeenth century to abolish it, with the result that in 1634 an Act was passed against ploughing by the tail. Nevertheless, the practice continued and was widely distributed. As late as 1949 a seventy-six year old man from Killinkere in Co. Cavan reported that his grandfather had been challenged by a policeman for ploughing in this manner.

There were substantial reasons for ploughing like this in what was called by English writers "the Irish manner" since much of the country where the practice occurred was hilly and the ground stony. In such conditions the 'long plough' favoured by the English which had the plough team harnessed in pairs and walking in tandem would not be suitable. With the horses harnessed abreast and the leader controlling them from in front in the Irish manner, rather than from behind, it would be possible to quickly detect when the plough struck an obstacle in the soil and stop the whole team. It was in this context of rocky soil, it was argued, tail ploughing came into its own. The horse, with the plough attached to its tail, quickly betrayed the nervous shock of encountering a rigid stone or rock and came to an immediate halt, thus saving the ploughshare from damage. The 'long plough' i.e. the plough with the lengthy team, would not allow the driver such control and, in the absence of ploughing by the tail, damage could be done by animals allowed to proceed in spite of obstacles. Nor was this thinking peculiar to Ireland. In eighteenth-century Scotland the advantage of the 'short plough' in rocky ground was perceived and a nineteenth-century account of the Highlands noted that "the horse's tail was regarded as a natural piece of harness evidently formed for the purpose".[4]

Ploughing in Ireland has a long history. Recent research in Co. Mayo has unearthed traces of plough marks under blanket bogs in field systems of neolithic date. The earliest ploughs were however drawn by oxen attached to head yokes, not by horses. Wither yokes which were introduced later were used to attach the horse to the war chariot but it was not until the introduction into Ireland of the rigid collar about the tenth century that the use of the horse in heavy farm work, other than by attaching the plough or cart to its tail, would have been possible. For evidence of early ploughing by the tail we turn away however from Ireland to Sweden where at Tegneby there are rock carvings probably dating from the middle of the second millennium BC showing ploughing by the tail. The phallic nature of the engravings makes it clear that ploughing was seen as a ritual act probably opening the virgin soil for the seed. In view of these correspondences it is possible to see the alleged cruelty of ploughing by the tail and the persistence of the Irish in adhering to the custom in a new light. One writer has bracketed it with other customs such as pulling the wool off living sheep and the burning of straw instead of threshing out the corn as possible relics of an ancient culture complex, a suggestion to which both legislators and commentators in the seventeenth century add weight. The earliest reference which we have to traction by the tail in Irish sources occurs in the annals in 1472. The animal in question in the account is not a horse but a camel. What is significant, however, is that it seems to have been accepted that the practice was possible.

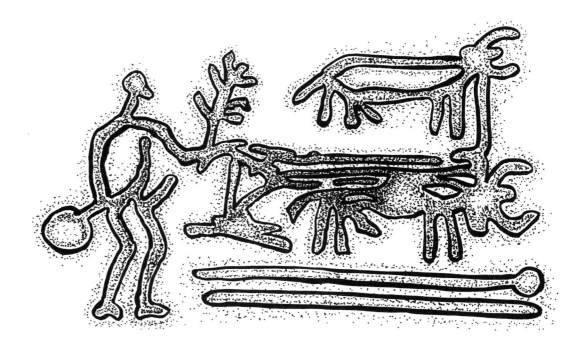

The Litsleby Ard, Sweden. The phallic figure, with the seed bag behind his loins, indicates that ploughing and sowing the seed were seen as ritual acts. The type of plough shown here was manufactured in Denmark as early as c. 1500 BC. *(Rock carving drawing after Glob)*

The indications are that the Irish were prepared to allow their horses to be damaged in certain situations which had, as they saw it, benefits for themselves. Horses might suffer for economic reasons or on account of warfare. There was also the question of deliberate damage to the horse in order to achieve ritual benefits. As we have seen, the line between these benefits and those of a more tangible nature might not be very clear. If there was an element of cruelty in ploughing by the tail it would not necessarily deter people from continuing with a practice which they saw as being economically necessary. The violence to the horse might even heighten for them the ultimate validity of the practice. The harvest must benefit where so much effort and pain had gone into its preparation.[5]

SEASONAL PRACTICES

The ultimate in ritual abuse of the horse perpetrated in order to achieve prosperity was horse sacrifice and some folk practices in Ireland seem to be related to this. Horse skulls, for instance, were sometimes placed in the foundation of houses in order to bring good fortune to those dwelling in the house. During the sowing of seed in Spring people were particularly concerned to ensure their good fortune. Until recent times a bonfire was lit annually in different parts of Ireland on the first of May. One of the main constituents of the fire was horse heads and horse bones, and the embers and smoke from the fire were believed to ensure the prosperity of all things which came in contact with them. The bonfire revived the horse species

Divided loyalties. Jacintha O'Halloran (6) from Celbridge, Co. Kildare, at the stables, RDS Horse Show, 17 July 1990. *(The Irish Times : Jack MacManus)*

and fertilised the earth. Appropriately the fire was lit just as summer was beginning, an important landmark in the agricultural year. Farm help was being hired, the fields were being prepared in order to yield meadow grass, the cattle turned out to graze and turf cutting begun. It was a period when expectations were at their height, a period of jollity when summer was welcomed, but it was also a period of concern that the bounty of the new season would not be missed, hence the bonfire. Cattle were driven through the embers or touched with torches taken from the fire and it was believed that the fields over which the smoke from the bonfire travelled would be assured of crops in plenty. In some places the ashes from the fire were scattered over the fields. Young men jumped through the flames in the belief that the crops would grow better as a result. Women did likewise and hoped for a better marriage. In the midst of the bonfire festivities the serious business of seasonal renewal was being pursued and hopes rekindled.

In other folk practices which involved the horse, the sacrificial element, if it ever existed, has been almost completely disguised. Harvest time in Ireland was marked by the Feast of Samhain at the end of October and beginning of November. It was a time of communal assembly when the gates of the Otherworld were considered to be thrown open and communal fortunes hung in the balance. In a manner reminiscent of the totemistic ceremonies to which we have alluded, the image of the horse was put on display. Processions were held, headed by the *Láir Bhán*, the White Mare, a figure enveloped in a white sheet having as it were, the head of a mare. This figure or Hobby Horse which survived in popular custom into the twentieth century also made its appearance in parts of the country at the festivities of May and St Stephen's Day. The Wren Boys from Tralee and the Dingle Peninsula in Co. Kerry, we are told, carried with them on St Stephen's Day a *Láir Bhán*. She was made from a wooden frame and white sheet and had a carved wooden head and dangling legs. The person carrying her could, by manipulating the strings, make her jaws snap and her legs kick out against those who were loath to make a contribution to the festive funds. The underlying reason, however, for the presence of the horse when people gathered together in this way at the approach of the New Year was not private greed but the public good.[6]

Clearly practices which required that the animal should be killed would pose a dilemma for a community that attached a premium to seeing the horse at the height of its powers on the racecourse. One of these practices would appear, from mythology which has come down to us, to have involved drowning the animal. But the folk imagination was able, it would appear, to devise methods of achieving the ritual benefits of drowning without its unfortunate consequence. Instead of killing the animal, the community was able to protect it.

Drowning, it would appear, was a method of sacrifice in the Indo-European world which was concerned with fertility in all its aspects. We have already considered instances of horse drowning in Irish mythology. In Greece the sacrificial drowning of horses is well-attested but the practice which sheds most light on Irish practices is a Cimbrian ceremony which took place after a victory over the Romans. Horses were drowned and valuables thrown into the water. In Ireland the animal was not destroyed but its otherworldly character was nevertheless asserted in a similar manner. It was the custom on the second Sunday of August every year to swim horses in lakes in the belief that it would render them healthy during the remainder of the year as in the following account from the Ordnance Survey Letters:

> At this Lough [Lough Keeraun, near Bohola, Co. Mayo] . . . there is usually a patron on the Sunday commonly called Garlic Sunday . . . the people, it is said, swim their horses in the lake on that day to defend them against incidental evils during the year and throw spancels and halters into it, which they leave there on the occasion.

Sometimes also races between the horses swimming in the waters were held at such assemblies.[7]

THE WINNING HORSE

Folklore reflects the importance which people attached to having good horses in their midst by highlighting remarkable individual horses. The names of some famous horses from several centuries back have survived to this day. In some instances there are peculiar circumstances which serve to heighten the public perception of the horse in question as a transcendent force for good in the lives of the people. This was certainly true of *Jenny Lind*, a mare from Co. Mayo named after the great Swedish soprano who was her contemporary. It was the time of the Great Famine in the mid nineteenth century and the people of Ireland were at the lowest ebb in their history. The English government in the interest of laissez-faire economics had largely turned a blind eye to their plight and when it decided to act it was too little too late. The one bright feature of this gloomy picture, as we have seen, was the action of some enlightened landlords who tried to assist their tenants and the people in their locale. One such landlord was Samuel Bournes from Rossport in Co. Mayo. In co-operation with the Quakers he provided large quantities of food for the needy of the area. Bournes was the owner of *Jenny Lind* and an excellent horseman, and on one celebrated occasion the well-known mare played an important part in the landlord's philanthropic activities and carved out for herself a place in the popular imagination as a result.

Bournes had been invited to a meeting in Belmullet by an official, to discuss means of alleviating distress in his neighbourhood but the letter informing him of the meeting had arrived late. He decided, however, that the meeting was of such importance that it warranted a journey to the town in the hope of a chance meeting with the gentleman concerned. For this he saddled up *Jenny Lind* who had already acquired a reputation for speed and jumping feats. It was a race against time and although the journey was accomplished in record time it appeared to be all for nothing. The gentleman had already left for Killala, thirty miles away, when Bournes arrived in Belmullet. Bournes was not easily beaten and he again took to the road, driving his horse to the limit. He arrived in Killala in time to meet the elusive official. As a result arrangements were made for transport by sea of food from Westport to the barony of Erris which was practically inaccessible by road. The meeting, so vital in saving lives during the ensuing year, had, however, taken its toll on the mare. The following morning her owner found her dead in her stable.

As well as using her great racing ability on the people's account, *Jenny Lind* had been very successful in sporting arenas also and stories are told to this day of her exploits. She was raced in Sligo, Ballina, Crossmolina and in other locations and on each occasion she was successful. Particularly notable was her jumping ability. She is reputed to have jumped the huge iron gates leading to Rossport House, Bournes' residence, as well as many other almost insurmountable obstacles and, if some of the alleged feats ascribed to her have a basis in fact, her reputation is truly deserved.

In the previous century the *Paidrín Mare* was carving out for herself an even more illustrious reputation on the racecourse and stories about her have remained in circulation well into this century. In 1745 and 1747 she won the Royal Plate at the Curragh in Co. Kildare, later to become the centre of Irish racing and training. Her victories came at a time when there was some formidable opposition. In 1745, for instance, three importers of the best blood in the first half of the eighteenth century—Lord Antrim, Lord Proctmore and Sir Edward O'Brien—had mares in contention, but despite this the *Paidrín Mare* carried the day. Her most famous victory was in 1760 when she was pitted against the most famous stallion of the time, *Black and All Black*. At the Curragh in 1751, for ten thousand guineas, the latter had beaten Lord March's *Bajazet*, a son of *Lord Godolphin's Arabian*, one of the three thoroughbred foundation sires, in one of the greatest matches ever witnessed.[8]

Such victories as that of the *Paidrín Mare* were of great importance to the people at the time and subsequently. For example, after this victory "bonfires were lit in many of the streets of Dublin and beer distributed." Great numbers of people

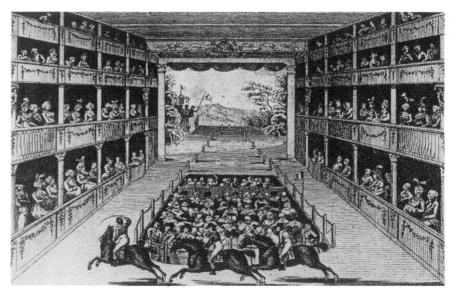

Left : *Arkle*'s trainer, Tom Dreaper, and owner, Anne Duchess of Westminster, at the unveiling of *Arkle*'s statue at Cheltenham. *(Gerry Cranham)*

Right : Pony races at the Theatre Royal, Crowe Street. *(National Library of Ireland)*

travelled to racecourses to see horses winning great battles and the folk imagination invested victories subsequently with extraordinary, even religious significance, as we have seen. The racecourse was, as in more ancient times, the location where, the people instinctively felt, their welfare was in the balance. The victory of a particular horse was an occasion for communal rejoicing, but failure spelt hardship. In view of this the horse's welfare was of particular concern. The line between success and failure at the racecourse was a fine one. The horse could be off colour on the day or could become quickly unsound and would either not be able to race or not be able to perform to the best of its ability. Moreover, it was more susceptible to such occurrences than most other animals, and folklore has frequent references to the horse being found in a lather of sweat for no apparent reason or unable or unwilling to move.

There were, of course, physical causes for symptoms such as these. Because of its small stomach, it could be quickly upset by unsuitable food. Its finely developed hoof and lower leg structure could also be easily damaged. The horse's lack of robustness was merely an inevitable consequence of its highly sensitive nature. But if the horse was very vulnerable physically it was also equipped with the senses to enable it to avoid occasions when it might be in danger. Particularly highly developed was the horse's sense of smell, giving it advance warning of things which might not be apparent to its rider. According to Job, "he smelleth the battle afar off". Every rider has at one time or another known his horse to startle or refuse to proceed for no apparent reason, only to find that something insignificant to which the animal is unaccustomed has frightened it. Because the horse was seen to be vulnerable and sensitive in this way and because human faculties were not often capable of discerning the factors behind the animal's behaviour, the folk mind envisaged the hand of otherworldly forces at work. (See marginal note.)

Refusal to yield to the spirit's wishes on such occasions was often ill-rewarded. A story, for instance, from Curlisheen in Co. Sligo tells how a horse which the owner refused to lend for a journey was found dead next morning in the stable. But there was no guarantee that the horse would be safe even if the spirits or their human accomplices got control of the animal. A story collected in Antrim in 1941 relates of a mare:

> After it had foaled someone saw a strange figure riding the mare around the fields, followed by the foal. Both mare and foal afterwards died.

In summary, therefore, the horse was seen to be open to otherworldly forces and usually these were seen by the folk mind to be malevolent if they gained control of the horse.[9]

But if the folk mind was preoccupied with the vulnerability of the horse and tried to explain this in otherworldly terms it also had to come to grips with the strengths which the horse clearly had. At the natural level it was of course possible to explain

From all parts of the country, even to this day, instances of the popular belief in the horse's ability to perceive spirits have been recorded. This belief arose out of many accounts of horses stopping along the road and refusing to go any further despite the best efforts of their riders. Usually the horse on such occasions becomes nervous and even begins to sweat, and popular imagination believes that the horse is in dread of the fairies it has seen. It was thought that the fairies and other otherworldly forces would damage the horse. One of the ways in which they would do this would be by stealing the animal or getting on its back and riding it hard, often at night. The unsuspecting owner coming to the stable in the morning would find his animal bathed in sweat. A frequent theme in these stories is the efforts made by the spirits to get on the horse's back even in the presence of the human rider.

the feats of a *Paidrín Mare* or a *Jenny Lind* in terms of good breeding lines, the high limestone quality of the soil or the talent of a good trainer, but these were factors, with the exception of the last, as we shall see, that folklore preferred not to handle. Better to suggest, as in the case of one of *Jenny Lind*'s escapades, that the animal was in the grip of forces which went beyond this world, with her rider hypnotised on her back and powerless to interfere with her headlong rush. An extreme example of this which we have come across already are the water horses in Irish tradition. Such horses were under the control of the fairies to such an extent that it was believed that they actually belonged to them. We have already seen that riders on such horses were, like *Jenny Lind*'s rider, hypnotised and unable to dismount. They were the finest horses of all but they would leave this world, if possible, and slip back into the water from which they came, bringing the rider with them. There was no suggestion of course that *Jenny Lind* or the *Paidrín Mare* were water horses. Folklore had however to explain their wonderful qualities. It did this by suggesting that these horses, which belonged essentially to this world, had an Otherworldly characteristic. In the case of *Jenny Lind*

> It is related that this extraordinary animal breathed through its anus as well as its mouth and that this is a trait or physical characteristic not possessed by one horse in a million. Any horse so distinctively endowed is supposed to be possessed of well-nigh supernatural staying power.

When the *Paidrín Mare* was killed they discovered that she too had something distinctive about her. An account of her death from Sligo recalls:

> When the mare was opened they found there a pair of wings attached to her heart. And people say that it was the wings that helped her to win.

Folklore collected in Co. Cork contains an indication of what was considered to have produced such wings. A wonderful stallion which had been killed, we are told, was also found to have them. This animal had, it would appear, been reared on goat's milk and it was believed that the milk was the cause of the wings on his heart. Taking the two accounts together, we see folklore ascribing the prowess of the horse, on the one hand to an otherworldly characteristic and on the other to a natural cause. The key to the apparent contradiction lies in the fact that folktales see the Otherworld as acting on this world through natural agents.[10]

FOLK PROTECTION FOR THE HORSE

As we have seen, Otherworldly forces could be either malevolent or benevolent in relation to the horse, and this variation is reflected in the effect which its human agents could have on the animal. The most feared of the injuries which could be done to a horse by a malevolent individual was the 'evil eye' or 'overlook'. Generally the horse would be struck down suddenly with an ailment which it was

At Cooley Show. *(Ruth Rogers)*

Superstitious practices geared to protect the animal from evil forces were particularly in evidence during ploughing and seed time when the damage to the horse would be most serious for the community. In some places the last handful of corn harvested during the previous year, the churn, was kept and given to the horses on the first day of ploughing to prevent this damage. There were elaborate instructions for the ploughman relating to his horses, a reflection again of superstitious belief. He had to turn his team on the headland in such a way that the sun travelled around it from left to right, a direction which from ancient times was held in Irish belief to be lucky. In addition, when he was yoking or unyoking the team it had to be facing southwards. Likewise the sower commencing his work had to observe certain procedures in relation to horses. He had to give them a handful of corn and throw a handful of earth over their rumps. At the end of the day, the residue from the sheaf of corn used for making the cross of St Brigid—a saint who was the Christian equivalent of the Goddess of Fertility of the same name—added to the bedding of the horses would, it was believed, ward off illness. Unruly horses could be tamed by using spancels made from the cross materials. All the superstitious practices did not relate to tillage, however.

not possible to explain. The blame would be laid on some unpopular person in the locale for 'overlooking' the horse or casting the 'evil eye' on it. The apparent absence of any concrete reason for the horse's indisposition did not necessarily point towards mysterious influences but the folk mind preferred to see mysterious forces at work in matters relating to the horse, rather than try to discover the physical causes of the problems. It was not, however, only concerned with evil agents and the damage they did to the horse. It counterbalanced these with agents which were benevolent. Society might have its evilly disposed people in its midst who would damage the horse but it also had its protective devices.

Given the value which the community placed on the horse, it is not surprising that buying and selling it has produced a range of stories in the folklore record and that many superstitious practices surround such transactions. Buying and selling were considered to be fraught with hazards, the belief being that the ignorant or unwary might suffer the loss of a horse or acquire one which was faulty in some way. As a result there is a great deal of folk wisdom—some from as early as the fifteenth century—concerning the significance for potential purchasers of the colour, markings and features of the horse. Particular importance during a transaction attached to the halter which was on the horse being purchased. It was believed that it brought good luck to the horse and to its new owner. It was therefore considered essential that it was not lost or given away. The vendor, for his part, also tried to retain it in his possession after the horse was sold. We might suspect, therefore, that, underlying the attachment to the halter and the belief in the good luck it brought, a more fundamental concern was at work. The scholar Marcel Mauss has noted the custom in the Vosges valley of a horse purchaser making a cross on the lintel of the stable door and retaining the halter which the horse wore when being sold, in order to detach the animal from its former owner. The concern on which these practices involving the halter throw light was with the bond and closeness which existed between horse and owner. The halter, almost like the chariot of old, shared in the nature of the horse. By possessing it, an owner possessed and controlled the horse.[11]

Attempting to gain control of the horse involved a struggle. A person had to establish contact and a close relationship with the animal and this involved conflict with unfriendly forces. These forces were seen to have an Otherworldly character, hence the superstitious practices attaching to the efforts to gain that control. Such control was considered vital for protecting or curing the horse. It would appear that protective contact between horses and people could be established not only through halters but through other means such as flowers attached to the bridles of horses. Amhlaoibh Ó Súilleabháin noted their use in his diary in May 1830: "The mail coach bedecked with a May bush; the horses adorned with beautiful little flowers; they are a glad sight."

The belief that such horse decorations had the capacity to protect and cure is conveyed in the following account collected in Mayo in 1942:

> The old people said that if a horse-nail and a wee red ribbon was tied to a horse's mane the horse couldn't be overlooked. I saw one horse one time in my life and he wouldn't eat anything. He was pining away every day. A man called Phil Gargan had the cure of the overlook. He would make a thread of wool, and he would say a prayer and put nine knots on the thread and put it around the animal's neck to save it from harm. He did the same for this horse and it cured him.[12]

One of the most famous of the wise old women or *caillechs* who were expert in such superstitious practices was Biddy Early from Clare who was born at the end of the eighteenth century and was once tried for being a witch. Her influence, like that of other *caillechs*, could take a malevolent turn. It was believed, for instance, that *caillechs* could overlook a horse. Biddy was indeed prepared to stop a horse in its tracks, in such a way that nobody else could get it to move, in order to demonstrate her power to a rival. This was a trick she had frequent occasion to play on a priest's horse after she had been criticised by the particular priest. On one such occasion the remedy which she offered to the priest in question, after he had made amends to her, required that he strike the animal on the right shoulder with cuttings from a whitethorn bush which she gave him. Thus, by extension, she made contact with the animal and it was freed.

From an early age Biddy had developed a reputation for her knowledge of fairies and for her ability to cure illnesses. To make contact with a sick person she sometimes used a bottle. People coming to her for remedies on behalf of sick relatives or friends would be given the bottle and a warning about possible dangers on the way:

> As you near the Black Wood, your horse will take fright. Take care not to be thrown. And be extra careful that the bottle is not broken.

Biddy's bottle, it was believed, contained her power and enabled her to make contact with those whom she wished to cure, and, as her warning implies, could exercise control of the horse. This control sometimes came under attack from evil forces as would appear to have been the case when one of the people who sought help from her was returning home. She had given him a bottle for a sick woman in Quin in Co. Clare and he noticed, we are told, on his journey there that his jennet became frightened at the same time as invisible people, unsuccessfully as it happened, attacked him to gain possession of the bottle. It was believed that Biddy knew how such invisible spirits could be thwarted in their attempts to gain control of horses and prevented from doing damage to them. Another story involving her tells of a splendid horse belonging to a man from Co. Clare. The horse, which was normally quiet, one day appeared inexplicably to be frightened and galloped continuously around the field until it was covered with sweat. When the owner

An interested spectator oversees discussions at Muff Horse Fair, held near Kingscourt in Co. Cavan, 13 August 1990. This fair is one of the oldest in the country, probably having its basis in a Lughnasa festival in honour of the god Lug. (*The Irish Times: Frank Millar*)

managed to catch it he rubbed it down with two sods of soft spongy turf until it calmed down and was dried. He then went to consult Biddy Early. Her diagnosis was:

> The fairies took your horse for a race. You made good work to catch him, and when you rubbed him down with the soft turf you knocked the jockey off his back, and that is why you were able to cool him down. If you had not done that he would have galloped until he dropped dead.

The superstitious practices and objects which, we have argued, brought Biddy Early and other practitioners close to the horse enabled such people to appear to transcend this life and to belong to and to understand the horse's world. Once in that world, an individual could protect the horse against the Otherworldly forces ranged against it, and thereby cure its ailment.[13]

The early training of a young horse with George Rogers (left) and John Davis. The Rogers family was responsible for many winners. Pat Rogers, George's father, bought *Master Robert* who went on to win the 1924 Aintree Grand National. Charlie, George's brother, discovered *Brown Jack*, the winner of the Queen Alexandra Stakes at Ascot for six successive years, 1929 to 1934. He also bred the 1937 Aintree Grand National winner, *Royal Mail*. *(Ruth Rogers)*

CONTROL AND MYSTIQUE

Science with its reliance on the cause-effect relationship would tend to cast doubts on the validity of such cures. But there is no doubting the firmness of the folk's belief in them. The horse had been injured in a mysterious way and it would be cured similarly. Where the physical sciences were somewhat at a loss was in dealing with the contribution which the curer's self-confidence made to the cure. The people believed that he could cure the animal. The prayer and the piece of thread in the account from Mayo we have quoted, or whatever other device was used, built up an atmosphere of mystery which fortified that belief and, more importantly, gave the curer the confidence that he was master of the situation. This undoubtedly had a calming effect on the horse, previously disturbed by the 'overlooker'. An animal quick to sense fear or the lack of confidence in humans is unlikely to be 'cured' by someone who is lacking in confidence. In fact, to the contrary, it is likely to become more disturbed.

So far we have dealt with the role of superstitious practices in protecting the horse from danger and maintaining it under the control of benevolent forces. There was a positive side to all of this and this concerned the training of horses. Individuals within the community were known to have the gift of being able to train or establish control over horses, but when we reach behind the welter of ritual and mystery with which they surround their activities we find that they make use of the same techniques as those which horse curers use. By means of some object or action they establish contact and develop a relationship with the horse. In this they are assisted by the highly developed sensitivity of the animal.[14]

The horse's keen sense of smell is a critical factor in many instances of apparent magic control of horses. One of the substances used by horse experts to exercise influence over the horse was the milt, a fibrous substance found in a colt foal's mouth when it is born:

> When a foal is born, ther's a pad in his mouth. And if yeh were quick enough, yeh'd get this pad—'tis a sort o' liver. An' if yeh have an'thin' to do with stall'ons or wicked horses, if yeh get that and preserve it—if yeh put it in yer pocket—the old people say that it quietens a stall'on. Yeh need only let him smell that an' he'll settle down. He connects it with the foal at once.

As well as quietening a troublesome horse, odorous substances could be used to stop a horse in its tracks or to attract it. In the case of the milt, in Britain oils were sometimes placed on it to give it a strong odour. In Scotland, where to this day horsemen are organised in a tightly-knit society where professional secrets are closely guarded, horsemen placed the milt under their armpits so that the milt carried their own odour.

The horse's sense of hearing, which is more highly developed than its sense of smell, provided an even more effective means of making contact with the horse. Hence the method of gaining control of the horse which was frequently used was that of whispering in its ear. It was believed that the horsemen had a secret word which when whispered in the horse's ear exercised control over it. Kevin Danaher gives the following personal experience:

> It was at a fair in Rathkeale that I saw for the first and only time the strange power of the horseman's word. A young colt, whether through fear or perverseness, was prancing and kicking wildly when a boy of about seventeen walked in and fondled the horse's nose, talking quietly. Immediately the colt became calm and the boy took the headstall and led him up and down as meek as a lamb. It was said, too, that as well as being able to quieten horses and break untrained animals in a matter of minutes, this boy could get a horse to stand still and not move for any force or persuasion until he or somebody else who had the power released it.

One of the most famous 'whisperers' was James Sullivan who lived in Cork at the turn of the eighteenth century. He had the reputation of being able to tame even the most intractable animal:

> When sent for to tame a vicious beast for which he was paid more or less according to distance, generally two or three guineas, he directed the stable in which he and the object of the experiment were placed to be shut, with orders not to open the door until a signal was given. After a tête-à-tête of about half an hour, during which little or no bustle was heard, the signal was made and upon opening the door the horse appeared lying down, and the man by his side, playing familiarly with him, like a child with a puppy-dog. From that time he was found perfectly willing to submit to any discipline however repugnant to his nature before.

As we might expect, one of Sullivan's successes was with a famous racehorse—*King Pippin*. Nobody could approach the stallion because of his fierceness. Sullivan, however, spent a night in the horse's stable sometime during 1804 and subsequently it emerged tame and could be entered for a race at the Curragh which he won.[15]

The activities of the Horseman's Society in Scotland to which we have referred and which was known as the Society of the Horseman's Word throws light on the nature of the Word. The Word or words were "Both in one" and referred to the bond which joined the horse and horsemen together. The Word was a closely guarded secret and was only revealed to young men when they were initiated into the society in an elaborate initiation rite. The society and its Word gave the young initiate the assurance that he could create with the horse the relationship necessary for its control.

Paul Darragh at home with *P. J. Carroll*, one of the fastest speed horses in the world in the late 1970s and early 1980s. *(Inpho)*

In Ireland there was no such tightly organised society as in Scotland. There are, however, clear indications that whisperers guarded the essential simplicity of their craft in much the same way. We are told, for example, that Sullivan learned the Horseman's Word from a soldier and that he had to swear to him that he would keep it a secret. The word was a convenient smoke screen for the secret of the ability to control horses. That secret was bound up with co-operation rather than fear. 'Capall le ceansacht' or 'treat your horse with kindness' was the conventional wisdom. Ploughmen sometimes sang to their horses in order to keep them going at an appropriate pace. In Kickham's novel *Knocknagow*, Matt the Thrasher sings 'Cailín Deas Crúite na mBó' to his plough horse. A prayer or whisper in a horse's ear, regardless of its content, was essentially an intimate occasion. In Wales whisperers generally intensified their contact with horses by massaging them all over, with the result that the horses relaxed completely in their presence.

Blowing down a horse's nostrils, a secret which Barbara Woodhouse learned from a 'Garanee' Indian in Argentina who used it to train his young horses, is also a method demanding a trust and intimacy with the animal. It is, according to Miss Woodhouse, a way of saying in the animal's language "How do you do".[16]

The fact that control of the horse was of such importance to the community meant that it was perceived to be a matter of otherworldly influence. One of the most important occasions when this control would be exercised would be when the horse was being ridden and it is clear from various stories that people believed that the best riders were either otherworldly figures or had connections with the Other-world. A case in point was Seán Boy, a very famous rider from Co. Mayo. He was so accomplished on horseback that it was believed that he was connected to the fairy people. Some people indeed believed that he was a fairy himself. His great riding skills are illustrated in one of the many stories told about Finnbheara the great Fairy King of the West of Ireland who had his residence, we are told, at Cnoc Meadha near Tuam in Co. Galway. Finnbheara, who was usually seen riding a superb black horse with red nostrils that appeared to breathe fire, sometimes, we are told, used to invite young men to ride with his fairy host and this is the reason, the people believed, why ever afterwards these young men were the most fearless riders in the countryside. He was very friendly with all the Galway landowners, the Kirwans, Blakes, Frenches etc., and the story which concerns us here fits into the general pattern which we considered earlier. The success or failure of the horse at the racecourse was of critical importance to the community, in this case the Kirwans of Castle Hackett in north Co. Galway. They had become very poor and the only thing which was likely to save their estates was the success of a valuable racehorse entered for a race at the Curragh in Co. Kildare. There was one problem however. Kirwans' jockey, while good, was unreliable and liable to get drunk before the race and be unable to ride. About a week before the race the owner of the horse encountered Finnbheara riding his black steed. The Fairy King told him that he had a very good jockey and he would make him available to Kirwan. As they parted the stranger said, "If you see my jockey putting his whip between his teeth you will know that he is going to win, but he is a strange little lad and he does not say many words to people. He speaks mostly to horses."

True to form on the morning of the race, Kirwan's jockey was drunk and Kirwan was about to scratch from the race when the fairy jockey Seán Boy appeared. When he saw the horse he walked around in front of it and they looked at one another, and Seán Boy whispered in the horse's ear. When he finished speaking the horse whinnied softly and Seán Boy put the whip between his teeth. The race was a foregone conclusion. Kirwan's horse was ten lengths ahead at an early stage and at the end the other horses were nowhere in sight. Kirwan's estates were saved.[17]

Training or riding the horse, it might be argued, is essentially about getting co-operation from the animal, and mutual trust is a necessity for this. It might further be argued that there is nothing essentially obscure about this and that any horseman would approach the horse in a manner calculated to develop this trust. But this is not the full story. In the first place the horse has managed to preserve an aura of unpredictability about him over the centuries. This is most apparent on the racecourse where the favourite is beaten and the experts confounded. There is, therefore, a premium on skill and a search for the secrets underlying that skill. Secondly, and of central concern in our story, is the history of man's relations with the animal. We have argued that in Ireland man's relationship with the horse has its basis in totemism and that in Irish eyes the horse acquired otherworldly characteristics. We pointed out that this relationship came under attack because of its central role in Irish life and we suggested that, instead of being destroyed, the core of the horse tradition was driven underground and retained its vitality, achieving, if anything, a clearer definition. It was natural in these circumstances that society would surround matters concerned with the relationship to the horse with a mystique, if only as a protection against attack. Knowledge of horses in the community was valued and would not be immediately available to the casual observer. It still retained the elements of a religion and it still had its priests.

Storm Bird, trained by Vincent O'Brien and ridden by Steve Cauthen, winning the Larkspur Stakes at Leopardstown, 20 September 1980. After this race, *Storm Bird* was installed as favourite for the Epsom Derby, but was maimed in his stable and did not race. (*Tony Parkes*)

Opposite page:
Jockey Walter Swinburn (left) out with the East Galway Hunt, with Michael Dempsey junior, Master. (*Ruth Rogers*)

Top: Millstreet International Horse Show 1984. Lungeing a horse during the Bank of Ireland Young Irelander Championship. (*Horseman Photography*)

Right: Killeagh Harriers' Point-to point, 24 January 1982. The winner, on the left, *King's Wagon*, ridden by T. O'Callaghan, is led over the last by *Search Warrant*, ridden by J. J. Mangan, who finished second. (*Horseman Photography*)

Bottom left: *Early Mist*, ridden by Bryan Marshall, takes the last fence to win the 1953 Aintree Grand National. (*Hulton-Deutsch Collection*)

Bottom right: Jessica Harrington and *Amoy* competing at Badminton Horse Trials in 1981. They were placed fifth. (*Czerny*)

8

The Development of Racing
to the Present Day

EQUESTRIAN SPORTS, THE CLERGY AND THE LAND WAR

BECAUSE equestrian sports enjoyed wide public appeal they were able to survive the strains imposed by such events as the influx of planters and the imposition of Penal Laws in the seventeenth century. These sports, however, had to face other threats in subsequent centuries. In the 18th and early 19th centuries landlords were dispensing with middlemen and letting their estates directly to tenants. This resulted in the increasing isolation of landlords as the bridge between them and the ordinary people was undermined by the disappearance of the middleman class. With this isolation went rural conflict which reached its peak in the Land League activities of the 1870s and 1880s.

The middlemen had served the function of popularising among the ordinary people the pursuits and interests of the gentry. With their removal, sports like hunting were in danger of being seen as the preserve of the few. Economic difficulties, culminating in the disastrously bad harvest of 1879, exacerbated these tensions. The Land League was established to fight for the rights of tenants who now began to see the landlords as alien. In the Land War which followed, hunting was a primary target. "Hunting or no hunting is landlordism or no landlordism", declared one of the leading clerical supporters in Co. Tipperary of a ban on foxhunting. In the same county a priest advised his parishioners to poison their lands—a type of action which, it would appear, achieved its objective in some places. The Tipperary Hunt Club, for instance, was forced to sell its pack. The counties of Kildare and Waterford were particularly badly hit and in many parts of the country hunts had to cease operations temporarily. Sportswriters complained of "the poisoning of poor inoffensive hounds and foxes" and the "prevention of hunting by organised mobs surrounding coverts, shouting, hooting, blowing horns and ringing bells." In Co. Limerick John Gubbins who was Master of the Limerick Foxhounds from 1880 to 1886 was prevented from following the hunt. On one occasion his hounds, which he kennelled at Bruree, were set upon by a gang with staves, rocks and stones. He took his pack home and hunted no more.

Priests' involvement in anti-hunting activities was in line with developments during the early part of the century. Many traditional forms of amusement were criticised by the Catholic Church as occasions of licentiousness, and some festivals

Thady Ryan, Master of the Scarteen Hounds, at the opening meet at Knocklong, Co. Tipperary, 16 October 1967. The hounds, which have a close relationship with the famous Kerry Beagles, have been associated for several hundred years with the Ryans of Knocklong. (*Horseman Photography*).

The Meath Hunt disappearing into the mist at Drumbarra, Kells, Co. Meath, 19 December 1989. (*The Irish Times: Paddy Whelan*)

and patterns were suppressed. Nor was the Catholic Church alone in this. The Presbyterian Church's list of offences included attending cock fighting and horse-racing as well as other forms of amusement such as card playing and activities at wakes. The Catholic clergy had for long denounced faction fights but it was not until the rural upper classes abandoned them that the way was clear to press for their suppression. The room for attacks by the Catholic clergy, however, on hunting or racing was very limited. In the early 18th century Catholic clergy generally came from the ranks of the gentry and, even in later periods, its background was generally one of some substance. In addition, some of the bishops knew that the priests themselves also shared the pleasures of the hunting field. Bishop Sweetman of Ferns who went on a visitation of his diocese in 1753 learned that in the parish of Rathgarogue "the Pastor minded dogs and hunting more than his flock". By the first half of the 19th century the popularity of hunting among the clergy had not waned. "The country priest now copes with the country squire [and] keeps sporting dogs", one commentator observed in 1834, and in the diocese of Kildare and Leighlin, it was later claimed, "there were priests who ejaculated 'Tally Ho' as often as 'Pax Vobiscum'." Bishops, however, in the first half of the century, on an individual and collective basis, took steps to deal with their clergy in this respect. In Kildare and Leighlin, for instance, priests were forbidden to attend horse-races, hunts or other places of amusement, and at the Synod of Thurles in 1850 similar regulations were given national application.

The tradition of the hunting priest, however, survived these regulations and in Glin in the 1870s we find an ardent huntsman, Fr Malone, as PP. Whenever the local hunt was meeting he used to run up the flag on the roof of the parochial house as a signal to the officers of the Royal Navy ships in the nearby Shannon estuary. The officers, seeing the flag, would come ashore and join the hunt. The effect of the Land League activities was to polarise opinion between landlord and tenant, and Fr Malone found himself in bitter enmity with the Knight of Glin and was forced to resign.

Landlords with a background in hunting, could also espouse the popular cause, and this probably was a significant factor in enabling hunting to recover its wide appeal and reassert itself after the difficulties of the Land War. In the middle of the century George Henry Moore, a landlord whose hunting exploits we have already noted, had become an MP and was reputed to have even taken the Fenian oath. Charles Stuart Parnell followed in the same tradition. When the Land League was formed he agreed to become its president. His background was upper-class. On the family estate of about 5,000 acres near Avondale in Co. Wicklow there were always horses, and as a young man he had hunted with the local pack. It would appear also that the man who would later advocate a policy of boycott against recalcitrant landlords was once part of the racing establishment, acting as a Steward at Laytown Races in 1876, races which were originally organised by the local parish priest until

Top left : Trainer Jim Dreaper on *Ten Up* at his farm at Kilsallaghan, near Dublin. *(Gerry Cranham)*

Top right : Seamus McGrath, trainer. *(G. A. Duncan)*

Bottom left : *Captain Christy* and trainer Pat Taaffe. *(Gerry Cranham)*

Bottom right : David O'Brien who as a 28-year-old was the youngest trainer to saddle an Epsom Derby winner—*Secreto* in 1984. Two years earlier he had another first to his name—trainer of the first horse, *Assert*, to win the Irish and French Derbies. In 1988 he retired from training. *(Inpho)*

the arrival of a reforming bishop put an end to his activities.[1]

Racing, too, suffered setbacks from the actions of the Land League. Lord Waterford's steeplechase course had to be shut down and in 1882 the Punchestown meeting had to be cancelled. No lasting damage was, however, done to the sport. In fact, the period 1870 to 1890 was the golden age of Irish steeplechasing.

PROFESSIONAL HORSE TRAINERS

A major factor in this was the encouragement given by landlords to professional trainers. Formerly many of the landlords had private parks, such as Lord Waterford's at Curraghmore, where their horses could be trained by their own staff. However, the economic position of the landlords changed radically in the last few decades of the century. Their grip on their estates weakened. Government legislation had sought to control the relations between them and their tenants, bringing about a reduction in rents. Funds were made available for tenants purchasing lands, commencing a process which, in the early years of the twentieth century, resulted in tenant purchase on a grand scale. As the big houses began to lose their acres, landlords realised that the days of private courses were gone and made alternative arrangements.

As we have seen, the gentry was prepared in the eighteenth and nineteenth centuries to admit into its ranks on the hunting field and at the racecourse horsemen of lower social standing. In the early part of the nineteenth century, for instance, members of the west of Ireland gentry had welcomed into their houses Tom Ferguson, a natural horseman who had started his career in a linen factory in the north of Ireland. "I know all the lords," he had boasted. In the difficult circumstances of the last quarter of the century professional trainers, self-made men also, began to play a major part in racing activities. Men like John Hubert Moore and Henry Linde had steeplechase courses laid out on their properties and were able to bring a business-like attitude to the training of the horses sent to them. Increasingly, men who had made their money in the cities and had no estates behind them were also coming into racing and required the services of trainers. Such men could send their horses to be trained, secure in the knowledge that it was not the pedigree of the owners but that of the horses which counted.

HENRY LINDE, THE BEASLEYS AND THE MOORES

Linde was one of the first of the trainers to whom the gentry sent their horses. With these horses he dominated steeplechasing in the last quarter of the nineteenth century achieving notable successes in Great Britain and France as well as in Ireland. Much of his success was due to the training methods which he adopted at his establishment at Eyrefield Lodge on the Curragh. His horses were given constant jumping practice over the private course which he had built there and which consisted of fences modelled on those to be encountered in competition in Ireland

and England.

Linde's horse purchases also demonstrated considerable acumen. He bought wisely and cheaply. In the 1870s he purchased the mare *Highland Mary* for £25 and she gave him his first real taste of success, winning at both Punchestown and Fairyhouse in April 1873. He also bought *Seaman* cheaply in a private deal and trained him to win both the Liverpool Hunt Steeplechase and the Grand Hurdle at Auteuil in 1881 before selling him. The horse was unsound and Linde did not believe that he was capable of taking steeplechasing's great prize—the Grand National at Aintree. In this he was, however, proven wrong. One year after his great victories for the Irish trainer, *Seaman* captured the honour for Lord Manners, ironically against opposition which included two of Linde's fancied runners. Thus was the Irish trainer deprived of a great hat trick, for in 1880 and 1881 he had saddled the winners of the race, *Empress* and *Woodbrook*.

A major factor in the success of his horses was the riding skills of the Beasley family on which he could call. The four Beasley brothers, Tommy, Harry, Johnny and Willy, had grown up near Athy in Co. Kildare a short distance from the Curragh where trainers Linde, Moore and Allen McDonough, a very successful rider earlier in the century, had their stables. From these trainers the brothers learned their craft.

Of the four brothers, Tommy had perhaps the most spectacular successes for he not only took three Aintree Grand Nationals, in 1880, 1881 and 1889, but also succeeded in winning the Irish Derby in 1889. His achievement in winning both this and the Grand National as an amateur in the same year is unlikely ever to be equalled. But Tommy never caught the public imagination in the same way as his younger brother Harry who was a more daring if less accomplished horseman. Harry became a particular favourite at Punchestown, scene of many of Linde's successes, winning the Conyngham Cup there no less than six times. But perhaps the most outstanding facet of his riding career was its duration. His commencement of training on the Curragh in the late 1880s by no means signalled the end of his riding career. In fact his long-awaited win in the Aintree Grand National did not come until 1891 when *Come-away*, trained and ridden by him, raced to victory. He continued riding until he was eighty-three, a living link, for those who attended Punchestown, with an earlier age when Punchestown and steeplechasing were in their prime. In 1923 at the age of seventy-two, forty-four years after his first winning ride there, he rode his own mare *Pride of Arras* to victory in front of a crowd which included the Governor General and the President of the fledgeling Irish Free State, William T. Cosgrave. Later the crowd which greeted his victory with a tumultuous reception carried him shoulder-high to be presented to the dignitaries.

The Beasley tradition did not come to an end with Harry. His son H. H. Beasley who was leading professional jockey in 1918 with forty-four winners on the flat and second with fifty-eight winners in 1919, had his first mount in a steeplechase on 17 March 1919. H. H.'s son, Bobby, who in 1951 at the age of sixteen was granted a

Gentleman Rider's permit went on to record, on both sides of the Irish Sea, successes which included the Cheltenham Gold Cup on *Roddy Owen* in 1959, the Champion Hurdle at Cheltenham and the Conyngham Cup at Punchestown in 1960. In the 1961 Aintree Grand National, he rode *Nicolaus Silver* to victory by five lengths bringing his owner over twenty thousand pounds, a figure well in excess of the prize of £1,680 which his grandfather won in 1891 for the same race.[2]

Just as Linde owed much of his success to the skills of the Beasley brothers, his neighbour at Jockey Hall on the Curragh, J. H. Moore was equally blessed in being able to call on the services of his sons, Garrett and Willie. Willie did much of his racing on the continent, however his most notable successes were the Irish winners of the Aintree Grand National of 1894 and 1896, *Why Not* and *The Soarer* respectively, with whose training he had assisted. Garrett's greatest victory was in the Aintree Grand National of 1879 on *The Liberator*, a horse owned jointly by his father and Mr Plunkett Taaffe. Because of a legal disagreement between the owners, the horse had to be registered in Garrett's name, giving him the distinction of being only the second owner-rider ever to triumph in the race. Garrett's exploits as retailed in stories told about him are reminiscent of those of the steeplechase riders of an earlier age. He was a happy-go-lucky man who was fond of drink and good food. A taste for the finer things in life would appear to have helped not only Garrett in his racing career but also, on one occasion, his horse. At the Curragh, Moore was observed, before a race, sharing a bottle of Jameson whiskey with his mare which duly went on to win at a canter.

J. J. PARKINSON AND MICHAEL DAWSON

The trainer who more than any other dominated the early years of the twentieth century was J. J. Parkinson. He had learned race-riding from Michael Dennehy of French House on the Curragh. Initially he had used Brownstown House, later to be the home of the McGrath empire, as his base, but, after a period in America in 1903, he returned and purchased Maddenstown Lodge and from there during the next quarter of a century he sent out a long list of winners both over obstacles and on the flat. Boss Croker was one of those who sent his horses to him and in 1905 and 1906 Croker, with Parkinson as his trainer, became the leading owner in Ireland. But when *Orby* was defeated twice as a two-year-old, Croker removed all his horses from Parkinson and installed F. F. McCabe as his private trainer at Glencairn in Co. Dublin. In 1917 and 1919 he won the Irish Derby with *First Flier* and *Loch Lomond* respectively.

One of the innovations which Parkinson had introduced as a rider and later as a trainer was the short leathers and forward seat favoured by American jockeys. John Thompson who was apprenticed to Parkinson and later retained by him as his stable jockey was the first important rider in Ireland to adopt this style. The innovation met with success for during the periods 1904–1907 and 1910–1912 Thompson was

Niall and Dotie Flynn lead in *Meladon*, ridden by Tommy Carberry, after winning the Daily Express Triumph Hurdle at Cheltenham in 1977. *Meladon* was the first Irish horse to win the event. *(Ruth Rogers)*

Ireland's leading professional jockey.

Parkinson's business was a high-volume one. His stable at Maddenstown Lodge was one of the biggest in Europe. During the first year after his return from America all his one hundred and fifty boxes were full. He had contacts all over the world and turned over his horses regularly. In 1923, one year after he had been appointed to the Senate by President William T. Cosgrave, he created a record by training one hundred and thirty-seven winners in the season. Nine years previously he had headed the Irish trainers' list having been runner-up for a number of years to his great rival, Michael Dawson, who had topped the list since 1906.

Before commencing his training career Dawson had been a very successful jockey. He had been apprenticed to one of the first trainers in Ireland to set up his own establishment, Pat Connolly of Curragh View. Assisted by his son, Tom, Connolly had trained such famous horses as *Barcaldine*, *Ben Battle* and *Bendigo*. When Rice Meredith succeeded Connolly at Curragh View, Dawson became his stable jockey. Meredith later moved to Rathbride Manor which he made into the finest yard in Ireland. With Dawson as his stable jockey, Meredith trained three Irish Derby winners, *Kentish Fire* (1890), *Roy Neil* (1892) and *Bowline* (1893). Two of these, *Kentish Fire* and *Bowline*, were owned by Mat Maher, a cousin of Valentine

Maher whose riding exploits we have already noted. They had been sired by *Torpedo*, a son of *Gunboat* and one of the most popular sires in the country. *Gunboat* had also sired Maher's most famous horse *Frigate* which on her sixth attempt in 1889 had won the Aintree Grand National with Tommy Beasley up. As far as the Beasley family was concerned, *Frigate* was common property. In three of the other attempts at Aintree she had been ridden by either one of the two other brothers.

On Rice Meredith's retirement, Maher continued to send his racehorses to Rathbride Manor where they became the responsibility of Dawson who had started training there. Thus, continuity from the early nineteenth century, when Pat Connolly first branched out on his own as a trainer, was maintained. It was a continuity that would extend well into the middle of the 20th century, for Dawson's son Michael took over from his father at Rathbride Manor, taking the Irish Derby in 1958 with *Sindon*.

During his training career, Dawson senior had, unlike his great rival, Parkinson, concentrated his energies at Rathbride Manor on a small number of horses. He preferred to train for owners who were prepared to give their horses time to develop. His results, including victories in four Irish Derbies, were excellent. He was leading Irish trainer eight times during his career and only ceded his position at the top of the list in 1914 to Parkinson. Among his owners was the popular James Daly, a horse dealer who in his youth had supplied British army remounts for the Crimean War. His Hartstown Stud was the first in Ireland to be run on modern lines and it was there that he bred *St Brendan* who, with Dawson as trainer, won the Irish Derby in 1902.[3]

In 1937 Hubert Hartigan, a nephew of Garrett and Willie Moore, broke the record established by J. J. Parkinson by winning £12,372 for the owners for whom he trained. Unlike his brother, Frank, winner of the Aintree Grand National in 1930 with *Shaun Goilin*, Hubert never moved his training operations permanently to England but at Melitta Lodge on the Curragh he managed to attract some of the most famous owners of his day. Among those who sent horses to him there were Prince Aly Khan and the Third Aga Khan and in 1948 their confidence in him was rewarded when *Masaka* bred by the Aga Khan in Ireland from *Nearco* won both the Irish and English Oaks.

THE AGA KHAN

The Third Aga Khan who entered the breeding and racing business in 1921 went on to found one of the most successful racing and breeding empires ever. He set up five studs in Ireland appointing as his first manager Captain Harry Greer who continued to hold the position of director of the Irish National Stud. Greer was instrumental in setting up in Ireland one of the most influential studs in the thoroughbred world, Sheshoon, for the Aga Khan. From Sheshoon flowed a succession of Irish and English Derby winners—*Dastur* (Irish Derby 1932), *Turkham*

The Begum Aga Khan with President Seán T. O'Kelly (right) presenting the Aga Khan trophy to Lt. Col. Nat Kindersley, Chef d'Équipe of the winning British showjumping team, at the RDS in 1958.

(Irish Derby 1940), *Nathoo* (Irish Derby winner 1948) and *Hindostan* (Irish Derby winner 1949). In 1939 the Aga Khan purchased Gilltown Stud which had been established in 1919 by Lord Furness. From *Americus Girl*, who was one of the first mares there, Furness had bred *Lady Josephine*. She in turn produced *Mumtaz Mahal*, 'The Flying Filly', whom the Aga Khan purchased and who was one of the fastest fillies ever bred. She was decisive in making him one of the world's greatest breeders. Her offspring included *Mumtaz Begum* who was the dam of *Nasrullah*, purchased by Joe McGrath and subsequently the most important sire ever introduced into America. Another daughter of *Mumtaz Mahal* bred the Aga Khan his third Derby winner *Mahmoud* whose record time for the Epsom race in 1936 still stands. Others of her descendants included *Abernant, Royal Charger*, the first stallion to stand at the National Stud in Tully, Co. Kildare, *Kalamoun* and the wonderful filly *Petite Étoile* who was bred at Gilltown Stud. But perhaps the most remarkable of all was *Shergar* of whom she was the seventh dam.

In 1981 *Shergar* won the Epsom Derby by a record ten lengths, the Irish Derby, King George VI and Queen Elizabeth Diamond Stakes and was returned to Ireland, where he had been bred, to stand at stud. The Fourth Aga Khan, grandson of the founder of the breeding and racing empire, had taken over control of these interests in 1960 and sold most of the Irish studs, including Gilltown in 1971, but had retained the Sheshoon and Ballymany studs. Ballymany, like Sheshoon, has produced many classic winners for the Aga Khan including the winner of both the Irish and English Derbies in 1988, *Kahyasi*. *Shergar* was placed at Ballymany where his stable companion was *Nishapour* a descendant of *Nasrullah* and winner of the French Two Thousand Guineas. His stay there was, however, short. On Tuesday 8 February 1983 he was kidnapped, ostensibly by the IRA—the illegal Irish Republican Army—and has never been found. There is little doubt but that he was killed.

R. C. DAWSON

The distinction of being the Aga Khan's first trainer belonged to an Irishman, R. C. Dawson who trained at Whatcombe in England. He had learned his horsemanship skills from Linde and like his mentor made excellent purchases of horses. In 1922 for 250 guineas he bought *Friar's Daughter*, later to be the dam of two of the Aga Khan's very successful horses, *Dastur*, the Irish Derby winner in 1932 and *Bahram*, the Triple Crown winner, who was bred at the Gilltown Stud. In 1897 he purchased *Drogheda* which he trained in England to win the Grand National in the following year. But his greatest purchase was that of *Blandford* in 1920 from its breeder, the National Stud in Tully Co. Kildare. *Blandford* which was kept by Dawson at his stud in Cloghran in Co. Dublin until the onset of the economic war between Ireland and England became the greatest sire of his generation having four Derby winners to his credit including two trained by Dawson—*Trigo* (1929) and *Blenheim* (1930), the Aga Khan's first winner of the great race. *Bahram* was also sired by *Blandford*, giving Dawson the distinction of having purchased the dam and sire of the great horse. Dawson was one of the greatest trainers of his generation. To others, his preparation of his horses seemed very severe but the results spoke for themselves. During the course of his career he had been champion trainer three times.

Mumtaz Mahal, the filly who provided the basis for much of the Aga Khan's breeding success and whom Dawson described as "the greatest horse I ever trained" had been sired out of *Lady Josephine* by the *The Tetrarch*, the 'spotted wonder', bred by Edward Kennedy at Straffan House Stud in Co. Kildare.

THE TETRARCH

The Tetrarch was trained by his owner, Atty Persse, a member of a Galway distilling family who in 1906 had moved from Ireland to England and had set up his training base at Chattis Hill in the Wiltshire village of Stockbridge where he trained four classic winners and became the best known producer of two-year-olds ready to run and win on their first outing. In this he was greatly assisted by the brilliant jockey Steve Donohue who had ridden for Boss Croker but had followed the path of most of those who worked for the Irish American and had been let go. With Donohue in the saddle *The Tetrarch* won all of his seven two-year-old races but in 1914, due to doubts about his fitness, he had to retire. He had never been defeated on the racetrack and his trainer was convinced that he never would have been beaten at any distance such was his phenomenal speed.

When he retired to stud, *The Tetrarch* was moved to Mountjuliet near Thomastown in Co. Kilkenny, the property of Persse's cousin, Captain Dermot McCalmont, who had acquired the horse and who had established Ballylinch Stud to house him. The Earls of Carrick from whom Dermot's father leased the stud, had kept hounds at Mountjuliet in the eighteenth century, hunting fox as well as deer and hare. Under the guidance of John Power, an influential Whig and Catholic emancipationist who was Master of the Kilkenny Foxhounds from 1801 to 1844, the sport in Kilkenny became legendary, attracting great numbers from England. Subsequent masters, including his son, kept up the great tradition established by Power and Kilkenny became known as the best scenting country in the world. Dermot McCalmont during his forty-seven years as master bred a superb hound and, when he inherited Mountjuliet, built the most efficient and most palatial kennels in the world there. In 1949 his son Victor became joint master and in 1968 sole master.

At Mountjuliet, *The Tetrarch* sired *Tetramena* who won the Two Thousand Guineas at Newmarket and who in turn sired *Mr Jinks* who won the same race in 1929. McCalmont also had many successes in Ireland culminating in Irish Derby victories in 1944 and 1945 with *Slide On* and *Piccadilly*. His son, Victor, who was appointed Senior Steward of the Turf Club in the early 1970s, retained Mountjuliet until 1987 when it was sold to become a leisure centre. Two of the stallions which attracted a large number of mares to the stud during the 1980s were *Jaazeiro*, trained by Vincent O'Brien to win the Irish Two Thousand Guineas, and *Scorpio* whose sire was *Sir Gaylord*. The stud's own mares also produced many winners.

THE BRITISH ARMY AND EQUESTRIAN SPORTS

One of the features of the McCalmont family has been its involvement with the British Army. Dermot's father was Captain Hugh McCalmont who emerged the winner of the Irish Grand Military Cup at Punchestown in 1873 after a controversial decision by the Stewards to disqualify the horse which had come in first. Hugh's brother, Harry, trainer of *Isinglass*, was also an army officer. Dermot served in the Seventh Hussars and Victor in turn followed in his father's footsteps and also joined the army. This family typified the link between the military and racing over the centuries in Ireland. In the nineteenth century, for instance, cavalry regiments played a leading part in steeplechasing. Part of the reason for this was that it provided an enjoyable form of training. A race from point to point across country approximated closely to the demands made on troops and officers on horseback. Closely associated with racing, as we have seen, was the sport of hunting, and officers were frequently found riding to hounds. Indeed military duties were not allowed to interfere very much with such pleasures. An officer's morning duties which usually consisted of parades and inspections could generally be left to NCOs

The Tetrarch's grave at Ballylinch Stud. (Horseman Photography)

Cheltenham, St Patrick's Day 1977, when trainer Mick O'Toole presented the Queen Mother with shamrock, the Irish there sang for her and the O'Toole-trained *Davy Lad* won the Gold Cup, beating *Tied Cottage*. *Davy Lad* was the sixteenth Irish winner of the trophy. (*Ruth Rogers*)

to undertake. Afternoons and evenings were usually free for sport and social engagements. Some officers hunted three times a week during the season while those stationed at the Curragh were within easy reach of several racecourses including one of the most popular, Punchestown.

Many British army personnel had racing interests on both sides of the Irish Sea and this contributed to the ties which existed between the sporting bodies in both countries. Such ties no doubt helped ensure that the Irish and English continued to mingle on the racecourse. Dermot McCalmont, for instance was a member of the Jockey Club in England as well as the Turf Club in Ireland. John Gubbins, a brother of Captain Stamer Gubbins, veteran of the Crimean War and trainer of the 1877 Irish Derby winner *Redskin*, achieved great renown through the successes of the horses he owned. When it suited he was prepared to send them to England to be trained retaining at the same time his studs at Bruree and Knockaney where *Seaman*, *Ard Patrick* and *Galtee More* were bred.

Sam Darling who trained for Gubbins in England also trained horses for Captain Harry Greer whose filly *Tragedy*, with Tommy Beasley up won the Irish Derby in 1889. Greer had his stud at Brownstown House on the Curragh and stood his famous stallion *Gallinule* there. *Gallinule* was the great grandsire of *Lady Josephine*, the dam of *Mumtaz Mahal* and had the distinction of siring every winner except one of the Irish Derby between the years 1895 and 1901. But his most famous progeny was undoubtedly *Pretty Polly* who was one of the greatest fillies ever to race and who carved out a firm place for herself in the hearts of the British race-going public.

PRETTY POLLY
The mare was foaled in 1901 at Eyrefield Lodge, the stud purchased in 1898 by Captain Eustace Loder, known as 'Lucky Loder' because of his enormous successes on the turf. When Loder left the army he retired to Eyrefield to supervise the business there, adding the Old Connell Stud to it in 1906. The list of winners emerging from these studs which have remained in the hands of the Loder family is impressive. *Pretty Polly* won the One Thousand Guineas, the Oaks and the St Leger. In 1906, *Spearmint* won the Epsom Derby and Grand Prix de Paris and subsequently went on to sire the 1920 Epsom Derby winner, *Spion Kop*, and *Zionist*, the Aga Khan's first Irish Derby winner. *Marwell* who was bred and owned by the present incumbent at Eyrefield Lodge, Edmund Loder, and who was by *Habitat* out of the *Tudor Melody* mare *Lady Seymour*, won ten prestigious races during her two- and three-year-old career in 1980 and 1981 netting over £200,000 in stake money.

THE IRISH NATIONAL STUD

But the ex-soldier who undoubtedly made the greatest long-term contribution to Irish breeding and racing was Colonel Hall-Walker. A Scotsman, Hall-Walker had competed successfully as a rider under pony rules in the late 1880s. In 1896 he bought the Irish horse *The Soarer* who won the Aintree Grand National for him in the same year. Two years later he bought a farm at Tully outside Kildare town on the edge of the Curragh and proceeded to breed thoroughbred horses and establish a Japanese Garden. Winnings from the progeny there showed an increase from the initial figure of £260 in 1900 to £27,400 in the 1905 season and for eleven out of the fifteen years during which he ran Tully he was in the top four of the list of breeders in the British Isles. Hall-Walker's views on breeding and racing were way ahead of his time and the practices he adopted regarding his own stock, although somewhat eccentric, were successful. He drew on astrological science, allowing his foals' horoscopes to dictate if they should be sold or retained and his mares' horoscopes to influence their matings. At Tully the horse-boxes were designed so that the horses could have a view of the sky and stars. "There is no royal road to success in breeding

acing at Cheltenham, 9 November 1974.
Gerry Cranham)

either by the aid of Astrology, Botany or Physiology," he pointed out in 1908, "but these all have their use if applied in an intelligent manner." Before the First World War he could point to such notable breeding successes as the Two Thousand Guineas and Epsom Derby winner *Minoru* which he had leased to King Edward VII, the One Thousand Guineas and Oaks winner *Cherry Lass* and the One Thousand Guineas winners, *Prince Palatine* and *Night Hawk*.

In 1915 Hall-Walker generously conferred all his bloodstock on the British Government on condition that it used the gift to found a National Stud and that it purchased his properties at Tully and in Wiltshire at a valuation to be drawn up by the government-appointed valuer, Captain Harry Greer. At Tully Colonel Hall-Walker had 6 stallions, 43 broodmares, 10 two-year-olds, 19 yearlings and more than 300 Shorthorn cattle. Among the mares there were very valuable animals of the calibre of *Black Cherry* and *Blanche* the dam of *Blandford*. He had frequently expressed strong views concerning the export from Ireland of some of the best bloodstock and his gesture in making the donation accorded with these views. The government at first hesitated to accept the priceless bloodstock but eventually was persuaded to incur the relatively small expense involved of £65,625. Greer became the first manager of the stud producing horses of the calibre of *Blandford, Big Game* and *Sun Chariot*. In 1943 after a prolonged dispute with the Irish government the British government removed all its stock from Tully to Gillingham in Dorset where it established its own National Stud. The land and buildings at Tully became the property of the Irish government which in 1945 set up the Irish National Stud Company.

The objective of the stud was to assist Irish breeders by providing the services of high class stallions at a reasonable fee. Mares approved to be mated with these stallions were selected by ballot. The first stallion purchased was *Royal Charger* a descendant of the Aga Khan's foundation mare *Mumtaz Mahal* and later one of the world's greatest stallions, siring among others *Turn To* in 1951 who became one of the best American stallions of his time. *Turn To*'s progeny included *Hail to Reason* and *Sir Gaylord*, sires of the Epsom Derby winners *Roberto* and *Sir Ivor* respectively, and *First Landing*, sire of the Kentucky Derby winner, *Riva Rouge*.

Other stallions which have stood at Tully include *Panaslipper*, trained by Seamus McGrath at Glencairn to win the Irish Derby in 1955 and *Tulyar* which was bred by the Aga Khan in Ireland and won the 1952 Epsom Derby and St Leger. *Tulyar* was the most expensive stallion of his day at £250,000 which was the sum paid by the stud to the Aga Khan. This was £50,000 less than the sum offered by an American syndicate to him for the stallion. Not for the last time would the Aga Khan seek to benefit the Irish horse industry, an acknowledgement perhaps of the role Ireland and, in particular, the National Stud had played in the inception of his breeding empire. The conversations which he had with Hall-Walker were one of the major factors which led to him becoming involved in racing and breeding in Ireland and

Left : Royal Charger at the National Stud, c. 1947. *(G. A. Duncan)*

Right : Mr What, 1961. *(G. A. Duncan)*

England. Hall-Walker invited him to visit Tully in 1904 where he was fired with an interest in the breeding theories of the Tully stud owner who, until his death in 1933, remained an advisor to him.[4]

The first manager of the National Stud was Major Cyril Hall who later followed in the footsteps of Captain Greer and worked for the Aga Khan. He was succeeded in 1954 by D. D. Hyde and sixteen years later Michael Osborne took over as manager. Among the measures Osborne adopted was the accumulation of a small group of high class mares, a policy which resulted in the production of *Tap on Wood*, winner of the English Two Thousand Guineas in 1979. In the same year Osborne had purchased the stallion *Ahonoora* for two hundred thousand pounds. The horse which had been sold to cover an outstanding debt to the Playboy Club in London quickly repaid the stud's investment with nominations to him costing twenty thousand pounds. In 1987 he was sold to the Coolmore stud for seven million pounds. Other wise stallion purchases made by Osborne included *Lord Gayle* and the sire of *Tap on Wood*, *Sallust*, bought for a quarter of a million pounds, about half his market value.

The twelve years of Osborne's enlightened management of the stud have seen developments in methods of housing, feeding and managing thoroughbreds and in the management of a foster mother service. He has placed great emphasis on education and there has been a ready market abroad for students of the horse breeding course at the stud. The Bord na gCapall farriery apprenticeship scheme and the Racing Apprentice Centre of Education, which provides residential training for apprentice jockeys, have also found a home at Tully. The stud has promoted equine research and done much to promote the appreciation of the Irish horse through its Horse Museum which houses the skeleton of *Arkle* and other exhibits illustrative of the history of the Irish horse. Every year many visitors from home and abroad avail of the opportunity of viewing the stud and the Japanese Gardens which are a feature of it.

WORLD WAR AND REBELLION

The early decades of the twentieth century were a period of disruption in Ireland. In 1916 while the rest of Europe was at war a small rising took place against British authority in Ireland. This was followed five years later by the controversial treaty negotiations which resulted in recognition of the Irish Free State, according it dominion status in the British Commonwealth. However the new state only encompassed twenty-six of the thirty-two Irish counties and civil war resulted.

Between the years 1916 and 1923 the danger was that equestrian sports would fall a victim to civil strife. Hunting and racing would be seen as the prerogative of one class and suffer the attacks of opposing sectors of the population. That danger was implicit in the landlord-tenant conflict a century before but lasting damage had been averted. The hunting field and racecourse remained, despite the tensions of the age, the locations of activities with which the different classes could identify. These activities had a transcendent character which was greatly valued by the people. In the turbulent early decades of the twentieth century determined efforts were made, as we shall see, to keep equestrian sport and racing in particular going, despite the disruptions which they faced. Implicit in these efforts was, it would appear, an appreciation that at the racecourse people of different backgrounds and beliefs could come together and that this was a value which transcended the ebb and flow of politics and war. Life would have to continue when the killing and destruction had ceased and, in Ireland, racing had always brought life.

During the 1914-1918 war the involvement of the British Army in the administrative side of racing in Ireland paid dividends in persuading the government of the necessity of saving racing from destruction. Also indicative of the spirit of the age was the alliance of the aristocratic Lord Decies, Senior Steward of the Turf Club, with William Nelson, a self-made man who wanted his horses to run, war or no war. Both men were united in their efforts to keep racing going. On a purely practical basis, the cessation of racing due to food rationing would have had disastrous consequences for horse breeders, many of whom operated on a small scale. In the event ninety-five race meetings were held in 1915, eighty-six in 1916 and in 1917 it was possible to hold eighty-one. The spirit of the times, typified by the alliance of Decies and Nelson was finely caught in the efforts of some of the spectators en route to Punchestown in 1918. On the first day of the race meeting the Irish Trade Unions had called a General Strike in support of the resistance to military conscription which had been organised, leaving the racegoers without trains. The struggle and 'larks' of the racecourse extended therefore to the means of transport employed in getting to the races. A young barrister, later to be appointed Chief Justice, for instance, together with two equally distinguished friends, drove on to the racecourse, to the applause of the crowd, in a hearse drawn by two horses. The hearse was the only vehicle they could hire to transport them from Dublin.

The difficulties in 1919 were more severe than those of the previous year. Members of Sinn Féin, an organisation dedicated to republican ideals, were interned in British jails and feelings were running high. Many big houses were burned by the Irish insurgents and the tactics used during the Land War some decades previously were revived. Outside Ulster hunting virtually ceased and point-to-point fixtures were abandoned. Five race meetings had to be cancelled owing to the actions of Sinn Féin. Despite this, a total of eighty-five meetings were held. Moreover the Sinn Féin tactics of directly attacking racing and hunting were not used again in the following years.

To many of the Irish people the British Army during the second half of the nineteenth century and early twentieth century was not the oppressive force which it was frequently represented to be. In 1916, for instance, British reinforcements arriving in Dublin to quell the rebellion were greeted by dozens of Irish women with tea and cakes. The rebels against whom the army was moving, on the other hand, had little support from the citizens of Dublin. A factor in the attitude of such people was undoubtedly the high proportion of Irish people who joined the British Army. In the nineteenth century, for instance, twice as many Irish people, proportionate to the population, joined as did English, Scottish and Welsh. There was one good reason for this high rate of recruitment. The army provided a livelihood. What was more, there was the prospect, even for an unskilled man, not only of relatively high wages but also of a pension. After fourteen years service a man could retire with a pension for life and a lump sum of £21. There were also charities to help the old soldier or his widow and children. The attraction of army life was therefore very strong. For many Irish men the only alternative would have been emigration.

In addition to the role of the army as an employer there was also the direct economic benefit which the army brought to many parts of Ireland. Up to forty towns had some military presence and the financial contribution which the army made was enormous. Shopkeepers, for example, in Fermoy in Co. Cork earned £30,000 per month from military spending and Buttevant owed 120 valuable civilian jobs to the presence of the army. Towns such as Fermoy benefited from the extra colour which the army brought to local life. Likewise the navy contributed greatly to social life in areas such as Glin adjacent to the Shannon estuary where its ships in the 1870s carried out manoeuvres. There were tennis parties, balls and, of course, hunting parties during which the locals, including sometimes the Knight of Glin's tenants, rubbed shoulders with the military. Also in Co. Limerick, a short distance from Bruree where the future President of Ireland, Eamon de Valera, was growing up, hunting meets were held attended by the officers of the Liverpool Regiment and Royal Artillery. Most of the "lords and ladies gay" of Limerick society and its environs were there. Two special trains travelled to Bruree, one from Mallow carrying the followers of the Duhallow Hounds. In 1912 and 1913 the military held their own races at nearby Clogher Hill. They set up camp there and raced their horses across the Limerick countryside in point-to-point competitions.

During the period of the 'Troubles', however, in the aftermath of the 1916 rising and executions, the British Army often came under attack from republicans. Officers travelling to race meetings were frequently the victims of these 'incidents'. The interests of racing, however, would appear to have won out. According to the commander of the British forces in Ireland, the threat of cancelling meetings throughout the country was sufficient to put an end to the harassment:

> I let it be known that on the next occasion on which any soldier was interfered with, either at or going to, or coming from, a race meeting, I would shut down racing throughout the country. The word went round and no further incidents occurred.

Nor did the preponderance of military figures in the ranks of the racing bodies prevent these bodies from acting, where it was appropriate, in an even-handed way in relation to the contending forces in the country. On 6 March 1919, for instance, the Secretary of State for War, Winston Churchill, was asked to move the British Army Remount Depot at the Irish Turf Club headquarters on the Curragh "to a more suitable place". Churchill did not comply immediately but the request clearly indicated that the racing authorities saw themselves as independent of the army.

What seems to have been generally appreciated was that the racecourse had a value as a place where even enemies could meet and suspend their differences. An illustration of this was provided during the period of the truce in 1921. One of the leading guerrilla leaders was Dan Breen and he had successfully evaded the efforts of Brigadier General Ormonde-Winter and of other officials to capture him. The Brigadier General recalls:

> I once rubbed shoulders with him after the Truce when we were both making a bet with Dan Leahy, the well-known bookmaker, at the Galway Races. I wonder if he had an automatic in his pocket at the time. I know I had.

Over the years the racegoing public had been determined to keep the racecourse free from divisive politics. The crowds had reacted hostilely in 1882 when the English King's representative in Ireland had made an unwarranted display of his

Point-to-pointing with the Scarteen Hunt.
(Ruth Rogers)

authority by driving straight across the course at Fairyhouse during the Grand Military there. Anti-royalist feeling, however, was also taboo. Three years later, when Prince Edward visited Punchestown, attempts at protest were quickly put down by the crowd.

Opposite:
Blue Wind, trained by Dermot Weld and ridden by Wallie Swinburn, wins the Irish Guinness Oaks in 1981. (*Horseman Photography*)

With the formation of a native Irish government, the good working relationship between the racing authorities and the civil authorities, which had proved of such value, could have been disrupted. Men who previously had been rebels were now in positions of power. The racing authorities, however, quickly adjusted to the change and accorded the new leaders appropriate recognition. Furthermore the tradition of civic leaders formally visiting the racecourse was continued. In 1923, the President, William T. Cosgrave, who like other members of the new Irish government became prominently associated with the racing bodies, attended Punchestown, accompanied by the Governor General appointed to Ireland by the British government. Cosgrave himself had taken the first step in bridge-building during the previous year by appointing, to the newly constituted Irish Senate, members who were prominently associated with racing and had links with the former British administration.

During the period of the 'Troubles' those in charge of racing seem to have realised its value, because of its acceptability to all, in providing a continuity between past and future, and to have appreciated the role which they could play in ensuring that continuity. It was important, during the period of military confrontation, that racing should not slip into anarchy if it was to exercise a stabilising influence when men laid down their arms. There was, therefore, a serious purpose behind the actions of the racing authorities in enforcing the rules of racing in the normal fashion while the country was in turmoil. In April 1922, for instance, as the anti-treaty forces commenced their resistance, the Irish National Hunt Steeplechase Committee which included the commander of the British forces in Ireland, General Sir Bryan Mahon, imposed fines on masters of the hunt for charging for motor cars being admitted to point-to-point meetings. In ensuring that the rules of racing continued to be observed whatever the state of the country, the racing authorities were not so much concerned with the arrangement of the deck chairs on the ship of state as with ensuring smooth waters for the vessel if and when it emerged from the storm.[5]

An Irish Hunter
(*Ruth Rogers*)

THE RULES OF RACING

The rules governing racing had evolved over a considerable period of time. Military riders who played such a prominent part in the early steeplechases before the evolution of the modern code of rules were, of course, subject to military discipline. Little need existed, therefore, in their case for a formal body of rules governing the sport. Others taking part in the early steeplechases were amateurs of means known as 'Gentlemen Riders' and their standards of conduct on the racecourse were largely dictated by pressures from the narrow social class to which they belonged or, in some instances, by local regulations. With the gradual acceptance, however, in the early nineteenth century of the Irish Turf Club as the body to which disputes relating to both flat and steeplechase races could be referred by officials at local meets and the formation of the separate Irish National Hunt Steeplechase Committee in 1869, it became necessary to codify the rules governing both branches of the sport.

Because some races—an increasingly small number from the middle of the nineteenth century on—were confined to gentlemen it was necessary to define what a 'Gentleman Rider' was for the purposes of the sport. In England army officers and members of various clubs including the 'Kildare Street or Sackville Street' clubs in Dublin were included in the definition. Such 'Gentlemen Riders' would, of course, not be accustomed to receiving any money for riding. A similar definition applied in Ireland to the Corinthian Races, the first of which was held at the Curragh in 1823, but in 1877, on the instigation of Lord Drogheda, the INHS Committee made it possible for those not belonging to specified clubs to be elected as 'Gentlemen Riders'. The emphasis was now on the honesty of the rider in paying his gambling debts and in never riding for hire rather than on which club, if any, he frequented.

In 1877 the number of steeplechase rules was 160, an increase of 86 since 1870. Two years later a further increase in the number to 187 was necessary in order to try and ensure uniformity between the flat and steeplechase authorities in both England and Ireland. The aim was to ensure that a person barred from one jurisdiction in either country would not be free to operate within another. By virtue of the changes also, 'Qualified Riders' could now be elected not only from among 'gentlemen' but also from the ranks of farmers with at least one hundred statute acres or from others who had been proposed by the INHS committee.

The pressure for the elaboration of the rules was not as great in Ireland as it was in England. In Ireland the natural tendency was to resist any steps towards central control of racing. In 1870, for instance, an attempt by the INHS committee to prevent horses which had competed at unauthorised meetings from running at meetings where its rules were in force, met with resistance. The oft-repeated claim that conditions in Ireland differed from those in England was voiced and the committee was told that local meetings should be left "to mind their own affairs". As a result

Michael O'Hehir, the voice of racing and Gaelic games for decades on Irish radio. *(Ruth Rogers)*

Right: J. McGrath's *Ellete* (G. McGrath up) winning from *Psittaha* (C. Roche up) No. 2 and *Mary Machree* (H. Cope up), Leopardstown Silken Glider Stakes, 1971. (*Horseman Photography*)

Overleaf page 230: *Shergar*, ridden by Lester Piggott, winning the Irish Sweeps Derby at the Curragh in 1981 from *Cut Above* and *Dance Bid*. (*Horseman Photography*)

Page 231 Top: Tom Taaffe senior, 1952. (*G. A. Duncan*)

Poster, 1833, proclaiming that men should not ride horses naked in the sea at Kilkee Strand, Co. Clare.

Bottom: Pat Taaffe (centre) with Tom Dreaper (right) and Gerry Annesley, horse owner, in 1961. (*G. A. Duncan*)

Bottom right: *Sir Patrick* winner of the first prize for thoroughbred stallions, RDS Horse Show 1897. Owned and bred by Michael Healy, Ballinaskea, Enfield, Co. Meath. Foaled 1890; sire *Ascetic*, dam *Minnie*. (*Photo courtesy of Dermot Forde, MRCVS*)

the committee accepted that it would not be possible to completely align the rules of both countries. There was always the danger that if the INHS Rules became too restrictive, illegal or 'flapping' meetings would occur outside the rules. Towards the end of the 19th century, 'flapping' meetings proved a problem for the authorities and horses running at them were banned from all INHS meetings. The INHS committee claimed, in terms which in varying contexts in Ireland have tended to betray a fear of losing control, that such meetings fostered 'immorality of many descriptions'. Owners, however, tried to get around the restrictions by entering their horses under different names.

DEVELOPMENT OF RACECOURSES

Along with the elaboration of the rules, significant changes were taking place in the character of racing. In the first half of the 19th century, as we have noted, steeplechase meetings were characterised by 'robust informality'. There were many small country races such as the 'tumble-down' affair at Lismore on 22 January 1819 or the four mile steeplechase at Bandon in July 1837 and at Roscommon in 1846. Such meetings were extremely popular and, increasingly during this period, were being mentioned in the Irish Racing Calendar. For instance, in March 1836, there was a Garrison Steeplechase at Ashbourne and in the following year the Kildare Hunt

See captions, page 229.

AT A MEETING
OF THE

Magistrates, Visitors & Lodge-owners of Kilkee,

Held on the 7th of August, 1833,

LORD MASSY BEING CALLED TO THE CHAIR,

The following Resolutions were adopted:

RESOLVED,

That we have witnessed the disgraceful practice of Bathing on the Strand of Kilkee, at all hours of the day, to the great annoyance of Females, who are, by such indecent exposures, prevented from exercising on the Beach.

That it is expedient that some measures be adopted to prevent a recurrence of the practice; and with this view, it is Resolved, that the Strand shall be divided into three parts; that two sides thereof, to the right and left, shall be appropriated to the use of the Female Visitors, for Bathing, and that the portion of the Strand, defined by Posts in the centre, shall be for the use of the Male part of the Visitors, up to the Hour of Ten o'Clock in the Morning of each Day, but after that Hour, no *Male Person* shall be permitted to Bathe on the Strand.

That we are determined, by every means in our power, to put an end to the shameful custom which prevails, of naked men riding horses through the water; and that the Police shall receive instructions to seize all persons so offending, in order that they may be prosecuted according to Law; and that all Male Persons, bathing on the Strand after the prescribed hour, shall be also prosecuted.

MASSY.

Lord Massy having left the Chair, and the Hon. Mr. Butler being called thereto,
RESOLVED,

That the thanks of this Meeting are due, and hereby given, to Lord Massy, for his Lordship's dignified and very proper deportment in the Chair.

T. F. W. BUTLER, *Chairman.*

Printed at CANTER's Paper and Account-book Ware-house, 12, Francis-street, Limerick.

held a steeplechase for its members. In 1838 there was a two-day meeting including a race for the Meath Gold Cup and we read that during the following year there were meetings at Carden, Westmeath, Ashbourne and Newcastle. Such races were still run in heats over natural country with spectators following the race on foot or on horseback. But changes were beginning to occur. In 1842 the Kildare Hunt Club ran its steeplechase without heats and eight years later the members of the hunt settled on Punchestown as the permanent venue for their annual meeting. A year later the Ward Union Hunt made a similar move and transferred from Ashbourne to Fairyhouse.

The selection of Punchestown by the Kildare Hunt was an important stage in the consolidation of steeplechasing as a popular sport in Ireland. Before the members had chosen it as their permanent venue they had held races at various locations. In 1834 they held them near Jugginstown Castle, in 1847 they were at Rathgorsa between Naas and Blackchurch, and in 1848 at Ballymea between Newbridge and Kilcullen. In 1854 the first two-day meeting was held at Punchestown and by 1861 the steeplechasing programme there comprised seven races including the National Hunt Steeplechase over three and a half miles for the biggest prize offered for a race in Ireland—£300 added to a £5 sweepstake. In 1862 this race was run over the course subsequently known as the Conyngham Cup Course which included the famous double bank which many intrepid sportsmen have attempted to 'fly', mostly without success. The royal visit in 1868, the first of many such visits, did much to add to Punchestown's popularity and confer on it the status of a national festival. Naas, we are told, was thronged with people for the arrival of Prince Edward and, at the racecourse, the crowd was estimated at 150,000. Even today shops and banks still close at lunchtime each day of the races and schools close down for the duration of the festival. For trainers and owners, Punchestown also had great attractions. The course there with its banks and ditches offered a valuable testing ground prior to the Aintree Grand National. In 1898, for instance, the Prince of Wales' horse *Ambush II*, bred in Ireland and trained at Eyrefield Lodge, had taken the Maiden Plate at Punchestown before going on to success at Aintree two years later. *Lovely Cottage*, the 1946 Grand National winner, also experienced success at Punchestown before going to Aintree. The great *Prince Regent*, the horse *Lovely Cottage* beat on that occasion, and *Workman*, the 1939 Aintree winner, also won at Punchestown before making their mark in England.

The officials at Punchestown had not ignored the needs of spectators in the development of the racecourse. In the 1860s permanent stands had been built and enclosures laid out. Until that time steeplechasing had been organised by gentlemen for gentlemen and little attempt was made to encourage spectators. However, in England commercial considerations had begun to play an important part in the sport and it was inevitable that Ireland would eventually have to follow suit. In 1860 the first enclosed park course had been established under the name of the

Howth and Baldoyle Race Meeting and had quickly prospered, threatening the standing of some of the long-established courses much to the disgust of some of the old guard of steeplechasing enthusiasts. In 1874 the Baldoyle Derby was run there for the first time and for a number of years it eclipsed the Irish Derby at the Curragh in importance. Such was the success of Baldoyle that in 1891 it became a limited company with capital of £10,000.

In 1869 the Ballybrit course was opened in Galway attracting huge crowds and proving a great success. The main feature of the meeting there was the Galway Plate, a steeplechase run over two and a half miles with eight fences, two of which were stone walls. Until 1922 when the civil war forced cancellation of the meeting, Galway races were held each year in an uninterrupted sequence. The problems of 1922 proved to have short-term consequences as far as Galway was concerned. Today Galway is the most popular of all of the holiday meetings. During the nine days of racing there each year a huge betting turnover is recorded making it the second largest venue in the country in terms of betting totals. Only Leopardstown, with twenty-two days racing, surpasses it since the demise of the Phoenix Park, with its seventeen days racing, in 1990.

One of the most important developments in the commercialisation of racing took place in 1888. In that year Leopardstown Racecourse catering for steeplechases, hurdles and flat races and with stands and amenities for spectators was established.

Kahyasi owned by the Aga Khan, ridden by Ray Cochrane on the right, winning the Irish Derby 1988 from *Insan* (T. R. Quinn). (*Horseman Photography*).

Its owner, Captain George Quin, had modelled it on the enclosed park at Sandown opened thirteen years earlier which had been an immediate success attracting large numbers of spectators. Improved facilities, transport by rail to the course and short races which were more interesting to the crowd and attracted increased betting activity, meant that the crowds, all of whom paid at the entrance, could share in the excitement of the races and enjoy them in comfort. The lavish advertising arranged by Quin for the opening day at Leopardstown proved only too successful and the facilities and trains organised for the occasion were completely inadequate. However an important milestone had been passed. The needs of the race-going public were now recognised as being paramount. An enclosed course which was within easy reach by train from Dublin and which had amenities and comforts for spectators would be able to afford higher stakes because of the gate receipts generated. The higher stakes in turn would encourage the best trainers and owners to enter their horses and better sport would ensue. At Leopardstown, for instance, a Grand Prix of £1000, the largest prize ever for a race in Ireland, was introduced. Leopardstown's success among trainers, owners and the race-going public had its parallel in the status of its meets as social occasions. A royal visit there in 1897 no doubt helped considerably. At the August meet in 1899 "a collection of beauty in the members' stand such as cannot be excelled, if equalled, elsewhere" could, according to *Baily's Magazine*, be seen there on the day preceding the Royal Dublin Society show.

Leopardstown marked the beginning of a new era for steeplechasing. Artificial fences had been built and races were shorter, a far cry from the original cross-country matches. The thinking behind these changes was that races would become more spectacular as the emphasis shifted from the stamina and jumping ability of the horses to their speed. Spectators would therefore be encouraged to travel to race meetings. Since the 1870s the steeplechase authorities had seen the direction into which these changes would lead the sport and had tried to prevent them. Genuine chasers would no longer be able to compete and would be forced out of the sport. Despite the opposition, the changes had come to stay and even Fairyhouse and Punchestown could not remain unaffected. The Grand National, for instance, which took place at Fairyhouse for the first time in 1870 has been run since 1939 entirely over bush fences and in 1959 the designation of the meeting was changed from 'Ward Union Hunt (Fairyhouse) Steeplechase' to 'Fairyhouse Races', reflecting the move away from natural country and banks. At Punchestown too a bush fence course was introduced in 1960, a hurdles course some years later and in 1964 the steeplechase for the Conyngham Cup was run for the last time. Two steeplechases which include banks as well as fences have however been retained thus helping to preserve something of the old appeal and character of the course. These changes met with opposition but for Punchestown the choice had been straightforward— adapt or die. Fewer horses were being produced to race over the walls, ditches and banks there, and fewer owners were prepared to risk their good horses over such courses. The old banks and ditches suited the horse which had special staying power and the cat-like agility to negotiate them but the bushes and hurdles coming into use meant that top class horses such as *Arkle, Mill House* and *Monksfield* which were popular with spectators could be seen in action.

The second half of the 19th century also saw the emergence of race meetings at Tramore and Cork Park. At Tramore the course was situated on the 'back strand' but, due to the incursion of the sea, the races there had to be moved to a new location in 1914. This subsequently became the venue for a holiday meeting of four days, held each summer. Cork Park fell a victim to industrialisation when the Ford Motor Company purchased it as a location for its factory. The loss to Cork was, however, made good in 1924 when Mallow was opened. The same year also saw the opening of Naas.[6]

SPONSORSHIP, THE IRISH HOSPITALS TRUST AND JOE McGRATH

In recent decades the size and quality of the fields at Punchestown and other courses have become critical to sponsorship. Unless the field is right sponsors are not interested. Probably the first instance of commercial sponsorship at an Irish race meeting occurred at Tralee in 1805 when 'the Gentlemen of the Profession of the Law of the County of Kerry' gave a prize of £50 for a race. Also in the 19th century

Above: Joe McGrath and Judge Wylie at the RDS in 1958. (*G. A. Duncan*)

Below: *Greek Star* led in by owner J. McGrath after winning the Phoenix Nursery. (*J. Cashman*)

the Guinness family began their association with Punchestown. The brewery used to close down completely for the two days of the meeting and the first Lord Iveagh used to take a party there from Kingsbridge by a special train. His carriage was marked with an XX, the Lord Lieutenant's with X. Guinness did not commence its sponsorship of Punchestown however until 1963 when it became a three-day meeting. The company which had inaugurated sponsorship there was Jamesons, the whiskey distillers, in the Gold Cup event. The period from the early sixties on saw a great increase in sponsorship at various Irish racecourses. Players, a cigarette manufacturer, sponsored the Navy Cut Stakes at the Phoenix Park in 1960, Guinness took over sponsorship of the Irish Oaks in the same year and Powers sponsored the Gold Cup at Fairyhouse. Another Irish company in the drinks market, Irish Distillers, commenced its sponsorship in 1971 of the Irish Grand National making it into one of the richest steeplechases run in Ireland. But the most significant sponsorship was that of the Irish Derby in 1962 by the Irish Hospitals Trust.

The Irish Hospitals Trust was founded by Richard Duggan, a leading bookmaker, as a result of the success of a lottery which he organised in 1918 to help the survivors of a German torpedo attack on the mail steamer *Leinster*. After some very successful lobbying, the Trust received government approval in 1930. Duggan's partners in the venture were Joe McGrath and Captain Spencer Freeman, all of whom made personal fortunes as well as benefiting the hospitals for which the Trust was set up. It was through his friendship with Duggan that McGrath became involved in racing both as an owner and breeder.

In 1941 he purchased the Brownstown Stud whose origins on the Curragh go back to the last quarter of the 18th century. *Sir Hercules*, the sire of *Birdcatcher* and *Faugh-a-Ballagh* stood there at one time. Greer and later Parkinson used it for their very successful training operations. McGrath installed *Smokeless* as his first brood mare there having purchased her from Richard Duggan who had won both the Irish One Thousand Guineas and the Oaks in 1935 with her.

McGrath provides us with an outstanding example of a one-time 'rebel' who through his racing interests and achievements could rub shoulders with and be accepted by those who were seen as belonging to the 'enemy' camp. Born in 1895, he was a paperboy on the streets of Dublin before going on to work in a chartered accountant's office and joining the Irish Transport Union at a time when the labour leader, James Larkin, was involved in a bitter struggle with employers. By 1916 McGrath was a member of the Irish Republican Brotherhood, an organisation committed to armed insurrection, and was one of those interned in 1918 by the British government. In the view of Michael Collins, the militant republican leader, he was "100 per cent reliable, and he thinks quickly in a tight corner". He was subsequently elected Sinn Féin member of parliament and was closely involved in the treaty negotiations which led to the emergence of the Irish Free State. W. T. Cosgrave made him Minister for Labour in his first government.

A man of considerable financial acumen and boundless energy, McGrath achieved great success in business and found time to take the necessary steps to propel himself to the top of the racing and breeding industry. He chose his horses wisely and sometimes paid high prices in support of his judgement. The price of twenty thousand pounds he paid for *Smokeless*, for example, was an Irish record. In 1939 he had purchased a colt called *Windsor Slipper* which, as a three-year-old, won the Irish Triple Crown, becoming only the second horse to do so. Because of the war he was however deprived of seeing *Windsor Slipper*, which his jockey, Morny Wing, considered to have been among the greats of the racecourse, race outside Ireland and thus attain its racing potential. In a typical gesture McGrath had issued a challenge before the Irish Derby to the owners of the top three-year-olds in England to take on his charge, a challenge which the transportation restrictions prevented any of them from taking up. After his final victory, *Windsor Slipper* was retired unbeaten to stud at Brownstown.

Between the years 1942 and 1946 McGrath was leading owner in Ireland. His purchase of *Nasrullah* for 20,000 guineas from the Aga Khan greatly assisted his breeding operations. In 1948 *Nathoo*, a son of the stallion, won the Irish Derby. When he sold *Nasrullah* to an American syndicate in the US in 1949 he fetched a price of £132,857. It was sales like this which kept McGrath in the racing game. Despite his spectacular successes, racing, he claimed, cost him £10,000 a year.

The British Press was, of course, not oblivious of his background. When his horse *Arctic Prince* won the Epsom Derby in 1951 and he was received by the Queen, the apparent anomaly of his position was not lost on the sub-editors. "Prison Breaker wins Derby. Queen 'charming' to ex-gunman", was the headline in the *Daily Express*. In 1955 his son Seamus trained *Panaslipper*, sired by *Solar Slipper* to take the Irish Derby and gain second place at Epsom. At the end of 1957 not only did Joe top the owners' list but he was also the leading breeder and Seamus was top of the list of trainers in Ireland. Seamus' greatest achievement came in 1969, three years after his father's death, when *Levmoss* won the Ascot Gold Cup and Prix de l'Arc de Triomphe. In 1973 he took the Irish Derby with *Weavers Hall*.

It is the promotional and administrative side of McGrath's work in the racing industry that is perhaps best remembered. In particular the present status of the Irish Derby can be attributed to him. The venue chosen for the initial running of the race in 1866 was the Curragh where racing had taken place in conjunction with the Curragh Fair since the earliest times. From the 17th century on, when organised racing became general, the Curragh could claim to be the focal point of Irish racing. According to the Earl of Clarendon who visited there during King James II's reign, "The common where the race is held is a much finer turf than Newmarket." The Irish Derby did not, however, initially attract great support from owners and trainers. In 1868, for instance, there were only two starters. In 1874 the length of the race was reduced from fourteen to twelve furlongs and, in order to save it from extinction, the articles of the race were altered to give a greater range of weights and to allow for penalties. These efforts met with success and Irish Derby day at the Curragh began to rival Punchestown as a social attraction. Not until 1946 was the race brought into line with the Epsom Derby and the penalties removed.

The event which was to change the Irish Derby from a race with little international importance into one of the most prestigious races in the world occurred sixteen years later when the Irish Hospitals Trust under McGrath's guidance contributed £30,000 to the prize money for the race. This sponsorship had the effect of raising the overall standard of racing in Ireland. Overnight Ireland was transformed into a country where competition of the highest standard was available. In 1986 Budweiser, the giant American beer manufacturer, took over the Derby sponsorship when the Irish Hospitals Trust was unable to continue it and Ladbrokes, the British bookmaking concern, decided to sponsor the Sweeps Hurdle at Leopardstown for which the Trust had been sponsor since 1969.[7]

BETTING

Sponsorship was one avenue for injecting finance into the Irish racing industry. There were others. Two of these were related, betting and the tote. Up to the second half of the 19th century racing had not assumed, it would appear, much of the character of an industry. Only gentlemen participated in the sport of steeplechasing and the wagers which they risked on the sport occurred largely without the intrusion of bookmakers. The betting public which had grown up in England in the wake of the Industrial Revolution did not exist in Ireland. The huge crowds which thronged to witness the sport of their betters in Ireland had no disposable income and were therefore only tolerated on the racecourse. The administration of the sport could therefore afford to be informal, as we have noted. People didn't stand to gain anything in financial terms from racing and had therefore little incentive to engage in sharp practice. Such bookmakers as there were, were not, it would appear, very busy. Harry Sargent, writing of a period about the middle of the century recalled one bookmaker: "He was named Mullins, and was often assisted by his wife; and even they had not sufficient betting to occupy all their time, so they worked a roulette-table as well."

Due to the commercialisation of racing and the emergence of the professional bookmaker in England the English Parliament had taken steps from the middle of the 19th century on to regulate betting. In 1906 the Street Betting Act was passed making the racecourse the only place where betting could take place legally. By this time, many of Ireland's racecourses had been established. Indeed, some of them were of very long standing. Both the Curragh and Bellewstown had featured racing since the first half of the seventeenth century. At Laytown in Co. Louth, according to the Irish Racing Calendar, racing on the strand had taken place at least as early as 1876. Today, Laytown is unique in Europe in that it is the only strand racing conducted under the approval of the governing bodies. A feature of it is that the time of racing is dictated by the tides. Nearer Dublin stood the Leopardstown and Baldoyle racecourses. At the Phoenix Park in 1902, on grounds formerly used for 'flapping meetings', the first official race meeting was held, with patrons coming in the main from the fashionable elements of Dublin society. With the growth of racecourses went illegal betting, but under existing legislation there was very little that could be done to control it. It wasn't until 1926 that the government acted. Off-course betting was made legal in that year and further acts establishing control over it followed in 1928, 1929 and 1931. Allied to these came the Totaliser Act in 1929 which gave a licence to operate the tote to the Irish Turf Club and the INHS committee. A year later despite opposition from bookmakers the tote came into operation at the Fairyhouse Easter meeting. During its first year of operation it had a turnover of £100,000.

It was hoped that prizemoney would benefit from the tote but, despite the assistance from this quarter, the amount of money available for prizes had gone into a decline in the mid twenties from which it did not recover for two decades.

Monksfield and Dessie Hughes land in front of *Sea Pigeon* and Jonjo O'Neill to win the Champion Hurdle for Ireland. (*Ruth Rogers*)

Flat racing, in particular, was at a low ebb in Ireland after the 1914-18 war during which many race meetings had been disrupted. In the decade 1922 to 1932 every Irish Derby except one was won by an English-trained horse. Racing attendances increased temporarily in the mid-twenties to a new record figure of 280,000 at 116 meetings and the number of races was rising but the resurgence was short-lived. By 1928 the Turf Club was reporting a loss on every Curragh meeting with the exception of Derby day which managed to make a profit of £15. Many other racecourses were in severe financial difficulties, with owners forced to contribute fifty per cent of prizemoney through entry fees. The betting legislation may have even compounded the problem by making off-course betting legal and, consequently, further depleting attendances. One casualty of the falling attendances was Navan Racecourse in 1934. But another factor was at work in Navan's demise. In 1933 De Valera who had just come to power had cancelled the land annuities which

Sale Day at Mallow — the international auction sales held under the auspices of Bord na gCapall — September 1974. *(Donal Sheehan)*

Irish farmers had been paying into the British exchequer as a kind of mortgage which would eventually make them owners of the land they farmed. The Irish leader's action provoked a retaliation from Britain who imposed a duty of forty per cent on Irish livestock imports including bloodstock. Horse exports from Ireland suffered a massive decline as a result. During the negotiations some of the best horses in the country, including R. C. Dawson's *Blandford*, were quickly shipped off to England before the new duties could take effect. Attendances at race meetings fell further away and the list of racing fixtures had to be curtailed. Exports of horses were badly hit with consequent repercussions on the breeding industry. Not until 1937 was De Valera able to announce the removal of the import duty.[8]

THE BREEDING INDUSTRY AND GOVERNMENT ASSISTANCE

From as early as the 17th century those interested in horse breeding appreciated that its fortunes were linked to those of racing. In 1673 Sir William Temple, as we have seen, had made proposals with a view to improving the quality of Irish breeding. One of his suggestions was that the king would present Plates for races which would be run near Dublin, a suggestion which was implemented. Eleven years later the first King's Plate in Ireland was instituted at the Maze racecourse at Down Royal in Co. Down where the first races had taken place as early as 1640 and in 1688 we read of races being held annually at the Curragh for a King's Plate. But circumstances in Ireland delayed the kind of developments in breeding which, with the importation of eastern stallions into England, had taken place in that country about this time. In Ireland, civil and religious strife meant that there could be little thought given to planning good breeding activities. From 1730 on, however, racing was in the ascendant in Ireland and by the year 1813 sixteen King's Plates, only six fewer than in England, were being run with the object of encouraging the breeding of horses capable of carrying weights over long distances. Up till that time breeding in Ireland had been approached in a haphazard manner with the nearest and cheapest stallions being patronised by owners. Moreover, it is clear from the Stud Book that many of the forty stallions whose services were advertised were employed in covering non-thoroughbred mares.

To many foreigners Ireland remained, for a considerable part of the 19th century a source for hunters and steeplechasers. The emergence in the first half of the nineteenth century of first class horses such as *Birdcatcher, Faugh-a-Ballagh*, in 1844 the first Irish winner of the St Leger, and *Harkaway* did little to change this perception of Irish horses. But, by the end of the century, Ireland could claim to have the basis of a first class breeding industry with studs of the quality of Knockaney, Eyrefield Lodge, Old Connell and Tully. These altered the picture significantly. In addition, in 1889 Captain Harry Greer purchased his great stallion *Gallinule* and subsequently allowed his services free at Brownstown to approved mares thus giving Irish breeding a much needed boost. In 1904 *Gallinule* was top of the English list of winning stallions and by 1907 horses sired by him had won a total of one quarter of a million pounds. The result of such developments was that in the early twentieth century Ireland was seen as a very important supplier of yearlings to the growing English commercial market. In the General Stud Book of 1901, for instance, Irish mares comprised nearly a quarter of the total. Twelve years later seventy-four of the three hundred and twenty-one yearlings sold at the Doncaster St Leger sales came from Irish studs. Also assisting the image of Ireland as a country of some standing in the thoroughbred world was the consolidation of the Irish classics racing calendar in the first quarter of the 20th century.

Assistance from government sources for the racing and breeding industry was slow in coming. In 1887 the then British government had begun to subsidise the breeding industry directly with an annual grant of £3,200 to be used by the Royal Dublin Society to award premiums to stallions distributed throughout the country and later to provide nominations to selected mares. The government's concern in this case, however, was not with the racing business but with ensuring that there was an adequate supply of remounts for its soldiers and of riding and harness horses for the growing number of people in Britain that required them. The commission appointed by the Irish government in 1935 to enquire into the horse breeding industry drew attention to the absence of high class sires and blamed income tax which was still being charged on stud fees in Ireland for the shortfall. Many race meetings no longer took place, the commission noted, and some racecourses were in grave need of financial assistance. Owners' expenses would have to be reduced so that they could afford to bring their horses to the tracks. The crowds, it was felt, would return and stakes could be increased if there were sufficient runners. Three years later a grant of £10,000 to be administered jointly by the two racing bodies was made by the Irish government. By virtue of this, racecourses were enabled to defray owners' transportation costs and the welcome from the industry was fulsome. As well as providing much needed financial aid, the scheme had another beneficial feature. It underlined once again how, in equestrian affairs, no border divided Northern Ireland from the rest of the country. Two of the racecourses which received assistance from the Irish government under the scheme, Down Royal and Downpatrick, were in Northern Ireland.

The special commission set up in 1942 by the Irish Turf Club and INHS committee to enquire into the state of racing and steeplechasing confirmed the findings of earlier inquiries—finance remained a problem and prizemoney was much too low. The periodic slumps aggravated by the Second World War had left Irish racing in a position where recovery was very difficult. The 1935 commission had argued that what was required was a central body which would purchase financially weak racecourses and dispense government grants. This body, the commission believed, would ensure that the industry did not go into irreversible decline as a result of war or recession.

THE RACING BOARD

Joe McGrath was also urging on the government the formation of a central body for racing about this time. Such a body, he argued, could be empowered to raise finance through a levy on betting and the tote and could channel its funds to the industry through increased prizemoney and reduced entry fees. In 1945 the Racing Board and Racecourses Bill was passed by the Dáil, bringing into being the Racing Board to provide for the improvement and development of breeding and racing. The bill envisaged that it would do this through better control of racecourses, over which it was given supervisory powers, the operation of the tote and the imposition of a levy on on-course betting. The Board's remit was, however, confined to finance and related matters. Not only were the Turf Club and INHS committee confirmed in their traditional roles but their powers were strengthened. The betting levy was initially set at two and a half per cent but in 1975, because of the inadequacy of the finance generated, further legislation was enacted to enable this to be raised. In that year the levy was increased to 6 per cent. Ten years later it was lowered to five per cent. The levy on the tote which rose to an all-time high of twenty two and a half per cent in the early 1980s was set initially at ten per cent and the revenue from this and the betting levy was applied to reducing admission charges to racegoers, to the improvement of facilities, to increasing prizemoney and to the payment of transportation charges for horses to race meetings. By virtue of the legislation in 1945 bookmakers were required to hold permits from the Board.

The effect of the Board's work on the racing industry was dramatic. By 1950 a sum of £300,000 had been given by it to the racecourses and prizemoney had increased dramatically. In that year it stood at £274,554 compared to £184,562 in 1946, an increase of nearly 50% in four years. Other improvements which the Board could point to were a reduction in race entry fees and better course facilities for the racegoing public. At Leopardstown Racecourse which the Board had taken over a major programme of reconstruction was undertaken prior to the reopening of the course in 1971. There were further developments there in 1987 with the completion of a major extension to the main grandstand concourse and the introduction of computerised tote facilities—the first step in the programme of computerisation at all racecourses. These and other Board activities have been partly funded by tote and on-course betting revenues which stood at £1.6 million and £5.4 million respectively in 1950 and, thirty five years later, at £16 million and £67 million.[9]

MY PRINCE, COTTAGE AND GOLDEN MILLER

In the period after the first world war steeplechasing had suffered less than flat racing from the ravages of war and recession. The sport has always had a firm place in the affections of the Irish people and, as a result, was able to weather the difficulties to which racing was subjected. In the last quarter of the 19th century, for instance, approximately three times the number of horses competed in steeple-chases as on the flat. Prizemoney for the horses that came out on top in steeplechasing was at least as good as that given to those engaged in flat racing. The popularity of steeplechasing in the 1920s received an important boost with Irish horses scoring successive victories in the Aintree Grand National. In 1920 *Troytown* bred and owned by Major Collins-Gerrard from Co. Meath was successful. The following year belonged to *Shaun Spadah* and in 1923 *Sergeant Murphy* became the oldest horse to win the race. The years 1928 to 1930 witnessed three successive Irish victories, *Tipperary Tim, Gregalach* and the Frank Hartigan trained *Shaun Goilin*. In 1930 all six horses finishing were Irish.

A feature of the Aintree Grand National in 1929 was that both *Gregalach* and the second-placed horse *Easter Hero* were by *My Prince*. In that year *Easter Hero* won the Cheltenham Gold Cup, the third time that an Irish horse had won it in its six year history and the first of *Easter Hero*'s two successive wins. From 1935 to 1937, *My Prince* horses were successful in all the Aintree Grand Nationals, *Reynoldstown* winning the race in 1935 and 1936 and *Royal Mail* in 1937. The 1930s, however, belonged not to any of these horses but to another Irish horse *Golden Miller*, sired by *Goldcourt*, grandson of Captain Greer's great stallion *Gallinule*. *Golden Miller*, bred

Left : Trainer Jim Bolger, pictured at Leopardstown on 27 October 1990, the day he broke Senator Parkinson's 1923 record of 137 home winners in a year with *Latin Quarter*'s win at Galway. On 3 November Jim broke Dermot Weld's 1985 record of 120 winners on the flat during one season when *Elementary* won at Down Royal. Sharing in many of his successes has been stable jockey Christy Roche who in 1990 equalled Michael Kinnane's record of 113 winners in a season. (*Horseman Photography*).

Right: *Caughoo* on Portmarnock Strand, Grand National winner 1947. (*G. A. Duncan*)

in Ireland and owned by the eccentric millionairess Dorothy Paget, was perhaps the greatest steeplechaser of all time. Like *Arkle* in a later age, he managed to capture the public imagination during his racing career. Between the years 1932 and 1936 he won five Cheltenham Gold Cups, a feat which is made all the more remarkable by the fact that in one of these great years, 1934, he also won the Aintree Grand National.

In the 1930s another sire of steeplechasers, *Cottage*, was beginning to assert his claims to greatness. Bred in France, he was purchased by Michael Magnier from Fermoy in Co. Cork for twenty five guineas in 1924. Fifteen years later one of his sons *Workman* won the Aintree Grand National after coming third in the previous year. Other *Cottage* winners of the great race followed. In 1946 *Lovely Cottage* took the race and two years later it was *Sheila's Cottage*'s turn. In the Cheltenham Gold Cup *Brendan's Cottage* was successful and *Cottage Rake* provided Vincent O'Brien with the unique series of successes which established his reputation, as we shall see. The reason, it would appear, that 'The Rake' is not numbered very frequently among the greats like *Golden Miller* and *Arkle* would seem to be that the end of his career was not covered in glory. He achieved nothing in England when his owner transferred him there out of O'Brien's care.

Golden Miller, G. Wilson up, winning the 1934 Aintree Grand National. *(Hulton-Deutsch Collection)*

PRINCE REGENT, ARKLE AND TOM DREAPER

The Grand National of 1946, in particular, marked the end of the domination exercised by *My Prince*'s progeny over steeplechasing. For the horse which *Lovely Cottage* beat on that occasion was the great *Prince Regent*, sired by *My Prince*. Although he had won the Gold Cup at Cheltenham in that year, *Prince Regent*'s career was effectively over. In the following year he again attempted to win at Aintree but was beaten into fourth place by the Irish horse *Caughoo*.

The man who had started *Prince Regent* on the road to greatness was the County Dublin trainer Tom Dreaper, a consummate horseman who absolutely refused to rush his horses. For two years, *Prince Regent* who was sent to him at the age of three by his owner Jimmy Rank was not allowed by him to compete. His first win came in a flat race at Naas in 1940 with his trainer in the saddle. In the following year he won three races, followed in 1942 by further success despite having to face opposition which was of a higher standard than would normally have been the case. Due to wartime restrictions on racing in England some owners such as Dorothy Paget had sent their horses to Ireland to be trained. Also adding to the keenness of the competition in Ireland were the restrictions on the international transportation of horses in force during the war. Another difficulty which *Prince Regent* had to overcome was the impositions of the handicapper which required him to carry twelve stone or more on each appearance. This did not prevent him winning the 1942 Irish Grand National from the formidable *Golden Jack* who, like *Golden Miller*, was sired by *Goldcourt* and owned by Miss Paget. *Prince Regent* had to concede twelve pounds to him.

Another brilliant horse with which *Prince Regent* had to contend was *Prince Blackthorn* who was the only horse to beat him in 1942—in the Avonmore Steeple-chase at Leopardstown when *Prince Regent* had to concede three stone five pounds to him. The return encounter in the following year at Baldoyle proved to be one of the best steeplechases ever seen in Ireland with huge crowds turning out to see it. With Tim Hyde up, *Prince Regent*, who was conceding two stone eleven pounds, did not disappoint his excited following. He managed to beat his rival by a neck. His achievements during the years 1943 to 1944 can be measured by the fact that despite the handicap of never giving away less than two stone four pounds he won five times out of ten starts. After the war he was sent to England with the results that we have noted. The years of giving away weights to good horses had taken their toll and only the horse's indomitable spirit ensured further victories. He was, as befits a horse with great heart, a favourite with the crowds. Pat Taaffe has recounted a story of how Dreaper asked a policeman at a crossroads in Dublin to hold up the traffic. "Is *Prince Regent* there?", asked the policeman. "He is," said Dreaper. "Right so," said the policeman, "I'll stop the whole lot of traffic, both ways."

Tom Dreaper with *Arkle*.
(*Bord Failte*)

Prince Regent was only one of many great Dreaper horses. He saddled the winners of Irish Grand Nationals in 1942, 1949 and 1954 and from 1960 to 1966 on seven successive occasions, a record unlikely ever to be beaten. In 1954 the horse in question was *Royal Approach* which seemed likely to rival *Prince Regent* by his achievements but injury put an end to his career. The successor to *Prince Regent* in the Dreaper stable was the gelding *Arkle* who had been bred by Mrs Mary Baker in Co. Dublin. Three years after his birth in 1957 he had been bought by Anne Duchess of Westminster who sent him to Dreaper. Dreaper did not rush the horse and in his initial two outings—bumpers at Mullingar and Leopardstown in December 1961— he was only placed. One month later the position had changed and the saga of *Arkle*'s great successes had begun. From December 1961 to 28 December 1966 he was out of the first four on only one occasion and he won twenty-two steeplechases, four hurdle races and one on the flat. These victories included the Irish Grand National in 1964 but for the public in that year *Arkle*'s greatest victory was not at Fairyhouse but in the Gold Cup at Cheltenham where he beat *Mill House*, the 1963 winner of the cup.

Arkle, left, ridden by Pat Taaffe, leads *Mill House*, ridden by Willie Robinson, over the second fence during the Cheltenham Gold Cup in 1965, which *Arkle* won with *Mill House* second. (S & G Press Agency)

This was the second of four encounters between the two great horses. In the previous year *Mill House* had beaten *Arkle* at Newbury in the Hennessy Gold Cup and was being hailed as the successor to *Golden Miller*. The contests between *Arkle*, Ireland's champion, and *Mill House*, the darling of the English crowds and media, began to acquire in Ireland and England, the dimensions of the age-old and deeply rooted struggle between the two countries. In view of *Mill House*'s origins, the public perception of these contests might appear strange. His trainer at Lambourn was Fulke Walwyn and his owner was an Englishman, Mr Gollings, but there was little else English about him. He had been bred in Co. Kildare by Mrs Lawlor and was generally ridden by the Irish jockey Willie Robinson. The racing public of both countries were, it would appear, only too happy to ignore the facts and identify their countries and themselves with the animals battling it out before them on the racecourse. *Arkle*'s jockey Pat Taaffe recalls the Irish crowd's excitement at the 1964 Gold Cup victory over the old enemy:

> We cleared the last two lengths in the lead and then came the Irish roar. Priests and farmers, lords and layabouts. When you are on the back of a fast running horse, you sometimes become oblivious to the sound of the crowd. But I heard that one all right.

In the following year *Arkle* confirmed his superiority when he won by twenty lengths in the Gallaher Gold Cup. There were also other victories. The Cheltenham Gold Cup of 1966 put him amongst the select company of *Golden Miller* and *Cottage Rake* who had won the event three years in a row. There were three Leopardstown Steeplechases in the years 1964, 1965 and 1966 and two Hennessy Gold Cups, but the memory of the struggles with his old rival *Mill House* has dominated all. Pat Taaffe who rode and respected both horses wrote:

> It's a rare occurrence when I visit the Curragh without popping in to see my old friend William Robinson. When we're alone we talk of the days that are gone. Then suddenly *Arkle* and *Mill House* come marching back and yesterday becomes today.

One of the factors which probably endeared *Arkle* to the crowds was his fallibility. Not only was he less than perfect in appearance but his jumping was characterised by frequent blunders from which he almost invariably recovered. When, in December 1966, he blundered at the fourteenth fence in the King George VI at Kempton Park the damage was irretrievable. He had fractured a pedal bone in his hoof forcing his owner to retire him.

PAT TAAFFE

As well as riding *Arkle*, Pat Taaffe had also some experience of his rival, *Mill House*, having ridden him in the first of the horse's many winning races. Pat's father Tom trained at Rathcoole in Co. Dublin and had taught Pat and his two brothers Willie and Tos to ride. Pat's first ride under Rules was as an amateur at the age of sixteen at the beginning of 1946 riding one of his father's horses at Baldoyle. Two years later he won the Kildare Hunt Cup at Punchestown and in the following year he won his first steeplechase for Tom Dreaper. It was the start of a great alliance. But it was for Vincent O'Brien that he scored his first great victory. He had turned professional in 1950 and five years later he rode the O'Brien trained *Quare Times* to victory in the Aintree Grand National. In the same year he achieved the unique double of winning both the Irish Grand National and the Galway Plate, the first rider to achieve this distinction since Tom Beasley in 1881. The years 1958 and 1959 proved very successful for the Taaffe family, with Pat winning the Irish Grand National on *Zonda* in 1959 and his father training the 1958 Aintree Grand National winner, *Mr What*. In the sixties *Arkle* put every other steeplechaser in the shade, but in 1968 *Fort Leney* gave Tom Dreaper his fifth Cheltenham Gold Cup and Pat his fourth. Two years later Pat crowned his career as a jockey with his second victory in the Aintree Grand National, this time on *Gay Trip*. In 1974 he scored his first major triumph as a trainer in the Cheltenham Gold Cup with *Captain Christy*. By that time there was another star Irish steeplechaser winning its way into the hearts of the English public. This was *Red Rum* bred in Ireland in 1965.

Quare Times, ridden by Pat Taaffe, passes the winning post in the 1955 Aintree Grand National.
(Hulton-Deutsch Collection)

RED RUM

Red Rum's pedigree did not give any hints regarding the magnificent career which he would have but it, nonetheless, revealed some interesting ancestors. His sire *Quorum* which stood at Balreask Stud near Dublin Airport traced back through sprinters like *Golden Boss* and eventually through it to *Orby*, the winner of the Irish Derby in 1907. On his dam *Mared*'s side, *Red Rum*'s great great grandmother, *Black Ray*, was a famous brood mare from whom Epsom Derby winner *Mill Reef* traced his descent. Also on his dam's side was blood which produced the great *Rheingold*, winner of the Prix de l'Arc and second to *Roberto* in the 1972 Epsom Derby. When *Red Rum* came for sale to Ballsbridge in 1966 he was purchased for 400 guineas, half the reserve, by the former great steeplechasing jockey Tim Molony, who had been training in a small way for six years in Leicestershire and who was acting on behalf of a Manchester businessman, Maurice Kingsley. Together with his brother Martin, Tim had carried off most of National Hunt's greatest prizes in the forties and fifties. As an amateur he had won over one hundred point-to-points and after the war, as a professional, he rode over nine hundred winners including four consecutive Champion Hurdles at Cheltenham and was five times champion jockey between the years 1948 and 1955. A courageous jockey, when Vincent O'Brien informed him before the 1953 Cheltenham Gold Cup that *Knock Hard* had a bad heart and could drop dead at any time, particularly when exerting himself over jumps, "He just laughed and said he wasn't worried," and went on to win the Cup. With Tim as his first trainer, *Red Rum* was in safe hands. He took care with the youngster as he drove him with long reins and backed him. He was being ridden at the canter while still a yearling against all the precedents of steeplechase training and, as a two-year-old, had come first in two races on the flat. In 1968 he was sold to Mrs Brotherton who had been trying for eighteen years to find a horse to win the Grand National. At that time a young Irish professional jockey, Tommy Stack, was working for her trainer, Bobby Renton, as a stable lad and it was Stack who partnered *Red Rum* in many of his outings. Their performance in these early outings gave little indication of *Red Rum*'s future greatness. Vets had even diagnosed chronic pedalosteitis, a kind of equine arthritis, which in lesser horses would have resulted in a premature retirement from the racing game. His early racing record, however, was far from poor. He won three races on the flat and three over hurdles and in two seasons of steeplechasing he had managed to clock up five victories. His owner's disappointment with him however led to his sale in 1972 to Noel Le Mare for 6,000 guineas.

His new trainer, Ginger McCain, confident that *Red Rum* would fulfil his childhood ambition to win at Liverpool, had paid six times more for him than he had for any other horse. He had his small stables at the back of his car showrooms on a busy street in Birkdale, Southport. These stables were close to the sea and, working in the soft sand on the beach, the horse thrived. The long series of great victories commenced. *Red Rum* won the Grand National in 1973 from the great Australian horse *Crisp*, who was favourite, and *L'Escargot*, who came in third. It was the manner in which *Red Rum* took the race which impressed. He smashed the generally accepted Aintree record established by *Golden Miller* in 1934 with a time of 9 mins. 1.9 secs., a speed of 29 miles per hour, on average, over the thirty biggest obstacles in Britain. *Red Rum*'s performance in the immediate aftermath of this gruelling race signalled further the horse's extraordinary class and courage. A fortnight later he smashed the course record at Ayr in a three-mile handicap chase. By the end of the 1973 season he was only £4,522 short of *Arkle*'s all-time record of stakes won by a 'chaser.

For the 1974 Grand National, *Red Rum* was severely handicapped to the top weight of twelve stone, penalising him more heavily than any previous first-time winner of the race. Once again he was victorious beating *L'Escargot* by seven lengths. To Tommy Carberry, the rider of *L'Escargot*, *Red Rum* appeared to have nine legs during the race. At the 26th fence the great horse should have fallen, but recovered and ran on too strongly for Carberry. As if to again underscore John Oaksey's comment that the 'rules do not apply' to horses such as *Red Rum*, he was entered in the Scottish Grand National at Ayr a mere three weeks later and won by four lengths. Ayr commemorated the great horse's achievement by commissioning, in the manner of Cheltenham's memorial to *Arkle*, a statue of him to stand at the course.

But the achievement had yet to reach its climax. In the Grand National in the following two years, *Red Rum* added to his Aintree record by coming second on both occasions. This was a remarkable achievement in view of the handicaps under which he now raced. In 1975 the victor was *L'Escargot* the horse which *Red Rum* had twice beaten in the race in 1973 and 1974. *L'Escargot*'s victory in 1975 was by a resounding fifteen lengths. For owner Raymond Guest it was the climax of twenty years of trying to win the race. However, in 1977, *Red Rum* came storming back becoming the first horse ever to win the race three times. The margin on this occasion was an incredible twenty-five lengths. After the race Tommy Stack commented, "Nothing can do justice to this horse, nothing I can say and nothing anyone can write; he is just beyond belief." *Red Rum* with his extraordinary presence had behaved as if he owned Aintree. Everyone at his stable knew that he would win. In the following year he was again entered for the race but had to be withdrawn due to a foot injury. This did not prevent him, however, from stealing the show when he was paraded before his adoring fans at the start of the race. As in the case of *Arkle* before him the adulation which *Red Rum* attracted took the form of enormous quantities of fan mail and led to some commercial exploitation. In Southport, for instance, where he is stabled there is a Red Rum Hotel and a Rummies Bar. The fame had not come easily however. Whereas *Arkle* had during his racing career the advantage of the attentions of one trainer, one owner and one jockey to guide him,

Red Rum (left) and *L'Escargot*, Grand National 1975. (*Gerry Cranham*).

Red Rum had to struggle with the vagaries of numerous owners, jockeys and trainers and an early crippling injury. *Arkle* had, as it were, been born with the silver spoon in his mouth but, to borrow Ivor Herbert's analogy, *Red Rum* had made it from rags.[10]

NATIONAL HUNT RACING 1974-1989

While *Red Rum* was earning his spurs in England Jim Dreaper was carrying on the tradition of his father, Tom, in Ireland. In the five years from 1974 to 1978 he trained the winners of four Irish Grand Nationals including *Brown Lad* who won it three times with Tommy Carberry in the saddle. Dreaper took the Cheltenham Gold Cup in 1976 with *Ten Up* and in the following year Mick O'Toole was also successful with *Davy Lad*. The subsequent years also saw great Irish victories at Cheltenham. In 1978 and 1979 the popular *Monksfield* took the Waterford Crystal sponsored Champion Hurdle. In 1980 as the Irish thronged to Cheltenham in great numbers *Monksfield* was once again favourite for the event. On the eve of the race the big poker schools in the town were driven underground and had to settle for a discreet presence in private rooms as the local police reminded hotel owners of the provisions of the 1968 Gaming Act. There was nothing subdued, however, about the Irish presence at the racecourse on the following day but this time *Sea Pigeon*, who on the two previous occasions had been runner-up to *Monksfield*, emerged the victor ridden by one of the best Irish National Hunt jockeys, Jonjo O'Neill.

Monksfield had been purchased in 1974 for 740 guineas by Des McDonagh who subsequently became the trainer of the horse, and against all the odds, guided him to his great victories. As Brough Scott watched *Monksfield* at Cheltenham he reflected that "the little colt with the swinging front leg, the big brave eye and the almost tangible will to win, had soon become a symbol of the soaring athletic courage that can lift racing far above mere animated roulette . . . how moved I was watching this little horse battle triumphantly up Cheltenham Hill, and surely the ability to excite the spectators is the ultimate test of the great horse."

There was another focus for Irish attention at the 1980 Cheltenham meeting. This was Gold Cup winner *Tied Cottage* trained by a great Cheltenham campaigner Dan Moore. The victory seemed like a fitting climax to the trainer's career but it quickly turned sour when the horse failed a dope test. As has often been the case, the prohibited substance had probably been unwittingly administered in the horse's food. As a young man Moore had been very much in demand in Ireland and Britain as a National Hunt jockey. He was leading jockey in Ireland six times and in 1940 was overall champion. As a trainer he experienced his greatest success with *L'Escargot*, only the second horse ever to win the Aintree Grand National and the Cheltenham Gold Cup which he won twice. Dan who had an excellent eye for a horse also selected many horses which went on to achieve great successes for other trainers. *Team Spirit* which he bought at Ballsbridge as a four-year-old won the

Grand National in 1964 for the stable of Fulke Walwyn to which he had been sent on Moore's selfless advice. The purchase of *Tied Cottage* was due to his son, Arthur, who like his father had been a leading jockey before becoming a trainer. As a fifteen-year-old he had shared the amateur championship with another young man who would also become an outstanding trainer, Dermot Weld. Since taking out a trainer's licence in 1972 Weld has trained over a thousand winners on the flat and over jumps. His victories abroad have included Group One events in each of the major European countries. At home, with champion Irish jockey Michael Kinnane in the saddle, he has achieved classic successes and is regularly at the top of the Irish trainers' list. In 1988 he succeeded in a major ambition when he took the Irish Grand National with *Perris Valley*, a horse owned by him in partnership with Michael Smurfit, Chairman of the Racing Board. In the following year he won the Cartier Million with *Caretaker*, bred by his mother. Kinnane, who was in the saddle on this occasion, added to the triumph by partnering the English-trained *Carroll House* to win the Prix de l'Arc de Triomphe on the following day.

Undoubtedly the national hunt horse which captured the public imagination during the early 1980s was *Dawn Run*, a daughter of the champion national hunt sire *Deep Run*. In the 1980-1981 season *Deep Run*'s progeny had won 61 races and prizemoney of £123,448 but five years later the number of his winners in the season had more than doubled and his money winnings had almost quadrupled. A major factor in these latter statistics was the performance of *Dawn Run* who in the 1983-4 season alone won eight of her nine races and amassed £149,000, more first-prize money than any other horse has won in a single jumping season.

As a three-year-old she had been bought at Ballsbridge Sales in November 1981 for £5,800 by Mrs Charmian Hill who at the age of 63 rode her to her first victory at Tralee Races in 1982. Tony Mullins, the son of the mare's trainer, Paddy Mullins, was then given the job of partnering her for Mrs Hill had been informed by the racing authorities that she could no longer continue to ride in races. In a hurdle at Down Royal the new partnership scored a resounding victory in November 1983 and later in the month *Dawn Run* was ridden by Jonjo O'Neill to victory at Ascot in the V. A. T. Watkins Hurdle. Jonjo, who had been champion jockey in England on two occasions, had the experience and qualities required by the novice's owner and trainer for their Cheltenham campaign and it was he who rode the mare to victory in the Champion Hurdle there in 1984. So enthusiastic was the reception awaiting Jonjo immediately after the victory that he greatly feared that he would lose the race through failure to weigh in correctly.

During the summer of that year Tony Mullins had taken the mare to France and ridden her to victory in the Champion Hurdle at Auteuil in Paris. Her margin of victory over the rest of the field on this occasion was twenty lengths. A leg injury delayed her second assault on Cheltenham but by December 1985 she had returned to winning form easily winning the Durkan Brothers Chase at Punchestown from some very good and experienced steeplechasers. Later in the same month at Leopardstown she renewed her rivalry with *Buck House* whom she had beaten at Cheltenham. Once again she asserted her superiority. A preparatory race at Cheltenham in January of the following year left her ready to take on the rigours of the Gold Cup there in March. Her victory in that race was a triumph of courage and determination and placed her name in the record books. No horse before her had ever won both the Champion Hurdle and the Gold Cup.

Like two other star *Deep Run* performers, *Ekbalco* and *Golden Cygnet*, *Dawn Run* was to die racing. In the French Champion Hurdle at Auteuil in 1986 she was killed from a fall at the fifth last hurdle.[11]

Deep Run, the leading Irish National Hunt stallion, at Grange Stud, Fermoy, Co. Cork, one of the Coolmore-Castle Hyde group of studs. *Deep Run* died in 1987. *(Gerry Cranham)*

Eddie Macken on *Carroll's Spotlight* at the Hickstead Derby Bank in 1981. This 16.3 hands chestnut gelding is by *Sunnylight* out of an Irish Draught mare. Eddie bought him from Michael Connors in Waterford where he was ridden in novice classes by his son Francis, now an international competitor. In 1980 Eddie won the Hamburgh Derby with him and in 1982 they won the opening class in the World Championships at the RDS in Dublin. *Source*: Peter Ayres.

ABOVE: Suzanne Donnelly and *Friendly Persuasion* in trouble in the National Championships at the Punchestown Three Day Event in 1990. *Source*: P. Zöller. LEFT: Simone Richter-Kals from Germany on *Bantu*, competing at the Punchestown Three Day Event in 1990. *Source*: P. Zoller. BELOW: *Source* Inpho. OPPOSITE PAGE: Competing in the One Day Event at Watergrasshill in Co. Cork. *Source*: Louise Parkes.

TOP: Punters at Punchestown Race Course. *Source*: Bord Fáilte. ABOVE: Jubilant scenes as *Dawn Run* is led in after victory in the 1986 Cheltenham Gold Cup. Included are jockey Jonjo O'Neill and owner Mrs Charmian Hill. *Source*: Gerry Cranham. LEFT: *Red Rum* ridden by Brian Fletcher lands over Becher's Brook in the 1974 Aintree Grand National which he won. *Source*: Gerry Cranham. BELOW: Spectators. *Source*: Inpho.

RIGHT: Pony Club Games, a feature of the RDS Horse Show. *Source*: Horseman Photography.
BELOW: Racing on the strand at Laytown, twenty-seven miles north of Dublin. It is the only strand racing in Europe conducted under the licence and approval of the governing bodies. The actual time of racing is controlled by the tide. *Source*: Inpho.

Rounding the home bend in a Phoenix Park bumper race. *Source*: Inpho.

The start of the first Cartier Million, Phoenix Park. *Source*: Inpho.

VINCENT O'BRIEN

In the four decades after the second world war the name of one Irish trainer stands out above all others. His record in both National Hunt and flat racing is so comprehensive that it would be invidious to claim that he excelled in one branch of the sport more than the other.

O'Brien's early years as a trainer were spent with national hunt horses in the main. At an early stage he was able to demonstrate both his confidence and the quality of his judgement in choosing horses for his owners. One of his first owners was a prosperous wool merchant, Mr Vickerman, whom Vincent persuaded to purchase *Cottage Rake*, one of *Cottage*'s progeny. Vincent had started training the horse in 1945 and had been greatly impressed by it. As it turned out *Cottage Rake* got Vincent's career to a dream start, winning the Cheltenham Gold Cup in 1948, 1949 and 1950. In the meantime Vincent had again purchased wisely and cheaply paying eighteen guineas at Ballsbridge Sales for *Hattons Grace* who before coming to Vincent had been ridden in bumpers by Colonel Dan Corry, for many years a prominent member of the Irish showjumping team. With *Hattons Grace* Vincent won three successive Champion Hurdles in 1949, 1950 and 1951, the first trainer to achieve this feat. By 1951 the time had come for Vincent to move from Churchtown where his late father had farmed and trained horses to the bigger canvas of Ballydoyle, forty miles away. Before moving, Vincent, who was meticulous in everything which he did, sought the advice of Hubert Hartigan and another trainer, Bob Featherstonhaugh, who warned him against setting up, as they had done, on the Curragh with its wide open spaces and little variety. The fields at Ballydoyle averaged twelve to fourteen acres but, using the most modern methods of land clearance, Vincent set about the arduous task of transforming it into one of the best training establishments in the world. Gallops with surfaces for all types of weather were gradually added, a covered ride erected, further land acquired and a private racecourse where all the distances, turns or gradients which would be encountered by horses in competition were first met at home.

The meticulous planning which went into Ballydoyle characterised all aspects of Vincent's horse management. From Ballydoyle winners of the Aintree Grand National flowed just as Churchtown had issued winners of the Gold Cup. In 1951 *Royal Tan* was second in both the Irish and English Grand Nationals and in 1952 *Alberoni* won the Irish Grand National. But it was another horse, *Early Mist*, imported into Ireland in 1946, which began the sequence of victories which gave Vincent a unique training record. *Early Mist* at one time belonged to Jimmy Rank the one time owner of *Prince Regent*, who had sent him to Tom Dreaper to be trained. At Rank's dispersal sale, O'Brien bought him for Joe Griffin, known as 'Mincemeat Joe' on account of one of the products of his business, and in 1953, under Vincent's guidance and with Bryan Marshall up he won the Grand National easily. In that year Vincent was top of the National Hunt list in England, taking his fourth Gold Cup and winning the Irish Derby with *Chamier*. Controversy surrounded the latter victory, however, as it was awarded to *Chamier* only after an objection against the first past the post horse *Premonition* was successful. His achievement in 1953 was followed by those of the following two years when *Royal Tan* and *Quare Times* won the Grand National at Aintree, making O'Brien the only trainer to send out three consecutive winners of the great race.

These victories meant a great deal to the Irish both at home and at Aintree. On the occasion of *Royal Tan*'s victory in 1954, according to Vincent's wife, Jacqueline, they 'went just delirious'. When *Quare Times* returned to Ireland he was paraded through Mullingar, his owner Mrs Wellman's home town, led by two bands and accompanied by a crowd of seven thousand. But Vincent was looking ahead. His ambitions lay with flat racing where the rewards from racing and breeding far outstripped those in National Hunt, dominated as it was by geldings. To 'chasing'

Royal Tan, right, ridden by Bryan Marshall, matches *Tudor Line*, ridden by G. Slack, stride for stride, and goes on to win the 1954 Aintree Grand National. *(Press Association)*

men of the old school, such a decision would have bordered on sacrilege. Jumping for them was a religion. Not so for Vincent. With typical thoroughness he applied himself to attracting and maintaining great American owners who would supply him with the horses on which he could hang his ambitions. The first of these was John McShain, a self-made Irish-American millionaire who, as a child, had lent his pocket money to his brothers and earned interest on the transactions.

McShain's initial requirement was for Vincent to buy yearlings for training in America but Vincent succeeded in retaining them in Ireland. One of the yearlings purchased by him was *Ballymoss* for whom he paid 4,500 guineas, a comparatively high price. It had been a gamble for a man who never bought yearlings before to buy this horse which was sired by *Mossborough*. "They are now gelding all the Mossboroughs," one expert informed him, but Vincent's gamble paid off. *Ballymoss* went on to win the Irish Derby and the English St Leger in 1957, the Eclipse Stakes and the King George and Queen Elizabeth Stakes at Ascot and the Prix de l'Arc de Triomphe in 1958. The English Derby of 1957 had, however, eluded him. At Epsom he was beaten by *Crepello* in the fastest time since *Mahmoud* established the record for the race in 1936. Parallel with the career of *Ballymoss* ran that of the great mare *Gladness* which McShain bought in 1957 and which Vincent trained to win the Ascot Gold Cup and the Ebor Handicap in the subsequent two years with the youthful Lester Piggott up. As well as providing Vincent with great horses to train McShain also gave him a valuable introduction to the Keenland Sales in Kentucky by having him buy yearlings for him there. Later Vincent, together with his partners, Robert Sangster and John Magnier, would travel to Keenland to carry out successful raids for the cream of the world's yearlings.

At Keenland, O'Brien met Raymond Guest, later American Ambassador to Ireland, who in 1968, with O'Brien as his trainer, became, like McShain ten years previously, leading owner on the flat in England. His first success was with *Larkspur*, a horse which Vincent had bought in Dublin and which won the remarkable Derby of 1962 in which seven horses fell at Epsom.

Vincent's alliance with Guest was no accident. Increasingly he was training horses for American owners. In America there was adequate finance available for massive investment in bloodstock and during the first half of the twentieth century America had purchased some of the best bloodlines. With American money Vincent was able to bring representatives of these bloodlines back to Ireland to train. The first of these great American winners which came to Ballydoyle and the one which copperfastened his American connection was Guest's *Sir Ivor*, son of *Sir Gaylord*, who had been sired by *Turn To*, originally from Co. Wicklow. In 1967 he took the Grand Criterium and followed this in 1968 with the Two Thousand Guineas, the Epsom Derby and the Washington International. Later Guest moved him to Clairborne Farm owned by Bull Hancock in Kentucky where he was retired to stud.

The Triple Crown which had only been won eleven times in the history of the turf was almost the only honour which still evaded Vincent. The horse which brought him this honour was the *Northern Dancer* colt, *Nijinsky*, which Vincent bought in Canada for the American Charlie Engelhard. When he made this purchase, *Northern Dancer* was barely known and his progeny, therefore, still inexpensive. There was something prophetic in the purchase. By the eighties *Northern Dancer* had become one of the most influential sires of the decade. *Nijinsky*'s racing record was magnificent. In 1970 he took the Two Thousand Guineas, the Epsom Derby, the Irish Derby, the King George and Queen Elizabeth Stakes and the St Leger. Like *Sir Ivor* he was also returned to stud in the US.

Vincent's next Epsom Derby was in 1972 with *Roberto*, also American bred and owned. By this time Vincent had gone into partnership with Bull Hancock in America and now owned some of the American horses which he trained. These first steps in ownership became giant leaps when he went into partnership with Pools millionaire Robert Sangster. Out of their partnership grew the Coolmore-Castle Hyde group of studs, one of the world's greatest breeding complexes. It stands many Vincent O'Brien trained winners including *Thatch, Gay Fandango, King's Lake* sired by *Nijinsky* and *Be My Guest* sired by *Northern Dancer*. *Be My Guest* has sired winners of three hundred and fifty races worth two and a half million pounds. *Northfields* one of Europe's most successful sires, *Godswalk, Ahonoora* and *Deep Run* who dominated National Hunt breeding in recent times have also stood there. The origins of the conglomerate go back to 1973 when O'Brien purchased two thirds of the Coolmore stud farm which was near his Ballydoyle training establishment in Co. Tipperary. Coolmore had belonged to Wing Commander Tim Vigors, a famous war pilot and horseman, and both he and O'Brien in 1975 enlisted the services of John Magnier, later to become O'Brien's son-in-law, to run Coolmore. Magnier who owned Sandville Stud jointly with Robert Sangster and ran it in conjunction with his own stud Castle Hyde was grandson of Michael Magnier of the Grange Stud in Fermoy, Co. Cork. In 1924 Michael, as we have noted, had the distinction of purchasing *Cottage,* in O'Brien's opinion "probably the greatest jumping sire of all time", for twenty five guineas.

The first major success of the O'Brien-Sangster syndicate was *The Minstrel* who won the Epsom Derby in 1977 and, later in the year, capped this achievement with the Irish Derby and the King George & Queen Elizabeth Diamond Stakes. In this horse, which he bought for $200,000 at Kentucky, Vincent was backing *Northern Dancer* blood on both the dam's and the sire's side. The success of *The Minstrel* is emphasised by the manner of his retirement to stud. He was valued at nine million dollars. When the O'Brien trained *Alleged* won the Prix de l'Arc later in 1977 the pressure was on O'Brien from his owners to capitalise on his charge's victory. O'Brien once again gambled and held out to keep the horse in training. A year later *Alleged* took his second Arc, a feat accomplished by only four horses since the 1914-18 War. He was syndicated in the US for thirteen million dollars.

Left : *Law Society*, trained by Vincent O'Brien and ridden by Pat Eddery, winners of the 1985 Irish Derby. In 1990 Pat, seven times British Champion Jockey, became the first since Sir Gordon Richards in 1952 to ride 200 winners on the flat in Britain. (*Horseman Photography*).

Right : Lester Piggott and Vincent O'Brien with Jonathan Irwin on the left. In 1990 the very successful partnership between Piggott and O'Brien was renewed, producing such results as a win in the Breeder's Cup Mile at Belmont Park in New York with *Royal Academy*. (*Ruth Rogers*)

To date as we have discussed owners, breeders, jockeys and trainers in Ireland we have noted how horsemanship skills are frequently a family concern and tend to be passed on from generation to generation. A young man, in particular, is inclined to pursue his father's interest in horses and emulate his achievements. The reason why success with horses would appear to have been frequently transmitted from parent to child may lie in the manner in which horsemen jealously guard their skills in Ireland. They only trust their skills, it would appear, to those who are closest to them and these are generally family members. As Vincent O'Brien prepared the *Nijinsky* colt he had purchased at Keenland, *Golden Fleece*, for the 1982 Epsom Derby his son David was training another horse in which Robert Sangster had an interest, *Assert* sired by *Be My Guest*. These two horses, both grandsons of *Northern Dancer*, provided the first two competitions between father and son. At Leopardstown, in both 1981 and 1982 *Golden Fleece*'s devastating burst of speed proved too much for David's charge. *Golden Fleece*, after the second of these two meetings sailed through a top class field at Epsom to take the 1982 Derby, setting the fastest time of 2 mins. 34.27 secs. since electrical timing was introduced in 1964 and almost equalling *Mahmoud*'s hand-timed record of 2 mins. 33.8 secs in 1936. Four days later, *Assert*, who had not been entered in the Epsom race, won the French Derby and then the Irish Derby. Both horses were retired to stud, each at a value of around twenty five million pounds. In the case of *Golden Fleece* the stud was Coolmore.

The great confrontation between father and son on Epsom Downs was not averted, only postponed. In 1984 both father and son saddled *Northern Dancer* sons—*El Gran Señor*, in whose dam the O'Brien-Sangster syndicate had a two-thirds share, for Vincent and for David, *Secreto*, owned by the Italian Luigi Miglietti. Vincent's horse was the favourite but at Epsom's final rise he failed to produce the expected surge forward and on the line, after a great struggle between the two, *Secreto* got his muzzle ahead. Paradoxically, the triumph of the 'winning father' was complete.

There was consolation for Vincent later on in the year in the victory of his charge in the Irish Derby. A year later one of *Alleged*'s progeny, *Law Society*, brought him another Irish Derby having come second in the English equivalent at Epsom.

If the O'Brien story demonstrates the importance of pedigree, both human and equine, the list of Vincent's jockeys also tells its own tale. Some of the most recent jockeys have made reputations which equal that of their master. Lester Piggott who was with Vincent until 1980 was in Vincent's opinion probably 'the greatest jockey of his generation'. One of Vincent's earliest riders, Pat Hogan, can, however, relate his achievement with the O'Brien-Sangster empire to a family involvement with bloodstock which began with his grandfather who lived in Rathcannon in Co. Limerick. Pat's father organised the local point-to-point meetings there in the 1930s. His greatest breeding success was *Limerick Lace*, one of Ireland's greatest showjumpers, who with Major J. G. O'Dwyer in the saddle played a key role in Ireland's victory in the Aga Khan Nations Cup of 1937 and 1938 at the Dublin Horse Show. As an amateur jockey, Pat set up a record in 1942 by riding thirty-two winners out of ninety-eight rides. His victories were not easily achieved. On one occasion he cycled to Kilkenny complete with saddle and lead cloth, stayed there overnight and on the following day went on to Carlow where he rode four point-to-point winners. On his way home he stopped off at Thurles races where he rode two winners, one for Vincent O'Brien. One of the many races which he won was the 1954 commemoration race for the first recorded steeplechase in 1752. His success with horses has continued and he is now a bloodstock agent with a key function in the Sangster breeding empire. One of his most noteworthy purchases was that of *Rheingold* as a yearling. *Rheingold* came second to *Roberto* by a small margin in the 1972 Epsom Derby and in the following year took the Prix de l'Arc de Triomphe. He is now a very successful sire.

When Vincent O'Brien won the Grand National in 1953 and 1954 with *Early Mist* and *Royal Tan* respectively the jockey in question, like Pat Hogan, was one who had learned his craft from the cradle. Bryan Marshall was a son of Mrs "Binty" Marshall who, in her day, was Ireland's leading horsewoman. Using a side-saddle she rode showjumpers for Lady Helen McCalmont, wife of Major Dermot McCalmont. Bryan won his first race at the age of thirteen and was later apprenticed to McCalmont's trainer in England, Atty Persse. A very big and powerful rider,

Marshall had initial difficulty in adjusting his strong riding style to suit O'Brien's *Royal Tan* but for *Early Mist* he was the "ideal rider" providing the firm guidance over the Aintree obstacles which the horse needed.

When Lester Piggott ceased riding for Vincent O'Brien at the end of 1980 Pat Eddery, the grandson of Jack Moylan who had ridden for both Vincent and his father, replaced the great English jockey. At the age of ten Pat had been mounted on the McGrath horses at Glencairn by his father, Jimmy, who never had any doubts about the boy's potential. In 1955 Jimmy had tasted brief glory as a jockey, riding *Panaslipper* to victory in the Irish Derby after finishing in second place at Epsom but his hopes for greater things lay with his son. Pat was apprenticed to Frenchie Nicholson in England before striking up a winning partnership with trainer Peter Walwyn. In 1974 at the age of 22 he had become the first ever Irish born English champion flat jockey under Jockey Club rules and the youngest since Gordon Richards in 1925. He managed to remain top of the table until 1977, a position he again achieved in 1986 and 1988. In 1975 he succeeded where his father had failed by taking the Epsom Derby. On the winning horse *Grundy* he was also successful in the Irish Derby, the King George and Queen Elizabeth Diamond Stakes and the Irish Two Thousand Guineas. Many classic victories followed and in 1981 the O'Brien-Sangster team made him a 'fantastic offer' which he accepted, beginning a sequence of 'musical saddles' among the top jockeys. As O'Brien's jockey, Pat partnered *Golden Fleece* and *El Gran Señor* to their great victories before signing a contract in 1986 to ride for Prince Khalid Abdulla. In that year he scored the second of three successive victories in the Prix de l'Arc.

Paddy Prendergast. *(Ruth Rogers)*

PADDY PRENDERGAST

The status of Ireland in the thoroughbred world owes a great debt to Vincent O'Brien but credit must also go to another great trainer on the flat in the sixties, Paddy Prendergast. As a National Hunt jockey in his youth, he had competed in England prior to taking out a trainer's licence at the Curragh in 1943. He was a superb trainer of two-year-old horses and at the beginning of his career he concentrated mainly on these. In 1950 he won the Irish Derby—the first of eight—with *Dark Warrior*. Other prominent winners of the race for him were *Ragusa*, belonging to Mr and Mrs J. R. Mullion, owners of Ardenode Stud near Ballymore Eustace in Co. Kildare, who won the race in 1963 and later went on to win the St Leger, and *Meadow Court*, part owned by Bing Crosby, victor in 1965. Like *Ragusa*, *Meadow Court* was later syndicated for £400,000. In 1963 Prendergast headed the English trainer's list, becoming the first Irishman ever to do so and held his position there until 1966 when he was replaced by O'Brien. Before his death in 1980 he had captured not only eight Irish Derbys but five Irish One Thousand Guineas, four Irish Two Thousand Guineas, one Irish Oaks and three Irish St Legers.[12]

GROWTH OF THE BREEDING INDUSTRY

The success of such trainers as Paddy Prendergast and Vincent O'Brien had highlighted Ireland as a significant country in the thoroughbred producing world thus accelerating trends which, as we noted, were developing from the early part of the century. Ireland had natural advantages of soil and climate which favoured bloodstock production and, from 1939 on, these were complemented by government incentives in the form of a favourable tax regime. In the 1939 Finance Bill income tax was removed from stud fees and thirty years later this concession was extended to take into account developments in the syndication of stallions. The sale of nominations and shares was now exempt from tax thus creating an environment in which some of the best bloodstock in the world would be located in Ireland.

A major factor in the growth of the Irish thoroughbred breeding industry has been the development of large studs of international repute such as Coolmore-Castle Hyde, already mentioned, and the Airlie-Grangewilliam-Simmonstown conglomerate which stands stallions of the calibre of *Habitat* and the 1980 Derby winner *Henbit*, both sired by *Sir Gaylord*. In 1979 these two large stud enterprises combined to sponsor the Irish Two Thousand Guineas while Goffs, the bloodstock sales company, agreed to sponsor the Irish One Thousand Guineas. Thus by the end of the seventies Ireland had a properly endowed Classics programme in keeping with its status as a leading producer of quality thoroughbreds.

The introduction of American bred horses to studs such as those at Airlie and Coolmore has contributed greatly to the Irish breeding industry. Massive investment from abroad in highly priced stallions and mares to breed from them has followed. In particular Arab investment has been great. Kildangan Stud, situated in Co. Kildare on some of the best horse breeding land in Ireland, was bought in the mid-eighties by a member of the Royal family in Dubai, Sheikh Mohammed, already the owner of the Woodpark and Derrinstown Studs. Massive investment under the direction of his manager, Michael Osborne, has followed, with over a hundred yearlings being prepared each year to go into training. The result of investments such as this has been that the thoroughbred horse industry has become an employer on a par with some of the largest industrial sectors in the country. The number of people directly employed in the industry in 1985, for instance, has been estimated at 12,000. This is equivalent to the combined totals at work in two of Ireland's star industrial performers, the electronics and pharmaceuticals industries.

Compared to the United Kingdom with its larger size and population, Ireland's rate of horse production has been extremely high. By the mid-eighties the country was producing more foals than its neighbour annually. The thoroughbred horse population has increased accordingly. In the four years to 1984 it has grown by 15 per cent. Traditionally much of the country's thoroughbred produce has been sold at English sales. In 1979, for instance at the Houghton Sales, the most select English

Sales, two hundred and twenty seven Irish bred yearlings were sold in comparison with one hundred and eighty two British breds. Moreover the selling prices did not reflect any diminution of quality. Much the same picture emerges five years later from sales figures indicating that 40 per cent of the turnover of British sales comes from the Irish-bred horses there. The strong Irish presence at these sales indicates a weakness however in the Irish industry and, in 1975, this led the Irish sales company Goffs, to reorganise with a view to encouraging Irish producers to sell their produce at home. It moved its sales centre from Ballsbridge in Co. Dublin to a new location in Kill, Co. Kildare, a short distance from the Curragh.

GOFF'S SALES AND THE PHOENIX PARK

The company owed its origins to Robert Goff who was appointed official auctioneer to the Turf Club in 1866. In August 1887 the first Goff's sale took place at Ballsbridge. Over the years Goffs had charge of many major sales including the auction of Henry Linde's Eyrefield Lodge in 1897, the sale of the bloodstock of Boss Croker and of J. J. Parkinson, one of the firm's directors, on his death in 1947. The list of horses which passed through the paddocks at Ballsbridge from the twenties to the fifties reads like a who's who of some of the best steeplechasers ever—*Golden Miller, Prince Regent, Easter Hero*, and *Arkle*.

The new Goff's company was chaired by Joe McGrath's son Paddy who had succeeded to some of his father's responsibilities, including the chairmanship of the Racing Board and of the Irish Hospitals Sweepstake and to membership of the Turf Club and the INHS committee. With Jonathan Irwin as its imaginative managing director until 1989, the company has succeeded in attracting the top international buyers to Kill and has proved a high currency earner. During its period of growth from 1979 to 1984 the company's sales went from 10.5 million Irish guineas to over 40 million.

In addition to his activities at Goffs, Irwin had taken on the responsibility of running the Phoenix Park Racecourse which was reorganised in the early eighties by a consortium which included Vincent O'Brien and Robert Sangster. Lying a short distance from the centre of Dublin, the racecourse set itself the target of bringing the crowds back to the Park by providing a varied programme both on and off the track. Sunday racing was even included in its programme. Losses, however, forced it to close in 1990. One of the major achievements of the new course was the amount of sponsorship which it has elicited from companies both at home and abroad—in 1985 as much as 40 per cent of the total sponsorship available to Irish racing. For instance the Heinz International held in August each year was the richest race for two-year-olds in Europe when it was launched and the Phoenix Champion Stakes provided the second largest racing prize in Ireland. However, the Cartier Million inaugurated in 1988 has eclipsed both of these events in glamour and prizemoney. The winner of the race receives half a million pounds, making this the richest race for two-year-olds in the world. In 1988 Tommy Stack, in his second season as a trainer, saddled *Corwyn Bay* to victory in the race. The horse had been bred at the Thomastown Castle Stud of which Tommy was the manager. Winning the 'Million', was for him his "greatest moment since riding *Red Rum* to victory in the 1977 Aintree Grand National."

DIFFICULTIES FOR IRISH RACECOURSES

Despite its success stories Irish racing, according to the 1986 Report of the Commission of Inquiry into the Thoroughbred Horse Breeding Industry, still remains in a "perilous financial state". Various aspects of the racing industry have seen growth. Sponsorship of racing, for instance, has continued to increase. Between the years 1981 and 1984 the average amount of sponsorship per race increased three-fold. In 1976 sponsorship represented nearly 8 per cent of total prizemoney but by 1985 this had increased to nearly 30 per cent. The overall level of prizemoney has increased as a result but, like sponsorship, this money has been unevenly divided among the country's racecourses. In 1985, for instance, 58 per cent of prizemoney was absorbed by meetings at the Phoenix Park, the Curragh and Leopardstown.

The problem for the less favoured racecourses has been exacerbated by an overall decline since 1981 in the real value of tote and on-course betting, a major source of racecourse funds. Off-course betting turnover, which is greater than both these combined, reached an all-time high in 1985 of £140 million. Racecourses, however, do not receive any benefit from this, a position which the 1986 Commission wished to see changed.

The result of inadequate financing is that racecourses, many of which date back, as we have seen, to the last century, do not have the funds necessary to improve amenities and prizemoney. As a result, the appeal of a day's racing to the public is in danger of diminishing. In the mid-eighties about one million people went racing each year, a decrease on the figure of a decade previously.

Compared to England, Scotland and Wales which, together, have a total of 63 racecourses, Ireland with its small population would appear to be more than well served with 28 courses, two of which, Downpatrick and Down Royal, are in Northern Ireland. These offer a great deal of variety. Some of the bigger courses, many of which lie close to Dublin, feature the cream of the thoroughbred horse world in pattern and group races which have a great deal of importance in the breeding world. At the opposite extreme, there are the small country meetings where the informal atmosphere still has much appeal for Irish people. The proliferation of venues has undoubtedly strained the available resources with many racecourses experiencing difficulties in devising programmes capable of attracting adequate crowds. But the size and number of the racecourses has, nonetheless, meant that much of the traditional and local character of racing has been preserved.

POINT-TO-POINT RACING

One branch of the sport which, more than any other, has thrived, is point-to-point racing, originally known as Redcoat Races. Organised by the hunting community, they were held over natural terrain and until the late twentieth century were free of INHS regulations. Gradually during the twentieth century they have gone much the same way as steeplechasing, becoming subject to increased control from the INHS committee and witnessing changes in the type of obstacles which their competitors negotiate. Prepared fences have tended to take the place of the banks and ditches of former times and in some cases the races are held over regular racecourses. Better facilities for spectators have resulted and the races, which take place mainly on Sundays, have proven very popular. Betting turnover, as a result, has continuously been on the increase and each year the number of horses competing has gone up. In 1985, for instance, 1179 horses competed at 71 meetings compared to 851 at 58 venues a decade previously.

One of the reasons for the growth of the sport is that it provides a proving ground for steeplechasers, with horses likely to make the grade normally changing to steeplechasing at the age of seven. Despite this 'nursery' aspect of point-to-pointing and the serious betting activity which it attracts, it still remains a sport for amateurs organised by amateurs. Frequently the horses competing, which are required by the regulations to be hunted regularly, are non-thoroughbred animals owned and ridden by local farmers at meetings where there is intense local rivalry. The thoroughbreds competing may go on to better things on the steeplechasing or eventing field and the non-thoroughbred may become a successful showing or showjumping champion but on the point-to-point field there is no distinction made between them. Frequently indeed the very good non-thoroughbred provides excellent competition for his more finely bred brother.[13]

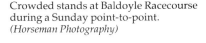

Crowded stands at Baldoyle Racecourse during a Sunday point-to-point.
(Horseman Photography)

Cross-country: Gerry Sinnott at
Bromont 1976. (*W. Ernst*)

9

Showjumping and Eventing

The changes in the type of courses over which steeplechasing and point-to-point races have been run have inevitably meant that the horse which took part formerly in these competitions is no longer found on the racecourse. When riders in centuries gone past took part in steeplechases, their horses' jumping ability over what could be very difficult natural country was more important than their speed. This has now changed and today the horse which most closely resembles such horses is the showjumper. In top class three-day eventing, the thoroughbred hunter-chaser is frequently found to the fore. Indeed some of the country's most successful three-day event horses have commenced their careers on the racecourse. *Amoy*, winner of the 1981 International Three Day Event at Punchestown, began her career in point-to-points. *San Michele*, who was on the Irish team in the Olympic Three Day Event in 1964, had competed as a Grade A showjumper and once came third in a steeplechase at Fairyhouse.

Sporting families in Ireland, like their horses, have frequently spread their efforts over several different equestrian fields. Pat Hogan trained with the Irish equestrian team for the 1960 Olympics for six months and would have competed in Rome had it not been discovered that, because he held a trainer's licence, he was ineligible. John Fowler who later achieved prominence as a national hunt trainer with horses such as *Banker's Benefit* competed internationally in three-day-event competitions on many occasions. In the 1967 European Championships when he was on the Irish team which came second his sister, Jessica Harrington, who subsequently achieved great success on *Amoy* came sixth in the individual placings on *Ginger Nut*. The owner of *San Michele*, Captain C. B. Harty, as we shall see, was a famous showjumping rider. His sons, John and Eddie, competed in Olympic Three-Day Event competitions for Ireland. The year before he competed in Rome on *Harlequin* and achieved individual 9th place, Eddie won the Conyngham Cup at Punchestown as an amateur rider on *Take Time*. In 1969 he accomplished a unique steeplechasing double by winning the Topham Trophy Chase on *Dozo* and the Aintree Grand National on *Highland Wedding*. One of the BBC commentators at Aintree on the day of the Grand National, David Coleman, later observed that Eddie gave him "the most graphic after-race interview ever". Eddie and his brother Henry were also trainers. After Henry's death in 1969 his daughter, Delma, who had been his assistant, took out a trainer's licence on her own account. In 1982 she became the first woman steward of the Turf Club.

The passing on of equestrian skills from parent to son or daughter is probably not a peculiarly Irish phenomenon but in Ireland, as we have noted, it is particularly in evidence. Horsemen have a great belief in their own ability to produce the winning horse and, as a rule, neither seek help from outside to assist them in this or are prepared to share their own expertise with others outside the family group. This individualism has, of course, been of value on the sporting field but it also has created difficulties for organisations involved in the equestrian world, having, as its basis, the competitive rather than the co-operative urge. Some of these organisations, nonetheless, have proven themselves of great value to equestrian sport and it is to them that we now must turn.

THE ROYAL DUBLIN SOCIETY

The organisation known since 1820 as the Royal Dublin Society was founded in Trinity College Dublin in 1731 by a group of men comprising landowners, professional men and members of the Irish Parliament, to promote the development of agriculture, industry and science. Over the years the promotion of agriculture remained to the forefront of the society's aims. It undertook many of the functions which the Department of Agriculture would later acquire. Included among its early schemes was the award of premiums in order to encourage the improvement of cattle and other livestock and in the second half of the 18th century this was extended to enable premiums to be awarded to the best imported stallions. In 1831 the first agricultural show was held and thirty years later agricultural horses were judged for the first time at the annual spring show. In 1864, in response to the considerable public concern about the deterioration of Irish breeds of horses, the RDS decided to experiment with a 'Show for Horses only', in all probability the first show in the world to feature an official jumping competition. This show met with success and in the following year it was held again with similar results. In 1866 it was decided to make it an annual affair.

The first horse shows were held at Leinster Lawns, the grounds of Leinster House where Dáil Éireann, the Irish parliament, now meets. Leinster House, which had been built about the middle of the eighteenth century had been intended initially for the Earl of Kildare. In 1815 the Dublin Society, as it was then known, acquired it. At the horse shows there, showjumping or 'horse leaping', as it was called in the programme, was introduced with a prize fund of £22, a cup and a riding whip. There were only two jumps, a wide leap over water and hurdles and a high jump consisting of three bars with an additional test over a stone wall for horses which had cleared 4 feet 6 inches. Later the stone wall championship was replaced by the high-pole jump, the forerunner of the modern puissance competition. Initially these competitions at the RDS were seen merely as a test for hunters. Few, if any, foresaw that eventually horses would be kept solely for competition purposes and that

MD ridden by Iris Kellett at the Double Ban the RDS in 1946. In this competition *MD* c third, probably the smallest horse to win a prize over the Double Bank.

Top right: Nat Galway-Greer who in 1964 the distinction of winning the three Champ Hunter classes at the RDS Horse Show, wi his winners, left to right *Great Moments* (Lightweight), *Treasure Hill* (Middleweigh and Supreme Champion) and *Twylight* (Heavyweight). (*G. A. Duncan*)

Bottom right: James Kernan and *Condy*, members of the Irish teams that won the A Khan Cup at the RDS Horse Show, Dublin 1977, 1978 and 1979. Here they are compet in 1977. (*Horseman Photography*)

Bottom left: Iris Kellett competing on *Mor Light* at Ostend in 1968. (*J. Bridet, Lausanne*)

'horse leaping' would be a sport on its own account and not seen solely as an appendage to hunting.

The sport quickly gained in popularity and more obstacles were added to the course. In 1881 the show was moved to the present headquarters of the RDS at Ball's Bridge, as it was then known. The competitions there must have been a success because in 1882 a larger continuous course was built. By 1885 competitors were jumping over the famous 'Ball's Bridge Course' which consisted of a hedge and ditch, a single bank, a stone wall, a double bank, a water jump and hurdle—a course which remained unchanged until 1935. In 1895 the competitions had become so popular that it was necessary to run off the competitors, who now numbered over two hundred, in pairs. These events, which were referred to as 'jumping' events, were by then sporting events in their own right and had found a place at local agricultural shows throughout the country. By the beginning of the new century they were attracting foreign riders to Dublin.

The rules for jumping the 'Ball's Bridge Course' were not very elaborate. There were stipulations regarding the minimum weights to be carried by the horses. For the champion stone wall event in the early 1880s, for instance, this minimum weight was 13 stone and riders had to weigh in with their saddles as in racing and eventing competitions of today. The time taken to complete a round did not matter, however, with the result that riders took plenty of time and care in ensuring that they presented their mounts correctly to the obstacles. It was expected that competitors would proceed at a fair 'hunting pace' but the original instructions for the 'leaping competitions' only specified that "obstacles are to be cleared to the satisfaction of the judges." In 1895 all rules and standards of judging were withdrawn and judges were left to express their own preferences. In these circumstances judges generally attempted to visualise how a particular horse would carry them on the hunting field. Inevitably, however, some of the decisions were arbitrary. One lady who asked what mistakes her horse had made was told that the horse had jumped well but that the judge did not like her hat. By 1921 a new system of judging was introduced in which mistakes with the forelegs, which tended to be critical on the hunting field, were penalised more heavily than mistakes with the hind.[1]

While the sport of showjumping was becoming established in Ireland through the efforts of the RDS, the first tentative steps were being taken, as we have seen, to support the breeding industry. The government had made little effort over the centuries to encourage better breeding of horses. Other more pressing concerns held its attention. But in the late 19th century horses were becoming a vital commodity. The British Empire was increasing in importance and needed the support of the army. The army, in turn, needed horses both to mount its men and to provide transport for the artillery. Britain was also the leading industrial country in the world and businessmen frequently aspired to be country gentlemen with a lifestyle which included horses. These factors help to explain the government's decision in

1887 to make a yearly grant to the RDS of £3,200 per annum in order to improve the quality of horse breeding in Ireland.

This money was directed initially towards solving the problem of the lack of good stallions available to service half-bred mares throughout the country. At the RDS annual show, owners of thoroughbred stallions were invited to compete for premiums of £200 each on condition that, if they were awarded to them, they would be then available, in areas designated by the RDS, to service a number of half-bred mares belonging to small farmers. The premiums were intended to encourage the breeding by farmers of "Hunters and other Half-Bred Horses" and for this reason the stallion owners had to agree to limit their fees to £1. An important element in this scheme was the involvement of sixteen local committees which inspected the mares in their respective districts and gave nominations to the stallions allocated to each. Later the RDS co-operated in the implementation of this scheme with local agricultural shows which, during the nineteenth century, had become established in different parts of the country and which, in the manner of the RDS, had also offered premiums of various kinds. These shows now held stallion classes at which prizes were awarded. An important benefit of this was that the examination of the stallions and the mares made owners conscious of the importance of soundness in their animals and taught them how to assess their own stock. Mare owners were also made increasingly aware of the importance of breeding to good stallions and they got to know where these stallions could be found. The concept of the travelling stallion developed and many farmers' mares were covered by stallions which would normally have been outside not only their financial but also their geographical reach.

The results of the scheme in its early years showed how effective were the incentives offered. The number of mares served by premium stallions had risen from 764 in 1888 to 841 in 1890. There were some problems however. Many good mares had failed to get nominations on account of their geographical location and the limited number of stallions. Clearly what was needed was a scheme whereby a large number of stallions certified as suitable for servicing half-bred mares would be available. In 1892 the RDS decided to move away from the premium scheme and to commence a registration scheme for thoroughbred stallions. In the first year of this scheme 147 stallions were submitted for registration and given veterinary inspections. Of these 102 were registered and a total of 1449 mares were serviced, a dramatic improvement on the number of matings under the previous scheme. The benefits did not stop there. By virtue of the scheme owners of mares not participating in the scheme now had access to a list of good quality stallions and were less likely to make breeding decisions based on ignorance of what was available.

It sometimes happened, before the development of the RDS schemes, that mares of small farmers were crossed with high quality stallions. Some landowners such as the Duke of Devonshire who owned the excellent stallion *Bacchus* were very generous to their tenants in arranging services for their mares. The RDS schemes, however, made some of these horses also available to other small farmers at a very modest fee. *Bacchus*, for instance, stood at a fee of £3. Edward Kennedy of Straffan in Co. Kildare, the breeder of *The Tetrarch*, registered his French-bred *Fortunio* who had won 19 races in France including the Prix d'Auteuil. Other notable owners with stallions registered were James Daly of Hartstown for whom *St Brendan* had won the Irish Derby in 1902 and John Widger whose *Wild Man from Borneo* had won the Aintree Grand National in 1895. The great horseman Captain M. A. Maher from Ballinkeele in Co. Wexford, a cousin of Valentine Maher, had three stallions registered including *Torpedo* who had sired many winners. *Red Prince* who was bred by Henry Linde and whose dam won the Grand National in 1875 was also registered. The Earl of Dunraven whose stables in 1900 boasted *Desmond*, a son of one of the greatest sires of all time *St Simon*, had also three registered stallions. In Donegal, *St Aidan*, who was also by *St Simon*, was standing at stud but this was not as a result of the RDS scheme. He was owned by the Congested Districts Board which had been founded in 1891 to cater for areas in which the rateable valuation was less than £1.10 per head. The Board was the greatest owner of stallions in Ireland but unlike the RDS its interest was not limited to thoroughbreds.

The concentration on thoroughbred stallions reflected the interests of the ascendancy class which predominated at the Royal Dublin Society. Army horses, light harness and riding horses were required in Britain and the RDS schemes were geared to satisfying that need. They took little account of the essential role which the working horse played in the Irish economy. Ireland was an agricultural country and needed to produce draught horses which would be capable of tillage and other agricultural work. The progeny of thoroughbred stallions mated with the type of mares found in many localities in Ireland did not suit this purpose. Moreover, the existing scheme discriminated in favour of certain parts of the country and left others at a loss. The whole of Co. Cavan, for instance, did not have a registered stallion in 1899. When the RDS decided to try to do something about this deficiency by purchasing stallions for placement in different parts of the country, only a small number were acquired and some of the most necessitous areas were ignored.

The RDS schemes could not fail to be affected by the move towards increased professionalism in the horse industry as well as in other areas of life in the late 19th century. In 1900 the Department of Agriculture and Technical Instruction was formed and gradually the RDS functions in relation to the registration of stallions and mare nominations were passed to it. Compared to the RDS, which had to run its programmes on a paltry sum, the new department's horse breeding schemes were well-funded. However, the impact of the RDS work could not be measured by reference to finance alone. Of necessity, the RDS schemes had, at times, revealed the hand of the amateur at work and reflected the interests of a narrow social class, but

Irish Draught mare and foal at the RDS Horse Show. *(Ruth Rogers)*

they had been extremely important in laying down the foundations for the work of the Department of Agriculture and of the semi-state body, Bord na gCapall, in relation to half-bred horses.

IRISH DRAUGHT HORSES

The Department of Agriculture realised that it was necessary to register heavy horses as well as thoroughbreds if the quality of horses for agricultural and heavy haulage work was to improve. Thus in 1901, Clydesdale and Shire horses were registered but three years later, as a result of lobbying directed against these breeds, the department agreed not to register any more of them except in Ulster and certain other areas. In the second half of the nineteenth century they had been imported from Britain into Ireland because of the inadequate number of horses in the country suitable for heavy work. The result of their importation was an increase in the amount of feather on the legs of Irish farm animals and there was a danger that their presence would lead to an irreparable coarsening of the Irish farm animal type. The Irish farmer needed a lighter animal than his British counterpart, an animal which he could yoke, drive and ride and the Irish Draught, the lobbyists were convinced, was such an animal.

In the late nineteenth century the characteristics of the Irish Draught horses as they were prior to 1850 had been described by Carden who had been a central figure in the RDS horse-breeding schemes:

> As regards conformation they were a long low build of animal, rarely exceeding 15.3 or 16 hands high, with strong short clean legs, plenty of bone and substance, short backs, strong loins and quarters, the latter however, drooping and inclined to be what is called 'goose rumped', slightly upright shoulders, strong neck and smallish head.

Carden admitted that breeding records for these animals were non-existent but put forward the opinion that they were the product of the "cross of the imported thoroughbred sires on the stronger, well bred mares of the country".

The attraction of the Irish Draught to Carden and to people today is that it is not essentially a draught horse but a multi-purpose animal which is particularly good in competition and hunting. "They had good straight and level action, without its being extravagant, and could trot, canter and gallop," Carden reported. "They were also excellent jumpers and this is generally recognised as being in some measure the result of their having the strong peculiarly formed quarters mentioned."

In 1905 the Department of Agriculture offered premiums of £50 to approved half-bred and Irish Draught stallions and by 1907 thirty-eight medium weight stallions, including some Irish Draughts, were admitted to the register. Three years later, after a series of inspections in different parts of the country, 13 stallions were registered as belonging to the Irish Draught type and 264 mares, whose owners were prepared to mate them with these stallions, were selected from a total of 5,040 as eligible for prizes and for registration.

The onset of the first world war stimulated the government into further assisting the Irish Draught. Horses were used in large numbers during the war although the days of cavalry operations had virtually ceased. The German army, for instance, had a total of fourteen million horses and a quarter of a million horses were lost by the British during the course of the war. Draught horses were used particularly with cannon which required up to twelve horses to draw it. Irish horses acquitted themselves well at this. The heavy draught breeds from other countries tired easily in drawing artillery and required a great deal of food whereas the Irish horses, particularly those from the south of the country where the Irish Draught was prevalent, were the most suited to artillery work. Lord Derby, the Secretary of State for War, stated succinctly his preference in 1917 for a "horse that will eat less, endure more and is quick enough for field artillery—really a cart horse that will trot", and suggested that such a type of horse should be encouraged. The Department of Agriculture responded by taking the first steps in forming a Book for Irish Draught horses. In that year 372 mares and 44 stallions were passed by inspectors as suitable for entry into the book. By 1938 the number of stallions registered had risen to 163

(G. A. Duncan)

and it could be argued that the scheme had been a success.

Unlike their thoroughbred equivalents many of the Irish Draught stallions still travelled widely at that time to cover their mares. *Boherscrub*, for instance, we are told travelled "to Ballinrobe on Mondays, Loughgeorge, Headford, Currindulla and Augheleggan on Wednesdays, Tuam on Saturdays, and at owner's stables on remaining days of the week". Many mares were the property of small farmers who could not have afforded to spare their mares from farm work in order to send them to the stallions. This problem had been particularly pronounced during the early years of the department's schemes when the number of stallions registered was small and the distance which some owners would have had to travel their mares for services would have been very great.

The years of the second world war once again demonstrated Ireland's dependence on its horses. With the increase in tillage work and the deterioration in other means of transport, the demand for the working horse grew and the government was forced to prohibit the export of horses suitable for work. By the end of the war the great decline in horse numbers had begun however. In 1945 the total number of horses in the country was 464,520. By 1951 this had dropped to 367,000 and at the beginning of the eighties there were only 68,500 horses in the country. The decline struck particularly at the Irish Draught. In 1944, 187 had been registered. 34 years later this number had declined to 63.

Reports into the horse industry over the years had highlighted the danger which threatened the Irish Draught. In 1935 a commission of enquiry into the horse breeding industry had expressed concern about the quality of such horses and when the survey team, established in 1965, reported, it warned of the danger of the extinction of the foundation stock of Irish Draught Mares. Fewer and fewer of them were being mated with Irish Draught Stallions. Farmers found it more profitable to cross them with thoroughbred stallions because the resultant progeny would fetch a better price than that of a mating between two Irish Draughts. It was clear that the inevitable consequence of this pattern of breeding would be the diminution of the Irish Draught strain. Five years after the survey team reported, the Irish government decided to act on its findings and established a semi-state body, Bord na gCapall, charged, as we shall see later, with responsibility for the half-bred horse industry.[2]

THE CONNEMARA PONY

Perhaps even more famous abroad than the Irish Draught has been the Connemara Pony. One of the reasons for this is that, like the Irish Draught, when crossed with thoroughbreds the Connemara mares have frequently produced excellent show-jumpers. *Dundrum*, as we shall see, was one of these. *Errigal* was one of the horses which made Diana Connolly-Carew internationally famous. *Stroller*, the 14.2 hands-high pony brought the English rider Marion Coakes the women's world champion-ships in 1965 and the individual silver medal in the Olympic Games at Mexico City in 1968.

The origins of the Connemara Pony are, like those of the Irish Draught, not clearly defined. When the Department of Agriculture instructed Professor J. C. Ewart in 1900 to study these ponies, he reported evidence of foreign influence, particularly from the East, in their breeding. Similar evidence of eastern influence on Irish horses had earlier been put forward by Dr R. F. Scharff after studying the skulls of early Irish horses found at Craigiewarren Crannog in Co. Antrim. Ewart categorised the horses he found into five different types and argued that the Clifden type in particular should be preserved.

One of Ewart's concerns was that the Connemara ponies should not be pampered in an effort to ensure the preservation of the breed. The ponies had acquired their celebrated resilience from having to survive in a landscape consisting mainly of bog, mountain and lake. In doing so they had "helped to gain for the Irish horse their widespread reputation for vigour, hardiness and intelligence". If given "rich food, much grazing, and warm stables they would ere long be as delicate as ponies reared in the ordinary way" and the reputation of Irish horses in general would consequently suffer.

At the time Ewart was carrying out his research, communications in Connemara were still of a primitive character. Many tracks could only be negotiated by riding and pack animals. Thus ponies played an important part in the economy of the region and farmers considered them essential for their livelihood. It was not until 1923, however, that steps were taken to implement Ewart's recommendation that good Connemara mares should be bred to chosen stallions. In that year the

Connemara Pony Breeders' Society was formed and after inspections of mares and stallions had been made the first volume of the Connemara Stud Book was issued.

Over the years the role of the Connemara pony has changed from that of a working animal to that of a riding animal. The pony has become well-known all over the world and an export trade has developed with many countries. Some countries, notably Britain, Denmark and the US, now have their own Connemara Pony Societies. So successful has been the export trade to some countries that the danger has arisen that the breed will cease to be distinctively Irish.

The continental market for ponies is a large one. In Britain, for instance the membership of pony clubs increased by 20 per cent in the years 1973 to 1978 and in Germany, where a Connemara Pony Society was formed in 1975, about 100,000 children participate in pony sport. Connemara ponies have been exported not only to Britain and Germany but also to many other countries in Europe. Outside of Europe there have been exports to the United States, Australia, South Africa and Canada. One country in the late seventies decided to use the Connemara pony in an effort to try to save its own herd of ponies. This was Lesotho, a mountainous country completely landlocked by South Africa. In the national stud there, two Connemaras are among the stallions servicing the local mares.

Two young riders with their show ponies. *(Ruth Rogers)*

THE ARMY EQUITATION SCHOOL

Parallel with the early involvement of the RDS in horse leaping competitions went the development of the Army Equitation School at McKee Barracks in the Phoenix Park in Dublin. The barracks which had been built during the years 1888 to 1892 for the British Army cavalry had been located in the Park on account of the training facilities which it offered. In 1922 the British army handed the barracks over to the Irish authorities and four years later the Irish Army Equitation School was established there under Major L. Hoolan with the aim of advertising Irish horses through army participation in international showjumping competitions at home and abroad. For this the RDS quickly provided a shop window at home.

In 1925, a Swiss army officer, Colonel Ziegler, suggested a means whereby Ireland could try to retain a dominant position in the horse trade over its rivals on the continent who were becoming a threat to Irish horse exports. Ziegler's interest in the matter could be attributed to the fact that Switzerland was a major importer of Irish horses. His proposal which was that Ireland should stage an international competition at Ball's Bridge was taken up by the RDS and in the ensuing competition between military riders from six countries, Ireland was beaten into second place by the Swiss. Riding all Irish horses, the winning army team took home the magnificent cup which the Aga Khan had put at the disposal of the RDS for the competition.

In the following year the Irish army team competed abroad for the first time, travelling to Lucerne and London. In 1928 the team received a great boost with the appointment of the Russian Prince Colonel Rodzianko, as the first instructor at McKee Barracks. He had been trained by James Fillis, the English dressage expert, and later had gone to the Italian cavalry schools at Pinerolo and Tor di Quinto where Caprilli, the inventor of the forward seat , had worked. He had ridden with the showjumping team of the Russian Imperial Cavalry which, under his guidance, won the King Edward VII Cup at Olympia in 1912, 1913 and 1914. At McKee Barracks he proceeded to train the officers in the riding methods advocated by Caprilli. In Ireland, as elsewhere, riders over steeplechasing and hunting obstacles had been accustomed to lean back in the saddle in order to ensure that they were not catapulted out of it on landing. This, as Caprilli showed, interfered with the natural jumping trajectory of the horse. The members of the army team, Captain Dan Corry, Captain C. B. Harty and Captain J. G. O'Dwyer, had all been selected from among officers with point-to-point experience and would have been schooled in the older riding methods. They were all very skilled riders and provided Rodzianko with excellent material on which to try out the new seat. O'Dwyer, however, stood out. "O'Dwyer was my best pupil," Rodzianko once revealed; "he was an artist," and it was he who replaced the Russian when he completed his term at McKee Barracks in 1931.

In 1928 the Irish team took the Aga Khan Cup for the first time. Four years later

The Irish Team which was narrowly beaten by Germany for the 1976 Aga Khan Cup at the RDS Horse Show: left to right Commandant Ned Campion and *Sliabh na mBan*, James Kernan and his father's horse *Spring Trout*, Captain Con Power and *Coolronan*, and Eddie Macken and *Boomerang*. This was the nineteen-year-old Kernan's first of many Aga Khan Cup appearances. *(Ruth Rogers)*

it repeated the performance, this time with O'Dwyer riding the great showjumper *Limerick Lace*. This very successful combination of horse and rider was on the winning teams again in 1935, 1937 and 1938. In 1936 the team was also victorious in the Aga Khan Cup competition but this time O'Dwyer partnered *Clontarf*. Abroad also the successes had been no less spectacular with the army team dominating the showjumping world. Total winnings in the years 1935 to 1937 were 12 Nations Cups and 61 first prizes in other international competitions. One of the most remarkable Irish performances was in Lucerne in 1935 when the team jumped 90 Nations Cup fences without fault.

During the period since the commencement of international competitions at Dublin the method of judging had evolved considerably. In 1921 the Fédération Equestre Internationale had been founded and had devised a system for judging military showjumping competitions. This system however took no account of the banks and walls which were a feature of the course in Ball's Bridge and did not differentiate between front and hind leg faults. It simply allocated faults when a fence was decreased in height or when a horse refused or fell. A points system was therefore devised for Dublin with all timber fences being judged by the FEI method and the banks, walls and water fences being judged by the Irish method.

At the Equitation School a special mounted corps was formed for the Eucharistic Congress taking place in 1932. Colourfully clad in its blue and saffron uniform it became known as the Blue Huzzars and performed escort duty for the President on state occasions. Part of the distinctive pageantry which surrounded the Nations Cup, for instance, required the Blue Huzzars to escort the President as he drove in an open landau from Áras an Uachtaráin to Ball's Bridge. This however ceased in 1948 when the troop was disbanded. At the outset of the second world war the school had been closed and the Dublin Horse Show discontinued but in 1945, with the end of the war, equestrian life was able to return to normality and in the following year Ireland once again took the Aga Khan Cup. Her victory three years later was to be the last for fourteen years. The army team which had brought Ireland the great victories in the thirties had retired and those who came after them in the fifties were unable to match their record. Colonel Fred Aherne, who was a member of many of the winning teams of the thirties, attributed the lack of post-war success to the background of the new recruits: "Before the war, we had the farmers' sons who had grown up with horses. Afterwards, we had the sons of Dublin shop-keepers—and many of them had never had their leg over a horse until they came to us." When Ireland again won the Aga Khan Cup in 1963 there was a new and important feature to the Irish team. It now consisted of civilian as well as army riders.

POLO

While the first steps were being taken at the RDS to establish the sport of showjumping another equestrian sport which could, however, never aspire to the same widespread support was gaining a small foothold in the country. Polo, which is one of the oldest team sports in the world, had been introduced into France by returning Crusaders about 1200 but had not become established in Europe until British cavalry officers who had played the sport in India founded the Monmouthshire Polo Club in 1872. In that year the first game was played in Ireland on Gormanstown Strand when the officers of the 9th Lancers played a team representing County Meath captained by John Watson. Watson's exploits were already well known. He came from a well known Co. Carlow hunting family and hunted with the Meath Foxhounds. He was a short-tempered man and during an auction of polo ponies he once threw the auctioneer off his rostrum. During the years 1891 to 1908, when he became master of the Meaths, he was reputed to have ridden six days a week with the hounds which he had bred himself.

In 1874 the All-Ireland Polo Club, now one of the most famous in the world, was founded in the Phoenix Park. The game became quite popular and at one time there were thirty-two clubs in the country. Crowds of up to 30,000 attending some of the big tournaments there were not unusual. The raw material for polo—spirited small horses of fifteen hands and upwards— is available in Ireland and many of the polo ponies required in Britain were once provided from Ireland. Between the years 1872 and 1914, Irish-bred ponies were among the most sought after in the world. This export trade has not continued however. The training of the ponies requires a great deal of time and patience and many of those participating in the sport in Ireland have found it more convenient and cheap to import them directly from Argentina. Polo is expensive with players needing at least two ponies for each game and in Ireland, where it was originally played by officers serving in the army, it has remained a sport associated with privilege. During the 1960s it nearly ceased altogether and today only about fifty people play it and the number of clubs has been reduced to three, one in Dublin, one in Waterford and one in Belfast. The season runs from April until the end of September and the main tournament of the year, the All Ireland Open Cup, which was first held in 1878, takes place in the Phoenix Park during the same week as the Horse Show at the RDS.[3]

EVENTING

In 1931 when the Governor General presented the Aga Khan Cup to Major Joe Hume-Dudgeon of the British team one old lady was reported to have said "Ah well; sure one of the Englishmen was an Irishman anyway and one of the English horses was an Irish horse." Such an assertion may not, of course, have been made on this particular occasion but there is no doubt about the the large Irish involve-

Polo at the Phoenix Park in 1964.
(G. A. Duncan)

Top left: Francis Connors on *Cherry Coin* in the early eighties competing at a local show. He is now a successful international rider. (*Horseman Photography*)

Top right: Taking the water jump at Castletown Horse Trials, 1952. In the background is Castletown House, the home of Squire Conolly in the eighteenth century. (*G. A. Duncan*)

Middle: Sheila Flannery, Bill Taaffe and Iris Kellett, winners at the Castletown Horse Trials, 1959. (*G. A. Duncan*)

Bottom left: Mona Croome-Carroll on *Croan* over the AVC bank at Punchestown Three-day Event, 1985. (*Horseman Photography*)

Bottom right: John Watson and *Cambridge Blue*. (*Horseman Photography*)

ment in British victories over the years. As we shall see, other countries such as Switzerland, the US and Italy have also used Irish horses to advantage. In the case of the 1931 British team the Irish-bred horse was *Irish Eagle* and the Irishman referred to was Hume-Dudgeon himself. He was born in Killiney in Dublin and had a distinguished career in the British army. He had been a pupil of Rodzianko and it was on his suggestion that the Russian was appointed to McKee Barracks. Riding British horses, Dudgeon was extremely successful as a showjumping rider. In 1938 he set up in Ireland the first private school of equitation at Merville, Booterstown in Co. Dublin where some of the early event competitions were held. The school was later moved to Burton Hall where it achieved a great reputation as a centre of excellence and attracted many top equestrian competitors from home and abroad. After training the British three-day event and showjumping teams for the 1948 Olympics, he trained the Irish three-day event team for the subsequent two Olympic Games. On each occasion the team included a horse owned by him and ridden by his son Ian.

Eventing owes its origins to a system of horse trials devised by the French army at a time when horsemanship skills were a military necessity. These trials were intended to test the horse's elegance and obedience for the parade ground, his speed for delivering dispatches and his courage and endurance for long marches, thus giving rise to the three disciplines of dressage, cross-country and showjumping. Ireland with its hunting and steeplechasing tradition was ideally suited to at least some of these three-day event elements and had riders who, in the early days of the sport in England, were prepared to 'have a go' with very little advance preparation. Penny Morton, for instance, who competed at the Mecca of three-day eventing, Badminton, for sixteen years between 1952 and 1968, on her first outing there rode *Vigilant* into fourth place without ever having competed in public before.

The premium, in Ireland, on the spectacular riding sometimes associated with the hunting, steeplechasing and showjumping fields has militated against success in dressage, an important discipline in the three-day event programme in its own right. The annals of Irish eventing are filled with tales of Irish riders compensating, with heroic feats on the cross-country course, for their poor performances in the dressage arena. Despite the national failing in dressage there have been over the years some spectacular successes. In 1965 at Badminton, *Durlas Eile*, ridden by Major Eddie Boylan, established a commanding lead in the dressage phase of the three-day event there and could not be overtaken. *Durlas Eile* had been bred by Phil Sweeney from Thurles in Co. Tipperary who sold him to the Army Equitation School. Before going to Eddie Boylan, he had been schooled by Seamus Hayes and had hunted for three years with the Fingal Harriers. In 1966, Eddie Boylan and *Durlas Eile* together with Penny Morton on *Loughlin*, Virginia Petersham on *Sam Weller* and Tommy Brennan on *Kilkenny* made up the Irish team which won the team gold at the World Championship at Burghley. In the following year at

Badminton, the great partnership managed to hold the dressage lead until the final day of the three-day event, when they were overtaken and beaten into second place. In the European championships which took place at Punchestown in the same year, Boylan again demonstrated the superb ability of his mount in dressage when he established a thirty points lead over everyone else and could not be stopped from taking the individual championship.

The strength of another member of the Irish team, Tommy Brennan, lay, however, in the showjumping and cross-country sphere. In the 1964 Olympics Tommy had ridden *Kilkenny* clear in the showjumping round and the team had managed to gain fourth place. Four years later, at the Olympics in Mexico, he was reserve rider on both the showjumping and three-day event teams. Pressed into service on the eventing team at the last minute, he had to compete in torrential rain on *March Hawk*, a horse he had never ridden before, and at one fence on the cross-country course both horse and rider were completely submerged and were in danger of drowning. Despite the intolerable difficulties, he managed with great courage to get his horse to continue as far as the eighth fence where he came to a complete halt.

Away from the eventing field Tommy has scored many successes on horseback. By the end of his equestrian career he had won a total of six point-to-points and fifty-five international competitions in showjumping, making him one of the most successful and versatile of Irish competitors.

Another rider who managed successfully to combine a showjumping with an eventing career was Bill Mullins who in the immediate post-war years was one of the most prominent of the showjumping riders. He was a member of the army team which took the Aga Khan trophy in 1949 and it was in showjumping that he made his reputation before turning his attention to eventing in the 1950s. In the 1956 Olympic three-day event competition he succeeded in coming tenth, of fifty-seven starters, riding *Charleville*. A distinctive feature of the Irish team on that occasion was that it contained not only Mullins, who was then serving as a commandant in the Irish army, but also two former British army captains, Harry Freeman-Jackson and Ian Hume-Dudgeon who as a young man had been commissioned in his father, Joe's, British cavalry regiment. Eventing like the other equestrian sports enabled participants to forget old historical rivalries and army officers seemed as concerned as the public in general to prevent divisive politics from interfering with their sport. Bill was not the only member of the Mullins family prominently involved in equestrian sport. With him competing in the World Championships of 1970 was his son Brian. Father and son achieved tenth and sixth place respectively as individuals. Equally illustrious, in his career as a national hunt trainer, has been Bill's brother, Paddy Mullins. Paddy has been one of the top Irish national hunt trainers in the 1980s, crowning his many achievements with the success of *Dawn Run*.

The Irish army involvement in three-day eventing has continued and some former members of the British army are deeply involved in the administration of

Diana Conolly Carew on *Barrymore* competing at the RDS Horse Show, 1964. (*G. A. Duncan*)

the sport. One family which has been closely identified with the development of eventing in Ireland has been the Conolly-Carews. The family home was formerly at Castletown in Co. Kildare which had been built by William Conolly, who was elected Speaker of the Irish House of Commons in 1715. Conolly's nephew Thomas was also an MP but it was as a horseman that he is best remembered. Known as 'Squire' Conolly he kept his own pack of hounds and entertained lavishly at Castletown. His descendant Patrick Conolly-Carew, during his days in the British Army, competed very successfully in showjumping and in 1971 was a member of the Irish team which took part in the Nations Cup at Hickstead. As an event rider he competed for many Irish teams in international events including a European and Olympic championship. In 1962, riding *Ballyhoo*, he was a member of the Irish team which took the silver medal at the European Championships at Burghley. In the following year his sister, Diana, was a member of the Aga Khan Cup winning Irish team, riding *Barrymore*, the horse which with *Errigal* made her internationally famous. Patrick has followed in the footsteps of his parents, Lord and Lady Carew, and has occupied a leading position in the administration of eventing. He has also served as President of the Equestrian Federation of Ireland.

The list of Irish competitors in the Olympic games in 1972 gives some idea of the extent to which equestrian sport has succeeded, where little else could, in drawing people from widely different political and religious backgrounds together to pursue the same object under the same flag. As well as Conolly-Carew the team consisted of an Irish army officer, Captain Ronnie McMahon on *San Carlos*, one of the most successful eventing combinations in the early seventies, coming second in their first appearance at Badminton in 1970, winning the three-day event at Fontainebleau, coming fourth in the three-day event World Championships and winning the Irish dressage championship, all in the same year, and winning the three-day event at Punchestown in the following year. Also in the Olympic team in 1972 riding *Benka* was Bill Buller from Scarva in Co. Down, a traditional Unionist and Protestant area in Northern Ireland. Bill also competed in the Irish team in the world championships of 1970. The fourth member of the team was Bill McLernon, a descendant of Mr O'Callaghan who competed in the first recorded instance of a steeplechase in 1752 from Buttevant Church to the spire of St Leger Church. In the steeplechase of 1954 which commemorated this race Bill, who was a proficient steeplechase rider, together with his brother, led the Killeagh Harriers to win the team prize. In 1971 he was a member of the bronze medal winning Irish team in the European championships and in the Olympic Games of the following year he rode the Bord na gCapall horse *Ballangarry*.

If *San Carlos* and Ronnie McMahon stole the limelight in the early seventies *Cambridge Blue* and John Watson were the heroes of the second half of the decade. John is the son of the equestrian historian Colonel S. J. Watson who numbers among his published works a history of Irish steeplechasing, a history of three-day eventing and a biography of Bianconi. In 1977, riding *Cambridge Blue*, John was a member of the bronze medal winning team in the European championships at Burghley in England. In the sweltering heat of the Lexington World Championships in the following year came his biggest prize, however. The sole Irish representative in the competition, he managed to guide *Cambridge Blue* to take the individual silver medal. In the following year he came fifth on the same horse in the European Championship at Luhmuhlen and, together with Helen Cantillon on *Wing Forward*, Lieut. David Foster on *Inis Meain* and Alan Lillingston on *Seven Up*, managed to capture the team gold for Ireland.

The Irish, as we have pointed out have, in general, shown little aptitude for dressage. Very few Irish riders, for instance, have attained the highest international levels in dressage competitions. In 1949 Patsy Hildebrand riding Colonel Joe Hume-Dudgeon's horse *Sea Forth*, did manage to win the Prix St George at the White City in London but overall the picture is a dismal one. Clearly the fault has been with the riders themselves and their trainers. Foreign-owned Irish dressage horses have frequently been very successful and Ireland is increasingly being seen by foreign buyers as a source of dressage horses. *Rathpatrick* has won several Grand

Left : John Watson on *Cambridge Blue* competing in the Dressage test at the Badminton Three-day Event. *(Horseman Photography)*

Right : Colonel Joe Hume Dudgeon, a very successful showjumping and eventing trainer, jumping a horse without the use of a bridle in 1952. *(G. A. Duncan)*

Prix events and taken the gold medal at the Pan American Games and the Swiss rider Claire Koch has been very successful on *Beau Geste*.

In the past the excuse for Irish failure to devote the time and effort required to bring horse and rider to a high standard in dressage could be made that, in Ireland, people have the privilege of enjoying the greater thrills associated with excellent hunting, point-to-pointing or racing at all times of the year. In other countries weather conditions may confine riders during the winter months to indoor riding schools whereas Ireland has a moderate climate. In addition, the elitist image which dressage has acquired has not helped its development. The fewer the numbers competing in the sport, the less likelihood of competitive standards being attained. Irish people traditionally, as we saw, have shied away from the formal attire which, in England, is accepted as an integral part of horsemanship. The top hat and tails of the dressage arena have, to some, appeared too forbidding. Increasingly, however, the leading showjumping riders and trainers have come to see dressage, which literally means 'training', as an essential part of their horses' preparations and this has brought a change in the perception of it in Ireland. Along with this increased awareness of the necessity of dressage has come greater opportunities for competitors in dressage.

In 1978 the Reducine National Dressage Championships, culminating in finals at the RDS, were inaugurated and have managed to increase their popularity since that time. In their first year, the championships had thirty finalists but by 1982 this number had doubled. Likewise, standards have improved so that Ireland, it is expected, will shortly have competitors at international level.[4]

THE RIDING CLUB MOVEMENT

One major factor in the increasing popularity of dressage has been the rise of the riding club movement. Other equestrian pursuits such as hunting, regarded in Ireland as one of the best amateur equestrian sports, lie outside the reach of many leisure riders. Not only can the cost of hunting be prohibitive but many hunts have been obliged to limit the numbers of those participating in order to maintain good relations with the farmers who own the land over which they hunt. Where the thrill of the hunting field is not attainable, dressage provides an alternative. It offers riders the opportunity to learn the fundamentals of horsemanship and participate in competition in a secure environment. The rider's financial outlay and the risk to the owner's horse are greatly reduced. While dressage is particularly suited to the leisure rider, it is only one among many branches of equestrian sport in which riding clubs participate.

The first riding club to be formed in Ireland was Foxborough which began in 1972 in the Dublin-Wicklow area. One of its founding members, Helen Mangan, later became National Secretary of the Association of Irish Riding Clubs which, by 1980, was co-ordinating the activities of a total of twenty-five clubs. By 1983 this number had grown to 39 with a wide geographical spread covering both sides of the border which divides the country politically. The increase in the number of clubs is

Leisure riding in County Cork.
(Bord Failte)

reflected in a large increase in the number of riding club members. In 1976 the clubs had a membership of approximately 800 but by 1983 this had grown to approximately 2,500. Encouraging the growth of the riding clubs and their activities has been the prevalence throughout the country of riding schools capable of providing members with the horses, facilities and instruction they require. By the early 1980s over forty riding establishments could offer their riders indoor riding facilities.

Many of the members of riding clubs are the products of the affluence of the late 1960s and 1970s. With more disposable income than Irish people of an earlier generation and with the leisure time available to devote to sporting interests they have turned to equestrianism for recreation. This development is hardly a surprising one. Traditionally Irish people have looked to the horse to provide them with recreation. Riding clubs have channelled the equestrian interests of their members into showjumping, dressage, hunter trials and cross-country events. In the sport of dressage, the riding clubs organise national competitions which culminate in a day of finals at the RDS each year.

The inter-club character of many of the riding club competitions adds greatly to their enjoyment. As well as affording an opportunity to members to improve and test their skills they are important social occasions. Where professional riders competing in national shows are primarily concerned with achieving results most riding club members, by way of contrast, tend to look on the sport as a social outlet. There is a practical side also to riding club activities. Some of the clubs, for instance, provide a great deal of assistance to the Riding for the Disabled Association which was formed in 1968 to make the benefits of riding available to those suffering from disability.

RIDING FOR THE DISABLED

From its very beginnings the riding club movement has been involved both in fund raising for the Riding for Disabled Association and in providing the personnel required by disabled children or adults while they are on horseback or learning the rudiments of horse management. Like the Association of Riding Clubs, the Riding for the Disabled Association has developed a series of graded tests for riders to encourage them to develop their potential and to enable them to measure their progress in horsemanship. An increasing number of people is participating in the association's activities and such has been its growth that in 1980 it changed from being a regional organisation under its parent body in England into a national organisation in its own right. The benefits of the sport to the riders are two-fold. It enables them to achieve a level of fitness otherwise perhaps not possible, to strengthen weak muscles and improve balance and co-ordination. But in many respects the related psychological benefits are more important. The horse physically raises its rider to a height not normally experienced by able-bodied or disabled alike. Riders generally gain great confidence from sitting on a horse or pony and looking down at the world. In addition the horse, as a living and feeling animal, has a unique ability to form relationships with the people around it. Its rider, whether able-bodied or disabled, benefits from the sense of harmony with it which the animal is capable of promoting.

EQUESTRIAN EDUCATION

The capacity of the horse as an educational and therapeutic tool has long been recognised in Ireland. As we have noted from the law tracts, young men in early Ireland were required to learn to ride and there were detailed provisions made for their education in this respect even during their period of fosterage. In the eighteenth and nineteenth centuries a young man from the landed classes had to be able to demonstrate skills in a number of equestrian fields. We noted also the provisions made for the young Art McMurrough Kavanagh in the first half of the nineteenth century to enable him to ride horses despite his severe disability. In more recent years the first steps have been taken in incorporating equestrianism formally into the curriculum of the Irish educational system. Charting the path in this respect has been Co. Kilkenny Vocational Education Committee which has included full-time courses designed to prepare young people for a career as riding instructors and horse farmers in its educational programmes. The school chosen to hold these

'Equestrian Education' — Does that mean I get to go to school? (*Ruth Rogers*)

Riding for the disabled.
(*Horseman Photography*)

courses under the guidance of the semi-state body, Bord na gCapall, the Irish Horse Board, is Thomastown Vocational School located in an area rich in horse associations. Nearby is the McCalmont stud at Mountjuliet where *The Tetrarch* once stood. Further south is Rossenara Stud where *Red Rum* was bred by Martyn McEnery. In nearby Goresbridge Paddy Mullins has his training stables and at Gowran a few miles from Thomastown national hunt and flat racing is held on one of the country's most attractive racecourses.

Further educational developments took place in 1989 with the launching of a certificate course in Equestrian Studies at Thomond College of Education in Co. Limerick. This course, together with the established programmes in Thomastown lay the basis for an educational structure which can claim to provide a modern equivalent of the more informal and long-standing traditional methods. They have the potential not only to cater for the needs of Irish people but to attract students from other parts of the world eager to learn in a country with a strong horse tradition.

But the early training of young people in equestrianism has not been left solely in the hands of the educational authorities. Many riding schools have the facilities and personnel to provide riders with both their initial riding introduction and with the training necessary to bring them to competition standard. A feature of the

Left : At the Millstreet International Horse Show Thoroughbred Stallion class, August 1980, were, left to right, Dermot Forde, Breeding Manager of Bord na gCapall, Judges Thady Ryan and Eileen Parkhill, and referee Jack Powell. In the background is the winner, *Mac Rocket*, and owner Denis Vaughan. *(Mary Tarry)*

Right : Leisure riding in Connemara. *(Bord Failte)*

programmes offered by these schools is the preparation which they provide for their pupils who take the examinations developed by both the British Horse Society and Bord na gCapall. Particularly well-known both in Ireland and abroad has been the Kellett Riding School situated a short distance from Naas in Co. Kildare. Originally located in the heart of Dublin city, the school numbered among its former pupils world class showjumpers such as Eddie Macken and Paul Darragh and managed to attract a significant number of students from abroad each year. The guiding light behind the school, until it was sold in 1989, was Iris Kellett, a former showjumping star who has an unrivalled reputation in Ireland as a trainer of horses and riders.

PONY CLUBS

For many riders in Ireland their first introduction to riding is through their pony club and the growth of the pony club movement, like that of the riding club, is an index of the extent to which riding has become a popular activity with all classes. In 1968 there were approximately 1,200 members but by 1977 this had grown to 2,400 spread over a total number of 29 branches. By 1983, the year in which the Irish Pony Club movement celebrated its fiftieth anniversary, the number of branches had increased to 41 with a membership of over 3,000. One of the important features of the pony club movement has been its widespread acceptance. Even remote parts of the country have their own pony club branch or are near to one and membership of clubs frequently bridges the social and economic classes. In Ireland pony club members frequently ride with their local hunts and, where these young people are the sons or daughters of farmers, this serves to create an important link between the hunt and the owners of the land over which the hunt is held, a link which goes some way towards explaining the generally harmonious relationship existing in Ireland between the hunt and the farmer. Tetrathlon, Mounted Games, Hunter Trials, Horse Trials, Dressage and Showjumping are also part of the Pony Club programme. At the RDS Horse Show the finals of the mounted games in which pony club branches compete against each other are held, adding greatly to the spectacle of the show. During the summer holiday period the clubs hold camps which involve the young people in a week's training and many pony club members take the examinations which are organised by the pony club. The success of the pony club movement is attested by the quality of its past members. For instance all four members of the successful Irish Aga Khan Cup teams from 1977 to 1979, Paul Darragh, Eddie Macken, Captain Con Power and James Kernan, have been in the ranks of the Pony Club.

BORD NA gCAPALL—THE IRISH HORSE BOARD

From the early 1970s until the period 1987-9, when the government abolished it, the body with the greatest resources at its disposal for the education and training of horse and rider has been the semi-state body Bord na gCapall. It was set up in 1971 in response to the recommendations of the survey team established by the government in 1965 "to examine all aspects of the horse breeding industry, except racing". The new body inevitably became involved in training and education. At an early stage a farriery training scheme was established and the tradition begun in 1889 by the RDS at its spring show of holding farriery competitions at Ball's Bridge was revived. Bord na gCapall also encouraged riding schools to improve their standards of horse management and riding instruction and organised courses for leisure riders, making available to them the best riding instructors in the country. Particular attention was also paid to the inauguration of an Irish certification scheme for riding instructors. Before 1977 the only examinations available which could be taken by riding instructors were organised by the British Horse Society. Bord na gCapall adapted these examinations to suit Irish conditions and, in conjunction with the BHS, acted as an examining authority. As indicated previously, the first steps have been taken by some educational authorities in developing the range of equestrian courses available and in carving out a place for equestrian education within the overall education system of the country.

But the educational sector was only one aspect of the non-thoroughbred horse industry which was in need of attention. Bord na gCapall realised that Irish horses had to be marketed effectively if Ireland was to compete with other countries for the increasing continental market for horses suitable for leisure riding. The English market which traditionally had absorbed the vast majority of Irish half-bred horses had contracted dramatically. In 1972 over 11,000 horses were exported to Britain but by 1977 this number had declined to just over 700. The Board devoted much of its resources in its early years to remedying this loss and in 1974 took the large step of organising its own sales. But it was the breeding area which had principally concerned the survey team when it reported in 1966 and which inevitably figured most prominently in the Board's activities.

Central to the Board's work was the production of the Irish Horse Register established in 1974. It became the basis for the identification of all half-bred stock. For ten years inspections were carried out annually, eligible mares registered and their progeny recorded. This meant that half-bred horses being sold abroad were equipped with passports which documented their breeding and, if relevant, their competitive performance, information which was of great importance to potential buyers. A feature of the development of the register since 1979 was the agreement between the Board and the Northern Ireland Department of Agriculture to make it a joint register for horses both from the Republic and Northern Ireland. This register formed the basis of many of the financial allocations to the industry made by the Board. In 1984, for instance, £47,600 in foaling premiums was paid to owners of registered mares.

Included within the register was a special section dealing with Irish Draught

Commandant Billy Ringrose competing on
Loch an Easpaig at the White City, London.
(*Photo courtesy of Louise Garland*)

Top right: Colonel Dan Corry competing on *Killaloe*, RDS Horse Show, 1952. (*G. A. Duncan*)

Top left: Commandant Gerry Mullins and *Rockbarton* competing at the Wolrd Showjumping Championships at the RDS in 1982. They were placed fourth in the individual competition. (*Tony Parkes*)

Bottom left: The winning Nations Cup Team at Lucerne in 1937: left to right Captain Dan Corry on *Duhallow*, Captain Fred Aherne on *Red Hugh*, Captain John Lewis on *Limerick Lace* and Lieutenant Jim Neylon on *Tramore Bay*.

Bottom right: Diana Conolly Carew competing on *Tubberoe* at Westport Show (*Horseman Photography*)

mares. The importance of the Irish Draught type as a sporting animal had been highlighted by Carden, as we have seen, and with the development of showjumping its importance became increasingly evident. The Irish Draught mare when crossed with a thoroughbred sire frequently had progeny which when crossed again with thoroughbred blood produced excellent jumpers. As with the Connemara pony, the focus of interest had shifted away from the horse's direct economic role as a work animal. Indeed the decline in the horse population was particularly pronounced in the case of working horses. From a total of 111,400 in 1967 they declined in numbers to 18,800 in 1980. Other half-bred horses have, on the other hand, been increasing in number reflecting the increasing interest in competitive and leisure riding. The Board's role in these circumstances was in the main to try to ensure that farmers continued to use the recipe for producing good jumping horses, namely cross their Irish Draught mares with thoroughbred stallions and cross the offspring with thoroughbreds. This in turn required that the Irish Draught continue as a type. In 1977 for the first time premiums worth £100 each were awarded to owners of suitable Irish Draught mares on condition that they produced live foals to approved

Left: David Broome on the Irish-bred *Queensway Sportsman*, RDS Horse Show, 1980. (*Horseman Photography*)

Right: Eddie Macken winning the Puissance on *Kerrygold* at the RDS Horse Show, 1977. (*Horseman Photography*)

James Kernan and
Kerrygold Country.
(*Irish Farmers Journal*)

Irish Draught stallions in the following year. By the mid-eighties when the amount of the premium had been increased to £150 about 50 premiums were being awarded each year. Meanwhile inspection of stallions, including both thoroughbred and Irish Draught, for inclusion in the list approved for the service of mares in the Irish Horse Register continued each year and subsidies and foaling premiums were paid to the stallion and mare owners respectively for foals recorded.[5]

Towards the end of the 1980s the production of the non-thoroughbred horse has assumed a great deal of importance in farming circles. Surpluses of such commodities as beef and milk have forced government and European Community officials to look to the horse industry as a possible area of expansion for farmers and to improve some of the incentives available for horse production. With the abolition of Bord na gCapall, responsibility for developments in this area lies, once again, with the Department of Agriculture.

Known as the 'Grand Master', John Boyne is a fourth generation Dublin farrier. Seen here with Owen Gilmore attending to *Glendalough* at the Army Equitation School, McKee Barracks, Dublin. John Boyne, Snr has been farrier to the army for eighteen years and for the past forty-five years to the Royal Dublin Society's Irish and international circuits. He has trained fifteen apprentices with the former semi-state body, Bórd na gCapall, many of whom now work abroad. His son, John, Jnr is also a farrier (fifth generation) and is training his own apprentice. (*Photo courtesy Brenda Boyne*)

SHOWJUMPING

For many people in Ireland equestrian competition means showjumping. The ultimate success for many breeders and owners is to produce a horse which will achieve international fame in the showjumping arena. Because the breeding of showjumpers is not overshadowed by considerations of breeding lines as in the case of racehorses there is always the possibility of the small breeder producing the great horse from relatively humble stock.

Early showjumping was, as we have seen, largely a military affair and all the Irish international teams were made up of military riders. One such rider, Colonel John Lewis, who partnered *Limerick Lace* on many occasions recalled seeing in his youth very good lady riders. Mrs 'Binty' Marshall of Limerick, mother of Bryan Marshall, was a very well-known rider. She rode side-saddle on Lady Helen McCalmont's showjumpers and, in the late 1930s, competed in London. Lewis also recalled seeing Mrs Wall of Dublin and Mrs McGee on her well-known horse *Nugget* which was still winning in Dublin at the great age of 30 years. In the early years of the century most principal towns in the country had an agricultural show with a jumping course intended to test hunters. Very little control was exercised over the sport, however, until 1942 when the Show Jumping Association of Ireland, known originally as the Riding and Encouragement Association, was founded. The new body included among its founder members showjumping star Iris Kellett's father, Harry, and General Liam Hayes who had purchased many of the horses which had helped the army team of the 1930s to the top of the showjumping world and whose son Seamus, would later become a very famous name in the showjumping arena, particularly through his association with the great horse *Goodbye*. The first chairman of the Executive Committee was Colonel Joe Hume-Dudgeon who in each subsequent year until he retired, shortly before his death in 1965, was unanimously re-elected to that position by the general body of the SJAI members. The association developed

Top : Eddie Macken and *Boomerang*. (*Ruth Rogers*)

Bottom left : Harvey Smith and the Irish-bred *Olympic Star*, later known as *Sanyo San Mar*, members of the 1976 British Nations Cup Team at the RDS Horse Show. (*Ruth Rogers*)

Bottom right : John Whitaker and *Ryan's Son* at the World Showjumping Championships at the RDS in 1982 in which they won the individual silver medal. "When I'm riding Ryan," John once explained, "I don't think about what I'm doing, or what I'm going to do; he's already done it." *Ryan's Son* was bred by Ned Byrne of Gorey, Co. Wexford, by the sire *Ozymandias*. (*Tony Parkes*)

a set of rules to govern competitions and the management of the sport. As the governing body for the sport in Ireland, both north and south of the border, it registers and grades competition horses and provides directions and advice to shows concerning the running of competitions.

After the war when the Army Equitation School reopened there were very few of the old guard of horses and riders which had dominated showjumping in the 1930s left. In their place, from the end of the forties on, came civilian riders. One of the most famous of these was Iris Kellett. Riding *Rusty*, which she and her father bought for £600, she won the premier event for ladies, the Queen Elizabeth Trophy at the White City in 1949, the first running of the event, and in 1951. Other great successes in the showjumping arena included the Irish Grand Prix at the RDS and in 1969 the European Championship at the same venue riding *Morning Light*. However, when she left the showjumping arena an equally successful career as a trainer of horse and rider commenced and some of Ireland's greatest riders of the seventies and eighties have learned many of their skills from her.

During the 1950s also Seamus Hayes was making a name for himself and soon was to join the ranks of the all-time great personalities of the showjumping arena. He had started riding in England in 1946 at the age of twenty-one and within three years he was leading rider, a position he again achieved in 1950 and 1952. In speed competitions in Britain in particular he was almost unbeatable and his many duels with Alan Oliver were unforgettable. When he returned from England he instructed the army team for a while before going into partnership with Joe McGrath. Out of this partnership grew his association with the world famous *Doneraile*, *Ardmore* on which he won the Imperial Cup in 1968 at the Royal International Horse Show and his best known mount *Goodbye*. *Goodbye* was bred in Kerry and worked on a farm in his early years before being bought as a four-year-old by Lord Harrington who sent him to Noel O'Dwyer, son of Major J. G. O'Dwyer, to be schooled. As a seven-year-old he was first ridden by Hayes in 1960, one year before the partnership achieved one of its most memorable victories—the inaugural Hickstead Derby. In subsequent years Hayes frequently had his audience on the edge of their seats as he executed superb feats of jumping. In 1964 Hayes and *Goodbye* were again very successful, beating Marion Coakes on *Stroller* for the Hickstead Derby. Two years later *Goodbye* won the puissance in Aachen, Dublin and Wembley. His performances over the high wall were excellent but it was his versatility which distinguished him and many other top Irish horses from the opposition. Competing in speed classes, Puissance and Grand Prix, *Goodbye* invariably delighted his fans.

Another great showjumping partnership was also formed in the fifties. In 1946 the Connemara Pony Breeders Society had bought a small thoroughbred horse, *Little Heaven*, to cover Connemara mares. One of *Little Heaven*'s progeny in 1952 was called *Dundrum* and, like many other famous equestrian champions, the 15.1 hands horse commenced his working career between the shafts of a cart, drawing milk.

Eddie Macken and *Boomerang* at the RDS Horse Show. *(Tony Parkes)*

Cashel man James Wade spotted him at local gymkhanas where he occasionally competed and he bought him for his son Tommy. Thus in the mid-fifties the partnership which ranks with that of *Arkle* and Pat Taaffe or *Boomerang* and Eddie Macken was formed, and for the next ten years the diminutive horse, with Wade as his rider, took on the best in Europe and beat them. Like *Goodbye* he was very versatile, excelling in a wide variety of competition types. Although very small in height he was capable of jumping seven foot obstacles. In 1961 he was Victor Ludorum at the Horse of the Year Show at Wembley, London, and in the following year he took the Grand Prix in Brussels and Ostend where he won every competition in which he was entered. His most successful year was undoubtedly 1963 when he was a member of the Irish Aga Khan Cup winning team at the RDS Horse Show and won the King George V Gold Cup at the White City and the puissance at the Horse of the Year Show for the second time. Three Irish partnerships had won the prestigious White City event before *Dundrum* and Wade but the riders had all been military men—Capt. John Lewis on *Tramore Bay* in 1935, Comdt. J. G. O'Dwyer on *Limerick Lace* in 1936 and Capt. Kevin Barry on *Ballyneety* in 1951.

1963, as we have noted, saw the emergence of civilian riders in the Irish Aga Khan Cup team. As well as Tommy Wade on *Dundrum* and Seamus Hayes on *Goodbye* there was Diana Conolly-Carew on *Barrymore*. The only member of the team from the Army Equitation School was Capt. Billy Ringrose, probably the most successful of the post-war army riders, on *Loch an Easpaig*. *Loch an Easpaig* by *Knight's Crusader* was bred in 1951 in Mullinavat in Co. Kilkenny out of a twenty-five year old Marshal Ney mare. Until he was seven, he was alternately worked and hunted before being bought by Mrs. B. Lawlor from Naas in Co. Kildare who sold him to the army. Ringrose had joined the army team in 1952 and with *Loch an Easpaig* he achieved great international success. In 1961 the partnership won the Grand Prix at Rome and competitions in Nice, London, Washington, New York and Toronto. The Grand Prix in Nice followed in 1965 and in 1966 the Grand Prix in London. When Ireland won the Aga Khan Cup competition again in 1967 Ringrose and *Loch an Easpaig* were again in the team together with Seamus Hayes on *Goodbye*, Capt. Ned Campion on *Liathdruim* and the heroes of the day once again, Tommy Wade and *Dundrum*. A few weeks later *Loch an Easpaig* died while competing in Ostend.

By the early seventies *Dundrum* had retired but already there were other stars on the horizon and a glorious era for Irish showjumping was commencing. Once again an army rider was to the fore. In 1973 Con Power began his career with the Army Equitation School and by the end of the decade he and the great *Rockbarton* were among the top combinations in the world. *Rockbarton*, formerly known as *Buccaneer*, had been bought by the army from David Mitchell of Comber in Co. Down. He proved a difficult horse to ride but there was ample compensation for this in the horse's great athleticism and scope. In 1976 Con was leading international rider at the RDS Horse Show and in the successive years 1977 to 1979 he was a member of

the Irish team which won the Aga Khan Cup a record three times. His team mates during these years were Eddie Macken on *Boomerang*, Paul Darragh on *Heather Honey* and James Kernan on *Condy*. The only changes in the team from one year to the next were the horses which he rode—*Coolronan*, *Castlepark* and *Rockbarton*. 1979 was a magnificent year for him with a total of twenty international wins.

When he retired from the army, his place as *Rockbarton*'s rider was taken by Capt. Gerry Mullins who had grown up in Co. Limerick in an area rich in equestrian associations. The new army combination was very successful taking fourth individual place in the World Championships in Dublin in 1982. In 1986 *Rockbarton*, at the age of seventeen, with Mullins again in the saddle, added further to his laurels at the RDS Horse Show by winning the prestigious Grand Prix of Ireland sponsored by the Irish government. The following year, however, they were beaten into second place in the competition by Paul Darragh riding *Carroll's Trigger*. The result on this occasion represented an unprecedented clean sweep for the Irish with Eddie Macken in third place on *Carroll's Flight*. In the Aga Khan Cup competition in the same year there was also an Irish success. This time *Rockbarton* and *Carroll's Flight* with their respective riders shared the honours with Captain John Ledingham who had a double clear round on *Gabhran* and Jack Doyle on *Hardly*. In 1988 *Rockbarton* was retired bringing to a close a superb international career.

Included in the victorious Aga Khan Cup teams of the second half of the seventies was *Condy* ridden by James Kernan, the son of horse dealer Frank Kernan from Crossmaglen in Co. Armagh, who had bought and sold many well known and

Left: David Broome and *Mr Ross*, at the RDS Horse Show, Dublin. *Mr Ross* was bred by Michael Loughlin in County Kerry, by *Carnival Night* out of a mare by *Sang Froid*. (*Horseman Photography*)

Right: Eddie Macken on *Pele* (later *Kerrygold*), second in the 1974 World Championship. (*The Horseman, Ansell*)

successful horses over the years including *Ambassador* and the great *Bellevue*. *Condy*, who was by *Conte Grande* out of an Irish Draught mare had been sold to him by perhaps Ireland's best known horse dealer Ned Cash. After his successes of the late seventies, *Condy* had to be laid off for a period due to illness but in 1983 was back on the winning trail with a victory in the Irish Showjumping Derby at Millstreet International Show in Co. Cork.

Paul Darragh was another Irish rider who commenced his very successful international career in the seventies. Trained by Iris Kellett he rode her great horse *Pele* to victory in the Hickstead Derby in 1975 commencing a period of Irish domination of that event. Before being bought by Miss Kellett, *Pele*, a gelding by *Go Tobann*, had been champion hunter at the Royal Hunter Show at Balmoral in Belfast and had won the ladies' championship under a side saddle at the RDS. With Eddie Macken, he would scale the heights of showjumping success. The horse, however, most closely identified with Paul Darragh was the courageous mare *Heather Honey*, owned by Jimmy Flynn from Ennis. She first came to prominence in the 1976 Junior European Championships when she took the gold medal with Brian McMahon in the saddle. When ridden by Paul Darragh she attracted the sponsorship of the cigarette manufacturing company, Carroll's, which also sponsored Eddie Macken's horses. In speed competitions she proved herself unbeatable but, in 1980, injury forced her out of senior international competition. Like *Condy*, she was back in the limelight in 1983, this time as a member of the Irish team which won the silver medal in the Junior European Championships.[6]

The great showjumping success story of the seventies and eighties was undoubtedly that of Eddie Macken. Born in Granard in Co. Longford in 1950, Eddie got early encouragement in his riding career from his father Jimmy who took part in local hunts with the Longford Harriers and rode in point-to-points and 'flapper' races. At five years of age Eddie had taken part in his first hunt and at the age of ten won his first class at the RDS Horse Show riding his pony, *Granard Boy*, later sold to the young Con Power. In 1969 he joined the Kellett Riding School and won international classes on such horses as *Maxwell, Morning Light, Oatfield Hills, Easter Parade* and *Pele*. In the following year he made his debut on the Irish Aga Khan Cup team.

At the Spring Show at the RDS in 1972 Eddie rode a horse which he later made famous, the Battleburn gelding *Boomerang*, which his breeder, Jimmy Murphy from Co. Tipperary, had sent to Iris Kellett to be trained. But *Boomerang* was sold and Eddie's early achievements were with *Pele*, later to be known as *Kerrygold* when sponsored by An Bord Bainne, The Irish Dairy Board. In the 1974 World Championships at Hickstead, Eddie on *Pele* took the equestrian world by surprise, leading for two of the three days of competition before Hartwig Steenken on *Simona* managed to pull back his lead and share first place with him, thus forcing a jump-off. Eddie was beaten into silver medal position in the ensuing struggle against the clock when

Pele who had to jump first had a fence down and four faults at the water jump.

A year later he turned professional and joined the German Champion Paul Schockemohle for a year in Oldenburg riding horses for Dr Schnapka, who owned the Ferrans Stud in Co. Dublin. In Germany he once again partnered *Boomerang* who through a series of circumstances was made available to him to ride. In 1972 Tommy Brennan had bought the gelding for £3,500 on behalf of Ted Edgar who wanted him for his wife Liz. Within a year he was sold on to the continent for £30,000 where he was ridden by, among others, Johan Heins who in 1977, mounted on another horse, pipped Eddie riding *Kerrygold* for the gold medal in the European championship in Vienna. *Boomerang* had been purchased in the meantime by Paul Schockemöhle and the manner of his passing from Paul back to Eddie once again gives the *Boomerang* story a fairytale quality. Before Wiesbaden Show in 1975 Eddie was without a horse to ride since all his horses were out of action. Paul Schocke-möhle offered him *Boomerang* in terms which, with hindsight, can be seen to have put a seal on his partnership with the horse: "Look, you keep *Boomerang* until you find a better horse." Eddie never found a better horse. For the next five years he dominated the showjumping world with this outstandingly consistent horse. Only the major championships eluded them. In 1978 at Aachen, Gerd Wiltfang won the World Championship gold medal, beating Eddie into second place. The fateful one quarter of a fault occurred when Eddie, riding another horse as required in phases of these championships, exceeded the time allowed on the course and incurred a time penalty.

The successes of Macken and *Boomerang*, however, were outstanding. They won the Victor Ludorum at Wembley in 1975, 1976, the year in which Eddie was Europe's biggest prize winner, 1977 and 1978. Four consecutive victories in the Hickstead Derby commenced in 1976 and three consecutive victories in 1977 as members of the Aga Khan Cup winning Irish teams. One of his most spectacular successes was in the *Sunday Times* Cup at the Horse of the Year Show in 1979. Eddie was last to go in a jump-off involving four others including *Ryan's Son* and *Heather Honey*, with only 0.3 seconds separating them. Eddie went clear and clipped 0.9 seconds off the leading time. Between Spring 1975 and Spring 1980 he won a record twenty-five Grand Prix type competitions and came second in eight, bringing *Boomerang*'s winnings to a record quarter of a million pounds.

At the beginning of the 1980s Eddie had to continue his showjumping career without his two great horses *Kerrygold* who had to be put down and *Boomerang* whose retirement he announced a few months later. A chestnut gelding, *Carroll's Royal Lion*, by the great jumping sire who once shared a class at Abbeyleix Show with *Dundrum*, *King of Diamonds*, brought Eddie his first great prize of 1980— £10,000 in the Rimas Challenge at Braintree in Essex. A very versatile horse and puissance specialist, *Carroll's Royal Lion* proceeded to win many valuable prizes for Eddie including the Hennessy Puissance Cup in 1983. In that year he jointly

Michael Whitaker on *Red Flight* watched by Gerry Byrne and Paul Duffy (trying to give him a leg up!), setting the World Bareback Showjumping Record at the Dublin International Horse Show at the RDS in 1982. This combination broke Maxi Scully's record set on *Drumlogan* in the previous year. *(Tony Parkes)*

established the Irish puissance record of 7ft. 3ins. at the RDS Horse Show.

As a result of Eddie Macken's performance in the World Championships of 1978, Dublin was the venue for these competitions in 1982. Gerry Mullins on *Rockbarton* came fourth in the individual competition but efforts to obtain world class horses for Eddie Macken and Paul Darragh before the championships had come to nil and neither of the Irish riders were in the final contention.

Ever since the Swiss army team won the Aga Khan Cup in 1926 riding Irish horses, the excellence of Irish horses in the jumping arena has been a two-edged sword in terms of international competition. Success has frequently attracted the attention of foreign buyers and horses which would have brought international victories for Irish riders have gone abroad. This pattern proved particularly damaging to the Olympic Games hopes of the Irish team in 1988 when one of the most exciting prospects, *True Blue*, was sold for a six-figure sum to become the mount of Paul Schockemöhle. *True Blue* had performed particularly well at Hickstead for his rider Trevor Coyle and had scored a double clear during the Nations Cup at Aachen before being snapped up a few months before the Olympic Games.

Some of the best performances recorded by Irish horses have been in teams from other countries. Not only have the Swiss teams invariably featured Irish horses among their Aga Khan Cup competitors but the British and Italians have frequently also relied heavily on horses which had been bred in Ireland. In 1962, for instance, the winning Italian team had three riders mounted on Irish horses. Among these was Piero d'Inzeo one of two brothers in the Italian army who carved out for themselves a special place in the affections of the RDS crowd. In 1960 Piero, riding *The Rock* had come second to his brother Raimondo in the Olympic Games in Rome. This great horse which was by *Water Serpent* included among his spoils bronze and silver medals in the European Championship, the Grand Prix at Aachen in 1961 and at Dublin and Lucerne in 1962. In those two successive years he had also taken the King George V Gold Cup. Raimondo who was not on the Italian team in 1962 had won numerous puissance events on another great Irish horse *Bellevue* which in 1981 made his final appearance at Dublin when Raimondo presented him to Iris Kellett. In 1960, riding another of *Water Serpent*'s progeny, *Gowran Girl*, which he had bought the previous year, Raimondo won the individual gold medal in the World Championships. One of his fellow Italians at the RDS in 1962 was Graziano Mancinelli who was mounted on the Irish mare *Rockette*, the alleged half-sister of *The Rock*. In the following year, with the same mount, he won the Men's European Championship and in 1972, riding the Irish-bred *Ambassador*, he took the gold medal at the Munich Olympics.

One rider who was never on the winning British Aga Khan Cup team at the RDS but who in the fifties made a very successful partnership with the Irish horse *Flanagan*, was Pat Smythe. In 1956 Pat, with this horse which once competed in the Badminton Three-Day Event, became the first lady rider to represent Britain in the Olympic Games. Together they won four Ladies European titles and in 1962 won the Hickstead Derby, the first time that the event had been won by a lady rider. The sixties were good years for British riders on Irish horses. In 1965 three of the winning British Aga Khan Cup team were on Irish horses. Harvey Smith was on *Harvester VI*, Marion Coakes on *Stroller* and Valery Barker on *Atalanta*. During the sixties *Mister Softee*, bought at the Dublin Horse Show by Andrew Massarella, took many of the major championships. In 1962 David Barker won the European championship on him and in 1967 and 1969 he was ridden by David Broome to victory in the same competition. Over the years with Broome in the saddle he captured many other prestigious prizes including the Hickstead Derby and the King George V Gold Cup and in the Mexico Olympics in 1968 he took the bronze medal behind Marion Coakes on *Stroller* who captured the silver. After he had ridden *Mister Softee* to his third European Championship in 1969, David Broome summed up his feelings on partnering the horse: "I wonder if people realise how lucky they are to see a horse like this." It was left to his listeners to speculate regarding David's feelings as his rider. Also included in the British squad in Mexico was the Irish-bred *The Maverick*, which had won bronze and silver medals for Alison Westwood in the European championships in 1969 and 1971 respectively, as well as taking the Hickstead Derby and the Queen Elizabeth II Cup in 1969.

In the World Championships in La Baule in 1970 the stars in the British team were once again mounted on Irish horses. David Broome on *Beethoven* was in gold medal position while Harvey Smith took the bronze medal riding *Mattie Brown*. Both riders have continued to record many successes on Irish horses. *Mattie Brown* took the Hickstead Derby and the King George V Gold Cup in the same year and in 1971 once again was successful at Hickstead. In 1970, the British Aga Khan Cup winning team in Dublin included this partnership together with Broome on *Manhattan*. Other very successful Irish horses for Broome over the years have been *Heatwave*, the *Chou Chin Chow* horse *Sportsman*, on which he regained the King George V Cup first captured for him by *Mister Softee*, and *Mr Ross*, a horse which was ridden in Switzerland by Gerrard Etter before being sold to Broome. In 1981 *Mr Ross* became the leading national and international money winner in Britain, winning the King George V Gold Cup and the Radio Rentals championship at the Horse of the Year Show.

Among the many other British riders who have ridden Irish horses to international success and have captured the imagination of their British audiences have been Paddy McMahon and Geoff Glazzard on *Penwood Forge Mill*, Ann Moore on *Psalm* and Malcolm Pyrah on *Towerlands Anglezarke* which had been purchased at Cahirmee Fair by Ken Taylor and which brought his rider the silver medal in both the European Championships of 1981 and the World Championships of 1982. But perhaps one of the most remarkable combinations of all has been John Whitaker and *Ryan's Son*. In 1976, 1980 and 1983 this small but great-hearted horse by *Ozymandias* was top of the British national and international money winner's list, including among their many achievements a silver medal in the 1976 Olympics, the Hickstead Derby and a silver medal in the European Championships in 1983. He was still competing until his death in 1987 from a fall after the Hickstead Derby.

Of the other European countries Switzerland has always been a dependable market for Irish horses. One of the most successful of Irish horses there in the seventies was the Kilkenny bred *Harley*. Ridden by Walter Gabathuler, he was Swiss national champion on five occasions and won many international events before being retired from competition in the early eighties. Irish horses have not been prominent among the top money winners in the US but in the 1980s there have been indications that this position may change. Three of the nine horses, for instance, on the US team at the RDS Horse Show in 1986 were Irish bred. One of these, *Leapy Lad*, had been sold at Ballinasloe Fair in 1980 and was on the Irish Aga Khan Cup team in 1983. One of the foremost horses in the US silver medal winning team at the 1988 Olympic Games in Seoul was *Mill Pearl*, one of Ireland's most exciting exports, which had been bred by Noel C. Duggan at his Equestrian Centre in Millstreet, Co Cork. Noel who has been the driving force behind the very successful Millstreet International Show since its inception in the late seventies had bought *Mill Pearl*'s mother for three hundred pounds in 1979 and crossed her with the Irish Draught stallion *King of Diamonds*. The resultant progeny, *Mill Pearl*, was sold to the United States for sixty thousand pounds but such was her success that at the time of the Olympics her value was estimated to be two million dollars.[7]

INGREDIENTS FOR SUCCESS

The successes of Irish horses internationally are, of course, extremely important in encouraging the growth of sales of Irish horses abroad. However, the prominence of Irish riders and their mounts on the international showjumping circuit has not been able to stem the decline in exports of half-bred horses from Ireland. These have decreased from over 10,000 in the early 1970s to about 1500 in 1985. This decline has taken place against the background of an increasing European market for medium-level horses suitable for sport and leisure. It has been estimated, for instance, that the number of riders in West Germany increased from over a quarter of a million to over 400,000 in the years 1973 to 1978. In Great Britain the number of riders over fifteen years of age increased by 15 per cent from 1971 to 1977. Clearly Irish horse producers have not been able to produce the well-trained animals required to cater for this demand or overcome the handicap of having to transport their horses across one sea to reach the British market and across two seas to reach the other European markets. Sea transport is still the norm in the non-thoroughbred horse industry.

Yet there is little doubt that Ireland has the resources to be as successful in the leisure riding market as it has been in the showjumping sphere. No doubt there are differences between the two. For instance, showjumping places a premium on the brilliant horse which every producer dreams of breeding one day, whereas to produce horses for the leisure riding market requires the more mundane commitment to the production and systematic training of the less spectacular but more numerous medium-level animal. With better educational opportunities, particularly for young people, in the horse industry this commitment should be forthcoming.

Top : Tommy Brennan competing on
Xenophon. (*Ruth Rogers*)

Bottom left : Tommy Wade and *Dundrum*
at the RDS Horse Show, Dublin, in 1963.
(*G. A. Duncan*)

Bottom right : The winning Irish Team
at the World Three-day Event
Championships at Burghley in 1966. Left
to right: Major Eddie Boylan on *Durlas
Eile*, Virginia Petersham on *Sam Weller*,
Penny Morton on *Loughlin* and Tommy
Brennan on *Kilkenny*. The Chef d'Equipe
is Captain Harry Freeman-Jackson.
(*Pony / Light Horse*)

Ireland has the advantage over many of its competitors of a long-standing horse tradition which ensures that equestrian skills and an interest in horses are passed on from generation to generation. To date this horse tradition has related mainly to hunting, horse breeding and National Hunt racing and much of the emphasis in competition has been on the survival of the fittest. But with more widespread access to education and training and with increased exposure in Ireland to equestrian knowledge from abroad there is a prospect of better equestrian skills taking root.

Irish people from the early times, as we have seen, placed a premium on equestrian skills. They jealously guarded these skills and surrounded them with mystique and superstition. There were practical reasons behind their care in this respect. It was considered important for society that the maximum benefit be obtained from horses and, if possible, that great horses should occasionally be produced. Training skills would help towards this end.

The key to training horses and harnessing their potential, people believed, lay in the relationship between man and horse. Irish people identified very closely with horses and this identification was so deeply rooted that it may have had a religious dimension. Political and religious matters were not separated in Celtic Ireland as they are today and the relationship between man and horse at an early stage found expression in political institutions. Eventually horses would become an essential part of what it meant to be Irish. Christian missionaries came to appreciate this as did the hostile invader. Horse and man could not be easily separated in Ireland.

Today the instinct to keep horses is still strong and widespread. The Agricultural Census of 1980, for instance, showed that there were over 11,000 holdings with horses and ponies in Ireland—a figure which had grown by nearly 40 per cent over the previous ten years. Yet it appears that commercial gain is not the main motivating factor for horse owners. Most of them keep only a small number of animals. Research into the non-thoroughbred horse industry in 1979, for instance, indicated that over 70 per cent of those keeping non-thoroughbred animals had only one or two horses or ponies. A similar distribution pattern prevails in relation to the ownership of thoroughbred horses. In addition the majority of racehorse owners earns no return from racing. Owning and training a racehorse is not on average a commercially viable proposition. Owners of non-thoroughbred horses, in general, would appear to keep horses also for non-commercial reasons. Only 11 per cent of horse farmers included in the 1979 survey kept horses primarily for commercial reasons. The study revealed that over 30 per cent had horses because they liked them; for 25 per cent horses were a hobby and 10 per cent kept horses because the tradition existed in their neighbourhood of doing so.[8]

The relationship between man and horse has proved resilient in Ireland. In times of difficulty in Irish history horse and man used the natural advantages of the landscape to thwart their enemies. The Irish environment still provides great advantages to the Irish and their horses. The climatic and soil conditions necessary for good horse production are a feature of the country. Young stock can remain out of doors almost all the year round and thus acquire the hardy constitution required for strenuous training. The limestone content of much of the soil gives the growing foal the calcium necessary to produce good bone. But in the past during much of Ireland's troubled history it was the impenetrable quality of the environment which proved of help to horse and man. The horseman living in inaccessible places frequently brought hope to an otherwise dejected people.

Today the struggles in the woods and mountains have been replaced by competition on the hunting field, racecourse, showjumping arena or eventing course. Much, however, has remained the same. The exploits of an Eddie Macken or Jonjo O'Neill can capture the imagination and bring pride to many Irish people. More importantly, equestrian activities in keeping with some other sports can help to bridge the gap between religious, political and social classes. The horse tradition, since it is not the prerogative of any one class alone, can be embraced by all. In a divided country where symbols mean so much the horse is a source of hope. In traditions to be found particularly in the south of Ireland, the returning horseman heralds the dawn of a golden age. In the north the image of King William and his horse, whether on a banner in a twelfth of July parade or on a gable end on Sandy Row in Belfast, provides a focus for the aspirations of northern Unionists. The content of their hopes may differ or even conflict but when dealing with horses, all in Ireland, whether rich or poor, Protestant or Catholic, have something in common.

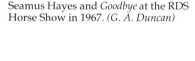

Seamus Hayes and *Goodbye* at the RDS Horse Show in 1967. *(G. A. Duncan)*

Chapter references

ABBREVIATIONS

I.H.S. Irish Historical Studies
I.T.S. Irish Texts Society
P.R.I.A. Proceedings of the Royal Irish Academy
R.C. Revue Celtique
R.S.A.I. Jn. Journal of the Royal Society of Antiquaries of Ireland
U.J.A. Ulster Journal of Archaeology

CHAPTER ONE

(1) T. F. O'Rahilly, *Early Irish History and Mythology*, pp 291-2.
(2) L. Duncan, 'Folklore Gleanings from Co. Leitrim', in *Folklore*, iv, p.182.
(3) M. Jankovich, *They Rode into Europe*, p.36; C. O'Rahily, *Táin Bó Cuailnge*, 3156-9, p. 324n.
(4) A. Ross, *Pagan Celtic Britain*, pp 411-12, 415-16.
(5) S. Pigott, *Ancient Europe*, p.92; T. F. O'Rahilly, *E.I.H.M*, pp 519-22;
(6) W. Sayers, 'Three Charioteering Gifts in Táin Bó Cuailnge and Mescad Ulad', in *Ériu*, xxxii, p. 166; C. O'Rahily, *T.B.C*, 1221
(7) T. Kinsella, *The Táin*, pp 147-155.
(8) C. O'Rahily, *T.B.C*, 964-72, 979-84
(9) C. O'Rahily, *T.B.C.*, 538, 4787.
(10) E. Durkheim, *The Elementary Forms of the Religious Life*, pp 206-13, 267-8.
(11) ibid. pp 114, 116-8, 134, 138-40, 209-10, 212
(12) ibid. pp 327, 329-30, 355.
(13) ibid. pp 68, 134-5, 139, 209, 247-8, 355, 261.
(14) T. F. O'Rahilly, *E.I.H.M.*, pp 291-2; T. J. Barron, 'Laragh Parish: I gCeartlár Sliabh na nDee', in *The Heart of Breifne*, 1978, pp 6-7;
(15) W. Stokes, 'The Prose Tales in the Rennes Dindsenchas', in *R.C.*, xvi, p.277
(16) F. J. Byrne, *Irish Kings and High Kings*, p.184; T. F. O'Rahilly, *E.I.H.M.*, pp 6, 9, 217-8, 295.
(17) Durkheim, *The Religious Life*, pp 276, 283-4.
(18) *Ancient Laws of Ireland*, v, pp 97, 123, 276; G. MacNiocaill, 'Tír Cumaile', in *Eriu*, xxii, p.84
(19) *Laws*, 1.74, iv, pp 3-5, v, pp 209-11, 269; D. Greene, 'The religious epic', in J. Carney, *Early Irish Poetry*, p.76
(20) T. F. O'Rahilly, 'On the Origin of the Names Erainn and Ériu', in *Ériu*, xiv, pp 6-17
(21) G. Dumézil, *Mythe et Épopée*, ii, pp 258-61, 297- 8, 316-22, 341-5, 351.
(22) Pigott, *Ancient Europe*, pp 80, 81, 130-3, 182; N. Chadwick & M. Dillon, *The Celtic Realms*, pp 10-12, 93.
(23) Pigott, *Ancient Europe*, p.180. But see, M. Dobbs, 'On Chariot Burial in Ancient Ireland', in *Sidelines on the Táin Age and other Studies*.

CHAPTER TWO

(1) Ross, *P.C.B.*, pp 254-5
(2) T. F. O'Rahilly, *E.I.H.M.*, pp 291, 293
(3) D. Ó hÓgáin, 'An Capall i mBéaloideas na hÉireann', in *Béaloideas*, 45-47, 215
(4) T. Kinsella, *The Tain*, p. 156
(5) G. MacNiocaill, *Ireland before the Vikings*, pp 3-4
(6) D. Ó hÓgáin, 'An Capall', pp 214-7
(7) Ross, *P.C.B.*, p.410; T. O'Cathasaigh, 'The Concept of the Hero in Irish Mythology', in R. Kearney, *The Irish Mind*, pp 80-1
(8) C. O'Rahily, *T.B.C.*, 442-6, 3120-3122, 3238-3240
(9) T. F. O'Rahilly, *E.I.H.M.*, p.296
(10) I. Finlay, *Columba*, pp 181-2
(11) H. O'Neill Hencken, 'Lagore Crannog: an Irish royal residence of the 7th to 10th centuries AD', in *P.R.I.A.*, 53c, p.3; W. Stokes, "The Prose Tales in the Rennes Dindsenchas', *R.C.*, xvi, pp 58-9
(12) W. Stokes, 'The Prose Tales' in *R.C.*, xv, pp 482-3, xvi p.152; P. W. Joyce, *Old Celtic Romances*, pp 68-70
(13) W. Stokes, 'The Edinburgh Dindsenchas', in *Folklore*, iv, p.475
(14) T. Ó Cathasaigh, 'Cath Maige Tuired', in P. de Brún, S. Ó Coileáin & P. Ó Briain (editors), *Folia Gadelica*, p.11
(15) J. Loth, *Les Noms du Cheval chez les Celtes en relation avec quelques problèmes archéologiques*, pp 17, 18, 26, 27
(16) F. Tripett, *The First Horsemen*, p.124; Ross, *P.C.B.*, pp 284- 5, 411
(17) L. Laing, *Archaeology of Late Celtic Britain and Ireland*, p.12; M. Duignan, 'Irish Agriculture in Early Historical Times', in *R.S.A. I.Jn.*, 74, p.142
(18) G. Eogan, 'Report on the excavations of some passage graves ... at Knowth Co Meath', in *P.R.I.A.*, 74c, pp 110; L. H. Van Wijingaarden-Bakker, 'The animal remains from the Beaker settlement at Newgrange Co Meath', in *P.R.I.A.*, 74c, pp 313, 348; M. Herity & G. Eogan, *Ireland in Prehistory*, p.131; H. O'Neill Hencken, 'Ballinderry Crannog No.1', in *PRIA*, 43c, p.233; Laing, *Archaeology of Late Celtic Britain and Ireland*, pp 12,149; H. O'Neill Hencken, 'Ballinderry Crannog No.2', in *PRIA*, 47c, pp 67-8
(19) J. Puhvel, 'Aspects of Equine Functionality', in Puhvel, *Myth and Law among the Indo-Europeans*, pp 164, 168
(20) J. O'Meara, *The first Version of the Topography of Ireland by Giraldus Cambrensis*, pp 93-4
(21) T. F. O'Rahilly, 'The names

Erainn and Ériu', pp 15-9.

(22) D. Binchy, 'The Fair of Tailtiú and the Feast of Tara', in *Ériu*, xviii, 123; F. J. Byrne, 'Kings and Commons in Gaelic Ireland', in B. Farrel, *The Irish Parliamentary Tradition*, pp 28, 30-1

(23) A. Lang, W. Leaf & E. Myers (editors), *The Iliad of Homer*, pp 412-422; Dumézil, *Mythe et Épopée*, i, pp 506,514-5.

(24) G. Dumézil, *Archaic Roman Religion*, pp 217, 225, 562; D. Dubuisson, 'L'équipment de l'innauguration royale dans l'Inde vedique et en Irlande', in *Revue de l'Histoire des Religions*, 1978, ii, pp 163-4

(25) Byrne, 'Kings and Commons', pp 30-1.

(26) Ó Cathasaigh, 'C.M.T.' ,p.8.

(27) M. O'Daly, 'The Metrical Dindsenchas', in Carney, *E.I.P.*, pp 65-7

(28) *Laws*, i, 128; E. E. Evans, *Irish Folk Ways*, p.255; P. Mac Cana, 'Early Irish Ideology', pp 64-5; O'Daly 'M.D.', p.67.

(29) Binchy, 'The Fair of Tailtiú', pp 123, 125-6;

(30) W. Stokes, 'The prose tales', in *R.C.*, xv, p.314

(31) T. P. Cross & C. H. Slover, *Ancient Irish Tales*, p.209

(32) Kinsella, *The Tain*, pp 6-7.

(33) G. Dumézil, *Mythe et Épopée*, i, pp 603-12.

(34) Puhvel, 'Aspects of Equine Functionality', pp 166-70; Ó Cathasaigh, 'C.M.T.', p.13; T. Ó Broin, 'What is the 'debility' of the Ulstermen?', in *Éigse*, x, pp 289-8.

(35) Dubuisson, 'L'équipment', p.163; Mac Cana, 'Early Irish Ideology', p.62

(36) P. Taaffe, *My Life and Arkle's*, p.53.

CHAPTER THREE

(1) J. L. Nelson, 'Inauguration Rituals', and D. Dumville, 'Kingship, Genealogies and Regnal Lists', in P. H. Sawyer & I. N. Wood, *Early Mediaeval Kingship*, pp 50, 72

(2) O'Daly, 'M.D.', p.61

(3) J. H. Todd, *St. Patrick Apostle of Ireland*, p. 422

(4) W. Stokes, 'The Life of St.Fechín of Fore', in *R.C.*, xii, pp 346-8

(5) F. Henry, *Irish High Crosses*, p.13-4, 19, 35, 40, 45

(6) C. O'Rahily, 'Marcach = Messenger?', in *Celtica*, vii, p.32

(7) Henry, *I.H.C.*, p.52

(8) P. Mac Cana, *Celtic Mythology*, pp 10, 24-6, 41-8, 127; Ross, *P.C.B.*, pp 180-201, 212-3, 405-6, 412; Henry, *I.H.C.*, p.51

(9) M. & L. de Paor, *Early Christian Ireland*, pp 125, 144; A. Dent & D. Goodall, *The Foals of Epona*, pl.17, pl.54, pp 88, 183

(10) Evans, *I.F.W.*, p.216; G. Evans, *The Pattern under the Plough*, p.195; G. Dumézil, *Rituels Indo-Européens à Rome*, pp 74-5; Ross, *P.C.B.*, p.99

(11) A. Otway-Ruthven, *A History of Mediaeval Ireland*, p. 18

(12) J. Clébert, *The Gypsies*, pp 100, 102

(13) Evans, *I.F.W.*, p.238; P. Somerville-Large, *From Bantry Bay to Leitrim*, p.180-1; D. Pochin-Mould, *The Aran Islands*, p.102

(14) Deuteronomy, 14.469

(15) G. Evans, *The Pattern*, p 197; Clébert, *The Gypsies*, pp 101- 2; Dent & Goodall, *Epona*, pp 31, 71; J. Graham-Campbell & D. Kidd, *The Vikings*, pp 96, 182; D. Ó Corráin, *Ireland before the Normans*, p.58; Somerville-Large, *From Bantry Bay*, p.181

(16) S. J. Connolly, *Priests and People in Pre-Famine Ireland*, p.106

(17) D. Ó hÓgáin, 'An Capall', pp 201, 207, 209; D. Ó hÓgáin, *The Hero in Irish Folk History*, pp 278-9; M. Ryan, *Biddy Early*, p.57; D. Corkery, *The Hidden Ireland*, pp 258,271

(18) D. Ó hÓgáin, 'An Capall' pp 210, 229, 236-7

(19) D. Binchy *Celtic and Anglo-Saxon Kingship*, pp 14-7; P. Mac Cana, *Regnum et Sacerdotum*, pp 446-7, 456, 477-8; J. Baudis, 'On the Antiquity of the Kingship of Tara', in *Ériu*, viii, p.104; D. Ó hÓgáin, *An File*, pp 265,334

(20) K. Simms, *Gaelic Lordships in Ulster in the Later Middle Ages*, pp 67-8; S. Ó Dufaigh, 'Cíos Mhic Mhathghamhna', in *Clogher Record*, iv, p.132

(21) D. Ó Corráin & F. Maguire, *Gaelic Personal Names*, pp 86-7; Byrne, *Irish Kings*, p.52

(22) ibid. p.54

(23) P. Mac Cana, *Regnum*, p.448, 457-8; Dent & Goodall, *Epona*, 104

(24) J. Carney, *The Irish Bardic Poet*, p.11

(25) Simms, *Gaelic Lordships* p.7; 'Life of Maedóc of Ferns', in C.Plummer, *Vitae Sanctorum Hiberniae*, B,ii, p.248; B.Ó Cuív, 'A Poem for Cathal Croibhdhearg Ó Conchubhair', in *Éigse* xiii, pp 196-7

(26) *Irish Texts*, Fasc. iv, p.52; N. O'Hare, *All about our Irish Horses*, p.8; M. A. O'Brien, 'A Middle Irish Poem on the Birth of Aedán Mac Gabráin and Brandub mac Echach', in *Ériu*, xvi, 166-8, 170; A. O'Sullivan, 'Triamhuin Ghormlaithe', in *Ériu*, xvi, 197

(27) Byrne, *Irish Kings*, 137-40

(28) 'ech', in *Contributions to a Dictionary of the Irish Language (Royal Irish Academy)*; O. Bergin, *Irish Bardic Poetry*, pp 259, 335; J. Carney, *Studies in Irish Literature and History*, p.335

(29) Byrne, *Irish Kings*, 63-4

(30) Ó Cathasaigh, 'C.M.T.', p.5; Mac Cana, *Regnum*, p.457

(31) K. Jackson, *A Celtic Miscellany*, p.256-7, 346n

(32) *Laws*, v., pp 61, 63, 67

(33) O. Bergin, *Irish Bardic Poetry*, pp 314, 315

(34) Jackson, *Miscellany*, p.143

(35) Corkery, *The Hidden Ireland*, pp 111, 117-8

(36) Carney, *The Irish Bardic Poet*, p.15

(37) Byrne, *Irish Kings* ,pp 15-21; J. O'Donovan, *The Genealogies, Tribes and Customs of the Hy Fiachrach commonly called O'Dowda's Country*, pp 109, 143-5, 434

(38) Mac Cana, *Regnum*, pp 452-3; Simms, *Gaelic Lordships*, pp 10-2, 30, 164; Plummer, *Vitae*, B,ii, 196-7; Byrne *Irish Kings*, pp 21-2

(39) Mac Cana, *Regnum*, pp 447-8

(40) Simms, *Gaelic Lordships*, pp 15, 31, 34-6; O'Donovan, *Genealogies*, pp 109, 139-45, 431; F. J. Byrne, 'Senchas', in *Historical Studies*, ix, pp 137-159; N. Ní Shéaghdha, 'The Rights of Mac Diarmada', in

Celtica, vi, p.164; Ó Dufaigh, 'Cíos', p.132

(41) M. Dillon (ed) *Lebor na Cert*, pp 5, 13-7, 79, 105, 127, 137; Byrne, *Irish Kings*, pp 43-4

(42) M. I. Finley, *The World of Odysseus*, pp 61, 95-8; M. Mauss, *The Gift*, pp 11,35,37

(43) Dillon, *L.C.*, pp 8, 85-7

(44) Finley, *Odysseus*, pp 98, 106, 120, 123; Mauss, *The Gift*, 4, 10, 22, 48, 54-7, 63, 77-9

(45) Dumézil, *Mythe et Épopée*, ii, pp 278, 296-8, 322

(46) Genesis, xlix; Byrne, *Irish Kings*, 139, 194-5, 288; Dillon, *Lebor na Cert*, p.155

(47) Binchy, *C.A.S.K.*, pp 3-4 ; *Laws*, iv.p.108-11

(48) *Caithréim Thoirdhealbhaigh* in I.T.S., xxvii, p.3; Simms, *Gaelic Lordships*, pp 112-3

(49) J. Todd (ed.) *Cogadh Gaedhel re Gallaibh*, p.97

(50) A.F.M. 1495; M. Cox, *Notes on the History of the Irish Horse*, pp 21, 68; F. J. Byrne, 'Tribes and Tribalism in Early Ireland', in *Eriu* xxii, pp 138, 143-4; Mauss, *The Gift*, p.28; Finley, *Odysseus*, pp 61-3, 122; Ó Cathasaigh 'C.M.T.' p.5

(51) K. Nicholls, *Gaelic and Gaelicised Ireland in the Later Middle Ages*, pp 37-9, 57, 65-7, 119; A. Chambers, *Granuaile*, p.102, 110; M. Cox, *Irish Horse*, p. 51; K. Nicholls, *Land, Law and Society in Sixteenth-Century Ireland*, pp 9-13, 21n

(52) Simms *Gaelic Lordships*, pp 106, 147; Nicholls, *Gaelic Ireland*, p.36; Otway-Ruthven, *A History*, pp 4-5

(53) Todd, *Cogadh*, pp 131-133; Simms, *Gaelic Lordships*, p.146

(54) Simms, *Gaelic Lordships* pp 47, 99,133-5,143-4,147; E.Ó Doibhlin, *Domhnach Mor*, pp 15-6, 21, 40-1

(55) *Calendar of the Carew Manuscripts*, ii, pp 435-7; Simms, *Gaelic Lordships*, pp 132; S.Ó Domhnaill, 'Warfare in Sixteenth-Century Ireland', in *I.H.S*, v. p.36; J. Carney(ed.), *A Genealogical History of the O'Reilly*, pp 81-8 , 90-1; Nicholls, *Land*, p.8

CHAPTER FOUR

(1) J. Lydon, *The Lordship of Ireland in the Middle Ages*, pp 82- 3, 283; B.Bradshaw, *The Irish Constitutional Revolution of the Sixteenth Century*, p.14

(2) G. A. Hayes-McCoy, *Irish Battles*, pp 27, 29; Lydon, *The Lordship*, pp 34-5, 58; F. X. Martin & A. B. Scott, *Expugnatio Hibernica*, pp 33-5, 247, 249; F. X. Martin & T. W. Moody (ed.), *The Course of Irish History*, p.129; Otway-Ruthven, *A History*, pp 58-9

(3) Hayes-McCoy, *Irish Battles*, p.27; Lydon, *The Lordship*, p.38

(4) O'Meara, *Topography*, p. 85; Lydon, *The Lordship*, pp 167-8; Martin & Moody, *Irish History*, p.137

(5) C. Oman, *History of the Art of War*, i, p.403-4; Hayes McCoy, *Irish Battles*, pp 17, 28; D. Ó Corráin, *Ireland before the Normans*, p.58; J. Todd (ed), *Cogadh*, pp 127, 145, 153, 201; F. X. Martin & A. B. Scott, *Expugnatio*, pp 115; A.F.M. (AD 1200) iii. 125; G. Orpen (ed.), *The Song of Dermot and the Earl*, p. 21; Dillon, *L.C.*, pp 69, 70; D. Binchy (ed), *Críth Gablach*, pp 6, 8

(6) Martin & Moody, *Irish History*, pp 123, 127, 137, 139; Lydon, *The Lordship*, pp 33, 37, 39, 41, 59, 60, 61-4, 87-91, 179; Hayes-McCoy, *Irish Battles*, p.28; Otway-Ruthven, *A History* pp 63-4, 94-5, 109, 115, 116, 253

(7) Ibid. pp 44, 59, 201-2, 229; J. Lydon, 'The Hobelar: An Irish Contribution to Mediaeval Warfare', in *The Irish Sword*, ii, pp 12-3; J. E. Morris, 'Mounted Infantry in Mediaeval Warfare', in *Transactions of the Royal Historical Society*, viii, pp 79-81; Lydon, *The Lordship*, p.59

(8) N. Browne, *The Horse in Ireland*, pp 25, 27; Dillon, *L.C.* pp 39, 69, 99, 131; Cox, *History of the Irish Horse*, 14, 23- 33, 35, 69-70; Ó Corráin, *Ireland before the Normans*, p.58; Hayes-McCoy, *Irish Battles*, p.27; Otway-Ruthven, *A History*, pp 49, 285-6; Lydon, *The Lordship*, pp 40-1, 100-1; 124, 257; J. Lydon,

'Edward I, Ireland and the War in Scotland 1303-4', in Lydon (ed.), *England and Ireland in the Late Middle Ages*, pp 47-9, 54; Lydon, 'The Hobelar', pp 13, 16; *Calendar of Documents Relating to Ireland 1171*, pp 3-6; J. Lydon, 'Irish Levies in the Scottish Wars 1296-1302', in *The Irish Sword*, v, pp 208, 211

(9) Lydon, *The Lordship*, pp 89-90, 130, 132-3; Lydon, 'Irish Levies', p.208; Lydon, 'The Hobelar', p.14; Lydon, 'Edward I', p.52; Lydon, 'An Irish Army in Scotland in 1296', pp 186-7

(10) J. Jolliffe (ed.), *Froissart's Chronicles*, p.363; K. Simms, 'Warfare in the Mediaeval Gaelic Lordships', in *The Irish Sword*, xii, p.107

(11) J. Jolliffe, *Froissart's Chronicles*, p.363-6; Lydon, *The Lordship*, pp 181-2

(12) M. MacNeill, *The Festival of Lughnasa*, pp 104, 152-3; D. Binchy, 'Mellbretha', in *Celtica*, viii, pp 149-52; J. Hennig, 'Some Early German Accounts of Schomberg's Irish Campaign', in *U.J.A.*, xi, (s:3) 71; F. X. Martin & A. B. Scott, *Expugnatio*, p.247

(13) Dent & Goodall *Epona*, pp 100-1; Nicholls, *Gaelic Ireland*, p.85; R. Haworth, 'The Horse Harness of the Irish Early Iron Age', in *U.J.A.*, xxxiv, 1971, pp 27, 41-2; P. Harbison, 'Native Irish Arms and Armour in Mediaeval Gaelic Literature, 1170-1600', in *The Irish Sword* xii, 192

(14) R. Frame, *English Lordship in Ireland*, pp 38-42; Lydon, *The Lordship* , p. 151; Bradshaw, *The Irish Constitutional Revolution*, pp 4-7, 11; Moody & Martin, *Irish History*, pp 154-5; E. Curtis & R. B. McDowell, *Irish Historical Documents 1171-1922*, p.53

(15) Lydon, 'The Hobelar', p.13; Otway-Ruthven, *A History*, pp 180-1; A. Cosgrove, *Late Mediaeval Ireland*, pp 57-60; Cox, *The Irish Horse*, p.46, 51

(16) Curtis & McDowell, *I.H.D.*, p.52

(17) Cosgrove, *L.M.I.*, p.72

(18) D. Ó hÓgáin, *The Hero*, p.114; Jolliffe, *Froissart's Chronicles*, pp 366-8

(19) Jackson, *Miscellany*, pp 236-7
(20) E. Curtis, *A History of Ireland*, pp 70-1
(21) Curtis & McDowell, *I.H.D.*, p.53
(22) J. P. Mahaffy, 'Two Early Tours in Ireland', in *Hermathena*, xl, p.7; Harbison, 'Native Irish Arms' pp 178, 183, 184, 188; Cosgrove, *L.M.I.*, 73-4;
(23) Nicholls, *Gaelic Ireland*, pp 84-5; D. Murtagh, 'Irish Cavalry 1. The Sixteenth Century', in *The Irish Sword*, i, 316-7; Hayes-McCoy, *Irish Battles*, pp 82-3; Curtis, *A History*, p.117
(24) Simms, *Gaelic Lordships*, p.733; Cox, *Irish Horse* p.39; G. A. Hayes-McCoy, 'The Army of Ulster 1593-1601', in *The Irish Sword*, i, p.116; G. A. Hayes-McCoy, 'Strategy and Tactics in Irish Warfare 1593-1601', in *Irish Historical Studies*, ii pp.260, 262
(25) D. Quinn, *The Elizabethans and the Irish*, p. 140; Mahaffy, 'Two Early Tours', p.8; R. Holinshed, *Chronicles of England Scotland and Ireland*, vi, 452, 459; R. Berleth, *The Twilight Lords*, pp 200-1
(26) Quinn, *The Elizabethans*, p.65
(27) Mahaffy, 'Two Early Tours', p. 7; Cox, *The Irish Horse*, pp 45-6; Nicholls, *Gaelic Ireland*, p.84
(28) E. McCracken, 'The Woodlands of Ireland circa 1600', in *I.H.S.*, xi, 273; Jolliffe, *Froissart's Chronicles*, p.363; Otway-Ruthven, *A History*, pp 208, 219; Hayes-McCoy, *Irish Battles*, p.120; Orpen, *The Song of Dermot*, 660-3, 1316, 1317, 1576-7
(29) Ó Domhnaill, 'Warfare in Sixteenth Century Ireland', in I.H.S., v, p.39; McCracken, 'The Woodlands', pp 273, 277, 283-4; L.Cullen, *Life in Ireland*, pp 58-9
(30) Ó Domhnaill, 'Warfare', pp 36-8, 40-5; Curtis, *A History of Ireland*, p.209; Hayes-McCoy, 'Strategy and Tactics', pp 257, 260, 262, 263, 265-6; M. J. Byrne, *Ireland under Elizabeth*, pp 78-81, 86-7
(31) Hayes-McCoy, *Irish Battles*, pp 93-7, 99-100, 119-120, 123; M.J. Byrne, *Ireland under Elizabeth*, pp 107, 109-110
(32) J.J.Silke, *Kinsale*, pp 53, 54, 115, 136; J. C. Beckett, *The Making of Modern Ireland*, pp 21-3
(33) Hayes-McCoy, *Irish Battles*, pp 156, 158-9, 163-9; Silke, *Kinsale*, pp 55, 106, 114, 126, 134, 142-5, 168-9
(34) Hayes-McCoy, *Irish Battles*, pp 164, 166, 169; Silke, *Kinsale* p.142; Hayes-McCoy, 'Strategy and Tactics', p.278; Nicholls, *Gaelic Ireland*, pp 84-5; D. B. Quinn & K. W. Nicholls, 'Ireland in 1534', in Moody, Byrne & Martin, *New History of Ireland*, iii, p.32; L. Price, 'Armed Forces of the Irish Chiefs in the early Sixteenth Century', in *R.S.A.I. Jn.*, lxii, p.206; K. Simms, 'Warfare', p.105
(35) *Cal. Carew Mss..*, v, pp 81-2; Hayes-McCoy, *Irish Battles*, pp 82, 156, 159
(36) ibid. pp 183-4, 189, 192-3; T. S. O'Cahan, *Owen Roe O'Neill*, pp 221-2
(37) Hayes-McCoy, *Irish Battles*, pp 204-5, 242; Murtagh, 'Irish Cavalry', p.321; T. W. Moody 'Introduction', in Moody, Byrne & Martin, *A New History of Ireland,*, iii, pp xlii-xliv
(38) Hayes-McCoy, *Irish Battles*, p.234; J. G. Simms, *Jacobite Ireland*, 160, 199; M.J. Culligan-Hogan, *The Quest for the Galloping Hogan*, pp 60-4
(39) Murtagh, 'Irish Cavalry', p.320; J. G. Simms, *Jacobite Ireland*, pp 220, 241-2, 247-9; Hayes-McCoy, *Irish Battles*, pp 259, 265-7

CHAPTER FIVE

(1) Ó hÓgáin, *The Hero*, pp 160-1
(2) C. J Jung, *The Collected Works of C.J Jung*, v, pp 274-5, 277- 9
(3) E. Davidson, *Scandinavian Mythology*, pp 45-6; Ó hÓgáin, *The Hero*, pp 144,151-4; B. Fitzgerald, *The Geraldines*, pp 272, 294
(4) C. S. Littleton, *The New Comparative Mythology*, p. 81; C. O Rahily, *T.B.C.*, 3319, p.324; T. F. O Rahilly, *E.I.H.M.*, pp 523-5
(5) J. F. Nagy, 'Heroic Destinies in the Macgnímrada of Finn and Cú Chulainn', in *Zeitschrift für Celtische Philologie*, xl, pp 22, 26-7, 31, 33, 35, 36; T. Woulfe, *The Right Stuff*, pp 56, 350
(6) Littleton, *Mythology*, pp 79-81; Woulfe, *The Right Stuff*, p.103
(7) Holinshed, *Chronicles of England, Scotland and Ireland*, vi, p.68
(8) J. A. Gaughan, *The Knights of Glin*, p.15, 22, 26-7, 33, 119- 22
(9) Holinshed, *Chronicles*, vi, p.68; Mauss, *The Gift*, p.35, 54, 123
(10) T. Peters & R. Waterman, *In Search of Excellence*, pp xxiii, 56, 60
(11) Woulfe, *The Right Stuff*, p.32-3; Jung, *Works*, v, p.421
(12) G. O. Sayles, 'The Rebellious First Earl of Desmond', in F. X. Martin, J. Watt & Morrall, *Mediaeval Studies presented to Aubrey Gwynn*, pp 204-5, 208, 213; Frame, *English Lordship*, pp 267, 297
(13) Nicholls, *Gaelic Ireland*, pp 26
(14) ibid. pp 9, 114, 115; Pigott, *Ancient Europe*, p.181; E. Spenser, *A View of the Present State of Ireland*, p. 179; Holinshed, *Chronicles*, vi, p. 269; C. A. Empey & K. Simms, 'The Ordinances of the White Earl and the Problem of Coign in the later Middle Ages', in *P.R.I.A.*, lxxv, p. 180
(15) Frame, *English Lordship*, pp 36-8, 37n.; Empey & Simms, 'Ordinances' p.180; Otway-Ruthven, *A History*, pp 97, 295
(16) *Cal. Carew Mss.*, iii, p.72; Spenser, *A View*, pp 33-4; Nicholls, *Gaelic Ireland*, pp 31-7; Otway-Ruthven, *A History*, p.249
(17) Empey & Simms, 'Ordinances', pp 178-180, 183-5; D.Binchy, 'Aimser Chue', in J. Ryan, *Féil-Sgríbhinn Eoin Mhic Néill*, pp 20-1
(18) Empey & Simms, 'Ordinances', p.185; Nicholls, *Gaelic Ireland*, pp 31-2, 34; K. Down, 'Colonial Society and Economy in the High Middle Ages', in A. Cosgrove, *A New History of Ireland*, ii, p.475; Holinshed, *Chronicles*, vi, p.257; H. J. Hore & J. Graves, *The Social State of the Southern and Eastern Counties*, p.150, 168; D.Quinn & K. Nicholls, 'Ireland in 1534', in Martin, Moody & Byrne, *A New History of Ireland*, iii, p.32; Price, 'Armed Forces of the Irish Chiefs in the early Sixteenth Century' in *R.S.A.I. Jn.*, lxii p.206; C. Falls, *Elizabeth's Irish Wars*, pp 60-1, 63, 65

(19) Hore & Graves, *Southern and Eastern Counties*, pp 90n., 150, 168-9, 171-2; Empey & Simms, 'Ordinances', p.185

(20) Nicholls, *Gaelic Ireland*, pp 53-4; Hore & Graves, *Southern and Eastern Counties*, pp 127, 128, 205, 207, 242, 270; A. T. Lucas, 'Irish Ploughing Practices', in *Tools and Tillage*, ii. p.70; 'The Presentments of the Jurors of the Counties of Kilkenny and Wexford...1537', in *The Annuary of the Kilkenny and South East of Ireland Archaeological Society* 1855, i,i, pp 42, 47, 48, 67-8

(21) Cox, *The Irish Horse*, p.57; Falls, *Elizabeth's Irish Wars*, pp 37, 41; Spenser, *A View*, p.145; P. Joyce, *Old Celtic Romances*, p.161; Quinn, *The Elizabethans*, p.151; D. Quinn, 'A Discourse of Ireland (circa 1599)', in *P.R.I.A.*, xlvii, pp 164-5

(22) Spenser, *A View*, p.75; Hore & Graves, *Southern and Eastern Counties*, pp 149-51, 168; Nicholls, *Gaelic Ireland*, p.32; Empey & Simms, 'Ordinances', p.185

(23) Spenser, *A View*, pp 75, 76; Hore & Graves, *Southern and Eastern Counties*, pp 161, 169-71, 173; *Cal.Carew Mss*, iii, p.72

(24) Cox, *The Irish Horse*, pp 36-7, 42; Hore & Graves, *Southern and Eastern Counties*, pp 81, 199, 222, 234; C. Lewis, *Hunting in Ireland*, pp 34, 37; Nicholls, *Gaelic Ireland*, p.34; Somerville-Large, *From Bantry Bay*, p.20

(25) Hore & Graves, *Southern and Eastern Counties*, pp 167-8, 227-8; Empey & Simms, 'Ordinances', p.179-82; Holinshed, *Chronicles*, vi, 269; Nicholls, *Gaelic Ireland*, pp 32, 34; Spenser, *A View*, p. 157; Berleth, *The Twilight Lords*, pp 61-2; Cox, *The Irish Horse*, p.35

(26) Nicholls, *Gaelic Ireland*, p.35; Hore & Graves, *Southern and Eastern Counties*, pp 154, 160-1, 170-1, 173; Otway-Ruthven, *A History*, pp 400, 402; 'Presentments', p.7; Frame, *English Lordship*, p.4

(27) Hore & Graves, *Southern and Eastern Counties*, pp 132-3, 173; 'Presentments', pp 48, 67, 68; H. Hore, 'The Clan Kavanagh, temp. Henry viii', in *The Kilkenny and South-East of Ireland Archaeological Society Journal*, ii, p.76; Nicholls, *Gaelic Ireland*, p.172; D. McCormick, *The Incredible Mr Kavanagh*, p.24

(28) ibid. pp 23-4, 35, 56, 116, 123, 142, 170; Nicholls, *Gaelic Ireland*, pp 171-2; Otway-Ruthven, *A History*, pp 338; Dent and Goodall, *The Foals of Epona*, pp 126, 278; J. Lalor, 'Elegy on the Death of the Reverend Edward Kennedy', in *The Kilkenny and South-East of Ireland Archaeological Society Journal*, i, p.119

(29) Empey & Simms, 'Ordinances', p.187; Otway-Ruthven, *A History*, pp 180, 275; R. Frame, 'War and Peace in the Mediaeval Lordship of Ireland', in J. Lydon, *The English in Mediaeval Ireland*, pp 130-1; Curtis & McDowell, *I.H.D.*, pp 33-5, 56, 57; Holinshed, *Chronicles*, vi, pp 323, 326

(30) Hore, 'The Clan Kavanagh', pp 74, 81, 84, 85; Hore & Graves, *Southern and Eastern Counties*, pp 281-3; Nicholls, *Gaelic Ireland*, p.173; Frame, 'War and Peace', pp 119, 126- 8; Frame, *The English Lordship*, pp 312, 314, 316; Otway-Ruthven, *A History*, pp 200, 201, 218-9, 242, 247, 255-6, 258n., 286; E. Curtis, *A History of Ireland*, pp 21, 59-60, 107-8, 121; D. Ó hÓgáin, *The Hero*, p. 161-3; Cox, *The Irish Horse*, p.53; Berleth, *The Twilight Lords*, p. 157

(31) Cox, *The Irish Horse*, pp 50-1, 53, 54; Ó hÓgáin, *The Hero*, pp 136-7, 147, 161-2; Holinshed, *Chronicles*, vi. pp 289-92; Spenser, *A View*, p. 74; J. E. Caerwyn Williams & M. Ní Mhuiríosa, *Traidisiún Liteartha na nGael*, p.164

(32) Empey & Simms, 'Ordinances', pp 179-180; Simms, *Gaelic Lordships*, pp 112, 113, 114-5; Hore & Graves, *Southern and Eastern Counties*, p.153; Woulfe, *The Right Stuff*, pp 101-3, 207

(33) Ó hÓgáin, *The Hero*, pp 119, 125-7, 134-7, 151; B.Ó Buachalla, 'An Meisiasacht agus an Aisling', in de Brún, Ó Coileáin & Ó Briain, *Folia Gadelica*, pp 74-7; Simms, *Gaelic Lordships*, pp 9-10; Jung, *Works*, v, p.278

(34) Ó hÓgáin, *The Hero*, pp 79-80, 125-7, 133, 142, 143, 146, 148, 149, 150, 152, 154; A. B. Scott & F. X. Martin (ed.), *Expugnatio*, pp 175, 293n., 313n., Ó Cathasaigh, *C.M.T.*, p.11

(35) Nicholls, *Gaelic Ireland*, pp 162-3; Ó hÓgáin, *The Hero*, pp 84-5, 146, 147, 149, 157-8; D. Ó hÓgáin, 'Gearóid Iarla', in *Cómhar*, May 1974, p.9; P.Ó Caithnia, *Scéal na hIomána*, pp 41-2, 290, 347, 381; K. Danaher, *The Year in Ireland*, pp 121-2

(36) Ó Cathasaigh, 'C.M.T.', p.9; Ó hÓgáin, *The Hero*, pp 142, 147, 148, 150-1, 156-7

(37) ibid. 144-5; B. Fitzgerald, *The Geraldines*, pp 255, 257, 258, 272, 281, 283; Hore & Graves, *Southern and Eastern Counties*, p.228; Berleth, *The Twilight Lords*, p.184, 186, 193, 205-6; Holinshed, *Chronicles*, vi, 452; M. Seoighe, *Dromm Athlacca*, p.191; Gaughan, *The Knights of Glin*, pp 72, 112

(38) R. Kearney, *Myth and Motherland*, p.10n.; N. Chadwick, *The Celts*, pp 169-173; A. & B. Rees, *Celtic Heritage*, 30-41; Ó hÓgáin, *The Hero* p.137-140; Ó Cathasaigh, *C.M.T.*, pp 8-14; Ó Buachalla, 'An Meisiasacht', pp 72- 4, 79; J. G. Simms, *Jacobite Ireland*, pp 236, 260

(39) Ó hÓgáin, *The Hero*, pp 56, 84, 131-2, 138-9, 140, 148, 149, 154; Ó Buachalla, 'An Meisiasacht', p.75; *Revelations*, 1.18, 19.11; J. S. Donnelly, 'Pastorini and Captain Rock: Milleniarism and Sectarianism in the Rockite Movement', in S. Clarke & J. S. Donnelly, *Irish Peasants*, pp 104-8, 110-1, 113-6, 117, 119-21; Woulfe, *The Right Stuff*, p.303; Samuel, 1.18

(40) Simms, *Jacobite Ireland*, pp 167, 258, 260; Cox, *The Irish Horse*, pp 92-4; Ó Buachalla, 'An Meisiasacht', pp 80- 1, 82-5; Corkery, *The Hidden Ireland*, pp 119, 201

(41) T. W. Moody, 'Redmond O'Hanlon', in *Proceedings and Reports of the Belfast Natural History and Philosophical Society*, i, pp 17, 19-21, 22, 24-5, 32; J. E. Walsh, *Rakes and Ruffians*, pp 84, 88; Cullen, *Life in Ireland*, pp 57-8; S. Ó Catháin, *Irish*

Life and Lore, pp 7-9; K. Danaher and J. G. Simms, *The Danish Force in Ireland*, p.34; Simms, *Jacobite Ireland* pp 198-9; Culligan-Hogan, *Galloping Hogan*, p.52

(42) Ó Catháin, *Irish Life*, p.8; Simms, *Jacobite Ireland*, p.199; Moody, 'Redmond O'Hanlon', pp 23-4; Danaher & Simms, *The Danish Force*, pp 56, 87, 98-100, 107, 110; T. Ó Fiaich, 'Filíocht Uladh mar Fhoinse don Stair Shóisialta', in *Studia Hibernica*, xi, p.116; Culligan-Hogan, *Galloping Hogan*, p.64; P. Roberts, 'Caravats and Shanavests: Whiteboyism and Faction Fighting in east Munster, 1802-11', in Clarke & Donnelly, *Irish Peasants*, pp 69n., 85-6

(43) Ó Catháin, *Irish Life*, pp 17-8; Holinshed, *Chronicles*, vi, p.446; Ó hÓgáin, *The Hero*, p.290; Culligan-Hogan, *Galloping Hogan*, pp 50-1

(44) Moody, 'Redmond O'Hanlon', p.32; Walsh, *Rakes and Ruffians*, pp 90; Ó Catháin, *Irish Life* , pp10, 11-2; Ó hÓgáin, *The Hero*, p.188

(45) Gaughan, *The Knights of Glin*, pp 62-3; Walsh, *Rakes and Ruffians*, p.85; Ó Catháin, *Irish Life*, pp 18-21

CHAPTER SIX

(1) L. M. Cullen, 'The Hidden Ireland: Re-Assessment of a Concept', in *Studia Hibernica*, ix, pp 15-6, 18; Corkery, *The Hidden Ireland*, p.145; C. Maxwell, *The Stranger in Ireland*, pp 61, 63

(2) K. Jackson, *Miscellany*, p.300; Corkery, *The Hidden Ireland*, pp 46-58

(3) Corkery, *The Hidden Ireland*, pp 117-21

(4) Ó Fiaich, 'Filíocht Uladh', p.125; B. O'Rourke, 'County Mayo in Gaelic Folksong', in B. O'Hara, *Mayo*, pp 157-9, 163; B. O'Hara, 'Some Famous Mayo People', ibid p. 292; Lewis, *Hunting*, pp 15, 41n., 61-2, 69; Cullen, *An Economic History*, p.7; D. Hyde (ed.), *Songs ascribed to Raftery*, p.98; Cullen, 'The Hidden Ireland', p.21

(5) L. M. Cullen 'Economic Trends 1660-1691', in Moody, Martin & Byrne, *A New History of Ireland*, iii, p.401; F. Mitchell, *The Irish Landscape*, p.198; Cullen, *Life in Ireland*, pp 110-2; Cox, *The Irish Horse*, pp 78; G. O'Brien, *An Economic History of Ireland in the Seventeenth Century*, pp 41, 63-5, 105, 212; A. Young, *A Tour of Ireland*, pp 15-7, 28; S. J. Connolly, *Priests and People*, pp 16-7; A. T. Lucas, 'Irish Ploughing Practices', ii, p. 71, iii pp 204-8; *Commission on Horse Breeding in Ireland (1896)*, pp 15, 28-9, 63, 70, 90; D. A. Chart, *An Economic History of Ireland*, p.117

(6) Cullen, *Life in Ireland*, pp 54, 74; L.M.Cullen, 'Man, Landscape and Roads: The changing eighteenth century', in W. Nolan, *The Shaping of Ireland*, pp 131-3; G. O'Brien, *The Economic History of Ireland in the Seventeenth-Century*, p. 212; L. M. Cullen, 'The Hidden Ireland', pp 40-1, 43; Corkery, *The Hidden Ireland* , p.258; Ó hÓgáin, 'An Capall', op. cit., p.208

(7) Cox, *The Irish Horse*, pp 69, 94, 95, 99; Simms, *Jacobite Ireland*, pp 55, 124-5; U. O'Connor, *Brendan Behan*, pp 89-90; G. O'Brien, *The Economic History of Ireland in the Eighteenth Century*, pp 24-5; J. Welcome, *Irish Horseracing*, pp 6-7; M. Wall, 'The Rise of a Catholic Middle Class in Eighteenth-Century Ireland', in *I.H.S.*, xi, p. 103; E. M. Johnston, *Ireland in the Eighteenth Century*, pp 36-7; R. B. McDowell, *Ireland in the Age of Imperialism and Revolution*, p.174

(8) E. Malcolm, 'Popular Recreations in 19th century Ireland', in O.MacDonagh, A. Mandle & P. Travers, *Irish Culture and Nationalism*, p.47; Cullen, *Life in Ireland*, pp 111, 141-2; D. Ó Muirithe, *A Seat behind the Coachman*, p.78; R. B. McDowell, 'Ireland in 1800', in T. W. Moody & W. E. Vaughan, *A New History of Ireland*, iv, p.675

(9) S. J. Watson, *Between the Flags*, pp 44-5; Welcome, *I.H.*, pp 24, 27, 28

(10) ibid. pp 119, 121, 123

(11) Malcolm, 'Popular Recreations', pp 42-3, 48-50

(12) ibid. pp 41-8; J. Barrington, *The Ireland of Sir Jonah Barrington*, p.172; Welcome, *I.H.*, pp 24, 26, 27, 65, 123

(13) Watson, *B.T.F.*, pp 67-8.

(14) ibid. pp 7, 37-8, 55-6.

(15) ibid. p. 7; Welcome, *I.H.*, p.7;

(16) J. E. Walsh, *Rakes and Ruffians*, pp 10-39, 42-4, 56-9; Watson, *Between the Flags*, pp 7, 12-3; Cullen, *The Emergence of Modern Ireland*, pp 133-4, 196, 200, 244-7; H. Morris, 'Marriage Customs', in *Co. Louth Archaeological Society Journal*, ii, No.3 p.323; K. Danaher, 'Some Marriage Customs and their Regional Distribution', in *Béaloideas*, 42- 4, pp 136-175; 'Marriage Customs in Co. Cavan in the Nineteenth Century', in *The Heart of Breifne*, 1978, p.27; C. Maxwell, *Country and Town in Ireland under the Georges*, p.20; Roberts 'Caravests and Shanavests', pp 69n., 85; Gaughan, *The Knights of Glin*, pp 76, 80

(17) ibid. p.119; Cullen, *Life in Ireland*, pp 54, 70; Cullen, *The Emergence*, pp 98-9; J. G. Simms, 'Connacht in the Eighteenth Century', in *I.H.S.*, xi, 116, 118, 120-1

(18) Maxwell, *Country and Town*, p. 50-54; S. Lynam, *Humanity Dick*, pp 51, 88-9; Simms, 'Connacht', op. cit., pp 129-30; Walsh, *Rakes and Ruffians*, p.29; Corkery, *The Hidden Ireland*, p.46; P. O'Donnell, *The Irish Faction Fighters*, p.27

(19) Malcolm, 'Popular Recreations', p.45; A. T. Q. Stewart, *The Narrow Ground*, pp 129-130; O'Donnell, *The Irish Faction Fighters*, pp 20-3, 27, 32-3, 36-7; Roberts, 'Caravests and Shanavests', p.87; J. L. McCracken, 'The Social Structure and Social Life 1714-60', in T. W. Moody and W. E. Vaughan, *A New History of Ireland*, iv, pp 47-8; Welcome, *I.H.*, pp 31-3, 83-5, 99-100; Watson, *B.T.F.*, pp 46, 47-8

(20) Welcome, *I.H.*, pp 38-9; Watson, *B.T.F.*, pp 51; Cullen, *The Emergence*, pp 23, 134, 247; Roberts, 'Caravats and Shanavests', pp 68, 70-2, 80; E. Bowen, *Bowen Court*, pp 125, 292, 308, 393; N. Ó Muraíle, 'An Outline History of County Mayo', in O'Hara, *Mayo*,

p.25; Gaughan, *The Knights of Glin*, pp 63-4, 114-5, 117-22; J. Hone, *The Moores of Moore Hall*, pp 137-8

(21) C. Maxwell, *Country and Town*, p.34, 56-8, 62-3; Corkery, *The Hidden Ireland*, pp 45-6; Watson, *B.T.F.*, pp 7, 48-9; McCracken, 'The Social Structure', p.47; Welcome, *I.H.*, pp 15-6, 88; Cullen, *The Emergence*, pp 98-9;

(22) J. S. Donnelly, 'Pastorini and Captain Rock: Milleniarism and Sectarianism in the Rockite Movement of 1821-4', in Donnelly & Clarke, *Irish Peasants*, pp 121-2; Cox, *The Irish Horse*, p 99; McCracken, 'The Social Structure', pp 47-8; Ó Buachalla, 'An Meisiasacht', pp 83-4; Barrington, *The Ireland of Sir Jonah Barrington*, pp 41, 44-5, 49-50

(23) ibid. pp 197; Watson, *B.T.F.*, pp 32, 43, 44, 49-53, 55; Welcome, *I.H.*, pp 36-8, 79, 82; Lewis, *Hunting in Ireland*, pp 106-107

(24) Bowen, *Bowen Court*, pp 268-9, 345, 346, 349, 366; M. Keane, *Good Behaviour*, pp 10-11, 14, 39, 78, 80-1, 97

(25) Maxwell, *Country and Town*, pp 24-5, 32-3, 42, 59-61; Lewis, *Hunting*, pp 41, 44, 53-4, 56-7, 84

(26) ibid. pp 56, 84; Seoighe, op. cit., p.161; Gaughan, *The Knights of Glin*, pp 119, 128, 152-5, 183; Maxwell, *Country and Town*, p.24

(27) Gaughan, *The Knights of Glin*, p.97; Bowen, *Bowen Court*, pp 170, 190, 196-203; Cullen, *The Emergence*, pp 243-4; Cullen, *Life in Ireland*, pp 59, 62; Lewis, *Hunting*, pp 111, 113; Margaret MacCurtain, 'Rural Life in post Cromwellian Ireland', in A. Cosgrove and D. McCartney, *Studies in Irish History: Presented to Dudley Edwards*, p. 135; Watson, *B.T.F.*, pp 4-5, 10; Cox, *The Irish Horse*, pp 98-102, 104-6

(28) Gaughan, *The Knights of Glin*, p. 167; Young, *A Tour*, pp 203-4; Watson, *Between the Flags*, pp 10-11, 32; C. Maxwell, *Country and Town*, p.24; Bowen, *Bowen Court*, pp 148, 171, 336, 340, 346; Cullen, *Life in Ireland*, p.154; Lewis, *Hunting*, p.113 W.A. Maguire, *Living*

like a Lord, pp 9, 25, 28, 30, 34, 37-8, 51-2, 61, 77, 80-2; J. Barden, *Belfast*, pp 71, 72; W. A. Maguire, 'A Resident Landlord in his Local Setting: The Second Marquis of Donegal at Ormeau 1807-1844', in *P.R.I.A.*, 83c pp 384 fig.1, 388-93, 397

(29) Maguire, *Living Like a Lord*, pp 84, 86, 89, 91-2, 95; Barden, *Belfast*, p. 72; J. Swift, *The Works of the Reverend Dr Swift*, pp 420-3; Cullen, *Life in Ireland*, pp 74-5; Maxwell, *Country and Town*, pp 56-61; Cullen, *The Emergence*, p.31, 47; Bowen, *Bowen Court*, pp 143, 146; Barrington, *The Ireland of Sir Jonah Barrington*, pp 130; Young, *A Tour*, pp 95-6; McDowell, *Ireland in the Age of Imperialism and Revolution*, pp 38-9, 500; Lynam, *Humanity Dick*, p.3

(30) Lewis, *Hunting*, pp 77 table 3, 80-1; Cullen, *An Economic History*, p.85; T. W. Freeman, *Pre-Famine Ireland*, p.228; Cullen, *The Emergence*, p.120

(31) D. Dickson, 'Middlemen', in T. Bartlett & D. W. Hayton, *Penal Era and Golden Age*, p.163, 165, 171-2; Cullen, *The Emergence*, 17-8, 33-4, 98-103, 120, 243-4, 246-7; Cullen, *An Economic History*, pp 56, 78-80, 82, 114-5; Barrington, op. cit., p.31-2; Corkery, *The Hidden Ireland*, pp 43-50; Cullen, 'The Hidden Ireland', op. cit., p.32

(32) Barrington, *The Ireland of Sir Jonah Barrington*, p.130, 32; Edgeworth, *Ormond*, pp 107-9, 126, 131-2; Ó Muirithe, *A Seat Behind the Coachman*, p.72-3

(33) S. Ó Tuama & T. Kinsella, *An Duanaire*, p. 169; Young, Op. cit., p.205; Cullen, *An Economic History*, pp 78-80, 82, 115; Cullen, *The Emergence*, pp 17-8, 33-4, 99-103, 214-5, 226, 227-33; M. Byrne, *Memoirs of Myles Byrne*, pp 17-8, 71; Gaughan, *The Knights of Glin*, pp 120-1; S. Ó Faoláin, *King of the Beggars*, pp 196-8; Cullen, *Life in Ireland*, p.111; Connolly, *Priests and People*, p.57; Maxwell, *Country and Town*, pp 176-8

(34) Jackson, *Miscellany*, p.295, 298-300, 348; Cullen, *The Emergence*, pp 28-9, 34, 177; Ó Tuama & Kin-

sella, *An Duanaire*, p.213; E. Dillon, 'The Lament of Arthur O'Leary', *Irish University Review*, i, 2, pp 198-9, 203; Connolly, *Priests and People*, p.148-50, 152

CHAPTER SEVEN

(1) *Laws*, i, pp 163-5 231, 235; ii, pp 155-61; iii, pp 181, 295; iv, p.97 v, pp 279, 477, 487; P. W. Joyce, *A Social History of Ancient Ireland*, ii, p. 411

(2) O'Meara, *Topography*, p.31, 34; *Laws*, v, p. 137; Ó Corráin, *Ireland before the Normans*, p.50; Cox, *The Irish Horse*, pp 84-5, 87; Dent & Goodall, *The Foals of Epona*, p.278; Pückler-Muskau, *Tour in England, Ireland and France in the years 1828 and 1829*, i, 279; *Commission on Horse Breeding in Ireland*, pp 31-2, 35, 48, 75, 81, 90-2, 200, 201; Barrington, *The Ireland of Sir Jonah Barrington* pp 79; F. O'Neill, U. Shanahan, M. Kennedy, T. McStay, *A Study of the Non-Thoroughbred Horse Industry*, pp 35-9

(3) Barrington, *The Ireland of Sir Jonah Barrington*, p. 172; Pückler-Muskau, *Tour*, p.204

(4) Lucas, 'Irish Ploughing Practices', ii, pp 73-9; iv, pp 195-8; E. E. Evans, 'Some Problems of Irish Ethnology: The example of Ploughing by the Tail', in C. Ó Danachair, *Folk and Farm* plates 3 & 4a, pp 34, 37, 38n.

(5) B. Ó Riordáin, *Antiquities of the Irish Countryside*, p.60; Lucas, 'Irish Ploughing Practices', i, pp 53, 55-6, 59-60, ii, p.80; R. Haworth, 'The Horse Harness of the Irish Early Iron Age', in *U.J.A.* xxxiv (1971), pp 38, 44n.; Ó Corráin, *Ireland before the Normans*, p. 57; K. Nicholls, *Gaelic Ireland*, p. 181; F. Mitchell, *The Irish Landscape*, p.193; P.J. Fowler, 'Early Prehistoric Agriculture in Western Europe: Some Archaeological Evidence', in D. Simpson, *Economy and Settlement in Neolithic and Early Bronze Age Britain and Europe*, pp 158; Simone de Beauvoir, *The Second Sex*, p.111n.; E. E. Evans, 'Some Problems of Irish

Ethnology' pp 34-5; A. Steensberg, 'Virgil's Wheel-Ard and the Two Mouldstrokers', in Ó Danachair, *Folk and Farm*, fig. 65, p.271; R. Rose, 'A Suggested Explanation of Ritual Combats', in *Folklore*, xxxvi, pp 322, 328-31; G. Dumézil, *Archaic Roman Religion*, pp 217-20

(6) Evans, *I.F.W.*, p.215, 273-5; Danaher, *The Year in Ireland* pp 86-8, 96, 102-3, 109, 133, 144, 146, 213-4, 247-51; Mac Cana, *Celtic Mythology*, p.127

(7) D. Ward, 'The Threefold Death: An Indo-European Trifunctional Sacrifice', in Puhvel, *Myth and Law among the Indo-Europeans*, pp 126, 130; A. Ross, *P.C.B.*, p.444n.; Danaher, *The Year in Ireland*, p 173; Thomas O'Conor August 1838—Mayo Ordnance Survey Letters, ii, p.368

(8) Ó Catháin, *Irish Life*, pp 39-45; Ó hÓgáin, 'An Capall', p.237; Cox, *The Irish Horse*, pp 107-14; Watson, *B.T.F.*, p.11; C. Lewis & M. E. McCarthy, 'The Horse Breeding Industry in Ireland', in *Irish Geography*, x, p.73

(9) Watson, *B.T.F.*, p.12; Cox, *The Irish Horse*, p.112; Ó hÓgáin, 'An Capall', pp 200-206, 239-40; P. Logan, *The Old Gods*, p.33; Ryan, *Biddy Early*, pp 56, 59; Ó Catháin, *Irish Life*, p.34

(10) ibid. pp 35, 41-2; Ó hÓgáin, 'An Capall', p.237-9; Logan, *The Old Gods*, pp 130-1

(11) Ó Catháin, *Irish Life*, p.34-49; Ó hÓgáin, 'An Capall', pp 207-9, 220-1, 229-36; Evans, *I.F.W.*, p.142; Danaher, *The Year in Ireland*, p.36; B. Ó Cuív, 'Fragments of Two Mediaeval Treatises on Horses', in *Celtica*, ii, Part 1, 42-4, 54-5; Mauss, *The Gift*, p.64

(12) T. de Bhaldraithe, *The Diary of Humphrey O'Sullivan*, p.82; Ó hÓgáin, 'An Capall', p.209

(13) Ryan, *Biddy Early*, pp 7, 20-1, 47, 55-60, 81-2, 100, 102; Ó Catháin, *Irish Life* pp 22-4; Ó hÓgáin, 'An Capall', pp 208- 10, 222, 229; Logan, *The Old Gods*, p.33; Ó hÓgáin, *The Hero*, pp 277-8

(14) G. Evans, *The Horse in the Furrow*, 249-50; Ó hÓgáin, 'An Capall',

p.240-3; G. Evans, *The Pattern under the Plough*, p.259

(15) G. Evans, *The Horse in the Furrow*, pp 251-3; G.Evans, *The Pattern under the Plough*, p. 204-12, 214-7; Ó hÓgáin, 'An Capall', pp 225-6, 227, 228

(16) G. Evans, *The Horse in the Furrow*, pp 241-3, 245-6, 249-50; *The Pattern under the Plough*, pp 213, 225, 232-3, 259; Ó hÓgáin, 'An Capall', pp 223, 226-7

(17) ibid. p 239; Logan, *The Old Gods*, pp 27, 31-2

CHAPTER EIGHT

(1) J. O'Shea, *Priests, Politics and Society in Post-Famine Ireland*, pp 13-4, 117; Watson, *B.T.F.*, pp 52, 54, 103; Lewis, *Hunting*, pp 57, 137; *Horse Breeding In Ireland*, pp 29, 102; L. P. Curtis, 'Stopping the Hunt, 1881-1882; J. Welcome, *I.H.*, pp 88, 133; S. J. Connolly, 'Religion, Work-Discipline and Economic Attitudes: The Case of Ireland', in T. M. Devine & D. Dickson, *Ireland and Scotland*, p.243; E. Malcolm, 'Popular Recreation' pp 45-6; Cullen, *The Emergence of Modern Ireland*, p. 134; de Bhaldraithe, *The Diary of Humphrey O'Sullivan*, pp 30-1, 45; Maxwell, *Country and Town*, p.158; S.J.Connolly, *Priests and People*, pp 40, 59, 66, 70, 72; Gaughan, *The Knights of Glin*, pp 130-2, 169- 70

(2) Watson, *B.T.F.*, pp 99-103, 107-8, 111, 117-8, 117-8, 125, 143, 164, 170, 188-9, 230, 280-3; Welcome, *I. H.*, pp 23, 38, 58, 70, 73, 77-9, 200; L. Cullen, *Life in Ireland*, pp 152-5; *An Economic History*, pp 149-50, 152-4; J. Hughes & P. Wilson, *Long Live the National*, p.203

(3) Watson, *B.T.F.*, pp 91-4, 112-3, 119-20, 131, 135, 307; Welcome, *I.H.*, pp 61, 64-5, 70, 112-3, 120-1, 123-4, 144, 188; Browne, *The Horse*, pp 46-8; G. St J. Williams & F. Hyland, *The Irish Derby*, p.63-4, 102, 104;

(4) Welcome, *I.H.*, pp 14-5, 47, 57, 80-1, 88, 76, 90, 95, 101, 111, 115-7, 135-6, 141-4, 155, 160-7, 171, 178,

183, 188, 206; Browne, *The Horse*, pp 49-50, 74, 77-8, 109, 111-2; R. Baerlein, *Shergar*, pp 21-2, 24-7, 31-4, 41-6, 71-2, 176; P. Willett, *The Classic Racehorse*, pp 54-5, 60, 92-5, 99; Kennedy & Doran-O'Reilly, *Horses of Ireland*, pp 23-5, 31-4, 101, 141-4, 166-7, 206; Williams & Hyland, *The Irish Derby*, pp 182-4; J. N. P. Watson, *British and Irish Hunts and Huntsmen*, i, 242-5; Watson,*B.T.F.*, pp 71, 120, 129-131, 294; M. O'Connell, *Shadows, An Album of the Irish People 1841-1914*, pp 113-4

(5) Watson, *B.T.F.*, pp 106-7, 157-8, 160-9; 183-6, 188-90, 196; Welcome, *I.H.*, p.137-9; M. O'Connell, *Shadows*, pp 111-2; Gaughan, *The Knights of Glin*, pp 106, 169-71; Seoighe, *Dromm Athlacca*, pp 161-4

(6) Watson, *B.T.F.*, pp 34-5, 37, 42-3, 45-6, 48, 56, 59-60, 63, 71-81, 83-90, 95-8, 113-5, 116, 126-8, 131-2, 220, 244, 285; Lewis, *Horse Breeding*, p.108; M. McCormac, *The Irish Racing and Bloodstock Industry*, pp 15-6, 162; Welcome, *I.H.*, pp 43-5, 55-6, 82-3, 107-10, 133, 140, 144, 154, 165, 172, 199- 200; *Irish Times*, 26 April 1980; J. O'Shea, *Priests*, p.15; Killanin, *Report of the Commission of Inquiry into the Thoroughbred Horse Breeding Industry*, p.71-2, Table 25; E. Murphy, 'Holiday Meetings', in *Sean P. Graham Racing Annual 1976-7*, pp 85-6; McCormac,*Irish Racing*, pp 18, 162

(7) Welcome, *I.H.*, pp 1-2, 4-6, 55, 80, 112, 132, 154-5, 161-2, 171, 200, 204, 206; Watson, *B.T.F.*, pp 15, 159, 165, 193, 248-9, 267, 289; Browne, *The Horse*, pp 13, 42; *Irish Times*, 26 April, 1980; Williams & Hyland, *The Irish Derby*, pp 10, 17-8, 21, 220, 240-2, 369-70; H. Dossenbach, *The Noble Horse*, p.249

(8) Watson, *B.T.F.*, pp 44-5, 71, 212, 221; Browne, *The Horse*, pp 47, 50-1; Welcome, *I.H.*, pp 133-4, 137, 141, 144-5, 149; Mac Cormac, *Irish Racing*, pp 20-2, 24, 25

(9) Watson, *B.T.F.*, pp 4-5, 136-7, 165, 168, 170, 172, 219, 226- 8, 238, 243, 247, 310; Welcome, *I.H.*, pp 14, 22, 81-2, 116, 124, 168; Willett, *The*

Classic Racehorse, pp 86, 93, 94; Dossenbach, *The Noble Horse,* p.248; Mac Cormac, *Irish Racing,* p.19, 28, 29; Lewis, *Horse Breeding in Ireland,* pp 11, 17-9; Killanin, *Report,* pp 59-60, Table 11; Browne, *The Horse,* pp 49, 53

(10) Welcome, *I.H.,* pp 70, 145, 146-8, 154, 162, 172-5, 177, 183, 187-8, 193-5, 208-9; Watson, *B.T.F.,* pp 89, 173-4, 202-5, 214-5, 272, 294-8; O'Brien & Herbert, *Vincent O'Brien's Great Horses,* pp 28-31, 40-2; P. Taaffe, *My Life and Arkle's,* pp 12, 78-9; Kennedy & Doran-O'Reilly, *H.I.,* p.95; I. Herbert, *Red Rum,* pp 17-8, 21-2, 34, 40-1, 48-65, 69, 107, 113-7, 126, 174-6, 205, 216, 225-6, 233, 237-8, 240-1, 245-63; Hughes & Wilson, *Long Live the National,* pp 28-9, 62-9, 133-6; Dossenbach, *The Noble Horse,* pp 286-7

(11) Welcome, *I.H.,* pp 209-10; R. Smith, 'A "last hurrah" dinner at the Don Pasquale—but the Champagne flows for Tommy Carmody on *Tied Cottage',* in *Sean P. Graham Annual,* 1980-1, p.87; Watson, *B.T.F..* pp 301; J. O'Neill, *Jonjo,* pp 167-9, 173, 176-7, 201; Kennedy & Doran-O'Reilly, *H.I.,* pp 132-3

(12) T. Fitzgeorge-Parker, *Vincent O'Brien,* pp 14, 18, 33, 42-3, 52, 63, 77, 85; O'Brien & Herbert, *Vincent O'Brien's Great Horses,* pp 17-33, 39-50, 54, 62-9, 70, 77, 80, 83-95, 100, 108, 126, 144-5, 147-8, 162-5, 167-9, 178, 192-3, 200-3, 210-11, 214, 216, 222, 224-5, 228-30; Welcome, *I.H.,* pp 154, 180-1, 184, 186, 198-9, 206; Browne, *The Horse,* pp 56-7, 94-5, 117; Kennedy & Doran-O'Reilly, *H.I.,* pp 27-30; Seoighe, *Dromm Athlacca,* pp 164-6; Watson, *B.T.F.,* pp 250, 262-3, 269-70, 274-6; Baerlein, *Shergar ,* pp 87; C. Poole, *Horseracing 1982,* pp 38, 155-6; J. Powell, 'Pat Eddery and the offer he could not refuse', in

Sean P. Graham Annual, 1980-1, pp 35-6; Williams & Hyland, *The Irish Derby,* pp 291-3, 377; Dossenbach, *The Noble Horse,* p.248

(13) Mac Cormac, *Irish Racing,* p.29; Kennedy & Doran-O'Reilly, *H.I.,* pp 39, 97-8; Willett, *The Classic Racehorse,* pp 97-8, 121; Dossenbach, *The Noble Horse,* pp 234, 236-7; Killanin, *Report,* pp 18-20, 38, 19, 50, 59 Table 11, 64-5, 66, 73, 75, 174, 177; Welcome, *I.H.,* pp 95-6, 198; Browne, *The Horse,* pp 131-2; Watson, *B.T.F.,* pp 131-3, 310-11; N. Ring, 'Point to Points—Pat Hogan continues to dominate', in *Sean P. Graham Annual,* 1980-1, p.64; Lewis, *Hunting,* p.121, 172

CHAPTER NINE

(1) S. J. Watson, *B.T.F.,* pp 284-5; *Three Days Full,* pp 33-37, 46, 91, 117, 126; M. Kennedy & Q. Doran-O'Reilly, *H.I.,* pp 85-8, 98, 136-7; Hughes & Wilson, *Long Live the National,* p.94 Dossenbach, *The Noble Horse,* pp 323-4; Browne, *The Horse,* pp 149-58

(2) Lewis, *Horse Breeding,* pp 17-23, 34-5, 37, 39-40, 51-3, 58, 60, 81, 85, 91, 93, 99, 102, 107-8, 121, 124, 126, 139, 144- 148, 159, 160-171, 176-80; N. O'Hare, *Our Irish Horses,* p.14-7; Kennedy & Doran-O'Reilly, *H.I.,* p.149; Dossenbach, *The Noble Horse,* p.170; *Bord na gCapall, Report and Accounts,* 1972, p.14, 1982 p.8; Browne, *The Horse,* pp 17-9

(3) Dossenbach, *The Noble Horse,* pp 200, 324-8; Browne, *The Horse,* pp 146, 166-7, 179-181, 194-9; N. O'Hare, *Our Irish Horses,* pp 23, 38-43; M. Tinsley, *The Aga Khan Trophy* pp 2-3, 12, 16-7, 33-4; M. Clayton & W. Steinkraus, *The Complete Book of Showjumping,* pp 19, 172-3, 178; Kennedy & Doran-O'Reilly., *H.I.* pp 77, 156-8

(4) Tinsley, *Aga Khan,* pp 33-41; Wat-

son, *T.D.F.,* pp 29-33, 37- 40, 42, 47-50, 53-6, 64, 67-9, 74, 78-9, 93, 96, 116-7, 126, 128-9, 131-2; Watson, *B.T.F.,* pp 25-6, 274-7; Browne, *The Horse* p.203; Kennedy & Doran-O'Reilly, *H.I.* pp 62-3, 129

(5) Kennedy & Doran-O'Reilly, *H.I.,* pp 65-6, 210, 223-5; J. Norton, 'A successful year for ponies', in *Irish Horse Yearbook* 1981, pp 27-9: *Irish Pony Club Yearbook* 1983 pp 11- 3; Bord na gCapall, *Report and Accounts* 1975, p.16; 1977, pp 3, 14; 1984, pp 2, 7; Lewis, *Horse Breeding,* pp 182, 184; Browne, *The Horse,* p.142

(6) Browne, *The Horse,* pp 162-3; Kennedy & Doran-O'Reilly, *H.I.,* pp 79-81, 139-40; M. Clayton & W. Steinkraus, *Showjumping,* pp 169-72, 210-12; Williams, *Great Moments in Sport,* pp 39-41; *Horse of the Year,* pp 132-3; Dossenbach, *The Noble Horse,* p.326; O'Hare, *One Hundred Irish Horses,* M. Seoighe, *Dromm Athlacca,* pp 168-9

(7) O'Hare, *One Hundred Irish Horses;* M. Ansell, 'Eddie Macken—Showjumping Superstar', in *Irish Horse Yearbook,* 1977, pp 11-2; Kennedy & Doran-O'Reilly, *H.I.,* pp 15-8, 54, 56, 58- 60, 115, 118, 139-40, 173-6, 180, 182-3, 187; Tinsley, *Aga Khan,* pp 16-7, 39-41; Clayton & Steinkraus, *Showjumping,* pp 204, 213, 218; Williams, *Great Moments in Sport,* pp 12, 24-6, 37, 39-40, 42-4, 65, 72-81, 107-8, 121; Dossenbach, *The Noble Horse,* p.329

(8) Bord na gCapall, *Report and Accounts* 1975, p.14; O'Neill, Shanahan, Kennedy & McStay, pp 35, Table 6.1, pp 21-2, Table 4.8; Central Statistics Office personal communication; *Report of the Commission of Inquiry into the Thoroughbred Horse Industry,* pp.65-6, Table 17, p.75.

Bibliography

ABBREVIATIONS

I.H.S. Irish Historical Studies
I.T.S. Irish Texts Society
P.R.I.A. Proceedings of the Royal Irish Academy
R.C. Revue Celtique
R.S.A.I. Jn. Journal of the Royal Society of Antiquaries of Ireland
U.J.A. Ulster Journal of Archaeology

Ancient Laws of Ireland , vols 1-6, Dublin 1865-1901
Annals of the Kingdom of Ireland by the Four Masters (AFM), edited by John O'Donovan, Dublin 1848 -51.
M. Ansell, 'Eddie Macken—Showjumping Superstar', in *Irish Horse Yearbook*, 1977, pp 11-4;
R. Baerlein, *Shergar*, London 1984.
T. de Bhaldraithe, *The Diary of Humphrey O'Sullivan*, Cork 1979
J. Barden, *Belfast*, Belfast 1982
J. Barrington, *The Ireland of Sir Jonah Barrington, selections from his personal sketches*, London 1968
T. J. Barron, 'Laragh Parish: I gCeartlár Sliabh na nDee', in *The Heart of Breifne*, pp 4-17, Monaghan 1978.
J. Barry 'Transport and Communications in Mediaeval and Tudor Ireland', in K.Nolan, *Travel and Transport in Ireland*, Dublin 1973, p.32-46
J. Baudis, 'On the Antiquity of the Kinship of Tara', in *Ériu*, viii, pp 101-7
Simone de Beauvoir, *The Second Sex*, Hamsworth 1975
J. C. Beckett, *The Making of Modern Ireland 1603-1923*, London 1966
O. Bergin, *Irish Bardic Poetry*, Dublin 1970
R. Berleth, *The Twilight Lords*, London 1979
M. O'C. Bianconi & S. J. Watson, *Bianconi: King of the Irish Roads*,

Dublin 1962
D. Binchy, 'Aimser Chue', in J.Ryan, *Féil-Sgríbhinn Eoin Mhic Néill*, Dublin 1940, pp 18-23;
D. Binchy, 'The Fair of Tailtiú and the Feast of Tara', in *Ériu*, xviii, 113-38
D. Binchy, *Celtic and Anglo-Saxon Kingship*, London 1970
D. Binchy (ed), *Críth Gablach*, Dublin 1941
D. Binchy, 'Mellbretha', in *Celtica* viii, pp 144-54
Bord na gCapall, *Reports and Accounts*
E. Bowen, *Bowen Court*, London 1964
B. Bradshaw, *The Irish Constitutional Revolution of the Sixteenth Century*, London 1979
N. Browne, *The Horse in Ireland*, London 1967
F. J. Byrne, *Irish Kings and High Kings*, London 1973
F. J. Byrne, 'Kings and Commons in Gaelic Ireland', in B.Farrel, *The Irish Parliamentary Tradition*, Dublin 1973, pp 26-36
F. J. Byrne, 'Senchas', in Historical Studies, ix, pp 137-159
F. J. Byrne, 'Tribes and Tribalism in Early Ireland', in *Ériu* xxii, 128-166
M. Byrne, *Memoirs of Myles Byrne*, Shannon 1972
M. J. Byrne, *Ireland under Elizabeth*, Dublin 1903
Caithréim Thoirdhealbhaigh in I.T.S., xxvii
Calendar of the Carew Manuscripts
Calendar of Documents Relating to Ireland 1171.
J. Carney(ed.), *A Genealogical History of the O'Reilly*, Cavan 1959
J. Carney, *The Irish Bardic Poet*, Dublin 1967
J. Carney, *Studies in Irish Literature and History*, Dublin 1955
N. Chadwick, *The Celts*, London 1977
N. Chadwick & M.Dillon *The Celtic Realms*, London 1967
A. Chambers, *Granuaile*, Dublin 1979

D. A. Chart, *An Economic History of Ireland*, Dublin 1920
M. Clayton & W. Steinkraus, *The Complete Book of Showjumping*, London 1975
J. Clébert, *The Gypsies*, London 1963
Commission on Horse Breeding, Ireland, Dublin 1897
S. J. Connolly, 'Religion, Work-Discipline and Economic Attitudes: The Case of Ireland', in T. M. Devine & D. Dickson, *Ireland and Scotland, 1600-1850*, Edinburgh 1983, pp 235-245
S. J. Connolly, *Priests and People in Pre-Famine Ireland 1780-1845*. Dublin 1982
Contributions to a Dictionary of the Irish Language, Royal Irish Academy, Dublin.
D. Corkery, *The Hidden Ireland*, Dublin 1975
A. Cosgrove, *Late Mediaeval Ireland*, Dublin 1981
A. Cosgrove (ed.), *Mediaeval Ireland 1169-1534*, A New History of Ireland, ii, Oxford 1987
M. Cox, *Notes on the History of the Irish Horse*, Dublin 1897
H. S. Crawford, *Irish Carved Ornament*, Dublin 1980
T. P. Cross & C. H. Slover, *Ancient Irish Tales*, Dublin 1969
L. M. Cullen, 'The Hidden Ireland: Re-Assessment of a Concept', in *Studia Hibernica*, ix, pp 7-47
L. M. Cullen, *An Economic History of Ireland since 1660*, London 1981
L. M. Cullen, *Life in Ireland*, London 1968
L. M. Cullen, 'Man, Landscape and Roads: The changing eighteenth century', in W.Nolan, *The Shaping of Ireland*, pp 123-34
L. M. Cullen, *The Emergence of Modern Ireland*, London 1981
M. J. Culligan-Hogan, *The Quest for the Galloping Hogan*, New York 1979

E. Curtis & R. B. McDowell, *Irish Historical Documents 1171-1922*, New York 1968

E. Curtis, *A History of Ireland*, London 1964

L. Curtis Jr. 'Stopping the Hunt, 1881-1882: An Aspect of the Irish Land War', in C. Philbin *Nationalism and Popular Protest*, Cambridge 1987, pp 349-402

K. Danaher, *The Year in Ireland*, Cork 1972

K. Danaher, 'Some Marriage Customs and their Regional Distribution', in *Béaloideas*, 42-4, pp 136-175

K. Danaher and J.G.Simms, *The Danish Force in Ireland*, Dublin 1962

E. Davidson, *Scandinavian Mythology*, London 1982

A. Dent & D. Goodall *The Foals of Epona*, London 1962

D. Dickson, 'Middlemen', in T.Bartlett & D. W. Hayton, *Penal Era and Golden Age*, Belfast 1979, pp 162-80

E. Dillon, 'The Lament of Arthur O'Leary', *Irish University Review*, i,2, pp 198-210

M. Dillon (ed) *Lebor na Cert*, I.T.S., xlvi, Dublin 1962

M. Dillon, 'The Inauguration of O'Conor' in F. X. Martin, J. A. Watt & J. B. Morrell, *Mediaeval Studies Presented to Aubrey Gwynn*, Dublin 1961, pp 186-202

M. Dobbs, 'On Chariot Burial in Ancient Ireland', in *Sidelights on the Táin Age and other Studies*, Dundalk 1917, pp 72-8

J. S. Donnelly, 'Pastorini and Captain Rock: Milleniarism and Sectarianism in the Rockite Movement', in S. Clarke & J. S. Donnelly, *Irish Peasants*, Manchester 1983, pp 102-43

H. & D. Dossenbach, *The Noble Horse*, Exeter 1985

K. Down, 'Colonial Society and Economy in the High Middle Ages', in A. Cosgrove (ed.), *New History of Ireland*, ii, pp 432-91

D. Dubuisson, 'L'équipement de l'innauguration royale dans l'Inde vedique et en Irlande', in *Revue de l'Histoire des Religions*, 1978, ii, pp 153-64

M. Duignan, 'Irish Agriculture in Early Historical Times', in *R.S.A.I. Jn.*, 74, pp 124-45

G. Dumézil, *Mythe et Épopée*, 3 vols, Paris 1968-1973

G. Dumézil, *Archaic Roman Religion*, London 1970

G. Dumézil, *Rituels Indo-Européens à Rome*, Paris 1954

D. Dumville, 'Kingship, Genealogies and Regnal Lists' in P. H. Sawyer & I. N. Wood, *Early Mediaeval Kingship*, Leeds 1979, pp 72-104

L. Duncan, 'Folklore Gleanings from Co. Leitrim', in *Folklore*, iv, 176-94

E. Durkheim, *The Elementary Forms of the Religious Life*, London 1976

M. Edgeworth, *Ormond*, Shannon 1972

C. A. Empey & K.Simms, 'The Ordinances of the White Earl and the Problem of Coign in the later Middle Ages', in *P.R.I.A.*, lxxv, pp 161-87

G. Eogan, 'Report on the excavations of some passage graves..at Knowth Co Meath', in *P.R.I.A*, 74c, pp 11-112

E. E. Evans, *Irish Folk Ways*, London 1976

E. E. Evans, 'Some Problems of Irish Ethnology: The example of Ploughing by the Tail', in C. Ó Danachair, *Folk and Farm*, Dublin 1961, pp 30-39

G. Evans, *The Horse in the Furrow*,

G. Evans, *The Pattern under the Plough*, London 1966

C. Falls, *Elizabeth's Irish Wars*, London 1950

I. Finlay, *Columba*, London 1979

M. I. Finley, *The World of Odysseus*, London 1977

T. Fitzgeorge-Parker, *Vincent O'Brien*, London 1974

B. Fitzgerald, *The Geraldines*, London 1951

P. J. Fowler, 'Early Prehistoric Agriculture in Western Europe: Some Archaeological Evidence', in D. Simpson, *Economy and Settlement in Neolithic and Early Bronze Age Britain and Europe*, Leicester 1971, pp 153-182

R. Frame, *English Lordship in Ireland*, London 1982

R. Frame, 'War and Peace in the Mediaeval Lordship of Ireland', in J.

Lydon, *The English in Mediaeval Ireland*, Dublin 1984, pp 118-41

T. W. Freeman, *Pre-Famine Ireland*, Manchester 1957

J. A. Gaughan, *The Knights of Glin*, Dublin 1978

J. Graham-Campbell & D. Kidd, *The Vikings*, London 1980

D. Greene, 'The religious epic', in J. Carney, *Early Irish Poetry*, Cork 1965, pp 73-84

P. Harbison, 'Native Irish Arms and Armour in Mediaeval Gaelic Literature, 1170-1600', in *The Irish Sword* xii, pp 173-99, 270-84

R. Haworth, 'The Horse Harness of the Irish Early Iron Age', in *U.J.A.*, xxxiv,1971, pp 26-49

G. A. Hayes-McCoy, *Irish Battles*, Dublin 1980

G. A. Hayes-McCoy, 'The Army of Ulster 1593-1601', in *The Irish Sword*, i, pp 105-17

G. A. Hayes-McCoy, 'Strategy and Tactics in Irish Warfare 1593-1601', in *I.H.S.*, ii, pp 255-279

J. Hennig, 'Some Early German Accounts of Schomberg's Irish Campaign', in *U.J.A.*, 3rd series, xi, pp 65-80

F. Henry, *Irish High Crosses*, Dublin 1964

I. Herbert, *Red Rum*, London 1974

I. Herbert & J. O'Brien, *Vincent and his Horses*, London 1984

M. Herity & G. Eogan, *Ireland in Prehistory*, Dublin 1977

R. Holinshed, *Chronicles of England Scotland and Ireland*, vol. vi, London 1808

The Iliad of Homer, trans. A. Lang, W. Leaf & E. Myers, London 1949

J. Hone, *The Moores of Moore Hall*, London 1939

H. J. Hore & J. Graves, 'The Social State of the Southern and Eastern Counties in the sixteenth century..', in *The Annuary of the Royal Historical and Archaeological Association of Ireland for the years 1868 and 1869*

H. Hore, 'The Clan Kavanagh, temp. Henry viii', in *The Kilkenny and South-East of Ireland Archaeological Society Journal*, ii, pp 73-92

J. Hughes & P. Wilson, *Long Live the National*, London 1983

D. Hyde (ed.), *Songs ascribed to Raftery*, Dublin 1903

Irish Texts, ed. J. Fraser, P. Grosjean, J. G. O'Keefe, London 1934

K. Jackson, *A Celtic Miscellany*, London 1967

K. Jackson, *The Oldest Irish Tradition*, London 1964

M. Jankovich, *They Rode into Europe*, London 1971

E. M. Johnston, *Ireland in the Eighteenth Century*, Dublin 1980

J. Jolliffe (ed.), *Froissart's Chronicles*

P. W. Joyce, *A Social History of Ancient Ireland*, 2 vols. Dublin 1913

P. W. Joyce, *Old Celtic Romances*, Dublin 1961

C. J Jung, *The Collected Works of C. J. Jung*, ed. H. Read, M. Fordham & G. Adler, London 1979.

M. Keane, *Good Behaviour*, London 1981

R. Kearney, *Myth and Motherland*, Belfast 1984

R. Kee, *Ireland A History*, London 1982

M. Kennedy & Q. Doran-O'Reilly, *Horses of Ireland*, Dublin 1982

Killanin, *Report of the Commission of Inquiry into the Thoroughbred Horse Breeding Industry*, Dublin 1986

T. Kinsella (editor), *The Táin*, London 1972

L. Laing, *Archaeology of Late Celtic Britain and Ireland*, London 1975

J. Lalor, 'Elegy on the Death of the Reverend Edward Kennedy', in *The Kilkenny and South-East of Ireland Archaeological Society Journal*, i, pp 118-43

C. Lewis, *Hunting in Ireland*, London 1975

C. Lewis, *Horse Breeding in Ireland*, London 1980

C. Lewis & M. E. McCarthy, 'The Horse Breeding Industry in Ireland', in *Irish Geography*, x, pp 72-5

C. S. Littleton, *The New Comparative Mythology*, Berkeley 1973

P. Logan, *The Old Gods*, Belfast 1981

J. Loth, *Les Noms du Cheval chez les Celtes en relation avec quelques problèmes archéologiques*, Paris 1925

A. T. Lucas, 'Irish Ploughing Practices, Parts 1-4', in *Tools and Tillage*, Vol.2, no.1 pp 52-62, no.2 pp 67-83, no.3 pp 149-60, no.4 pp 195-210

J. Lydon, *The Lordship of Ireland in the Middle Ages*, Dublin 1972

J. Lydon, 'The Hobelar: An Irish Contribution to Mediaeval Warfare', in *The Irish Sword*, ii, pp 12-6

J. Lydon, 'Edward I, Ireland and the War in Scotland 1303-4', in Lydon (ed.), *England and Ireland in the Later Middle Ages*, Dublin 1981, pp 43-61

J. Lydon, 'An Irish Army in Scotland 1296', in *The Irish Sword*, v, pp 184-190

J. Lydon, 'Irish Levies in the Scottish Wars 1296-1302', in *The Irish Sword*, v, pp 207-217

S. Lynam, *Humanity Dick*, London 1975

P. Mac Cana, 'Early Irish Ideology and the Concept of Unity', in R. Kearney, *The Irish Mind*, Dublin 1985, pp 56-78

P. Mac Cana, *Regnum et Sacerdotum*, London 1981

P. Mac Cana *Celtic Mythology*, London 1970

D. Mac Iomhair, 'The Battle of Fochairt, 1318', in *The Irish Sword*, viii, 192-209

G. MacNiocaill, 'Tír Cumaile', in *Ériu*, xxii, p. 84

G. MacNiocaill, *Ireland before the Vikings*, Dublin 1972

W. A. Maguire, 'A Resident Landlord in his Local Setting. The Second Marquis of Donegal at Ormeau 1807-1844', in *P.R.I.A.*, 83c, pp 377-99

W. A. Maguire, *Living like a Lord*, Belfast 1984

J. P. Mahaffy, 'Two Early Tours in Ireland', in *Hermathena*, xl. 1- 16

E. Malcolm, 'Popular Recreations in 19th century Ireland', in O. Mac Donagh, A. Mandle & P. Travers, *Irish Culture and Nationalism*, Dublin 1983, pp 40-55

F. X. Martin & A. B. Scott, *Expugnatio Hibernica*, Dublin 1978

F. X. Martin & T. W. Moody (ed.), *The Course of Irish History*, Cork 1967

M. Mauss, *The Gift*, London 1954

C. Maxwell, *Country and Town in Ireland under the Georges*, Dundalk 1949

C. Maxwell, *The Stranger in Ireland*, Dublin 1979

Mayo Ordnance Survey Letters, ii, p.368, Thomas O'Conor August 1838

D. McCormick, *The Incredible Mr Kavanagh*, New York 1961

M. McCormac, *The Irish Racing and Bloodstock Industry*, Dublin 1978

E. McCracken, 'The Woodlands of Ireland circa 1600', in *I.H.S.*, xi, pp 271-296

J. L. McCracken, 'The Social Structure and Social Life 1714-60', in Moody and Vaughan, *A New History of Ireland*, iv, Oxford 1986, pp 31-56

Margaret Mac Curtain, 'Rural Society in post Cromwellian Ireland', in A. Cosgrove and D. Mc Cartney, *Studies in Irish History: Presented to Dudley Edwards*, Dublin 1979, pp 118-36

R. B. McDowell, 'Ireland in 1800', in Moody & Vaughan, *A New History of Ireland*, iv, Oxford 1986, pp 655-712

R. B. McDowell, *Ireland in the Age of Imperialism and Revolution 1760-1801*, London 1979

M. MacNeill, *The Festival of Lughnasa*, London 1962

F. Mitchell, *The Irish Landscape*, London 1976

T. W. Moody 'Introduction', in Moody, Byrne & Martin, *A New History of Ireland*, iii

T. W. Moody, 'Redmond O'Hanlon', in *Proceedings and Reports of the Belfast Natural History and Philosophical Society*, i, pp 17-33

H. Morley (ed.), *Ireland under Elizabeth and James 1*, London 1890

H. Morris, 'Marriage Customs', in *Co. Louth Archaeological Society Journal*, ii, no.3 pp 323-4;

J. E. Morris, 'Mounted Infantry in Mediaeval Warfare', in *Transactions of the Royal Historical Society*, viii, pp 77-102

E. Murphy, 'Holiday Meetings', in *Sean P. Graham Racing Annual 1976-7*, pp 85-6

G. Murphy & S. O'Sullivan, 'Review of the Songs of John Mac Codrum', in *Béaloideas*, ix, pp 135-38

D. Murtagh, 'Irish Cavalry 1. The Sixteenth Century', in *The Irish Sword*, i, pp 316-17

J. F. Nagy, 'Heroic Destinies in the Macgnímrada of Finn and Cú Chulainn', in *Zeitschrift für Celtische Philologie*, xl, pp 23-39

J. L. Nelson, 'Inauguration Rituals', in P. H. Sawyer & I. N. Wood, *Early Mediaeval Kingship*, Leeds 1979, pp 50-71

K. Nicholls, *Gaelic and Gaelicised Ireland in the Later Middle Ages*, Dublin 1972

K. Nicholls, *Land, Law and Society in Sixteenth-Century Ireland* Dublin 1976

J. Norton, 'A successful year for ponies', in *Irish Horse Yearbook* 1981, pp 27-29

G. O'Brien, *The Economic History of Ireland*, New Jersey 1972

G. O'Brien, *The Economic History of Ireland in the Seventeenth- Century*, Dublin 1919

G. O'Brien, *The Economic History of Ireland in the Eighteenth- Century*, Dublin 1918

M. A. O'Brien, 'A Middle Irish Poem on the Birth of Aedán Mac Gabráin and Brandub mac Echach', in *Ériu*, xvi, 157-170

T. Ó Broin, 'What is the 'debility' of the Ulstermen?', in *Éigse*, x, pp 286-99

B. Ó Buachalla, 'An Meisiasacht agus an Aisling', in de Brún, Ó Coileáin & Ó Briain, *Folia Gadelica*, Cork 1983, pp 72-87

T. S. O'Cahan, *Owen Roe O'Neill*, London 1968

P. Ó Caithnia, *Scéal na hIomána*, Dublin 1980

S. Ó Catháin, *Irish Life and Lore*, Cork 1982

T. Ó Cathasaigh, 'Cath Maige Tuired', in P. de Brún, S. Ó Coileáin & P. Ó Briain (editors), *Folia Gadelica*. Cork 1983, pp 1-19

T. Ó Cathasaigh, 'The Concept of the Hero in Irish Mythology' in Kearney, *The Irish Mind*, Dublin 1985, 79-90.

M. O'Connell, *Shadows, An Album of the Irish People 1841 - 1914*, Dublin 1985

P. O'Connell, *The Diocese of Kilmore*, Dublin 1937

U. O'Connor, *Brendan Behan*, London 1972

D. Ó Corráin, *Ireland before the Normans*, Dublin 1972

D. Ó Corráin & F. Maguire, *Gaelic Personal Names*, Dublin 1981

B. Ó Cuív, 'Fragments of Two Mediaeval Treatises on Horses', in *Celtica*, ii, Part 1, 30-63

B. Ó Cuív, 'A Poem for Cathal Croibhdhearg Ó Conchubhair', in *Éigse* xiii, pp 195-202.

M. O'Daly, 'The Metrical Dindsenchas', in Carney, *Early Irish Poetry*, Cork 1965, pp 59-72

E. Ó Doibhlin, *Domhnach Mor*, An Omaigh 1969

P. O'Donnell, *The Irish Faction Fighters*, Dublin 1975

J. O'Donovan, *The Genealogies, Tribes and Customs of the Hy Fiachrach commonly called O'Dowda's Country*, Dublin 1844

S. Ó Domhnaill, 'Warfare in Sixteenth-Century Ireland', in *I.H.S.*, v. pp 29-54

S. Ó Dufaigh, 'Cíos Mhic Mhathghamhna', in *Clogher Record*, iv, pp 125-32

S. Ó Duilearga, *Leabhar Sheáin Uí Chonaill*, Dublin 1977

S. Ó Faoláin, *King of the Beggars*, Dublin 1980

T. Ó Fiaich, 'Filíocht Uladh mar Fhoinse don Stair Shóisialta', in *Studia Hibernica*, xi, pp 80-129

B. O'Hara, 'Some Famous Mayo People' in O'Hara, *Mayo*, Galway 1982, pp 256-300

N. O'Hare, *All About Our Irish Horses*, Dublin

N. O'Hare, *One Hundred Irish Horses*,

D. Ó hÓgáin, 'An Capall i mBéaloideas na hÉireann', in *Béaloideas*, 45-47, pp 199-243

D. Ó hÓgáin, *An File*, Dublin 1983

D. Ó hÓgáin, 'Gearóid Iarla', in *Cómhar*, May 1974

D. Ó hÓgáin, *The Hero in Irish Folk History*, Dublin 1985

C. Oman, *History of the Art of War in the Middle Ages*, 2 vols., London 1924

J. O'Meara, *The first Version of the Topography of Ireland by Giraldus Cambrensis*, Dundalk 1951

D. Ó Muirithe, *A Seat behind the Coachman*, Dublin 1972

N. Ó Muraíle, 'An Outline History of County Mayo', in O'Hara, *Mayo*, Galway 1982, pp 10-35

F. O'Neill, U. Shanahan, M. Kennedy, T. McStay, *A Study of the Non-Thoroughbred Horse Industry*, Dublin 1979

H. O'Neill Hencken, 'Ballinderry Crannog No.1', in *P.R.I.A*, 43c, pp 103-239

H. O'Neill Hencken, 'Ballinderry Crannog No.2', in *P.R.I.A*, 47c, pp 1-76

H. O'Neill Hencken, 'Lagore Crannog: an Irish royal residence of the 7th to 10th centuries AD', in *P.R.I.A*, 53c, pp 1-247

J. O'Neill, *Jonjo*, London 1985

C. O'Rahily, 'Marcach=Messenger?', in *Celtica*, vii, pp 31-2

C. O'Rahily, *Táin Bó Cuailnge*, Dublin 1967

T. F. O'Rahilly, *Early Irish History and Mythology*, Dublin 1946

T. F. O'Rahilly, 'On the Origin of the Names Erainn and Ériu', in *Ériu*, xiv, pp 6-28

B. Ó Ríordáin, *Antiquities of the Irish Countryside*, London 1979

B. O'Rourke, 'County Mayo in Gaelic Folksong', in B. O'Hara, *Mayo*, Galway 1982, pp 153-200

G. Orpen (ed.), *The Song of Dermot and the Earl*, London 1892

J. O'Shea, *Priests, Politics and Society in Post-Famine Ireland*, Dublin 1983

A. O'Sullivan, 'Triamhuin Ghormlaithe', in *Ériu*, xvi, pp 189-99

S. Ó Tuama & T. Kinsella, *An Duanaire*, Portlaoise 1981

A. Otway-Ruthven, *A History of Mediaeval Ireland*, London 1968

M. & L. de Paor, *Early Christian Ireland*, London 1964

T. Peters & R. Waterman, *In Search of Excellence*

S. Pigott, *Ancient Europe*, Edinburgh, 1965

C. Plummer, 'Life of Maedóc of Ferns', in *Vitae Sanctorum Hiberniae*, B, ii, p.248

D. Pochin-Mould, *The Aran Islands*, Devon 1972

C. Poole, *Horseracing 1982*, London 1982

J. Powell, 'Pat Eddery and the offer he could not refuse', in *Sean P.Gra-*

ham Annual, 1980-1, p.16

'The Presentments of the Jurors of the Counties of Kilkenny and Wexford...1537', in *The Annuary of the Kilkenny and South East of Ireland Archaeological Society* 1855, i,i, p.42, 47, 48, 67

L. Price, 'Armed Forces of the Irish Chiefs in the early Sixteenth-Century', in *R.S.A.I. Jn.,* lxii, pp 201-7

Pückler-Muskau, *Tour in England, Ireland and France in the years 1828 and 1829,* London 1832

J. Puhvel, 'Aspects of Equine Functionality', in J. Puhvel, *Myth and Law among the Indo-Europeans,* Berkeley 1970, pp 158-172

D. B. Quinn, *The Elizabethans and the Irish,* New York 1966

D. B. Quinn, 'A Discourse of Ireland (circa 1599)', in *P.R.I.A.,* 47c, no.3, pp 151-166

D.B.Quinn and K.W.Nicholls, 'Ireland in 1534' in F.X.Martin, T.W.Moody and F.J.Byrne, *A New History of Ireland,* iii, pp 1-38

A. & B. Rees, *Celtic Heritage,* London 1961

N. Ring, 'Point to Points—Pat Hogan continues to dominate', in *Sean P.Graham Annual,* 1980-1

P. Roberts, 'Caravats and Shanavests: Whiteboyism and Faction fighting in east Munster, 1802-11', in Clarke & Donnelly, *Irish Peasants,* Manchester 1983, pp 64-101

R. Rose, 'A Suggested Explanation of Ritual Combats', in *Folklore,* xxxvi, pp 322-31

A. Ross, *Everyday Life of the Pagan Celts,* London 1970

A. Ross, *Pagan Celtic Britain,* London 1974

M. Ryan, *Biddy Early,* Dublin 1978

W. Sayers, 'Three Charioteering Gifts in Táin Bó Cuailnge and Mescad Ulad', in *Ériu,* xxxii, pp 163-7

G. O.Sayles, 'The Rebellious First Earl of Desmond' in F. X. Martin, J. A. Watt & J. B. Morrell, *Me-*

diaeval Studies Presented to Aubrey Gwynn, Dublin 1961, pp 203-29

N. Ní Shéaghdha, 'The Rights of Mac Diarmada', in *Celtica,* vi, p.156-172

M. Seoighe, *Dromm Athlacca,* Limerick 1978

A. Sexton, 'Marriage Customs in Co. Cavan in the Nineteenth Century', in *The Heart of Breifne,* Monaghan 1978, p.27

J. J. Silke, *Kinsale,* Liverpool 1970

J. G. Simms, *Jacobite Ireland,* London 1969

J. G. Simms, 'Connacht in the Eighteenth Century', in *I.H.S.,* xi, pp 116-133

K. Simms, *Gaelic Lordships in Ulster in the Later Middle Ages,* PhD Thesis (TCD) 1976

K. Simms, 'Warfare in the Mediaeval Gaelic Lordships', in *The Irish Sword,* xii, pp 98-108

R. Smith, 'A "last hurrah" dinner at the Don Pasquale—but the Champagne flows for Tommy Carmody on Tied Cottage', in *Sean P.Graham Annual,* p.87, 1980-1

P. Somerville-Large, *From Bantry Bay to Leitrim,* London 1974

E. Spenser, *A View of the Present State of Ireland,* ed. W. Renwick, London 1970

A. Steensberg, 'Virgil's Wheel-Ard and the Two Mouldstrokers', in C. Ó Danachair, *Folk and Farm,* Dublin 1961, fig. 65, p. 271

A. T. Q. Stewart, *The Narrow Ground,* London 1977

W. Stokes, 'The Prose Tales in the Rennes Dindsenchas', in *Revue Celtique,* xv, pp 273-336, 418-484

W. Stokes, 'The Prose Tales in the Rennes Dindsenchas', in *Revue Celtique,* xvi, pp 31-83, 135-167, 269ff-

W. Stokes, 'The Edinburgh Dindsenchas', in *Folklore,* iv, pp 471-97

W. Stokes, 'The Life of St. Fechín of Fore', in *Revue Celtique,* xii, pp 313-353

J. Swift, *The Works of the Reverend Dr*

Swift, ed. G. Faulkner, Dublin 1772

P. Taaffe, *My Life and Arkle's,* London 1972

M. Tinsley, *The Aga Khan Trophy,* Dublin 1979

J. H. Todd, *St. Patrick Apostle of Ireland,* Dublin 1864

J. H. Todd (ed.) *Cogadh Gaedhel re Gallaibh,* London 1867

F. Tripett, *The First Horsemen,* Netherlands 1974

M. Wall, 'The Rise of a Catholic Middle Class in Eighteenth-Century Ireland', in *I.H.S.,* xi, 91-115

J. E. Walsh, *Rakes and Ruffians,* Dublin 1979

D. Ward, 'The Threefold Death: An Indo-European Trifunctional Sacrifice?', in Puhvel, *Myth and Law among the Indo-Europeans,* Berkeley 1970, pp 123-46

J. N. P. Watson, *British and Irish Hunts and Huntsmen,* 2 vols. London 1984

S. J. Watson, *Between the Flags,* Dublin 1969

S. J. Watson, *Three Days Full,* Dublin

J. Welcome, *Irish Horseracing,* Dublin 1982

L. H. Van Wijingaarden-Bakker, 'The animal remains from the Beaker settlement at Newgrange Co Meath', in *P.R.I.A,* 74c, pp 313-383

P. Willett, *The Classic Racehorse,* London 1981

J. E. Caerwyn Williams & M. Ní Mhuiríosa, *Traidisiún Liteartha na nGael,* Dublin 1979

D. Williams, *Great Moments in Sport: Showjumping,* London 1973

D. Williams, *Horse of the Year,* Canada

G. St J. Williams & F. Hyland, *The Irish Derby, 1861-1979,* London 1980

T. Woulfe, *The Right Stuff,* New York 1980

A.Young, *A Tour of Ireland,* ed. C.Maxwell, Galway 1983

Index

PUBLISHER'S ACKNOWLEDGEMENTS

We wish to thank all who facilitated us with picture research, and especially those photographers and others who supplied us with pictures for reproduction. We have credited the illustration sources in the relevant captions. In a few instances where we have been unable to identify copyright holders, we request them to contact the publisher. Thanks also to Aileen Caffrey for drawings on pages 15, 40, 42, 43, 187 and the title page.